THE SMART OFFICE

Turning Your Company on Its Head

by
A.K. TOWNSEND

GILA PRESS

P.O. Box 623, Olney, MD 20830-0478
301-774-0917

Gila Press
P.O. Box 623
Olney, MD 20830-0478

Gila Press is an imprint of the Sustainable Development International Corporation. This book is printed on 100% recycled Halopaque paper with soy-based inks.

Although the author & publisher have made every effort to ensure the accuracy and completeness of information contained in this book, we assume no responsibility for errors, inaccuracies, omissions, or any inconsistency herein. Any slights of people, places, or organizations are unintentional. In addition, any products or companies mentioned herein are for the purpose of illustration only, not for advertising purposes.

The photograph shown on the front and back covers is of bamboo.

Library of Congress Cataloging-in-Publication Data

Townsend, A.K.
    The smart office: turning your company on its head / by A.K. Townsend — 1st edition.
        p. cm.
    Includes bibliographical references, glossary, and index.
    ISBN 0-9657081-0-1
    Library of Congress Catalog Card Number: 96-95460
        1. Business.   2. Architecture.   3. Environment.   4. Green products. I. Townsend, A.K. II. Title.
        1997

FOREWORD

Buildings in the United States account for 36% of the nation's primary energy consumption, 35% of CO_2 emissions, and 35 million tons of construction waste each year. These figures do not include the energy embodied in the production and transport of building materials, nor the impact of demolition waste at the end of a building's life cycle. The environmental and economic impacts associated with the construction and powering of buildings are so enormous that even modest gains in efficiency can provide substantial benefits.

The Smart Office is a timely and comprehensive guide for architects, engineers, building owners, and businesses on how to reduce the environmental impacts of our building stock while saving money and increasing the health and productivity of the work force. A wealth of practical information gleaned from government reports, academia, the experience of forward-thinking designers, and the author's own research is provided in a single, well-organized compendium. A valuable tool now exists for those wishing to create more sustainable offices and homes. This work represents a substantive contribution to the literature of the green movement.

Ronald D. Judkoff
March 1997

Mr. Ronald D. Judkoff directs the Buildings and Thermal Systems Center at the National Renewable Energy Laboratory. The views expressed here are entirely his own and are not given as an agent of the National Renewable Energy Laboratory.

This book is dedicated
in loving memory
to
Dr. Richard Trumbull

ACKNOWLEDGMENTS

My most sincere thanks go to the many people who have taken time to answer questions along the way, providing information in person and by mail, phone, and the Internet. In particular, I would like to thank Mr. William Browning (Rocky Mountain Institute), Mr. Gregory Franta (ENSAR Group), Mr. Michael Myers (Department of Energy), and the late Dr. Richard Trumbull (Office of Naval Research, retired) for their thorough, thoughtful, critical reviews and suggestions. Because of them, you hold a better book in your hands. Thanks, also, to Mrs. Jean B. McConville, whose fresh, unbiased mind and skillful editing uncovered my many grammatical blunders, large and small.

I am grateful to Mr. Ronald D. Judkoff of the National Renewable Energy Laboratory for taking the time to write this book's Foreword and to Mr. Arun Vohra of the Department of Energy (Office of Buildings Systems, Energy Efficiency and Renewable Energy) for his support and encouragement; to Environmental Construction Outfitters in New York City for allowing me to dismantle, rearrange, and photograph just about everything in the store; to Real Goods Trading Company's Solar Living Center in Hopland, California, and My Organic Market in Rockville, Maryland, for allowing me to photograph various products; to the Oklahoma Waste Reduction Resource Center for their information on waste exchanges; to Ms. Christine Blanke and the staff at Thomson-Shore for their patience and assistance in producing this book; to Mr. Michael Perez and Mr. Richard Perez, who spent time they didn't have to graciously take the cover photo; to Mr. Robert Townsend and Ms. Margaret Holmes for their ongoing help; and to Ms. Elizabeth Trexler and Mr. Ramin Assa for their help in updating contact information.

And, finally, I offer my deepest gratitude to my family and friends, whose suggestions helped provide some mental turning points for me, who were patient when I fell out of touch and thought of nothing but the latest efficient, non-toxic, and recycled products, and without whom this book would not have happened.

TABLE OF CONTENTS

PART ONE: INTRODUCTION

PART TWO: THE EFFICIENT OFFICE

PART THREE: THE HEALTHY OFFICE

PART FOUR: SETTING UP SMART PROGRAMS

PART FIVE: ADDITIONAL INFORMATION

PART SIX: APPENDICES & REFERENCES

PART ONE

• • • • • • • • •

INTRODUCTION

INTRODUCTION

By reducing pollution, you greatly increase your company's profits, productivity, and competitive edge.

THE SMART OFFICE

Welcome to *The Smart Office*. **A smart office is one that is both healthy and efficient in its use of resources.** It is a place characterized by no (or low) toxicity, less wasteful work practices, and energy efficiency. As a result, it saves money, is a more pleasant place in which to work, and goes easier on the environment.

This book provides information on many of the hidden costs of today's businesses and offers strategies to overcome them. Many companies have used similar strategies, increasing their profits, productivity, and competitive edge. As the case studies in this book show, whenever an office is turned into a smarter one, the payback of any expenses is often much quicker than projected because of a great increase in employee productivity. When employees feel that their work environment is healthy and stimulating, it's inspiring what they can accomplish! And it makes their employers more competitive, too.

WHY A SMART OFFICE?

Running a business can be challenging and rewarding. One of the biggest challenges is streamlining your operations to save time and use resources as efficiently as possible while keeping employees happy and productivity high.

Many companies, however, become caught up in administrative and other details at the expense of efficiency and health. This can be detrimental to companies, costing them enormous amounts of money that they could otherwise apply to advertising, R&D, downsizing prevention, wage increases, and general growth.

Some companies, have discovered where their inefficiencies lay and have saved hundreds of thousands of dollars annually by becoming more efficient, healthier places in which to work.

SICK EMPLOYEES, LOST PROFITS

If you're like many people, you spend much of your time in an environment that doesn't foster your health. In fact, many working environments can be harmful.

As an employer, you want to ensure that your employees are comfortable and able to perform their best. At the same time, you want to profit as much as possible. After all, that's probably why you're in business. But poor working environments can make your employees sick, decreasing their motivation and productivity and significantly decreasing your profits.

As an employee, you want to work in an environment that is healthy and supportive. You want adequate lighting, clean air, and a healthy workplace. Without these things, it can be difficult to concentrate on getting your work done. Lighting that is inappropriate for the tasks at hand and poor ventilation that circulates the latest flu or the toxic chemicals from your carpets can leave you with a variety of symptoms that interfere with your ability to do your job well. Work-related health problems can be expensive for both you and your employer, particularly when doctors' bills or sick days are the result or when your productivity drops.

WHAT *THE SMART OFFICE* DOES

The Smart Office is a business survival guide and source book filled with comprehensive, detailed, practical information. It can help any business create a more efficient, healthy, and profitable workplace, including corporate headquarters, government facilities, home offices, hospitals, museums, factories, boutiques, shopping malls, and airports.

This book is divided into six parts and is organized as follows:

Part One: Introduction

Chapter 1: The Hidden Costs of Business explains how inefficient and unhealthy workplaces became the norm. It outlines the expenses — from utility bills to medical bills — that come from operating many of today's workplaces.

Chapter 2: Smart Success Stories provides examples of companies that have saved money and improved their workplace environments simply by overcoming inefficiency and toxicity.

Chapter 3: Getting Started toward a Smarter Office discusses the importance of a workplace audit. It also explains how to establish smarter company policies, set healthier goals, and enlist the help of others in making it all happen.

Part Two: The Efficient Office

Chapter 4: The Costs of Inefficiency shows you just how expensive inefficiency can be and how much money it may be costing you and your company.

Chapter 5: Energy-Efficient Lighting explains how to save money and improve employee morale and productivity through daylighting and by using energy-efficient lighting that is appropriate for the tasks at hand.

Chapter 6: Energy-Efficient Office Equipment gives detailed information on the energy use of today's office equipment, from PCs, printers, modems, and fax machines to refrigerators and vacuums. It also explains what to look for when purchasing new equipment.

Chapter 7: Efficient Building Systems offers information on smarter alternatives to conventional insulation as well as heating, ventilation, and cooling systems. Not only can you improve the comfort of your work environment, but you can save money doing it. Waste treatment alternatives and ideas for efficient water use also are discussed.

Part Three: The Healthy Office

Chapter 8: The Costs of an Unhealthy Workplace discusses the severe indoor air pollution that today's toxic office materials can create. It also examines other health concerns (chemical sensitivity, EMFs, ergonomics, eye strain, radon, sick building syndrome,

stress, water pollution) that can result from unhealthy workplaces and offers ideas on how to overcome them.

Chapter 9: Smarter Building Materials gives information on healthier, more efficient building materials, including bricks, carpentry, concrete, doors, drywall, flooring, metals, pavement, roofing, siding, and wood. It discusses readily available products and their sources.

Chapter 10: Smarter Carpets & Flooring discusses the toxins commonly found in today's carpets and flooring and offers several sources for healthier alternatives.

Chapter 11: Smarter Paints & Wallcoverings provides information on some of the health risks associated with paints and wallcoverings. It also has an extensive list of smarter alternatives.

Chapter 12: Smarter Furniture examines some of the problems associated with much of today's furniture. It explains the importance of purchasing non-toxic furniture made of sustainably harvested or reused woods and lists several sources for smarter woods, finishes, and furniture.

Chapter 13: Smarter Office Supplies provides alternatives to conventional office supplies — from chlorine-free, recycled paper and non-toxic correction fluid and markers to smarter personal-care products used in restrooms.

Chapter 14: Smarter Cleaners & Pest Control offers healthier alternatives to today's toxic cleaners and pest-control methods.

Chapter 15: Smarter Daycare & Child Care lists sources of non-toxic children's products, from clothing and bedding to toys and games, that can help any child-care facility find better alternatives to less healthy children's products.

Part Four: Setting Up Smart Programs

Chapter 16: Office Recycling explains how to set up a recycling program. It highlights the many items that can be recycled (e.g., paper, toner cartridges, metals, shoes), going beyond simply putting aluminum, glass, and paper into bins.

Chapter 17: Smarter Office Lawn Care & Landscaping discusses ways to eliminate chemical pesticides, waste water, and inefficient landscape practices, offering better alternatives to help you save money and create a healthier outdoor environment.

Chapter 18:   Smarter Transportation & Telecommuting offers information on alternatives to driving your car to work. It discusses hypercars, the revolution in autodesign, as well as using alternative fuels for your current vehicle. It also details many of the pros and cons of telecommuting and how you can start your own telecommuting program at work.

Part Five: Additional Information

Chapter 19: Smart Investing discusses important issues to consider when investing your money to ensure that you're supporting smarter products, services, and technologies.

Chapter 20: Surfing the Internet gives information on some of the hottest sites on the Internet, covering topics ranging from energy efficiency and helpful government programs to non-toxic office products.

Part Six: Appendices & References

Appendix A: Directory of Suppliers gives addresses and phone numbers for the smarter product manufacturers, distributors, and suppliers listed in this book.

Appendix B: Helpful Government Programs offers telephone numbers for many of the government's voluntary programs that have been designed to help businesses become smarter and save money.

Whether you're renovating or designing a new building or lease or own your office space, my hope is that this book will give you some of the tools that you need to create a healthier and more efficient place in which to work.

CHAPTER 1

THE HIDDEN COSTS OF BUSINESS

"Pollution prevention has a much higher rate of return than most investments your company is now making."
Romm, 10

THROWING YOUR MONEY AWAY

THE INEFFICIENT WORKPLACE

Inefficiency is expensive. And for a company, it can be deadly since it dramatically reduces the company's competitive edge. Unfortunately, most companies lose a great deal of money through inefficiency.

The smarter and more efficient your company's use of resources, the more competitive it can be. And the money saved from efficiency goes directly into your company's profits.

In addition to saving money, efficiency is good for your company's image. Not only does it show that you're smart with your money and materials, but it is one way to increase employee morale and productivity while being ecologically responsible. These days, that's something that most of your customers, employees, and shareholders will appreciate.

How Did the Inefficient Workplace Become the Norm?

Inefficiency is common to most companies, and it's not difficult to understand why. After all, the prosperity of the U.S. was built upon the country's abundance of natural resources, and conservation often was not a high priority. Although the idea of waste has become a concern for some, many companies still are plagued by inefficiency.

Due to inefficient work practices, U.S. companies unnecessarily lose a considerable amount of money. Even compared with other industrialized nations, U.S. companies use about twice as much energy to produce one dollar's worth of goods. In addition, U.S. companies create about five times more waste per dollar of goods produced than do Japanese companies and over twice the waste of German companies.

But changing to efficiency can be difficult for some. Current accounting methods that ignore the costs of inefficient and unhealthy practices can rule out profitable, proactive measures. They also can make it nearly impossible to see sources of waste and how much money this inefficiency is costing companies. Non-communicative management styles also can hinder information flows that would help companies to become more profitable and competitive through increased efficiency and better health.

THE UNHEALTHY WORKPLACE

Just as inefficiency is expensive, so is a toxic workplace. The use of unhealthy furnishings, paints, and supplies has cost many people more than just the purchase price — it has cost them in health costs, sick leave, and decreased productivity.

Many of today's furnishings and other materials contain numerous toxins. The glues used to hold together pressed wood furniture and building materials, adhere laminated surfaces to furniture, and keep floors and carpets in place often are poisonous. Paints, particularly those that are oil-based, often are another source of toxins in the workplace. The toxins emitted from carpets, furniture, and plastics through "offgassing" can create a variety of health problems in anyone exposed to them. So, being sealed into our office buildings with the toxic chemicals that offgas from these furnishings and other materials can make us and our co-workers sick.

But toxicity isn't the only health problem present in the workplace these days. Poorly designed lighting is another. It can result in eye strain, headaches, and higher than average work errors, which are very costly to productivity. Too much or too little light — or lighting that is not designed for the tasks at hand — actually can impair worker vision or make it more difficult to get the job done right.

How Did the Unhealthy Workplace Become the Norm?

Today's tightly sealed buildings were designed to keep the effects of outdoor temperature and humidity outdoors. As a result, most buildings have inoperable windows and little ventilation using outside air. Although there are ways to ventilate buildings while keeping them energy-efficient, most are not designed with the health of the occupants in mind. As a result, indoor pollutants often are shut inside and left to circulate within the buildings.

In many buildings, the air intake (which is supposed to bring in fresher outdoor air) is placed by the loading dock. As a result, fumes from delivery trucks and other vehicles are left to circulate within the buildings. Noise, bad light, poor air, ugly smells, bad water, dry/overheated/uniform environments, electro-magnetic fields (EMFs), and the dominance of visual information, computer glare, and artificial lights can result in sickness and sensory deprivation.

Looking back, the industrial and technological revolutions are recent occurrences. Many of the products made today haven't been around long enough for their effects on human health and the environment to be fully understood. Experience has taught us that once these impacts are known, it can be difficult to get companies to change the way they make things or undertake costly replacement.

With the increasing number of work-related health problems, some of which you may have experienced yourself, many of us are just starting to realize that the materials used in our office construction and furnishings are harmful to our health. A few of the health problems that can result from toxins in the office are: Sick Building Syndrome (SBS), Chemical Sensitivity (CS), electromagnetic radiation, and radon poisoning. (For more information on these health problems, turn to Chapter 8: "The Costs of an Unhealthy Workplace.")

Dirt-covered windows at a printing factory not only help to create an uninspiring work environment but also can contribute to eye strain, work errors, and the need for additional lighting from artificial sources.

Chapter 2

Smart Success Stories

"As professionals who shape the built environment, we have an imperative to redefine our role on this planet from one of exploitation to one of stewardship. We want architects to change the way they design, to think about everything they do in terms of what it means for future generations."
Susan Maxman, past president, American Institute for Architects in *Gunts*, June 20, 1993

Overcoming Inefficiency

Henry Ford was obsessed with efficiency. Two of his main contributions to today's work practices were interchangeable parts and the moving assembly line, both of have which saved a great deal of time and resources. Ford stressed the importance of squeezing everything we can out of time, material, and energy.

No doubt, Ford was an efficiency addict because he understood some of the costs associated with wasted resources and time. Reusing scrap is great, but planning for its prevention is even better and saves energy, resources, and money. After all, efficiency and health are the keys to a smarter work environment.

For a highly productive, efficient, healthy workplace, your company needs to have an understanding of the life cycles of the products it purchases. A life-cycle analysis looks at the phases and costs of a product from its beginning to its end: from the gathering of its raw resources to its transportation (to the factory) and production and packaging to its transportation (to the store) to its purchase to its use and maintenance to its discard (cradle-to-grave) or reuse (cradle-to-cradle) and the associated transport. Looking at the costs of a product over its lifetime will help you to understand its true costs — not just its initial cost (purchase price) — thereby allowing you to make smarter purchasing and other business decisions.

The issue of looking at life-cycle costs for products (from pencils to buildings) has become an important one. If a product's purchase price was based on its real costs, consumers would find that the least expensive products tended to be those that were made more efficiently and were healthier. Concerned over the enormous burden and costs of undoing the negative ecological damage that has resulted from various industrial practices, the U.S. Commerce Department is interested in developing an alternate Gross Domestic Product calculation that takes into account the impact of long-term environmental damage (e.g., deforestation, pollution).

The root of such damage lies in inefficiency. Even environmental managers, hired by companies to handle pollution and other ecological issues, often use expensive, inefficient methods that do not get to the source of the pollution. In 1994, *Industry, Technology, and the Environment*, a report by the Congressional Office of Technology Assessment, found that most environmental managers have been trained in reactive, end-of-the-pipe measures rather than prevention. And most environmental equipment vendors still sell end-of-the-pipe equipment rather than products that work toward prevention, even though prevention is generally much less expensive.

These managers may not know that smart companies depend on proactive measures that prevent inefficiency. One study of 84 companies compared those that had been proactive in dealing with pollution through recycling, energy efficiency, and waste minimization with those that hadn't. *The companies that had been environmentally proactive had a 4% higher rate of return on investment, a 9% higher sales growth, and a nearly 17% higher operating-income growth* (Romm, 4).

Efficient Building Examples

Let's take a look at how some companies have saved money by making smarter purchasing decisions. The examples below first discuss how companies have worked toward efficiency and then outline how some have achieved healthier buildings. Of course, a smart building does not focus on one aspect to the exclusion of the other.

Boeing

Many companies that have become smarter are proving time and again that efficiency really does save money and gives them an edge over their competitors. To save money and increase its efficiency, the Environmental Protection Agency helped Boeing cut its lighting energy use up to 90%. The lighting changes that Boeing made saw a two-year payback, a 53% return on investment. Additionally, the lighting redesign has minimized glare and helped the employees to work more productively, creating fewer defects and greater comfort.

Compaq

In the 1980s, Compaq Computer's facilities manager saved the company about $1 million a year simply by cutting back on energy use. The company's chief financial officer, having a long-term view for the company, believed in spending money to save money. And that's exactly what the facilities manager did. He went to Compaq's financial staff, establishing the first contact between financial and facilities people at Compaq.

The facilities manager was able to get beyond the traditional, two-year payback time for investments working, instead, with a new goal of five to seven years. The financial staff did a life-cycle analysis, examining the total cost (energy use, operations, maintenance) over several years of changes in energy use. Compaq discovered that, by investing a little more money up front, its later savings would be significant. By doing this life-cycle analysis of the proposed energy changes, Compaq came to realize what many companies are beginning to understand. Even if you do spend a little more early on, if you do it right, your savings can be great in many ways.

Compaq's changes were designed to remove the blockages to worker productivity through increased daylighting and other actions, and it worked. In 1985 alone, productivity rose by 55%. Because of this experience, Compaq's people began looking not just at the purchase and installation costs but at the life-cycle costs of the whole system.

Another move toward efficiency at Compaq is worth mentioning. One of the central cooling plants circulated a large quantity of water to all of the company's buildings. Someone hired to improve Compaq's heating, ventilation, and air conditioning (HVAC) systems suggested turning off the secondary pumps. There were eight of these pumps that used a total of 240 horsepower. While turning off these pumps took only four hours to do, it saved the company about $100,000 every year. And when the time came to replace the cooling towers, Compaq replaced them with towers about 10 times more energy-efficient than the old system. Compaq's philosophy is, "Anything less than a year's payback is free." (Romm, 66)

Comstock

Comstock is another company that has become more competitive and environmentally friendly just by being smarter. Using an interdisciplinary design team, Comstock's 10-story building was designed and constructed within 18 months, cost $500,000 less than was budgeted for, and operates at half the cost of one of the company's other, less-efficient buildings (Romm, 87).

Dow Chemical

Dow Chemical has saved a great deal of money through efficiency. Since 1982, in its Louisiana Division, Dow has enjoyed an average annual return of 204% on investments in 575 projects designed to reduce energy use and waste. Every year since, Dow has saved over $110 million.

Dow Chemical also set up an employee suggestion program. In 1982, its Louisiana Division ran a contest for energy-saving ideas that required under $200,000 and would pay for themselves in less than one year. That first year, there were 27 winners; Dow spent $1.7 million and got an average return of 173% on its investments. The next year, there were 32 winners. About $2.2 million was spent with an average return of 340%, resulting in $7.5 million savings the first year and every year after that. The program was so successful that, in 1984, the $200,000 cap was taken off the investments, and gains from any type of efficiency, not just energy, were included (Romm, 42-43).

Florida Solar Energy Center

The Florida Solar Energy Center is located at the University of Central Florida/Brevard Community College campus. Focusing on efficiency in lighting and the HVAC systems, the New Energy Center (34,000 square feet) is expected to use two-thirds less energy than any comparably sized office building that meets Florida energy codes. The building, a long rectangle, runs east-west, reducing the time that the building's walls and windows are exposed to direct solar radiation. All offices receive natural light, and controls dim electrical lights when sunlight is available and brighten them when the sky is overcast. Motion sensors turn off lights when spaces are unoccupied. The white roof reflects 80% of the sun's heat, greatly reducing the need for air conditioning (*ASHRAE Journal*, Oct. 1995, 6).

Harrah's Hotel and Casino

Las Vegas' Harrah's Hotel and Casino now saves $70,000 a year at no cost. How? It simply asked its guests if they wanted their sheets washed each day, and most said "No." As a result, they were able to reduce their energy and water costs.

Headquarters, Inc.

This Missoula, Montana, company renovated a 20,000 square foot building. It restored the old building's facade to its original, historic appearance and reused some of the artifacts it found. Cork insulation was reused in peg boards for the new office space; storefront glass was re-cut for storm windows; concrete chunks from demolition were used in landscaping for retaining walls and as fill. By simply reusing or recycling what was free and readily available, Headquarters, Inc., deferred $30,000 in construction cost, $10,000 of which was saved by avoiding the landfill fees by recycling construction material (Watkins-Miller, 32).

Kraft General Foods

One point that is not stressed nearly enough is that creating a smarter work environment can save jobs. Some companies, such as Kraft General Foods, have actually avoided closing down plants and laying off workers simply through efficiency.

In the late 1980s, Kraft planned to close some of its older and least-productive plants. To cut costs, one plant that employed 200 people went to a four-day workweek, and closure was impending. Fortunately, this plant's manager had an extensive energy audit done for the plant. This audit suggested $3.6 million in changes to improve energy efficiency. But only after the utility Boston Edison offered to repay the expense of the upgrades (their unique scheme guaranteed that Kraft would get a full payback in one year) did Kraft go through with the improvements. Not only was Kraft able to keep the plant open, but the energy saved was enough to power 1,000 houses (Romm, 59-62).

Lockheed-Martin

Lockheed-Martin built a $50-million engineering design and development facility that resulted in a $300,000-$400,000 savings on energy bills EVERY YEAR. In addition, employee productivity went up 15%, and absenteeism dropped by 15%. In just one year, the drop in absenteeism, alone, covered the extra $2 million that Lockheed-Martin had paid for its new energy system (Romm, 96-98). The rise in productivity increased the company's competitive edge, and all of it was accomplished by working with architects who simply used smart design techniques. The resulting workplace environment used more sunlight and increased the possibilities for workers to interact.

National Audubon Society

Just a few years ago, the National Audubon Society needed to move its New York City headquarters into a larger space. Rather than buy a new building, which would have cost $9 million more, Audubon decided to retrofit an existing building in Manhattan. The non-profit organization held a two-year campaign to raise the $14 million it needed to purchase and retrofit the 100-year-old, eight-story, $10 million building (partially financed through tax-free bonds). The building was gutted, and the original materials were reused or recycled, keeping in place 300 tons of steel, 9,000 tons of masonry, and 560 tons of concrete. Then, it was renovated.

To be consistent with its conservation mission, Audubon wanted to make its new space an environmentally responsible one. But it had a big decision to make. Did it want to seek out the latest, most eco-friendly prototypes of "green" products? Or did it want to buy products that were easily available to anyone, even if they weren't the most eco-friendly? Audubon decided that, while it wanted to be as environmentally responsible as possible, it also wanted to serve as an example to other businesses that being smart is easy. It wanted to show that anyone can create an efficient, non-toxic workplace without struggling to find smarter products and without spending more money.

The resulting retrofit made Audubon House 60% more energy-efficient than a conventional office building. Audubon originally projected that the savings would pay for themselves within three to five years; however, the energy efficiency (from heating, cooling, lighting) saved $100,000 each year, making the system pay for itself in under three years (Lemonick, 38).

Motion sensors with manual buttons were installed in each room to control the lights, and zone sensors were placed in open areas. Long, rectangular pendant fixtures were hung from the ceilings, reflecting light off the ceilings and shining it in all directions. GE's efficient T-8 bulbs were used, which dim as the sensors detect sunlight. Audubon's lighting, alone, has saved the organization at least $60,000 each year over conventional lighting (Randall, 32). Task lighting (arranged specifically for the tasks at hand) was used to minimize waste from unnecessary, general lighting.

During the summer months, air conditioning in most buildings doubles electricity consumption. In the winter, electric heat also doubles power consumption. But the gas-powered heater/chiller that Audubon purchased saves $36,000 each year by using gas over electricity (Nasatir, 3). Unlike most air conditioners, it heats and cools with natural gas. When installed, the unit was only one of about three in New York City. It uses no chlorofluorocarbons (CFCs), and the thermal shell and other energy-efficient features resulted in a $72,000 rebate by Consolidated Edison, the local utility (Randall, 134).

The heater/chiller is relatively small and sits on the top floor of Audubon's offices. It results in cleaner air that is circulated 6.5 times every hour (the heater/chiller has the capacity to exchange the air up to 18 times per hour). Most offices only circulate their air about four times per hour.

National Wildlife Federation (NWF)

In 1988, the National Wildlife Federation established an Environmental Quality Task Force. This Task Force is a voluntary, open forum, and action-oriented group, focusing on both purchasing decisions and staff awareness. Since the establishment of its Task Force, NWF has made several moves toward a smarter office.

NWF recycles its aluminum, glass, cardboard, computer paper, laser printer cartridges, and kitchen scraps. Between its Washington, D.C., and its Virginia offices alone, NWF recycles 30 tons of paper each month (13 tons of office paper, 11 tons of cardboard, over 5 tons of computer paper, and nearly one ton of newspapers and phone directories). NWF purchased a baler to bale cardboard, saving $28,700 in disposal costs, and made $5,000 selling recyclable materials in 1990. In addition, NWF set up a local recycling center (McIntosh, 29).

NWF cut its water use by 3% each year since the inception of its Task Force. Lawn watering has been reduced to 300 gallons each year, mostly for new plants. All of the plumbing fixtures were fitted with water-saving devices to increase its water efficiency, and NWF even offers water-saving kits to employees at cost for home use (McIntosh, 30).

NWF replaced its incandescent bulbs with fluorescent ones, saving 3% on its energy bills. (Bulbs are offered to employees at cost for home use, too). It also reduced its lighting by up to one-half in some work areas. Employees have become more conscientious about turning off lights as well. The light switch plates are stickered, reminding employees to off lights, and security guards often turn lights off in unoccupied areas.

To cut down on pollution, NWF switched from plastic to wooden coffee stirrers and from chlorine-bleached (toxic) to unbleached coffee filters. NWF also stopped buying adhesive notes since these notes cannot be recycled. To save paper, photocopying was reduced by 40% in less than a year thanks to double-sided copying, the circulation of memos (rather than giving one copy of all memos to each person), and overall paper conservation (McIntosh, 30). Over the past several years, NWF's recycled paper use has gone from 2% in 1986 to nearly 100% in 1991. NWF has switched to using recycled paper for its holiday cards and packaging materials as well (Workman, 29).

NWF's Washington, D.C., office uses motion sensors to turn lights off and on. In addition, energy use has been cut by 15% due to the building's wall, window, and roof design. Between $1,200 and $1,400 is saved each month by the ice-storage air conditioning system alone.

Shuttle service is provided between NWF's Virginia building and the nearby subway station. In place of free parking, employees at the Washington, D.C., office receive a cash transportation subsidy to encourage the use of public transportation.

The National Wildflower Research Center

The National Wildflower Research Center was the brainchild of Lady Byrd Johnson. Her interest in conservation inspired her to create a place for the research and protection of wildflowers and the genetic diversity that they offer. Located outside Austin, Texas, the complex was designed in an integrated fashion, with the architect, the landscape architect, and others working together toward a concordant design. The Center includes several smart features aimed at creating as little impact as possible on the surrounding natural systems. The design included, but was not limited to, the following:

- Construction waste reduction plan
- Efficient lighting/daylighting
- Good indoor air quality
- Minimization of materials
- Minimized site impact
- Non-toxic materials and pest-control methods
- Passive solar energy
- Rainwater catchment
- Recycled materials
- Site analysis
- Sustainable lumber
- Xeriscaping

Natural Resources Defense Council (NRDC) – New York

Just a few years ago, NRDC retrofitted its Manhattan office after gutting most of its building. The organization incorporated many skylights and windows into its office space. All of the windows are triple-paned, the center pane being a heat mirror of finely spun polymer (coated on both sides on those windows facing south and west) that reflects out infrared rays. These windows also have blinds, a simple and effective means to energy efficiency, that reflect light out in the summer and provide extra insulation in the winter. NRDC's windows have the same insulation rating, R-11, as the walls. The roof's rating is R-30, which is highly efficient.

In its first year of operation, NRDC saved 75% on lighting costs. This allowed the system to pay for itself within two to three years. While more expensive up-front (at $69 per square foot vs. inefficient lighting at $52 per square foot), the single electronic ballast, fluorescent lighting fixtures last much longer and are much more energy-efficient than are conventional fixtures. With reflectors behind and louvers in front, they offer more diffuse light with no glare. Although lights generally contribute up to 50% of a building's heat, the octron gas (rather than floron) lamps are triphosphore-treated and reduce the building's heat load so that there is less to cool.

NRDC also bought motion sensors for each office. These detectors have a built-in override feature and can be turned off manually. Only two hallway lights are left on constantly in case of emergencies. There is a skylight in the conference room, and the hallways and interior offices receive ambient light through glass panels installed above windowed-office doorways.

The organization believes that the originally projected three-year payback on lighting took place well under three years due to the energy-conservative behavior of employees, who often turn on their lights only when necessary and shut them off without waiting for the motion sensors. As a result, NRDC uses about 30% of the energy of a typical office rather than the 50% originally projected.

NRDC uses energy-efficient appliances as well. For instance, there is a Sub-zero® refrigerator in the kitchen that is well-insulated. The freezer is on the bottom and the motor on the top (since heat rises). The Kitchen Aid dishwasher has an energy-efficient cycle.

As is common in most of New York City, NRDC's heat comes from radiators and a basement boiler. A cost-benefit analysis done before the organization's retrofit showed that there were no good heating alternatives available that were worth the cost of modification.

Within five to six years of the retrofit, NRDC expects that the costs of the entire retrofit (heating/cooling, thermal

upgrade, non-toxic environment, and financing) will be recovered. After that time, NRDC will save at least 50% in annual energy costs. Over the next decade, NRDC's savings in energy, operations, and maintenance will exceed $1.2 million.

NRDC sends its unused stationary to its printer, who cuts it in half and puts adhesive along the edge, turning it into note pads. Finally, white paper, cans, and bottles are recycled through a state-of-the-art recycling system and then given to We Can, a homeless organization that recycles to finance its soup kitchen. The trash is taken to New Jersey, where it is separated under the state's strict regulations.

Regal Fruit and Bonneville Power: Utilities and Companies Working Together toward Efficiency

In 1989, Washington State's Bonneville Power Administration talked with the state's Regal Fruit Co-op. Regal Fruit keeps about 1.25 million bushels of Washington State fruit at its facility. Bonneville Power, interested in pollution prevention and energy efficiency, proposed a plan (compiled by Washington State University researchers) to decrease Regal's energy demand. The researchers had discovered that the fans circulating the air in the storage facility actually created 60% of the heat that they were trying to cool.

Regal's solution was a computer-controlled monitoring system that runs the fans only six hours each day. This allows the fans to be off 75% of the time rather than running 24 hours every day. Since efficiency is in their best interest, the Bonneville Power Administration paid for over half of the expense for the new equipment, which cost $104,000. And, while the projected energy savings were $13,000 each year, the actual, measured savings surpassed that projection by $2,000-5,000 each year. As a result, the investment paid for itself in only three to four years.

But that wasn't all. Productivity increased, and so did the quality of the fruit. The temperature was raised from 31 to 33 degrees Fahrenheit, eliminating the freezing, defrosting, and resulting shrinkage of the fruit, which is normally stored from five to nine months before going to market. Instead of selling about 100 partially dehydrated apples in every bushel, Regal sold about 85 plump ones, saving even more money. As a result, the money saved because of better quality fruit far exceeded, possibly by a factor of 10, any savings on energy. This increase in productivity made the system pay off in under one year, from energy savings alone, rather than the three or four years originally projected (Romm, 36-37).

Why would a utility help people to save energy? Because it's more efficient, creates less pollution, and is cheaper than having to build a new power plant. *Pollution prevention, by the way, is a high-yield investment that beats other investments with comparably high rates of return because there is very little or no present or future risk, less waste, and increased productivity as a result.*

Republic Engineered Steels

Republic Engineered Steel's largest, money-saving idea came from its employee suggestion program. The idea was for a better way to recycle its scrap steel. Rather than paying freight on waste, the company decided to recycle or keep its scrap steel and make money from it. As a result, the company saves almost $3.6 million every year just by more efficiently recycling its steel. Between that and increased water efficiency, the company has saved a great deal of money (Romm, 51). And because Republic is an employee-owned company, its employees benefit from the company's smart investments.

VeriFone

The company responsible for making phone credit card verification systems, VeriFone, built a smart building for its headquarters in Costa Mesa, California. So far, the building has seen a 50% reduction in energy costs and a 48% drop in absenteeism.

Designed at $39 per square foot, the building uses ergonomic office systems, high-efficiency mechanical system, low-VOC (volatile organic compound) building materials, and skylights. Because of the natural lighting, the building's light sensors rarely turn on the electric lights except at night. The T-8 lamps, electronic ballasts, and occupancy sensors further cut operating costs as does the high-efficient gas-absorption chiller used for mechanical cooling.

Outdoor air provides indoor ventilation (25 cubic feet per person per hour). The air flow is slow enough to allow water to drop out of air before it's distributed, thereby preventing moisture build-up. According to a Rocky Mountain Institute study, employee absenteeism went from 14.3 hours to 7.5 hours as a result of the building's smart design, and employee feedback has been so positive that the company has decided to retrofit an older, adjacent building.

The White House

On Earth Day in 1993, President Clinton announced an initiative toward a smarter White House. Already, the increased efficiency through smarter lighting has seen a 65-70% savings in lighting costs; as a result, the lighting paid for itself within six months. In addition to energy efficiency, the White House initiatives have focused on improving indoor air quality, water conservation, heating and cooling processes, and better methods of both landscaping and reducing and handling solid waste.

Over 100 energy, architecture, environment, engineering, and building experts have come together to work on this project. For the next 20 years, the National Park Service and other agencies have been put in charge of overseeing the long-term White House improvements. If you're interested, a CD-ROM of the White House initiatives is available through the Center for Renewable Energy and Sustainable Technology (CREST). For more information, contact them at:

CREST
1725 K Street, NW
Suite 402
Washington, DC 20006
202-289-5370/ Fax: 202-289-5354
Internet: solstice.crest.org/environment/gotwh/

See Chapter 20: "Surfing the Internet" to discover how you can find out more about the changes to the White House.

WHAT YOU CAN DO

If you are considering retrofitting your workplace, call your local utility and local and federal government agencies to find out about tax breaks or other advantages and incentives to become more efficient. Increased profits from retrofits can come in a variety of ways, including:

1. Paying attention to what your building's end users want shows them that you care, that they can work with you, and helps you to stay in touch and maintain good rapport.

2. A company's concerns over a healthy office, its efficient use of resources, and its elimination of waste means a lot to employees. It's good for morale and often increases productivity. In addition, creating a non-toxic, efficient, healthy work environment is more motivating, and employees feel better. If you're working toward a smarter office, take advantage of valuable employee knowledge and suggestions. These

can lead to reduced resource use and costs since employees in different positions may have smart suggestions for their particular areas or for the whole workplace. You may find that some of your imaginative, innovative employees already have made adaptations to their immediate work environments that can be applied throughout the workplace.

3. Improving process efficiency everywhere can make your company a much smarter and more competitive one. And, of course, increased productivity and profit are what most companies are all about.

There are inexpensive and even free things that you can do to be smart. Yet, in spite of the inarguable advantages of being smart, many people still are under the impression that being smart has to cost money and means sacrificing comfort. A small business survey found that people actually still thought energy efficiency meant cold and poorly lit buildings.

An increasing number of companies, however, are realizing that a smarter workplace means increased comfort and money saved. One generally unexpected money-saver is the increased employee productivity that often accompanies positive, smarter office changes. *Time and again, when a workplace is made more energy-efficient and less toxic, increased profits from heightened employee productivity have been over 10 times the energy savings.* In one example after another, the common results of a smarter work environment include:

• An increase in profits, often with a much higher rate of return than any other investment
• An increase in worker productivity
• A re-education in employee errors
• Better worker health, which minimizes or eliminates the unnecessary health costs resulting from a toxic environment

Making your office the smartest it can be requires the unending participation of everyone involved. It's a team effort that needs to focus on the workers, who are the end users of a workplace, and allow them fuller control over their work environment. Being smart means reviewing and revamping your whole production and work process. And when you improve your processes, you cut waste and increase productivity.

By making yours a smarter office, you can avert the need to downsize by reducing the non-labor costs of doing business. Becoming healthier and more efficient can save jobs, boost employee morale, increase your company's profits and competitive edge, lead to a healthier environment, inside and outside, and improve your company's image.

OVERCOMING TOXICITY: CREATING A HEALTHIER WORKPLACE

HEALTHY BUILDING EXAMPLES

As one article in the *ASHRAE Journal* reported, "Poor indoor air quality has wide-ranging consequences and imposes a staggering cost. In a 1989 report to Congress, the U.S. Environmental Protection Agency estimated that medical care for major illnesses resulting from indoor air pollution cost more than $1 billion annually. Lost productivity from those illnesses cost between $4.7 and $5.4 billion. Further, lost productivity and increased sick leave time as a result of IAQ-related illnesses carries an annual price tag as high as $60 billion" (Fedrazzi, 37).

Obviously, the costs of unhealthy buildings are enormous. But healthy work environments have been shown to raise employee productivity by approximately 10% through less sick leave taken and healthier employee attitudes. "If the average office worker in New York costs $40,000 a year and occupies 200 square feet of space, that means the employer's cost is about $200 per square foot per person." A 10% productivity increase would mean a $20 per-square-foot increase in rental value (Holusha, 3).

Sometimes, it helps to know who has tried what and what works. Many companies are realizing the long-term and short-term economic, health, and environmental benefits of being smarter. Below are just a few examples of those that have created healthier workplaces.

Durst Building

The Durst Organization is building mid-Manhattan's first new office building to go up in years. The company is committed to designing a smart building, which will be located at 4 Times Square, at 42nd and Broadway.

The Durst Organization wants the building to be environmentally responsible and has taken several steps to make that happen. The 48-story building's features will include: energy-efficient lighting, well-sealed and insulated doors and windows; water conserving plumbing fixtures and water, energy, and sewage treatment sys-

tems; recycling chutes for paper and wet trash; and carbon dioxide-level sensors. An automated energy management system will manage smart heating/cooling,
individual fan units, and variable air volume (Durst
Organization fact sheet).

Not only will it recycle its demolition materials, but its
tenant guidelines promote smart office material use to
maintain good air quality. Conde Nast, the travel magazine publisher, will be Durst's anchor tenant. The company will occupy one-third of the building's 1.5 million
square-foot office space. Conde Nast's executive in
charge of relocation, Charles H. Townsend, said, "The
tenant benefits from a green building. The Dursts supply us with high-quality air and low noise levels. It is our
intention to carry on the environmental theme in the
build-out and furnishing of our space." The publisher will
focus especially on adhesives, carpeting, paint, and
wallcoverings, some of the materials primarily responsible for poor indoor air quality (Holusha,1).

Douglas Durst, president of the Durst Organization, says
environmental virtues have a double benefit — "A pleasant interior space is attractive to prospective tenants,
and careful attention to conservation actually saves
money, despite somewhat higher initial costs." The company is committed to being smart. "Being environmentally responsible is part of our lifestyle," Durst said. "We
were pleased to learn that the economics made sense
as well."

The building's energy costs will be 25-30% lower than
those for buildings built in the 1980s and 15-20% better
than current government standards require. The building's lower operating costs will be passed on to tenants
(Holusha,1). As far as the building's air quality and
employee health, Durst is optimistic about the cost savings. "Eight percent of most employers' costs are for
personnel," Douglas Durst said. "If you reduce absenteeism in an environmentally friendly building, it can
have a big payoff" (Holusha,3).

National Audubon Society

As mentioned earlier, the National Audubon Society's
"new" building, Audubon House, served as an example
of energy efficiency. But it also provides a good example of a non- or low-toxic workplace.

When the National Audubon Society first retrofitted its
New York City offices, it claimed to have the most environmentally sound office building in the world. Audubon
now saves $1 million each year in rent and $100,000
each year solely through energy savings. The staff likes
Audubon House so much that it comes to work earlier,

keeps the desks neater (which, by the way, are cleaned
with citrus oil rather than toxic cleaners), and stays later.

To contribute to Audubon House's retrofit, a number of
companies donated environmentally benign products.
The National Audubon Society's status as a non-profit
organization helped to fund the retrofit. Consolidated
Edison rebates for the air conditioning ($72,000), high-
efficiency motors ($7,820), and lighting ($30,895)
helped offset the costs of the retrofit (Randall, 34).

Although some of the new products' initial costs were
higher than conventional ones, Audubon required that
they ALL pay for themselves within five years. The
materials used (furniture, carpets, etc.) were relatively
eco-friendly, with little or no toxicity. The mahogany in
Audubon's tables was certified by the Rainforest
Alliance as sustainably harvested and containing no
polyurethane, which is a hazard to those applying it. A
wipeable (reusable) board and pens hang inside a
movie-screen box on a conference room wall. (This box
takes the place of paper easels and takes up very little
space — it's about three-by-two feet and extends a mere
four inches from the wall.)

Only low-VOC paint was used. The natural carpets and
pads were tacked to the floor, avoiding the chemical offgassing that would have occurred had they been glued.
Carpets are 100% virgin wool and were made without
chemicals or dyes (wool carpet lasts much longer than
does synthetic carpet, so the carpeting will not need to
be replaced as quickly). The carpet padding used is natural, made of jute fibers encased in recycled paper.

The GTE floor tiles were made of recycled glass, left
over from lightbulb manufacture. They're much harder
than most, which means that they won't need to be
replaced as often. In addition, their pigment is mixed in
so they are impregnated with color. The tiles are non-
porous, won't scratch, and don't need waxing. While
more expensive up front, the tiles require less care and
last longer than most.

- The non-toxic insulation materials include:
- Homasote (recycled newspapers mixed with water and
  compressed with heat) used under the floors
- Multiple layers of fiberglass on the roof

Six inches of air-krete (made from magnesium salts and
whipped seawater, which is pumped in as a liquid; its
foam fills crevices and hardens into a non-toxic and non-
flammable insulation) in the walls. The air-krete offers
an insulation factor of R-18, which is three times higher
than required by New York City's building code, the second strictest next to California's.

Audubon's windows use a reflective film and are triple-paned, having two panes of glass with polymer plastic and inert gas in between them. They reflect out ultra-violet (UV) rays while retaining the building's heat and actually provide better insulation than do the brick walls. In addition, the windows open so that there is more individual control over the work environment.

Each desk has three slots for recycling, and there is an 80% recycling goal for all materials leaving Audubon House. In each kitchen, there are doors to four chutes:

• High-quality paper (Audubon estimates 42 tons/year)
• Aluminum/plastics
• Off-white paper
• Organic materials, which are then composted in a rooftop garden.

Glass is collected separately, to eliminate the breakage that would result from dropping it down the chute. The chutes empty into a basement recycling center. Whenever the door to a chute is open on another floor, the red light over the chute door on all the floors goes on. This is a warning so that, for instance, one person putting a hand in the organic materials chute on the third floor doesn't get nailed by a flying banana peel coming down from the fourth floor. This basement recycling center cost $185,000 and, although it was built for environmental reasons, it could become a profit center as markets for recycled products develop.

All materials brought into the building, from file folders and stationery to food packaging, meet strict purchasing guidelines specifying that they must contain recycled material and must be recyclable/compostable. And to be an easy example for others to follow, Audubon still purchases easily available materials rather than prototypes. While it has compiled a catalogue from Boise-Cascade and other distributors of the smartest office materials, it has met some resistance to change from those accustomed to more conventional products.

The building's air intake is on the roof, where the air is cleaner, rather than over the loading dock as many building intake vents are. The Audubon system filters out 80% of the particles in the air intake, twice the New York City code. The stairs between the floors were built to encourage increased communication among those working on different floors and to save electricity. (Glass walls were built around each floor's stairs to pass fire inspection.)

Natural Resources Defense Council (NRDC)

NRDC's ventilating system has four American Standard stand-alone roof units that bring in fresh air. This air is cooled in the summer by a Honeywell, computer-run water chiller on the roof that individually cools each floor by passing air around chilled, rooftop water. When it's muggy, the air conditioner helps, but the condensers are used only in July and August. These units can do up to 27 air exchanges each hour, resulting in fresher, healthier air. NRDC's air is filtered and, typically, exchanged 18 times each hour, far more than the average office's four to five air exchanges each hour (Gill, 58).

The air conditioning is controlled and monitored by a central computer that indicates such things as the outdoor temperature, when a filter is dirty, and each floor's air conditioning status. While the air conditioning system was expected to pay off five to seven years from completion, it paid off after only four years of use.

On the air conditioning is a two-hour button. If someone is working at night and is warm, that person can hit the button for five seconds, and the air conditioning will turn on for two hours at its last setting. Rather than cooling the whole office space, this is done on a floor-by-floor basis so as not to waste electricity.

The organization's carpets, made of 80% wool and 20% nylon, are backed with jute rather than foam and are tacked down rather than glued. These carpets are not treated chemically. Outside offices are not carpeted but have wood floors instead. The wood floors are coated with polyurethane. Fiberboard work stations were laminated to prevent the offgassing of toxic chemicals. In addition, the paint used throughout NRDC's offices was water-based, latex paint, which is less toxic than oil-based paint (Russell, 6).

Conference room furniture includes oak chairs and ranch-grown cherry wood that are stained to look like rosewood, an endangered species. More companies are beginning to experiment with lesser known species and making exotic-looking woods without contributing to environmental degradation and the further loss of biological diversity.

Unbleached paper towels are used. For its copy machine, NRDC uses paper with the highest post-consumer content it can find. Its stationary is recycled and unbleached.

University of Michigan Study

According to one *Business Week* article, Stuart L. Hart, director of the corporate environmental management program at the University of Michigan-Ann Arbor Business School, did some research. He studied the impacts of 1988-1989 pollution reduction on 1988-1991 financial performances of 127 companies on Standard & Poor's 500 stock index. He found that the majority of these companies could reduce pollution emissions up to 70% before receiving diminishing returns.

Way Station

In 1991, Way Station, Inc., opened the doors of its new 30,000 square-foot building. This place for voluntary treatment and rehabilitation of people with long-term mental illnesses was designed to be a healthy, efficient building. Although the company wanted to create a healthy environment for its building's users, its limited budget and the promise of savings through energy efficiency were hard to ignore.

ENSAR Group, an architectural firm out of Boulder, Colorado, designed the company's new facility. Rather than having architects, designers, building owners, and others work independently of one another, ENSAR Group brought together these people to create a fully integrated building design. It also used computer simulation to help design lighting, insulation, solar gain, and daylighting. The walls' insulation has an R value of 24, and the roof's is R-30 to R-35. Following its completion, the Way Station building was chosen by the American Institute of Architects as one of the United States' five most energy-efficient buildings. The electric lighting, for instance, uses 75% less energy than that of conventional building lighting systems.

The building includes a greenhouse just over one thousand square feet, which helps to contribute to the passive solar gain. Adding to solar gain is the 2,500 square feet of south-facing glass (e.g., windows). The building uses only 22,700 Btu/square-foot/year (66% less than conventional).

Other resource-efficient features include roof monitors, no west or east window glazing, skylights with daylight trackers, thermal mass (tile flooring in 80% of the building, masonry wall in the greenhouse to absorb heat during the day and release it at night), water-efficient plumbing fixtures, windows with Heat Mirror™ glazing, highly efficient lighting and controls, and an energy management system. In addition, the building uses daylighting, greenhouse and atrium plants, low-toxicity paints and fabrics, ceramic (not vinyl) tile, and low- or non-toxic cleaning materials and floor wax. Ongoing ventilation controls humidity and air quality.

The building cost $111 per square foot, a fair price for comparable facilities in that area. Although the added energy and solar features cost $170,000 more than a conventional building, they were offset by $37,655 energy savings every year. The payback was estimated at 4.5 years, an investment that would yield a 22% annual return for the company. The money saved on energy costs could be spent by the building's owners on other products and services in the local economy. In addition, the good indoor quality provided by high ventilation rates, low- or no-toxicity products, and plants helps the well-being of the building's users.

The reduction of fossil fuel use (associated with cancer and lung disease) contributes to the health of the general population. In Maryland, about 20% of the energy comes from nuclear power and 80% from fossil fuels. The Way Station does not annually emit many of the byproducts that a conventional building would, including:

6,600 pounds of sulfur dioxide
2,200 pounds of nitrogen oxide
660,000 pounds of carbon dioxide

The integration of solar and other energy-efficient features raised the cost of the building about five percent over that of a similar, conventional building. However, the annual costs of operating the Way Station's new facility are compared to a conventional building's below:

Energy Bills	Way Station (1992 bills)	Conventional
Heating (space, water)	$2,939	8,800
Cooling (electric, light)	16,672	47,100
Water heating	734	2,100
Total	20,345	58,000

Aside from the cost savings, many simply appreciate the open design, passive solar features, and lighting changes that occur throughout the day according to the sun's angle. According to Tena Meadows O'Rear, the facility's Chief Operating Officer, "Our members deal with a lot of restriction, depression and mental walls in their live. It makes a tremendous difference being in a building that embraces the natural world and feels expansive and sunny" (Thayer, 24).

FINANCIAL FEEDBACK: INSPIRATION FOR A SMARTER OFFICE

You may not realize this, but anything that cuts your employees' productivity is costing you an enormous amount of money. If you make changes in your workplace that cause employee productivity to rise just 1% per square foot, you will save more money than you pay for all other per square foot costs combined (rent, heat, light, etc.). That can make a huge difference!

Companies would be smarter if they understood the costs of inefficiency. Unfortunately, many companies have their waste handled by an environmental department. Or else, the costs of inefficient, unhealthy offices are incorporated into other expenses rather than being linked directly to their sources. The way companies' infrastructures are designed often makes it hard to track the origins and the real costs of inefficiency and toxicity. Since it can be difficult to know where the waste and inefficiency are occurring, it's tough to stop it.

Here's an example. Not long ago, there were some houses built in the Netherlands. Some of these were built with electric meters installed in their hallways. Others were built with the meters installed in their basements. In the houses with meters in the hallways, 30% less energy was used on average than in the houses with meters in the basements (Romm, 45). The only difference between the groups of houses was the presence of obvious feedback. When people can see a meter every time they walk down the hallway, it's easy for them to see the immediate results of their energy uses and adjust their behavior accordingly.

When we get immediate, obvious feedback, its easier to prevent inefficiency and an unhealthy work environment. But there are some other benefits that are hard to project — the accident that never happens, the employees that remain healthy in a non-toxic work environment, the customer that is not lost, the savings in environmental costs, the decrease in corporate liability to employees and customers.

While all of the benefits of having a smart office may not be obvious at first, many will become apparent quickly. For example, as we've seen, a good lighting retrofit will not only see savings in electric bills, but it will also improve lighting quality (which increases productivity) and lower air pollution. If you become involved with an energy-efficient program such as the Environmental Protection Agency's Green Lights Program (see Chapter 5: "Energy-Efficient Lighting"), you'll receive outside recognition of your smart office efforts and successes. And that's something else that will reflect on your management skills and your company's image internally and externally.

When such incredible changes are made so simply, rapidly, and inexpensively, the end goals that once seemed impossible are within reach. For instance, you can attain that 85% decrease in product defects, 20% increase in productivity, and 70% reduction in heating, lighting, and cooling costs that you had hoped for.

U.S. DEPARTMENT OF ENERGY'S LOW-COST INSULATION

The Department of Energy has developed a new, low-cost, exterior insulation retrofit process for existing houses with no wall cavities (e.g., homes constructed of adobe or cinder blocks). Houses of this type comprise a significant percentage of the low-income housing in the South and Southwestern United States. Many Native Americans, for instance, live in such houses on tribal lands where fossil fuels are not affordable or available and firewood is scarce. There are no commercially available low cost insulation systems for houses in such circumstances.

Adobe has poor insulating properties. As a result, these houses provide little protection against the harsh winters of the high sierra. During the winter of 1986, three Lakota Sioux elders of the Pine Ridge Reservation in South Dakota froze to death in their homes. Improving the energy efficiency and living conditions in adobe homes represents a difficult design challenge. Natural gas and other conventional heating fuels are either unaffordable or not available in many parts of the Southwest and West. Because these homes are often in remote locations, it is cost-prohibitive to use skilled labor or specialized expensive equipment to retrofit additional house insulation. Materials used should be available in building supply stores or distributors within a reasonable distance. The process used should be such that work crews, using minimal construction trade skills, should be able to perform it in a reasonable time. Because driving times may be as much as 2 hours, the number of work trips to the house should be as small as possible.

In August 1995, a demonstration wall insulation system using pumice was constructed on one wall of an adobe house in Santa Fe, New Mexico, with an insulation value of R=16 at a cost of $3.76 per square foot. The cost is expected to fall below $3.00 per square foot as the process is refined. This insulation retrofit demonstration has proven to be cost effective and structurally sound, and it also preserves a deteriorating wall from falling apart, as shown by photos taken during the construction process in August 1995 and at the end of June 1996. The insulating wall has gone through two winter seasons with no evidence of significant defects.

The process uses sandbags filled with pumice, a naturally occurring lightweight volcanic ash that has an insulating property (R value) of 1.02 per inch. Pumice is available abundantly in the Southwest where adobe homes are reported to comprise 80 percent of the low-income housing stock. The construction of the new retrofit insulation technology process is as follows:

1. 4" x 4" pressure-treated wood posts are installed in the ground at the ends of the wall so that the outer surface of the posts is at a distance equal to the width of the filled bags from the surface of the wall (16 inches).

2. A layer of crushed stone 6 inches deep and 3 feet wide is wrapped in a layer of geosynthetic felt fabric made of non-woven polypropylene and placed on grade against the base of the wall between the corner posts. The crushed stone is leveled and tamped down so that it settles. The geosynthetic fabric prevents the crushed stone from being washed away or moving.

3. Sandbags made of polypropylene are filled with 3/8-inch graded pumice and stacked against the existing wall. The sandbags rest on the 6-inch layer of crushed stone wrapped in geosynthetic felt fabric. The bags are patted down so that the pumice settles. Then, 3/8-inch-wide plastic straps are nailed to the wall with 6 inch long spiral nails on a grid 2 feet wide and 1 foot high and tied around the bags. The straps provide the sandbags with lateral support. The bags are stacked up to the top of the wall.

4. The lumber used to help support and define the ends of the wall are the 4" x 4" pressure-treated corner costs and a 2"x 12" lintel above the window. The insulation bags support themselves. The tops of the corner posts are tied together with polypropylene rope at the topmost layer of sandbags.

5. Chicken wire mesh is stretched the length of the wall and nailed to the corner posts. The wire mesh is supported by the sandbags by tying it to the ends of the straps around the sandbags, every 2 feet. It is anchored with 3 feet long steel reinforcing rods woven through the lower 12 inches of mesh and then driven into the ground. A layer of glass-fiber reinforced portland cement stucco with a minimum thickness of 3/4-inch is applied to the wire mesh.

6. The top of each corner post is tied to the adjacent pole with polypropylene rope to prevent the bagged pumice walls from pulling away from the house. The bagged pumice wall cannot fall inward because the existing wall will prevent this from happening.

Geosynthetic fabrics or geotextiles – an industrial strength textile designed for civil engineering and soil construction – are inexpensive and have many desirable properties. Geotextiles are made commonly of polypropylene and can be woven or non-woven fabrics. Polypropylene has a high tensile strength, is so light that it floats on water and is unaffected by soil and water. Sandbags manufactured from polypropylene woven geotextiles cost about 22 cents each. The non-woven polypropylene used to wrap the crushed stone sub-base is used as an underlayment in highway construction and costs about 6 cents per square foot.

The key cost-saving ideas in this process are that it uses no foundation or structural supports and needs a very small amount of lumber. No digging or pouring of a reinforced concrete footer is needed. The insulation supports itself and the weight of a stucco skin and does not add any additional structural loads to the existing house wall. Expensive machinery and specialized equipment are not needed. Standard construction trade skills are used. The materials used are readily available and should easily pass fire-resistance ratings of most of the model Codes.

The thermal insulating values of uninsulated walls of different construction are surprisingly similar: R=3.5 for 10-inch thick adobe; R=3 for 8-inch thick block wall; and R=3.4 for a wood frame wall with 2x4-inch studs. A revised DOE-2 computer energy simulation (July 1996) shows that the pumice wall reduces the heating cost from $570 to $275 for a saving of about 50%. It assumes propane for heating at $.95 per gallon and 74.1 percent heating efficiency and electricity for the furnace fan at $.0924/kWh, the current costs in rural New Mexico. The life spans of stucco and polypropylene are over 30 years.

The Savings to Investment Ratio (SIR) is 1.2. This house has a cellar and floor 2 feet above grade. If the house had a floor on grade and no cellar, the SIR increases to 1.4. The Cost of Conserved Energy for propane is $1.04 per gallon of Propane, which is 9% higher than the price of propane.

CHAPTER 3

GETTING STARTED TOWARD A SMARTER OFFICE

"Without courage, you can't practice any other quality consistently."
Maya Angelou

THE IMPORTANCE OF BEING SMARTER

**Efficient + Healthy Workplace =
Increased Profits + More Competitive Company**

Businesses spend an enormous amount of money on electricity, paper, and other resources. Not only is an inefficient use of resources expensive for businesses, but the environmental impacts can be enormous. Each year, because of inefficiency, buildings and power plants in the U.S. emit 14% of the gases that contribute to global warming, release millions of tons of sulfur dioxide and nitric oxide (accounting for over 15% of U.S. acid rain), use 30 million trees each year through wasteful practices, and consume 12.5% of all electricity used. Fortunately, smarter technologies and products increasingly are available, making it easier to find alternatives to more resource-intensive standbys.

Many businesses concerned with efficiency, health, and the environmental impacts have created new organizational policies and behaviors. Some have established internal task forces to address such issues as energy efficiency, sick building syndrome (SBS), recycling, purchasing policies, and smart office behavior.

Efforts have been made to create healthier business environments, switch to more ecologically friendly products, and increase employee awareness of the impacts that individual behaviors have on conservation. Educational "green bag" lunches have been used by some ecologically oriented companies, and weekly electronic mail (e-mail) messages have been sent to everyone in the company to raise awareness on a variety of issues related to office health and efficiency.

Most companies that have made their workplaces healthier and more efficient have found that they needed an overarching framework of internal policies and goals to guide them. Use your creativity to come up with your own, or look to other companies' guidelines to help you create a framework that will be useful to you and your company.

ESTABLISHING THE SMART OFFICE AS A COMPANY PRIORITY

Once you've decided that having a healthy, resource-efficient workplace is an organizational priority, it will be easier to follow up on decisions that are beneficial to your company. It also can help to orient new employees to your internal, smart office goals and strategies.

To create a smarter working environment, there are three important things that you need to keep in mind:

- Be proactive
- Focus on the end results
- Improve constantly

You've seen how being proactive has helped smart companies succeed, but what do I mean by focusing on the end results? Think about what it is that you're really after and then look into the smartest alternatives that can get you there. In designing better alternatives to your current situation, focus on the needs of the end user and on your desired end results. Then, create the smartest design that you can.

TAKE THE FIRST FEW STEPS

Survey Employees

You may want to conduct an employee survey as a part of your smart office audit. Your employees are great sources of information on how they feel at work and suggestions on how to improve processes and save money.

Conducting employee interviews offers the human perspective that air quality tests, for example, cannot. They can offer details on physical symptoms resulting from Sick Building Syndrome, eye strain from poor lighting (which can include poorly designed, too much, or too little lighting), or suggestions on how to make simple improvements. Your employees may spend many of their waking hours living and breathing in the work environment and have a vested interest in making it healthy.

In addition to formal surveys, there are many informal ways to get employee feedback regarding the work environment. Concerns, ideas, and suggestions can be collected through meetings, by phone, in the hallways, via suggestion boxes and through electronic mail. You can do general surveys or thematic ones (air quality, energy efficiency, etc.).

Whatever you choose to do, be alert and sensitive to the first indications that employees are experiencing difficulties. They may differ greatly in allergic reactions, responses to stress, and other health and production problems. Rather than resenting their complaints, find the source of trouble. Just as mine operators were able to avoid massive costs by heeding your canaries' warnings, don't take for granted the benefit of your more sensitive employees. You might be happy to have them there; rather than resenting them for their sensitivity.

Use Science to Save Money

There also are scientific ways to measure certain compounds in the air, electromagnetic fields emitting from electronic equipment, and how much light falls on a given area. Consider using the information from these measurements in working toward a smarter office.

The Smart University

For university students and faculty interested in creating a smarter campus, *Campus Ecology* is available. Put out by a student environmental action coalition, this manual explains how to conduct environmental audits for campuses. Contact SEAC at: 919-967-4600. E-mail: seac@igc.org or seac@unc.bitnet

Green Seal wrote the Campus Green Buying Guide to help universities use their purchasing power beneficially. Contact Green Seal at: 202-331-7337.

SMART OFFICE PROGRAMS

There are many government programs that have been designed to help commercial building owners and tenants design, retrofit, and maintain smarter buildings. These programs are voluntary and can offer invaluable assistance to people with varying degrees of expertise. A few are outlined below:

Clean Cities

This program provides technical assistance to cities and offers information on financial resources for using alternative fuel vehicles (AFVs). Since the program's beginning, there has been a 300% increase in alternative fuel refueling facilities across the United States.

Climate Challenge

A joint effort of the Department of Energy (DOE) and the electric utility industry, the Climate Challenge program was created to minimize or eliminate greenhouse gas emissions. It works toward "energy improvements in end-use, distribution, transmission, and generation; increased use of energy-efficient electro-technologies; fuel switching to lower carbon fuels such as natural gas, nuclear, or renewable-energy; transportation actions, including greater use of vehicles power by natural gas and electricity; forestry actions; recovery of methane from landfills and coal seams; and, the use of fly-ash as a Portland cement substitute." Contact: 202-586-6210

Climate Wise

This partnership of the Department of Energy, Environmental Protection Agency (EPA), and industry was developed to cut greenhouse gas emissions across industries by adopting voluntary energy-efficiency, renewable-energy, and pollution-prevention technologies. The DOE offers information through the Climate Wise Clearinghouse and seminars/workshops. Contact: 202-260-4407

Energy Star Computers and Office Equipment

This voluntary program was designed to help reduce the energy demands of computers and other office equipment. Contact: 202-233-9114

Energy Star Buildings

In the United States, energy used to operate buildings costs about $70 billion each year. Aside from the expense of using non-renewable energy, it also contributes to global climate change, smog, and acid rain.

In 1995, the Environmental Protection Agency launched its new Energy Star Buildings program. This program, an expansion of the agency's Green Lights program (discussed in Chapter 5: "Energy-Efficient Lighting"), includes buildings' electrical and mechanical systems. Through this program, the EPA and willing building owners and facility managers work together on a five-part building improvement process:

"Stage 1: Green Lights
• Install energy-efficient lighting technologies

Stage 2: Building Tune-Up
• Check and adjust building systems
• Develop and implement an ongoing preventative maintenance plan

Stage 3: HVAC Load Reductions
• Install window films, reflective coverings, and more effective roof insulation
• Buy energy-efficient computers, monitors, and printers that have the EPA Energy Star label

Stage 4: Fan System Upgrades
• Upgrade constant-air-volume systems to VAV systems
• Upgrade variable-air-volume (VAV)
• Reduce fan system oversizing
• Replace existing motors with smaller, high-efficiency motors

Stage 5: HVAC Plant Improvements
• Replace or upgrade chillers
• Retrofit water pumps and compressors with VSDs
• Replace electric resistance heat where possible"
(Energy Star Buildings fact sheet).

Energy Star Buildings volunteers are asked to upgrade their buildings' systems where profitable. In return, the EPA will provide support, including the Energy Star Buildings Manual, software that plans and schedules upgrades, software that calculates savings from upgrades, a database of financing programs for upgrades in efficiency, case studies showing savings from upgrades, indoor air quality information, and other information. Contact:

Energy Star Buildings Program
U.S. EPA (6202J)
401 M Street, SW
Washington, DC 20460
888-STAR-YES
Fax (24-hour): 202-233-9659
Internet: www.epa.gov/docs/GCDOAR/EnergyStar.html

Federal Energy Management Program (FEMP)

This program makes Federal buildings throughout the country more efficient through energy efficiency, renewable energy, and water conservation. FEMP also has a Renewable Energy Working Group of over 100 Federal and renewable energy industry representatives. Under this program, each Federal agency is to develop at least one renewable "showcase" project to serve as a model for its agency. Contact: 202-586-5772

Geothermal Heat Pump Consortium

This is an organization of the DOE, EPA, Consortium for Energy-Efficiency, electric utilities, equipment manufacturers, and industry associations. It works to increase efficiency and geothermal heat pump sales, reduce greenhouse gas emissions and tenant costs, and create a viable market for geothermal heat pumps that is not reliant on rebates or government incentives.

Industrial Assessment Centers (IACs)

Industrial Assessment Centers are located at 30 U.S. universities. They offer one-day, free assessments for small- and medium-sized manufacturers (20-499 employees) and training in energy-efficiency management. Comprehensive reports are created for each company detailing its energy-conservation and waste-reduction potential.

Motor Challenge (U.S. DOE)

The Motor Challenge program teaches industries and local governments about energy-efficient motor systems. Contact: 202-586-7234

Municipal Energy Management Program (MEMP)

This grant program supports local government projects. It helps communities become smarter by using smart technologies, energy-efficient transportation, and designing sustainable energy programs.

National Industry Competitiveness through Energy, Environment, and Economics (NICE3)

This grant program works to raise industry competitiveness through energy efficiency and waste reduction.

Partnerships for Affordable Housing

This collaboration among the Department of Energy, Department of Housing and Urban Development, and Habitat for Humanity and other low-income housing organizations was designed to encourage and implement the construction of smart, affordable housing. It provides technical assistance for both energy efficiency and renewable energy.

Rebuild America

Rebuild America offers technical and sometimes financial assistance to reduce energy use in commercial and multi-family buildings. Contact: 202-586-9424

Utility Photovoltaic Group (UPVG)

Through this program, public utilities work together to reduce greenhouse gas emissions by using photovoltaic generating systems.

Weatherization Assistance Program (WAP)
Administered through grants, WAP works to increase the residential energy efficiency of low-income citizens.

SMART OFFICE STANDARDS

Some organizations have designed standards by which to measure a building's health and efficiency ratings. These ratings focus on the health of the building itself as well as the building's local and global impacts.

BEPAC

One such program is Canada's BEPAC (Building Environmental Performance Assessment Criteria) program. This is Canada's first comprehensive process for measuring the environmental performance of existing and new commercial buildings. It was created as a way to determine a building's impact on the global, local, and indoor environments. Modeled after the United Kingdom's BREEAM, this voluntary program was developed at the University of British Columbia in December 1993, and other regions across Canada have developed similar programs since then.

To determine a building's performance, several factors are taken into account. The environmental criteria evaluated are divided into five primary topics, and within each of these topics are specific criteria. They are:

- Environmental impact of energy use
- Indoor environmental quality
- Ozone layer protection
- Resource conservation
- Site and transportation

The BEPAC Foundation developed a version that enables companies to do an in-house evaluation of their own buildings rather than rely on a third party. It contains a BEPAC document, a program to train users, and software spreadsheets. For more information, contact:

BEPAC Foundation headquarters:
301-1770 W. Seventh Street
Vancouver, British Columbia
Canada, V6J 4Y6
604-736-0013/ Fax: 604-736-4277
Internet: greenbuilding.ca

BREEAM

Another rating program is Britain's BREEAM program. "BREEAM" stands for Building Research Establishment Environmental Assessment Method. It was established to assess indoor environmental quality and covers a wide range of buildings, from superstores and supermarkets to new and existing offices.

BREEAM is a voluntary program that allows building owners and occupants to find out about their impacts on a variety of environmental factors, including ozone depletion, global warming, and the destruction of rainforests and other resources. It also illuminates a number of other building issues, from noise and air pollution to lighting and hazardous materials. For more information on BREEAM, contact:

BREEAM Project Manager
Building Research Establishment
Garston
Watford
WD2 7JR
United Kingdom
0923-89404/ Fax: 0923-664010

U.S. GREEN BUILDING COUNCIL

The U.S. Green Building Council is a non-profit coalition dedicated to encouraging the development of healthy and efficient buildings. The Council has developed a rating system for buildings that looks at asbestos, daylighting, energy conservation, indoor air quality, and temperature. Of course, a good rating could increase a building's resale value while encouraging others to retrofit or design new buildings with these factors in mind.

CONDUCTING A SMART OFFICE AUDIT

Before you start a campaign to make your workplace healthier, you should conduct a smart office audit. This audit is a systematic way to determine the good and bad aspects of your work environment. A complete, smart office audit looks at a variety of things, including:

Air Quality
- Ventilation (how often air is exchanged/hour, fresh air sources (e.g., loading dock)
- Toxins (paints, carpets, glues, resins, plastics, pesticides used on indoor plants, manufacturing processes)

Ergonomics
- Keyboards
- Chairs
- Desk arrangements

Heating/Cooling *
• Cost
• Method
• Efficiency

Lighting *
• Efficiency
• Quality (glare, color)
• Degree of manual or automated control

Materials Used
• Virgin vs. recycled
• Toxic vs. non-toxic

Production Processes
• Indoor toxins
• Open loop manufacturing processes (characterized by unnecessary waste)
• Direct mail/publications (recycled/recyclable papers, soy-based inks)

Check with your local utility to find out if it offers free or inexpensive energy audits. In addition to knowing what to look for in your lighting, heating, and cooling, your utility may help to pay for the changes it recommends.

DESIGNING SMART COMPANY POLICIES

While creating a smarter office is a worthwhile task, be aware that it requires a shift in thinking. To create a smarter office, you have to understand the impacts that your purchasing decisions and individual behaviors have upon employee health, customer/client health, ecology, and your company as a whole. Increasing employee awareness throughout the organization and developing smart policies is a good first move.

You can design smart company policies regarding everything from environmental policies to choosing and working with suppliers. To get an idea of some beneficial policies that your company could develop, take a look at what some other businesses have done.

GENERAL
The CERES Principles

Many companies, including some major corporations, have joined the Coalition for Environmentally Responsible Economies (CERES) and adopted their CERES Principles. Originally known as the Valdez Principles, the CERES Principles were developed in 1989 after the Exxon Valdez oil spill. The following information should provide a clear idea of what the CERES Principles are all about.

The Coalition

CERES promotes the CERES Principles, a model corporate code of environmental conduct. Environmental groups and institution investors controlling $150 billion in assets designed the principles.

Companies endorsing the CERES Principles pledge to monitor and improve their behavior to regarding:

• the biosphere
• the sustainable use of natural resources
• the reduction and disposal of wastes
• energy conservation
• risk reduction
• safe products and services
• environmental restoration
• informing the public
• management commitment
• audits and reports

Endorsers agree to decrease their waste, use resources efficiently, market safe products, and take responsibility for their past harms. They also call for an environmental expert on each corporate board and an annual, public audit of a company's environmental progress.

These groups asked companies to subscribe to the principles, implicitly suggesting that eventually investments could be contingent on compliance. Several companies have signed the CERES Principles, including Sun Oil and H.B. Fuller (a chemical company).

The Principles
"Introduction
By adopting these Principles, we publicly affirm our belief that corporations have a responsibility for the environment, and must conduct all aspects of their business as responsible stewards of the environment by operating in a manner that protects the Earth. We believe that corporations must not compromise the ability of future generations to sustain themselves.

We will update our practices constantly in light of advances in technology and new understandings in health and environmental science. In collaboration with CERES, we will promote a dynamic process to ensure that the Principles are interpreted in a way that accommodates changing technologies and environmental realities. We intend to make consistent, measurable progress in implementing these Principles and to apply them to all aspects of our operations throughout the world.

1. Protection of the Biosphere

We will reduce and make continual progress toward eliminating the release of any substance that may cause environmental damage to the air, water, or the earth or its inhabitants. We will safeguard all habitats affected by our operations and will protect open spaces and wilderness, while preserving biodiversity.

2. Sustainable Use of Natural Resources

We will make sustainable use of renewable natural resources, such as water, soils and forests. We will conserve non-renewable natural resources through efficient use and careful planning.

3. Reduction and Disposal of Wastes

We will reduce and where possible eliminate waste through source reduction and recycling. All waste will be handled and disposed of through safe and responsible methods.

4. Energy Conservation

We will conserve energy and improve the energy efficiency of our internal operations and of the goods and services we sell. We will make every effort to use environmentally safe and sustainable energy sources.

5. Risk Reduction

We will strive to minimize the environmental, health and safety risks to our employees and the communities in which we operate through safe technologies, facilities and operating procedures, and by being prepared for emergencies.

6. Safe Products and Services

We will reduce and where possible eliminate the use, manufacture or sale of products and services that cause environmental damage or health or safety hazards. We will inform our customers of the environmental impacts of our products or services and try to correct unsafe use.

7. Environmental Restoration

We will promptly and responsibly correct conditions we have caused that endanger health, safety or the environment. To the extent feasible, we will redress injuries we have caused to persons or damage we have caused to the environment and will restore the environment.

8. Informing the Public

We will inform in a timely manner everyone who may be affected by conditions caused by our company that might endanger health, safety or the environment. We will regularly seek advice and counsel through dialogue

with persons in communities near our facilities. We will not take any action against employees for reporting dangerous incidents or conditions to management or to appropriate authorities.

9. Management Commitment

We will implement these Principles and sustain a process that ensures that the Board of Directors and Chief Executive Officer are fully informed about pertinent environmental issues and are fully responsible for environmental policy. In selecting our Board of Directors, we will consider demonstrated environmental commitment as a factor.

10. Audits and Reports

We will conduct an annual self-evaluation of our progress in implementing these Principles. We will support the timely creation of generally accepted environmental audit procedures. We will annually complete the CERES Report, which will be made available to the public.

Disclaimer

These Principles established an ethic with criteria by which investors and others can assess the environmental performance of companies. Companies that endorse these Principles pledge to go voluntarily beyond the requirements of the law. The terms may and might in Principles one and eight are not meant to encompass every imaginable consequence, no matter how remote. Rather, these Principles obligate endorsers to behave as prudent persons who are not governed by conflicting interests and who possess a strong commitment to environmental excellence and to human health and safety. These Principles are not intended to create new legal liabilities, expand existing rights or obligations, waive legal defenses, or otherwise affect the legal position of any endorsing company, and are not intended to be used against an endorser in any legal proceedings for any purpose."

The above principles were taken from CERES' Internet home page. For more information on the CERES Principles, contact the Coalition for Environmentally Responsible Economies (CERES):

Coalition for Environmentally Responsible Economies
711 Atlantic Ave.
Boston, Massachusetts 02111
617-451-0927/ Fax: 617-482-2028
Internet:www.dep.state.pa.us/dep/deputate/pollprev/ceres/ceres.htm

The Hannover Principles

Another example are the Hannover Principles. These were developed by William McDonough Architects for EXPO 2000, the World's Fair, in Hannover, Germany.

"1. Insist on rights of humanity and nature to co-exist in a healthy, supportive, diverse and sustainable condition.

2. Recognize interdependence. The elements of human design interact with and depend upon the natural world, with broad and diverse implications at every scale. Expand design considerations to recognizing even distant effects.

3. Respect relationships between spirit and matter. Consider all aspects of human settlement including community, dwelling, industry and trade in terms of existing and evolving connections between spiritual and material consciousness.

4. Accept responsibility for the consequences of design decisions upon human well-being, the viability of natural systems, and their right to co-exist.

5. Create safe objects of long-term value. Do not burden future generations with requirements for maintenance or vigilant administration of potential danger due to the careless creation of products, processes, or standards.

6. Eliminate the concept of waste. Evaluate and optimize the full life cycle of products and processes, to approach the state of natural systems, in which there is no waste.

7. Rely on natural energy flows. Human designs should, like the living world, derive their creative forces from perpetual solar income. Incorporate this energy efficiently and safely for responsible use.

8. Understand the limitations of design. No human creation lasts forever and design does not solve all problems. Those who create and plan should practice humility in the face of nature. Treat nature as a model and mentor, not an inconvenience to be evaded or controlled.

9. Seek constant improvement by the sharing of knowledge. Encourage direct and open communication between colleagues, patrons, manufacturers and users to link long-term sustainable considerations with ethical responsibility, and re-establish the integral relationship between natural processes and human activity" (William McDonough Architects, 5).

These principles can be tailored to suit your company's needs, or you can design your own.

A Smart Mission

Many companies are beginning to take environmental, human rights, and other factors into account in their day-to-day operations. A few are mentioned below.

Calvert Group

The following was taken from the Calvert Group's (a socially responsible investment firm) mission statement.

Mission

"Calvert Group's mission is to become a premier asset management company recognized for our quality programs and for our commitment to positive social change.

Operating Philosophy

Calvert Group is committed to constant improvement. We choose to make a difference in our world by working to improve the quality of life for our customers, employees and the communities in which we live and work. We strongly believe that the spirit of Calvert Group is embodied in our Shared Values. Our growth and long-term success will directly result from meeting the continually changing needs of our customers and employees with unflinching integrity. All decisions are made with consideration given to their effect on all of Calvert Group's constituents, balancing our growth and our responsibilities to society with fair profits" (Social Venture Network, 2).

Tom's of Maine

Tom's of Maine sells all-natural, personal-care products, from toothpastes to deodorants. The company's mission statement is:

"Serve customers by providing safe, effective, innovative, natural products of high quality.

Build a relationship with customers that extends beyond product usage to include full and honest dialogue, responsiveness to feedback, and the exchange of information about products and issues.

Respect, value, and serve not only customers, but also our co-workers, owners, agents, suppliers, and our community; to be concerned about and contribute to their well-being, and to operate with integrity so as to be deserving of their trust.

Provide meaningful work, fair compensation, and a safe, healthy work environment that encourages openness, creativity, self-discipline, and growth.

Acknowledge the value of each person's contribution to our goals, and to foster teamwork in our tasks.

Be distinctive in products and policies which honor and sustain our natural world.

Address community concerns, in Maine and around the globe, by devoting a portion of our time, talents, and resources to the environment, human needs, the arts, and education.

Work together to contribute to the long-term value and sustainability of our company.

Be a profitable and successful company, while acting in a socially and environmentally responsible manner" (*The GreenMoney Journal*, Spring/Summer 1995 issue).

Environmental Policies

Some companies have designed policies specific to the environment.

Patagonia

This U.S. outdoor clothing company recognizes individual environmental activists and publicizes over 100 organizations working toward positive environmental change. Since 1984, Patagonia has donated 10% of its pre-tax profits to such groups.

World Wildlife Fund – United Kingdom

In order to be consistent with its own smart policies, World Wildlife Fund (UK) developed twelve specific goals for 1992. Each of these goals is broken down into specific strategies (see #1 for an example). These goals are described below:

1. Reduce electricity consumption by 10% (based on 1989/90 figure).

- Check whether you can reduce overhead lighting at your desk.
- Switch off the lights when they are not needed.
- Switch off all electrical equipment when you are not using it (except for shredders, water urns, photocopiers, mainframe computers, fax machines, and snack machines).
- Switch photocopiers to standby after use.
- Avoid fans and fan heaters.
- When buying any new electrical equipment, ask for its power rating.
- Future issues include replacing lightbulbs with more energy-efficient ones, existing button operated electric hand dryers, adapting lighting to be movement sensi-

tive, removing Klix drink machines.

The other eleven goals (not including their associated strategies) are:

2. Reduce fuel consumption of road travel for business by 20% (based on 1989/90 figure).

3. Reduce air miles traveled for business by 5% (based on 1989/90 figure).

4. Reduce stationery consumption by 10% in value (based on 1990/91 figure).

5. Extend procedures for recycling waste.

6. Reduce waste paper resulting from WWF's direct mail operations.

7. Improve purchasing accuracy.

8. Avoid buying or selling any product that could contribute to the destruction of wildlife or the non-sustainable use of biological resources.

9. Assess the environmental impacts of paper and all stationery products and identify the best options.

10. Improve the average "Green Rating" of the Gift Catalogue by 5% (for both 1992 catalogues compared to their 1991 equivalents).

11. Improve the average "Green Rating" of licensed products by 5% (based on 1990/91).

12. Decide whether to relocate Head Office, having carried out a fundamental review of all the environmental considerations involved (WWF-UK 1992 policies).

In addition to coming up with these smart, internal policies and goals to fulfill them, WWF (UK) created a Green Action Project Team (GAPT). This team helps to ensure that the organization's policies and goals are carried out.

The GAPT gives its policy manual to new staff and talks to them of the Eco-Standards and Practices developed at WWF (UK). The GAPT also answers questions and provides annual reviews for WWF (UK)'s goals. It also acts as an advisory group, promotes an unending dialogue within the organization, and developed WWF's Pledge and Standard. The GAPT representatives also lead small discussion groups periodically both for ideas and to keep the greening momentum going.

As an incentive for being smarter, the GAPT is thinking of awarding a quarterly Green Award to employees. There also is hope that employees will monitor their own progress. The GAPT meets quarterly to review the organization's progress, producing a "short, and light-hearted, Quarterly Update" to be circulated to everyone. This Update includes the staff's best ideas and amendments to Staff Guidelines. It also will show electricity consumption, gas money reimbursed, air fares, and amounts of stationery used for the previous quarter.

Choosing & Working with Suppliers

You may believe that as just one company there is not much you can do to choose the products that your suppliers carry. Increasingly, however, companies are finding that they can have a strong and positive impact while increasing their own product options.

Co-op America's Programs

Co-op America, founded in 1982, focuses on economic strategies and education to help individuals and businesses address social and environmental problems. It has Green Business, Consumer Education and Empowerment, Corporate Responsibility, and Sustainable Living Programs. It also publishes the National Green Pages – an inexpensive (free to members), annual directory of smart companies in the U.S., Boycott Action News, Socially Responsible Financial Planning Guide, and Co-op America Quarterly, consumer magazine with information on improving housing, work, food, the environment, and other social issues.

1612 K Street, NW
Suite 600
Washington, DC 20006
202-872-5307
1-800-58-Green

Green Seal Environmental Partners Program

You can ask your suppliers if they carry smarter products that have been certified by Green Seal or another certification organization. Green Seal, a non-profit company, awards seals of approval to products that are more environmentally friendly than their peers. This generally means that they are less toxic, more efficient, made of recycled materials, etc. You can become a Green Seal Environmental Partner to be recognized for your efforts

Patagonia's Santa Barbara, California, store offers clothing and outdoor products and informs its customers about organic cotton and other issues.

in being environmentally friendly and creating a smarter workplace.

What to Ask Your Suppliers

You can call to ask what smarter products your suppliers carry, or you can send a simple, one-page form for them to fill out. Let them know that you are trying to reduce your resource use and create a less toxic workplace. Ask them what they can do to help, and be sure to ask:

1. What types of supplies do you carry?

2. Are they made from recycled, non-toxic, or sustainably harvested materials?

3. What are your products' impacts on environmental/ human health?

4. Will they biodegrade, or will they remain a part of the recycling/waste stream?

5. How are they packaged?

6. What packing do you use (boxes filled with newspaper, styrofoam, biodegradable corn starch peanuts)? Is it recyclable?

8. May we return used packaging to you to be reused or for credit?

9. Are the people who make your products paid fairly, and do they work in suitable conditions?

10. Does your company have and practice smart policies internally and externally?

Ben & Jerry's

According to the Ben & Jerry's Ice Cream Company, "The purpose of developing progressive supplier relationships is to move our social mission beyond simply giving away a share of our profits by making our business dealings themselves reflective of our philosophy" (Social Venture Network, 111).

The company works with a variety of suppliers including:

Greyston Bakery (Yonkers, NY) – This bakery is managed by a Buddhist monk who hires and counsels homeless people or those about to become homeless. Greyston Bakery produces the fudge brownies for Ben & Jerry's Chocolate Fudge Brownie ice cream; this has created twenty-five jobs.

Community Products, Inc. – Ben & Jerry's buys cashews and Brazil nuts harvested by indigenous Amazonian peoples. It offers a sustainable alternative to non-renewable resource use that allows indigenous inhabitants to remain in and sustainably use their ecosystem.

Maine Blueberry Company (Maine) – Ben & Jerry's uses these blueberries for its ice cream. The blueberry company is owned by Passamaquoddy Indians, who use the profits for economic and educational development in their community (Social Venture Network, 111).

SETTING SMART GOALS

After defining your company policies, you'll need to set goals. A policy may look great on paper, but if there is no strategy to back it up, follow through may be difficult.

Setting goals is important in working toward a smarter office. It gives you something specific to work toward, and that makes it easier to monitor your own progress and find out what works best for you. It also reminds employees, shareholders, and customers of your continuing efforts on their behalf and can increase their cooperation in helping you achieve your goals. Setting specific goals that are consistent with your company's policies is important, too.

- Define smart criteria, and identify products and behaviors that fit these criteria.
- Choose your target areas (e.g., electricity, paper products, air quality), and develop short- and long-term goals for improvement.
- Develop strategies to reach these new goals.

COMING UP WITH YOUR OWN GOALS

When establishing company goals, be as specific as possible. Let's say your first goal is to improve indoor air quality. Choosing the goal Improve Indoor Air Quality is a great start. Next, you'll need to come up with the steps you will take to get there. For instance, replacing your current, toxic office supplies with non-toxic ones might be one way you choose to follow through on your air quality goal.

So, under Goal 1: Improve Indoor Air Quality, your first steps may be to:

1. Meet with your office supplies representatives, and urge them to carry non-toxic products if they don't already.

2. If your current office supply companies don't offer non-toxic office products, order from one that will. Remember that a toxic office is not only hard on everyone who works there, and it is hard on the health of those that manufacture it. It also can be quite costly to remedy and expensive in terms of your company's liability.

It might take a little effort on your part, but healthier alternatives to products that we've been using for a long time are available. They are much easier to find these days, and can help you avoid the many costs associated with indoor air pollution.

Another goal might be to reduce the amount of paper that each person uses. If you decide to cut back on paper use within the next 12 months, for instance, let everyone in the company know your goal and how they can help you achieve it by using electronic mail, double-sided copying, etc.

LOCAL GOVERNMENTS & SMART BUILDINGS

Private companies are not the only ones interested in smart building. Some governments, local and Federal, have seen the benefits of smart building and are taking advantage of them.

Just like companies, government budgets often are limited and not forgiving of waste. So, it makes sense for them to design or renovate buildings with an eye toward resource efficiency and no toxicity.

DESIGNING SMART CITY PRINCIPLES

According to Michael Myers (Department of Energy) who worked with the City of Austin, Texas, to design its guidelines, cities interested in creating sustainable development principles should take the following steps:

"Examine local government policies and procurement procedures for inclusion of green building measures.

Develop a demonstration green building project or local sustainable building design competition.

Require that government building projects incorporate renewable energy and energy-efficient systems, indoor-air-quality guidelines, and waste and water-efficiency measures.

Survey and review other cities with green building projects, programs, and standards.

Assemble a multidisciplinary team within the community to discuss the possibility of developing a green building program.

Develop a green building awards program; co-sponsor the program with the local utility and local chapters of design, engineering, and property-management societies.

Survey and publish the community's green building resources.

Initiate a conference or series of lectures on green building issues.

Assemble a green building resource library within an existing library or municipal office.

Initiate a green building computer-based bulletin board or Internet site" (U.S. DOE, 1997, ix).

EXAMPLES OF SMART CITY PRINCIPLES

Some governments have created guidelines for renovation and for building new. The City of Austin is considered one of the cutting-edge governments as far as smart building and community design go. Below are their building design guidelines, adopted February 24, 1994.

City of Austin's Sustainable Building Guidelines Resolution

"Whereas, sustainability means satisfying our present needs without compromising the ability of future generations to meet their needs; and

Whereas, sustainable or "green" building practices conserve energy, water and other natural resources, preserve local and global environmental quality, strengthen the local economy, promote human health and safety, create higher quality enduring structures, and offer cost reductions in maintenance, solid waste disposal and energy; and

Whereas, the citizens and the government of Austin have continually demonstrated a commitment to the preservation of our natural resources and to quality of life; and

Whereas, the existing internationally recognized Austin Green Builder Program for residential building has been well received by the public and the building community; NOW, THEREFORE,

BE IT RESOLVED BY THE CITY COUNCIL OF THE CITY OF AUSTIN:

That City staff develop guidelines for sustainable building practices for non-residential buildings within 6 (six) months of approval of this resolution. The Environmental and Conservation Services Department shall be charged with overseeing the development and application of the guidelines to all municipal facilities and with providing necessary training and guidance for affected staff and consultants; and

BE IT FURTHER RESOLVED:
That the City shall encourage voluntary compliance with its sustainable building guidelines in the private sector

through educational and promotional endeavors, with the ultimate goal being that of making Austin a model "Sustainable City"; and

BE IT FURTHER RESOLVED:
That the City Council expresses its support for using green builder projects to provide opportunities for youth through apprenticeship programs such as the Casa Verde Program sponsored by the American Institute for Learning with the assistance of the Environmental and Conservation Services Department; and

BE IT FURTHER RESOLVED:
That the Environmental and Conservation Services Department shall monitor compliance with the Resolution and shall annually report to the City Council, with the first report being given not later than February 25, 1995."

City of Portland's Sustainable City Principles

Of course, Austin isn't the only city that understands the benefits of being smarter. Others, including Portland, Oregon, have created development guidelines. Portland's were adopted in November 1994. They are:

Goal
"City of Portland will promote a sustainable future that meets today's needs without compromising the ability of future generations to meet their needs, and accepts its responsibility to:

• Support a stable, diverse and equitable economy
• Protect the quality of the air, water, land and other natural resources
• Conserve native vegetation, fish, wildlife habitat and other ecosystems
• Minimize human impacts on local and worldwide ecosystems

City elected officials and staff will:

1. Encourage and develop connections between environmental quality and economic vitality. Promote development that reduce adverse effects on ecology and the natural resource capital base and supports employment opportunities for our citizens.

2. Include long term and cumulative impacts in decision making and work to protect the natural beauty and diversity of Portland for future generations.

3. Ensure commitment to equity so environmental impacts and the costs of protecting the environment

do not unfairly burden any one geographic or socioeconomic sector of the City.

4. Ensure environmental quality and understand environmental linkages when decisions are made regarding growth management, land use, transportation, energy, water, affordable housing, indoor and outdoor air quality and economic development.

5. Use resources efficiently and reduce demand for natural resources, like energy, land and water, rather than expanding supply.

6. Prevent additional pollution through planned, proactive measures rather than only corrective action. Enlist the community to focus on solutions rather than symptoms.

7. Act locally to reduce adverse global impacts of rapid growth of population and consumption, such as ozone depletion and global warming, and support and implement innovative programs that maintain and promote Portland's leadership as a sustainable city.

8. Purchase products based on long term environmental and operating costs and find ways to include environmental and social costs in short term prices. Purchase products that are durable, reusable, made of recycled materials, and non-toxic.

9. Educate citizens and businesses about Portland's Sustainable City Principles and take advantage of community resources. Facilitate citizen participation in City policy decisions and encourage everyone to take responsibility for their actions that otherwise adversely impact the environment.

10. Report annually on the health and quality of Portland's environment and economy" (City of Portland, Sustainable City Principles, 1).

EXAMPLES OF SMARTER CITIES

Other cities are thinking smart, too. A few that are developing and implementing smart building guidelines are New York, San Diego, San Francisco, Seattle, and Hennepin County, Minnesota.

Several cities have published smart design guidelines. You may want to turn to them for ideas. They include: Maryland's Department of Education's *Building Ecology and School Design,* Austin's *Sustainable Building Guidelines,* Portland's Solid Waste Department of Metro's *Guide to Recycled Products for the Building and*

Construction Industry, and Denver's *A Sustainable Design Resource Guide.*

Build it and....

Chattanooga, TN

Over 2,600 Chattanoogans were involved in ReVision 2000, defining the city's environmental renovation goals and offering suggestions for Chattanooga's development. Plans include building and renovating public facilities as model smart buildings, creating eco-industrial parks and greenways, and including smart technologies in Chattanooga's trade center.

Maryland Public Schools

The Maryland Department of Education and Maryland Public School Construction Program created policies to minimize the negative environmental and energy impacts of school construction and operation. They include:

- Annual energy use reports
- Daylighting must be used when possible.
- Designers are encouraged to follow certain indoor air-quality guidelines.
- Energy monitoring
- New construction and retrofits must incorporate life-cycle costs for the buildings' systems.

Montgomery County, MD

Montgomery County, Maryland, adopted energy design guidelines in 1989. As a result, new and renovated government buildings use 50% less energy without higher initial building costs. Energy saving measures include:

- Electronic energy management systems
- High-efficiency lighting systems
- High-performance glazing systems
- Ice-storage systems for cooling

Rebuilding Smart in the Midwest

Following the Midwestern floods of 1993, the towns of Valmeyer, Illinois, and Pattonsburg, Missouri, are taking advantage of passive solar design to rebuild both municipal and residential buildings. In Valmeyer, the Illinois Department of Energy and Natural Resources is teaching residents how to use passive solar features, super insulation, and efficient heating and cooling systems. Because of this, 40% of the town's new homes' annual heating bills are projected to be under $200. In addition, the emergency services and municipal building relies on passive solar design as do a mutli-family complex and a senior center. Residents in Pattonsburg, Missouri, are

learning about passive solar design in their home design selection, and the city has developed a passive-solar land use plan (U.S. DOE, 1997, IV.135).

Santa Barbara, CA

The county developed a voluntary program to help residents and businesses save money through smarter residential and commercial building design. Santa Barbara created a Building Review Committee to provide assistance on smart building design that will exceed California's energy standards by 15% for residential and 25% for commercial buildings (U.S. DOE, 1997, IV.137).

San Francisco, CA

The city's main library was completed in 1996. Because indoor air quality was of primary concern, the design team worked to eliminate opportunities for poor indoor air quality. As a result, adhesives, carpets, furniture, paints, and copy machines were selected carefully.

San Jose, CA

The San Jose City Council asked the Environmental Services Department to research the advantages and costs of adopting solar access guidelines. The Department found that high energy savings and reduced carbon dioxide emissions would result. As a result, San Jose adopted voluntary solar access guidelines, and it offers workshops encouraging use of the guidelines to architects, builders, city employees, and developers.

Keeping Buildings & Cities Smart

Although building design and renovation are important, many building owners don't take into account how they will operate and maintain their buildings throughout their lives. Below are examples of some groups that have tackled this issue.

Austin, TX

Austin's Environmental and Conservation Services Department wrote the *Sustainable Design Guidelines Manual* for Austin's new airport. This report offers some non-toxic alternatives to chemical pest controls.

Denver

Denver's new international airport minimizes waste by using low-flow toilets, drought-resistant grass, efficient lighting, recycling ethylene glycol from de-icing facilities, and telecommuting.

Maryland

The Department of Education (School Facilities Branch) developed a technical series of publications on smart building maintenance, including, "The Maintenance of

Heating, Ventilating and Air-Conditioning Systems and Indoor Air Quality in Schools."

Pennsylvania

The Slippery Rock Foundation's *Guidelines for Sustainable Development* were written to help government and private building owners and tenants understand and maintain air quality, appliances, energy systems, lighting, recycling, water conservation, and smart product purchasing.

Portland, OR

Portland is working toward a 10% increase in energy efficiency for retrofitted buildings by the year 2000. The city trains facilities operators to run their facilities with increased efficiency, and its efforts are paying off.

FIND OUT WHAT YOUR CLIENTS WANT

A 1991 survey of some of the United States' top companies found that only 22% always or nearly always use customer wants and needs to help suggest and develop new products and services (Romm, 121). This compares with 58% of Japanese companies. While keeping in touch with your clients is a necessary part of business, finding out and giving them what they want is often an overlooked way of being more competitive and efficient with resources, and of saving money.

GETTING EVERYONE ON BOARD

Once you've developed some principles and accompanying strategies to create a smarter office, you will need to get office-wide support. Working toward a smarter office will be much easier when everyone works together. Companies have developed a variety of ways to keep in touch with employees and work toward smarter offices. Do whatever works for you.

MANAGEMENT

If you're the boss, get together with your employees and tell them that you want to create a smart office. Tell them why it's important – it means a healthier and more comfortable work environment for them, and a more efficient,

profitable, competitive company (which also can mean increased job security).

If you'll be conducting an environmental audit and surveying employees, let them know so they understand what's going on. It will require their cooperation, so it's important that they understand why you're doing this and how they can benefit and help (e.g., turning off lights whenever they leave their offices, double-sided copying). Keep them up-to-date on the progress you're making, too, so they won't feel that their efforts are in vain. They will be quick to sense a token effort or short-term, uncommitted show.

Regardless of the methods you use to keep employees involved and informed, the most important thing is to keep your smart office goals from falling by the wayside.

EMPLOYEES

If you're an employee, it can be a challenge to get your company to sign on to smart policies. Understanding your company's internal politics is important. You don't want management to feel as though you're trying to stage a coup or go over their heads in determining how they should run the company.

You may want to raise smart office ideas with your boss first. Tell her or him about the benefits of a smart office. Offer to share successful smart office case studies with your boss. Letting management know what other companies have done and how much they have saved may prove reassuring.

Or you can talk with the facilities manager, send an electronic mail (e-mail) message to others who may be interested, raise the idea of a smart office at an informal lunch meeting or brown bag lunch or even at a formal meeting if it will not be perceived as a threat. Some companies are open to employee suggestions, and others tend not to be. Be aware of your company's probable response to your suggestions, and strategize accordingly.

KEEPING TRACK OF YOUR PROGRESS

Keeping track of your progress is really important – it can help keep you inspired on the road to a smarter workplace. I cannot emphasize how important this is, especially if you or some of your employees start losing steam. Besides, seeing what you have accomplished can feel great!

If you lease your office space, you may feel limited in the smarter changes you can make on a building-wide scale. If you rent your office space and cannot carry out building-wide renovations that offer increased energy efficiency, decreased indoor air pollution, and other environmental benefits. However, you may be able to work with your building management company to make some environmentally beneficial changes, including:

1. Cutting energy use (you may want to contact local utilities and the EPA's Green Buildings program for support and information)

2. Consider turning off your building's air conditioning a few hours earlier each day.

3. Retrofitting exit lights with energy-saving, fluorescent bulbs.

4. Conserving water through adjustments to the building's water fixtures to conserve water.

WHISTLE-BLOWING

We cannot talk about creating smart offices without raising the issue of whistle-blowing. If your company is knowingly harming people -or the environment and efforts to correct matters have been resisted, consider informing the public and/or appropriate authorities of your company's poor practices. Before doing this, however, think hard, and evaluate the risks. You could get fired for whistle-blowing and black-listed from working for other businesses, too. But there can be personal and public rewards for doing what you believe is right.

If you decide to go ahead, consider the following suggestions:

- Weigh the risks.
- Get advice from a lawyer, union, professional association, state agencies, and co-workers you can trust or from other whistle-blowers.
- Check your rights under the law, and find out how you are protected or vulnerable.
- Do your homework. If you don't have all your facts and evidence straight, your risk may be for nothing. You could even get sued.
- Send your information where it will get the best results. For example, decide whether you should work through the system, talking with the company superiors of

increasing importance until you're heard, or whether you should go directly to the media or the government. Decide if you want to supply the information anonymously.
- Consider your timing – a change of administration, for instance, might improve your chances of success of working out change internally and peacefully.
- Be persistent. It could take years to get violations corrected (Anderson, 1990, 207).

FINAL COMMENTS

If you feel comfortable, lobby management to create a committee to monitor your company's in-house and outside efficiency and environmental performance. Suggest purchasing policies that take into account the environmental records of your vendors. Try to discourage company pension plans and other investments that support businesses that harm the environment or are otherwise detrimental. Also, support your company's moves toward investing in smarter, socially responsible technologies and products.

Remember that new technologies and increasing environmental regulations are on your side in creating less wasteful, healthier workplaces. Many states and cities are creating development principles that your company may be able to tap into for ideas and support.

Work with your local utility for suggestions on how to improve your building efficiency. With the reregulation of utilities, you also may be able to work with utilities that offer cleaner power that can contribute to savings for you and a cleaner outdoor environment for your community.

With utility restructuring comes increased competition among the utilities and increased choices for energy consumers. Each utility has a portfolio of the sources of energy that it uses. For instance, one utility may rely heavily on a combination of nuclear and coal power while another buys 70% hydroelectric power from Company XXX, 20% solar power from Company YYY, and 10% wind power from Company ZZZ. The cleaner, sustainable technologies will come from the latter utility that focuses on renewable resources.

These basic issues should be kept in mind when renovating or designing a smart office. Don't be discouraged if smart office concepts are new to your company; remember that many others are working on such efforts globally. Don't try to re-invent the wheel. Instead, network heavily, and create alliances with your legislators, utilities, environmental protection and energy agencies, other companies, product suppliers, and company col-leagues. Capitalize on and contribute to the growing body of anecdotal experience and hard, quantitative data on creating smart offices. It is only by building on shared knowledge that we will make any great strides.

PART TWO

• • • • • • • •

THE EFFICIENT OFFICE

CHAPTER 4

THE COSTS OF INEFFICIENCY

Pollution = Waste
It comes from using a resource incompletely.

townsend, 1995

With today's intensive energy demands, a cityscape such as this one represents a great amount of waste.

In the United States, we use an enormous amount of energy. And the technology that we employ to create this energy often is inefficient, wasteful, and unhealthy. For instance, our reliance upon fossil fuels for transport and electricity is inefficient and highly polluting. And right now, the single, largest source of air pollution from burning coal, oil, and natural gas is not from cars or factories but from the generation of electricity.

Of course, it's difficult to do a quick comparison of energy use among countries whose lifestyles differ greatly. However, that's partly the point. Even compared to other industrial nations with similar standards of living, the U.S. is the most wasteful. Not only is this costly on a global level, but it is costly to most companies as well.

ENVIRONMENTAL DEGRADATION

One of the biggest costs of inefficiency is pollution. Pollution results from an incomplete use of resources. This was a lesson learned in Silicon Valley, the heart of the U.S. semiconductor industry. Since 1981, there have been over 100 toxic chemical spills in Silicon Valley. The density of Superfund sites is higher in that county than in any other in the United States.

Making computers in Silicon Valley also has resulted in terrible pollution due to the inefficient use of natural resources in making computer parts. The production and use of the world's well over 115 million personal computers contribute to environmental degradation, negatively affecting climate change and the ozone layer, creating water and air pollution, and creating millions of tons of nonrecyclable, toxic solid waste.

Additionally, just the number of computer diskettes that are used and later discarded is enormous. In 1991, over one billion diskettes were sold in the United States alone. Although diskettes are relatively small, the number that ends up in landfills is not small and represents an unnecessary waste of resources that could be used for something else.

Many other forms of pollution, including electrical fields from video display terminals (VDTs), televisions, computer monitors, and metal ducts, static from synthetic fibers, and especially smoking and polluted, dusty, dry air, cause negative ions (positively and negatively charged molecules) to be depleted. This can create an unhealthy environment in which to live and work.

ENERGY USE

For a long time, computers have been great consumers of electricity. Of course, this has been environmentally destructive. According to the Environmental Protection Agency, computers and their components use 3-5% of all commercial power. By the year 2000, they're expected to use nearly 10%. The rate at which office equipment energy demands are growing is faster than any other type of U.S. commercial building energy demand.

According to the Worldwatch Institute, U.S. energy consumption is:

- Twice that of Germany
- Over twice that of Japan
- Six times that of Mexico, Turkey, or Brazil
- Thirty-five times that of India or Indonesia
- One hundred forty times that of Bangladesh

For many businesses, this has proved to be enormously expensive. This high energy use costs U.S. businesses $2.1 billion every year. And if you include the energy that it takes to cool the excess heat created by office equipment, U.S. businesses' annual electricity usage is estimated at 36 billion kilowatt-hours (kWh). If we con-

tinue at our current rate, U.S. office equipment energy use is expected to quintuple over the next decade.

Despite the incredible wastes incurred by inefficiency, when companies are deciding on the office equipment they will purchase, many ignore the money that can be saved with more efficient equipment. Instead, purchase price, speed, and operating quality are often the only factors used in deciding what equipment to buy.

But not only will you save money buying energy-efficient office equipment – you also will prevent the additional pollution that would have occurred with less energy efficiency. If the 36 billion kWh/year electrical consumption of U.S. companies were cut in half simply by using already available energy-efficient technologies, the amount of carbon dioxide (CO_2) kept out of the air would equal the removal of six million cars from the U.S.

Using energy-efficient equipment makes sense. First, it requires less of an electrical load, which creates less of a strain on your office or building wiring. Second, your workplace comfort level probably will be higher due to the minimization or elimination of wasted heat and fan noise (this often is the case). Third, newer technology creates an increased flexibility in the workplace. Notebook computers, for instance, are portable, and don't tie people down to their work stations. Fourth, electromagnetic fields (EMFs) are reduced. Fifth, equipment costs go down as people share printers through networks. Sixth, federal regulations are beginning to demand the reduction of energy consumption. For instance, by the year 2000, federal agencies, under Executive Order 12902, are required to cut energy use by 30%. In addition, each agency must have one building as a prime example of energy efficiency and water conservation, a smart building.

To get a better idea of the tangible cost differences among an inefficient, a more efficient, and a very efficient office, read the following examples from the Electric Power Research Institute (EPRI).

EPRI'S SMART OFFICE EXAMPLE

In their *Guide to Energy-Efficient Office Equipment*, EPRI provided a great example to show the differences in cost among three different office equipment scenarios. One is a High-Energy-Use Office, the second is a More-Energy-Efficient Office, and the third is Today's Energy-Efficient Office.

Let's say that your company leases a space for 200 employees, and each employee has a PC and access to a printer, fax machine, and copier.

High-energy-use Office

Here is the first, inefficient scenario. Your company buys the following for its 200-person office:

• 200 desktop microcomputers
• 100 laser printers
• 20 laser facsimile machines
• 20 heat- and pressure-fusing copiers

With a Monday through Friday, nine-hour workday, computers and printers are left on all the time. Each employee prints 30 pages every work day on printers without energy-saving modes. Each employee also makes about 30 copies every work day on the energy-saving copiers, but the energy-saving, power-down modes have not been enabled. Copiers are left on all the time, too, and the machines' duplexing capabilities are not used. Every employee gets about five pages of faxes each day.

For one year, the energy cost for equipment operation, electricity use, and the additional air conditioning needed to make up for the waste heat generated by the equipment is about $44,050. In order to create the building's capacity to handle the air conditioning and the continuous power supply, there is a one-time cost of $59,250. Each year, paper costs are about $13,750 (ACEEE, 1996, 76).

Energy-Efficient Scenario

Your company buys the following:

• 200 Energy Star microcomputers
• 20 combination printer/fax machine/scanners combinations with networks of 10 microcomputers per machine
• 3 high-volume Energy Star copiers

Employees turn off computers at night and on weekends. Machines are power-managed for 5.5 hours each day. Combination printer/fax machine/scanners are turned off at night and on weekends and are power-managed for 4.5 hours each day. For each employee, combination equipment prints about 22 pages each day with 50% of all print jobs being double-sided. They copy about 18 pages per day per employee with 80% of all copy jobs double-sided. Plain paper fax capabilities are used, and the paper is reused.

The total, annual energy cost, with the same features as mentioned before, is about $1,650. One-time air conditioning and power supply costs are about $8,800, and paper costs are about $4,650 (ACEEE, 1996, 76).

The costs mentioned above are direct costs only. They only take into account the paper costs and equipment purchase prices. The energy-efficient office will see a savings of $150,000-300,000. Look at the graph to see how they compare.

ANNUAL & ONE-TIME COSTS FOR OFFICE SCENARIOS

	High-Energy Scenario	Energy-Efficient Scenario
Annual Direct Energy Cost	$33,536	$1,150
Annual Indirect Energy Cost	10,515	510
Total Annual Energy Cost	44,050	1,650
Annual Paper Cost	13,750	4,650
Total Annual Cost	57,800	6,300
Total One-Time Cost	*59,250*	*8,800*

Taken from ACEEE, 1996, 78

CHAPTER 5

ENERGY-EFFICIENT LIGHTING

High quality energy-efficient lighting cuts pollution, saves money, and helps people to see better. When people can see what they're doing, productivity and quality increase while mistakes decrease.

The effective use of daylight with high quality visibility is the first step in good lighting design and is further described later in this chapter.

LIGHTING BASICS

Believe it or not, about one-quarter of all generated electricity in the U.S. goes to lighting. Lighting is an integral part of any work environment. And although it allows us to see what we're doing, poorly chosen or designed lighting can cause glare, visual discomfort, unwanted shadows, and additional heat. Lighting is one of the main sources of heat gain, especially in commercial buildings; as a result, your lighting choices will affect your choice of HVAC equipment.

LIGHTING TYPES

You are probably familiar with the various types of lighting available. The most obvious is sunlight. Increasingly, architects are taking advantage of "daylighting" (using windows, skylights, and other methods to bring daylight indoors) in commercial and residential buildings to provide natural light and reduce (or eliminate) the need for electric lighting.

Electric light comes from three primary sources – *incandescent filament, fluorescent,* and *high-intensity discharge (HID)* lamps.

Incandescent Filament Light

Incandescent filament lighting uses electric current to heat a thin, metal filament until it glows and emits light. They are not nearly as energy-efficient as fluorescent lights and are shorter lived.

About 80% of the energy consumed by the average, incandescent lightbulb wafts away as heat. And although heat is destructive to the

bulb, making it short-lived, incandescent bulbs still are heavily used. Why? Many people don't realize the incredible savings and benefits of smarter lighting.

Fluorescent Light

In fluorescent lighting, light is emitted when electrons flow from one cathode (electrode) to the other, colliding with mercury along the way. The ballasts in fluorescent lamps regulate the current while giving the necessary starting operating voltage. While ballasts make a humming noise, the volume is graded from A (quietest) to F (loudest) so that you will know ahead of time what you're buying. Fluorescent lamps last many times longer than do incandescent ones.

You may remember that some of the older fluorescent bulbs had a flicker. These days, the electronic ballasts are supposed to prevent this. The ballast regulates the current and voltage that feed a fluorescent bulb – it also helps prevent the flicker associated with older fluorescent lighting. Some fluorescent tube lighting uses ballasts that are not built in.

Compact Fluorescent Lights (CFLs)

Lawrence Berkeley National Laboratory created a more efficient bulb, known as the compact fluorescent (CFL). The CFL bulb wins hands down in energy savings over the old incandescents. Although compact fluorescents are more expensive, they use one-fourth the energy used by an incandescent for the same amount of light. They also last about 10,000 hours instead of an incandescent's 500-1000 hours. Experts agree that you can save anywhere from $20 to $50 on each bulb during its lifetime. And if you receive coupons from your electric utility some companies still provide, the savings are even greater. It doesn't get much easier than that.

If you choose a CFL bulb instead of an incandescent one, over its lifetime the CFL will offset the burning of about 528 pounds of coal, the release of one ton of carbon dioxide, 20 pounds of sulfur dioxide, and the equivalent of a barrel of oil. In addition, it will prevent the need for 10-13 times its weight in metal, glass, and packaging from entering landfills. Just one bulb.

According to Environmental Protection Agency estimates, "If everyone in the United States switched to energy-efficient lighting, 202 million tons of carbon dioxide, 1.3 million tons of sulfur dioxide, and 600,000 tons of nitrogen oxides would be kept out of the atmosphere" (Anzovin, 47).

If all U.S. households switched one incandescent bulb with one compact fluorescent bulb, one nuclear power plant could be shut down. According to the Rocky Mountain Institute, a leading "think tank" for energy efficiency, if U.S. homes switched all of the 500 million incandescent bulbs with compact fluorescent ones, *the U.S. instantly would be an energy-exporting nation.* Some experts estimated that if we use the most efficient lighting available in the U.S., we will cut our yearly energy bill by at least $30 billion.

Those of you with home offices should know that the energy used to heat and light the "average" home in the U.S. results in annual carbon dioxide emissions of almost 11 tons. Of course, inefficient offices increase that number significantly and help to contribute further to global warming. In the nearly century-and-a-half that global temperatures have been monitored, the 1980s saw five of the world's warmest years on record. The 1990s have not been much different.

CFLs Past and Present
You may remember the compact fluorescents of the past. When they first came on the market, some lamps could not use CFLs because of the size or shape of the bulb. Check again – this is one market that has changed quickly. And rest assured that the colors emitted from the CFLs these days are much better than the old, bluish tones. CFLs come with the electronic ballasts built in, which prevents a flicker.

High-intensity Discharge Lights (HIDs)

Like fluorescent lamps, HID lamps discharge an electrical arc through a metal/gas mixture, require ballasts, and last much longer than do incandescent lights. Unlike fluorescent lighting, the HID's electrical discharge occurs within a small area, and HIDs produce brighter light. There are three types of HID lamps – high-pressure sodium, mercury, and metal halide. The mercury lamps tend to have poor color; metal halide lamps have better but inconsistent color and are shorter-lived than the other two.

Due to recent lighting innovations, both fluorescent and HID lamps can be dimmed safely although HIDs dim more slowly than do fluorescent lamps. Their ability to dim means that these lamps can be integrated into daylighting design.

VISUAL DISCOMFORT

Discomfort from poor lighting generally occurs when the eye must adapt to rapid, repeated changes in brightness. In a work environment, there should be enough light for employees to distinguish details on the work objects. However, too much brightness (glare) can decrease visual accuracy. While not all glare interferes with visual accuracy, it can result in visual discomfort, causing headaches, eye strain, and other symptoms of visual stress.

Since our eyes adjust to the brightest spot within our field of view, high brightness differences cause visual discomfort. With visual demands for computer and paper tasks in office environments, a soft ambient light with individual task lighting can provide a more comfortable working environment.

OFFICE LIGHTING DESIGN

According to Fuller Moore, author of *Environmental Control Systems*, there are a number of factors that should be considered when designing lighting.

HOW WILL THE SPACE BE ORGANIZED VISUALLY?

Through lighting design, you can mandate what areas and objects in a room will be lit and which will be in shadow. Brighter areas can draw attention to areas of interest and activity, or they can reinforce the room design visually.

Accent Lighting
• Determine the main areas of attention (such as a painting, a work area, etc.), and design your lighting so that these focal areas will be apparent.
• These areas should be lit 5-10 times brighter than their surrounding areas, depending on how much attention you want to call to them.

Level of Stimulation
• Use warm colors to stimulate occupants and cool colors to soothe them.

- If you use lighting under about 3 cd per square foot (or 10 fL), it may be reminiscent of dusk, or surfaces may look dingy.
- Tinted colors are less stimulating to occupants than are saturated colors.
- For a relaxing ambiance, you can use darker areas but for a dramatic contrast, consider accenting focal accents with lighting.

Occupied Area

- When this is the main activity area, lighting design should be designed for the tasks at hand. Comfortable lighting should maintain a good balance between the occupied, perimeter, and transition areas.

Overhead Area

- Use a well-designed lighting pattern to reinforce the design emphasis of the space (activity zones, circulation patterns, spatial hierarchy, structural elements...)

Perimeter Area

- To create a peaceful ambiance, the perimeter should be brighter than the overhead area. Keep the lighting visually simple; this also allows the focal area to remain a place of visual interest.

Transition Areas

- When you want there to be little visual differentiation between transition areas and activity areas, keep the lighting ratio at about 3 to 1 or less.
- If you want to have a more visual difference between activity areas and adjoining areas, lighting differences should be more than the above ratio.
- To create a clear, visual distinction, a 10-to-1 lighting ratio can be used; a 100-to-1 or greater ratio creates abrupt visual differences and typically should be avoided.
- Using varying color lighting (different shades of white, for instance) also can create a visual break between areas.

STANDARDS FOR EFFICIENT LIGHTING

To save money and resources, we can support the development and use of the most energy-efficient, non-toxic technologies available. Fortunately, there are three efficiency programs that strongly influence lighting design:

- Demand-Side Management Programs (DSM)
- EPA's Green Lights Program
- The Energy Policy Act (EPACT)

DEMAND-SIDE MANAGEMENT PROGRAMS

These utility-sponsored programs encourage customers toward energy efficiency by offering financial incentives. Check with your local utility to find out what incentive programs are available to you.

EPA'S GREEN LIGHTS PROGRAM

Because of this intensive energy use, the Environmental Protection Agency's (EPA's) Green Lights Program was established in 1991 to encourage large businesses and other institutions to use energy- and cost-efficient lighting. Generally, energy-efficient lighting not only increases lighting quality but also yields 20-30% annual rates of return. That is better than most investments your company could make and much less risky.

This program enters into a voluntary agreement with companies and works with them to improve their energy efficiency as long as it is financially beneficial to the company. In this way, it is treated as an investment for the company rather than as an expense.

To become a Green Lights Partner, interested companies must sign a Memorandum of Understanding with the EPA, agreeing to install energy-efficient lighting within five years and in 90% of their space *where it is profitable* and *where lighting quality will be improved or maintained*. In other words, the EPA wants to promote energy efficiency, and it knows that the only way that it can do this successfully is to ensure that your company saves money. In return, the EPA provides a variety of services to assist in the lighting upgrade. For more information, call: 202-233-9230

ENERGY POLICY ACT (EPACT)

This act is designed to promote energy efficiency. Although most of EPACT deals with alternate fuels for transportation (see Chapter 18: "Smarter Transportation & Telecommuting" for the transportation hotline number), EPACT also supports the creation of efficient HVAC systems, lighting, motors, and windows. For more information, call: 800-363-3732

Easy Steps Toward Better Lighting

Who's Responsible: Me or the Lightbulb?

One of the easiest and most often overlooked ways to save money on your utility bills is to, whenever possible, turn off the lights whenever you leave a room. It's amazing how many people overlook this obvious energy-saver or are too lazy to lift a hand to flip the switch. And, contrary to the popular myth, turning on and off lights does not use more energy than it saves.

Of course, you're not going to turn off the lights whenever you leave a room full of fellow workers, but turning off the light switch does work when you've got your own office or lighted cubicle space. For shared work spaces, taking advantage of sunlight and using task or section lighting with switches that control various lighting sections are two ways that you can save energy and money while creating a more pleasant work space. Use automatic controls for occupancy and daylight.

Take Advantage of Sunlight

Nature has provided us with a giant lightbulb that runs for free and does not need to be replaced – the sun. Without it, we wouldn't exist. It lights our days, and its reflection off the moon softly lights our nights. Yet, many tend to overlook the obvious when it comes to what will light our offices.

You may not realize it, but daylighting is viable, practical, and increasingly widespread in its use. It makes sense to use this truly renewable resource over most other options currently available. A well-designed daylighting system can cut electric lighting energy use up to 70%.

In addition to its economic benefits, daylighting is an important component of good health. Until the industrial revolution, when electric lights became commonplace, people spent a good deal of time exposed to natural light. Now, most people in industrialized areas are exposed to only 90 minutes of lighting levels over 2000 lux each day.

Exposure to sunlight is important for many reasons. For one, it is vital for internal time-keeping that help to regulate human cycles (changes in daily body temperature, etc.). Those that lose that connection with natural light

Our dependence on non-renewable resources continues to be a costly enterprise. It is an expensive way to produce energy, and the costs of both pollution cleanup and enhanced global climate change that result from the burning of fossil fuels are enormous.

are more prone to fatigue, insomnia, and other disorders. Seasonal Affective Disorder (SAD) and daylight deprivation are clinical diagnoses for individuals exposed to too little sunlight.

A study of employees that worked within a windowless factory found that they had a much higher incidence of sickness, headaches, and faintness than those who worked in a similar but windowed factory (Franta and Anstead, 40, Spring 1994).

Sunlight provides full-spectrum light, which provides brightness and contrasts and values that are always changing. These changes in the light require the human to constantly adjust, helping to decrease eye fatigue. Although brightness and reflection need to be controlled indoors, the eye can adjust to high levels of luminance without discomfort.

Windows are the best way for employees to connect with the outside world visually. Windows allow the eye to focus on long-range objects. Keeping in touch visually with the outdoors also helps workers know the time, weather, and orientation to the rest of the world. It also provides more realistic color rendering and helps to better define tasks and spaces. The lack of a visual connection to the outdoors is one of the largest sources of dissatisfaction for building occupants.

A number of European countries require that workers be no more than 27 feet from a window. In Switzerland and Scandinavia, these windows also must be operable. Automatic sensors are placed within the air diffusers in individual offices, and when windows are opened, the sensors pick up the change in air pressure and turn the heat of for those rooms automatically as long as the windows are open.

Natural lighting's physical and psychological benefits can be helpful to those in hospitals, nursing homes, and other health-related environments. The elderly, in particularly, may adapt more slowly to lighting changes and have a difficulty with glare, and sunlight can make seeing a little easier.

Skylights and SunPipes®

Using skylights and SunPipes can bring natural, free lighting into your workplace and limit your need for paid lighting. Although you are probably familiar with skylights, you may not know about SunPipes. These are aluminum pipes that are installed in the roof. Lined with mirrors, they reflect sunlight into the room below. When comparing the costs of skylights and SunPipes, remember to include the installation cost in the overall price.

Windows

If there are windows in your workplace, you have a great opportunity to use free lighting. A three-by-five-foot office window in direct sunlight lets in more light than 100 60-watt incandescent bulbs (Anzovin, 46). And it's free. Just be sure that your windows are well-insulated so that you do not inadvertently affect indoor temperature while you are gaining light.

Lockheed-Martin found that using sunlight in one of its San Francisco-area buildings not only saved energy but increased the productivity of its workers. The building's architect was alert to many factors, including the building's orientation and layout, ceilings, and window placement and glazing. The end result was a space that allowed indirect sunlight deep into the building. In an area where half of a building's energy goes to lighting, Lockheed's building consumes about 20,000 Btu/ft²/year, which is only half that allowed by California's 1980 energy code. While the lighting design cost an extra $2 million, Lockheed claimed that the productivity gains in the first year offset the extra cost (Romm, 96-97). For more information on windows, see Chapter 7: "Efficient Building Systems."

LIGHTING UPGRADES

Upgrading lighting for individual offices and cubicles can be pretty straightforward. But what can you do if you have many people with different tasks working in one large space? Examples abound of factories and other large spaces in which the lighting is too high up or is otherwise poorly designed or located to illuminate the tasks

at hand effectively. Often, there are only a few switches to control the many lights in a room. Whenever a few people are working in a large room in which the lights are kept on always or a third of the room is lit when workers are in one small area, light is being wasted.

To be most efficient and healthy, use lighting systems designed specifically with the end users in mind. In other words, lighting needs to be directed to areas where it will be needed. Often, that means there should be less lighting in areas that people simply pass through and more lighting where work is being carried out. When planning or retrofitting your lighting, keep the following in mind:

- Ask your local utility about coupons or other financial incentives for more efficient lighting.
- Check into using the next lowest wattage when replacing bulbs. Not only will you use less power and create less heat that requires cooling, but you may cut down on glare.
- Be sure that you don't have too much lighting, which can cause eye strain.
- Try task lighting, focusing it only where necessary. And keep in mind this rule of thumb: light your computer area only about three times brighter than the room's ambient lighting. When setting up the task lighting, be careful to avoid glare on computer monitors. This can cause eye strain, lower production, and increased errors.
- Install motion or heat sensors. If you try motion sensors, be aware that if you remain very still for a specified period of time, the lights may go out until you move again. Some people seem to get a chuckle when this happens since they're happy to see that their energy-efficient lighting is doing its job. However, heat-sensitive sensors and dual sensors are effective and won't turn off the lights when a room is occupied.

Halogens, while not quite as efficient as CFLs, are two to three times more efficient than incandescent bulbs and last four times longer, giving off a warm light closer to sunlight. They work well for desk lamps since they're compact and light and are only two to four times more expensive than their near-equivalents in incandescent bulbs. You can use a 20-watt halogen in place of a 60-watt incandescent.

More efficient than halogens are the new CFLs. Like halogens, they can screw into any lamp socket. And the latest models don't have the radioactive trace elements that the earlier types did. While a 15-watt CFL gives off about the same light as a 75-watt incandescent bulb, it lasts 10-13 times longer. The new CFLs also give off little heat, which means that less air conditioning will be required.   Since about 30-50% of workplace energy goes simply to cool the extra heat produced by lighting, that makes a big difference.

Each of these things takes a different degree of effort and commitment. But one, turning off lights whenever you leave your office space, is something that you can start now, for free. All it takes is the flip of a switch.

Just a Few Examples....

Pennsylvania Power & Lighting

A decade ago, Pennsylvania Power & Lighting Company was worried about a large workspace (12,775 ft^2) used by its drafting engineers. Light bouncing off the work surface caused an indirect glare. This created veiling reflections that made it difficult to see contrasts on work surfaces. Because the drafting work was difficult to see well, errors were made. In addition, employees suffered from eyestrain and headaches, resulting in increased sick leave, and overall productivity dropped.

A lighting upgrade with energy-efficient bulbs and ballasts was done in a small area within the room. Unlike the old setup, the new lighting ran along the ceiling in the same direction as the work stations. It was encased in eight-cell parabolic louvers, which are metal grids that reduced lighting glare.

The new design provided better light for the tasks at hand. This reduced glare, and workers needed less light to see their work. Lighting that had been controlled with just one switch was now on several circuits, allowing some lights to be turned off when not in use. While the total cost of changes was $8,362, the energy used for lighting dropped by 69%.

Under the new lighting, productivity rose 13.2%, which was worth $42,240 each year. When energy savings, maintenance savings, and productivity improvement were combined, the payback went from 4.1 years to 69 days. Not only did the operating costs drop by 73% per year, which would have paid for itself in just over four years, but the 24% increase in productivity gave the lighting investment a 540% return (Romm, 92).

New England Office

One office in New England spent $863,475 replacing 7,023 lighting fixtures with energy-efficient ones. Not only did the company get a $405,688 rebate from the local utility, but the new lighting required 63% less energy. The company's savings were $183,341 each year. These savings, alone, made the retrofit pay off in 2.5 years; however, the reduced glare on the computer screens increased worker productivity, which made the payback time even shorter (Romm, 79).

What a Difference You Make

As you've seen, you don't have to work in the dark to save money through efficiency. Upgrading your lighting and turning off the lights when you leave the room can shave an enormous amount off your energy bills. Of course, your savings go straight to your profits.

You may not believe that your small actions – like switching to more energy-efficient bulbs or turning off the lights whenever you leave a room – will make much difference in the long run. Especially if you've got a smaller space, like a home office. But it doesn't take long to realize what a difference we're making already (albeit a negative one) on our business expenses and on the global environment through inefficiency.

Remember that every time you turn on a light switch, you're creating a demand that a utility has to feed. And, if more demand is created than can be met, utilities have to find ways to meet it. If they cannot convince their customers to save energy through efficiency, they are forced to find other ways to provide energy for their resource-intensive customers – like building more dams for hydro-electric power or drilling for oil in areas such as the Alaska National Wildlife Refuge.

Unfortunately, using the non-renewable resources upon which we've come to depend (e.g., coal, oil, natural gas, hydro) results in the further destruction of habitat (including ours) and the loss of species. Not only does this degrade the quality of life for all species, but it's also an expensive proposition for all of us taxpayers and businesses who will pay for the negative impacts of our resource use, manufacture, and waste disposal in the long run. And, as businesses are increasingly held accountable for their non-smart behaviors through government regulations, cleanup will be an increasingly costly proposition relative to prevention.

Using renewable energy, using energy-efficient equipment, and remembering to turn off the lights whenever you leave your work space are very simple and powerful ways for your business to save on its utility bills. These savings will directly increase your profits and may increase your company's productivity. And the power saved has a positive and far-reaching impact on the global environment, too.

HELPFUL RESOURCES

INFORMATION

Building Connections, Energy and Resource Efficiencies
American Institute of Architects, 1993. Washington, D.C.: AIA.

Dana Duxbury and Associates
16 Haverhill Street
Andover, MA 01810
508-470-3044
Contact for a fluorescent lamp recycling company list.

Daylighting Design & Analysis
Claude Robbins, 1986. New York: Van Nostrand Reinhold Co., Inc.

ENSAR Group, Inc.
2305 Broadway
Boulder, CO 80304
303-449-5226/ Fax: 303-449-5276

EPA's Green Lights Program
Washington, D.C.
202-233-9230

Glazing Design Handbook
Greg Franta, et al., 1997. Washington, D.C.: American Institute of Architects. (AIA Committee on the Environment)
This is a design guide for selecting and specifying window characteristics related to solar heat gain, daylight transmittance, heat loss/gain, and reflectance values.

Daylighting Design: Energy, Environment & Architecture
Eunice Noell, 1992. Washington, D.C.: American Institute of Architects.

Rocky Mountain Institute
1739 Snowmass Creek Road Snowmass, CO 81654
970-927-3851
Internet: www.rmi.org

PRODUCTS

For addresses and phone numbers, refer to *Appendix A: Directory of Suppliers.*

COMPACT FLUORESCENT LIGHTS
Environmental Light Concepts, Inc.
North American Philips Information & Literature Center

Panasonic Industrial Co.
Phillips Lighting
Real Goods Trading Corp.
Sylvania GTE
Teron Lighting Corp.

EMF-SHIELDED BULBS/FLUORESCENT BULBS
Brownlee Lighting
Ecoworks
Environmental Construction Outfitters
Nuclear Free America
Osram-Sylvania Inc.
Real Goods Trading Corp.
Seventh Generation
Trendway

ENERGY MANAGEMENT SYSTEMS
Carrier Corp.
Home Automation, Inc.
Unity Systems, Inc.
Honeywell, Inc.

FULL-COLOR SPECTRUM LIGHTS
Environmental Light Concepts, Inc.
Westgate Enterprises

MANUAL PROGRAMMABLE LIGHTING SYSTEMS
Litetouch
Crestron

OTHER LIGHTING PRODUCTS
Chapman Studio Lighting
Natural Lighting Co.
SunPipe

SENSORS
Rocky Grove Sun Company
Solar Light Company, Inc.

Summary of Recommendations

Daylighting

• Take advantage of sunlight, and design your workspace so that all workers have access to natural light.

Electric Lighting

• Turn lights off when not in use.

• Replace incandescent bulbs with compact fluorescents. Retrofit old fluorescent fixtures with electronic ballasts and "T-8" lamps.

• Install light sensors.

• Use dimmer switches to be sure you get as much lighting as you need for the task at hand.

• Check into using the next lowest wattage when replacing bulbs.

• Be sure that you don't have too much lighting.

• Use task lighting, focusing it only where necessary.

• Use halogens, or better yet, use compact fluourescent bulbs rather than incandescents.

• Become an EPA Green Lights Partner.

• Contact your local utility for rebates and other incentives for your lighting upgrade.

• To avoid glare from windows, keep computers out of direct sunlight, tilt monitors away from the window.

• Use top-silvered blinds, and, when possible, use transparent materials (e.g., glass) along the tops of office partitions and the interior walls of windowed offices.

Chapter 6

Energy-Efficient Office Equipment

"The choice of technology, whether for a rich or a poor country, is probably the most important decision to be made."
George McRobie, Oct. 1976 (quoted in Rodes and Odell, 30)

Energy-efficient, well-designed lighting and smart behaviors are only some of the steps you can take toward a smarter workplace. There are many others. Chances are, you have a lot of office equipment around. Computers, copiers, printers, fax machines, and even refrigerators are just a few of the pieces of equipment common in today's workplace and can consume vast quantities of energy.

Standards for Efficient Equipment

The EPA's Energy Star Office Equipment Program

Because of the costs of inefficiency, in June 1992 the EPA announced its new Energy Star program. This program was created to encourage the development of energy-efficient office equipment.

The first phase of the program covers personal computers (PCs). Many PCs are left on 24 hours every day, requiring an enormous amount of energy to keep them running. Because the EPA wanted to cut this power consumption, it created the Energy Star Program as an incentive to computer manufacturers to produce PCs that go into a sleep mode whenever they are inactive for a specified period of time.

Under the Energy Star program, PCs and monitors that power down to 30 watts or less when inactive are allowed to carry the Energy Star logo. This lets buyers know that they are getting a PC that's not an energy hog all of the time and is more eco-friendly, which has been another good selling point.

Manufacturers of the Energy Star computers sign a voluntary agreement with the EPA to use its Energy Star logo on labels and in promotional materials. Computers were allowed to use the logo beginning in June 1993, so the earlier machines with energy management capabilities do not carry the Energy Star logo. However, these would have been easy to identify, as they were the only desktop computers at the time (late 1992) to advertise power-management capabilities and could be identified through such advertising.

Because the new Energy Star program is a federal (EPA) program, all federal PC procurements must comply with the Energy Star requirements (a $4-billion market).

The Energy Star requirements state that PCs can use no more than 30 watts of power when inactive.

All notebooks already do this to conserve battery power, but desktops of the past have been very energy-intensive. Several vendors already have products that meet EPA's new requirements, and many more are ready to join the Energy Star program.

The EPA predicts that by the year 2000, the Energy Star computers may save about 25 billion kilowatt/hours of power. This is the total, annual amount of energy used by Vermont and New Hampshire combined. These PCs should save nearly $1 billion each year in electric bills. They also prevent emissions of:

- 20 million tons of carbon dioxide (global warming)
- 140,000 tons of sulfur dioxides (acid rain)
- 75,000 tons of nitrogen (acid rain) (Anzovin, 41)

Be aware that the Energy Star program does not require PCs to be energy-efficient all of the time. It also doesn't specify how long the period of inactivity is before the machine powers down. It only specifies that Energy Star machines power down when inactive and that they power down to use no more than 30 watts when inactive. The time of inactivity, however, is up to the user to set.

Also, an Energy Star computer does not have to be shipped with its power-down features enabled. You might assume that the machine is power-managed when it's not. So, if you're buying a new computer, be sure to double-check before you take it to the office. Also, once you get your new Energy Star computer, you can experiment with its delay settings to be sure your PC doesn't wait too long during inactive periods before powering down.

Keep in mind that not all Energy Star models are the same. Call the manufacturers of the PCs you might be interested in to find out about their energy use. Or, take a look at back issues of *PC Magazine* and other publications that have compared the energy ratings of several PC models. According to EPRI,

"A computer that consumes 25W at full power, 5W at low power, and is default managed to be at low power 70% of a nine-hour day, would consume 90% less energy (256 kWh) than another Energy Star computer that consumes 160W at full power, 25W at low power, and is default managed to be at low power only 30% of a nine-hour day" (EPRI, 19).

As you can see, not all Energy Star computers are alike, so be sure to ask about the energy use of different PCs when you are shopping for one. The Energy Star program's second phase was announced in January of 1993. Since June 1993, it has allowed energy-efficient printers to use the Energy Star logo. For more information on Energy Star printers, see the "Printers" section in this chapter.

NATIONAL TESTING AND INFORMATION PROGRAM FOR COMMERCIAL OFFICE EQUIPMENT

This is another program that promotes energy-efficient office equipment. Through the Energy Policy Act of 1992, Congress created a program to inform consumers of office equipment energy use. As a follow-up, a private sector program was created that would design testing procedure specifications for various types of equipment. The program covers a number of things, including PCs, copiers, faxes, and printers.

GENERAL TIPS FOR ENERGY SAVINGS

There are many things that you can do to save money through efficiency. We'll get into specific office equip-

ment shortly, but let's go over some basic, energy-efficiency information.

The first and easiest thing that you can do is something you already know – turn off your equipment when you're not using it. According to the American Council for an Energy-Efficient Economy and the Office Technology Consortium, your average PC (not including the monitor) uses 70 watts of power. Just by turning off the PC at the end of the work day, you can cut its energy use by more than 75%. And you can save even more by turning it off whenever you're not using it – not just at night and on weekends. If you know that you're going to a meeting, out to lunch, or you just won't be using it for awhile, go ahead and turn it off.

You can do this for other equipment, too. I know the thought of getting up and running around your office to turn off every piece of equipment that's not being used can seem a little intimidating. But there are alternatives.

Power-management devices (either external devices plugged into your power supply or internal hardware or software) can turn either your equipment or its components off at set times or whenever they are not being used. By using power-management devices, you can reduce your computer consumption by an additional 50% during working hours.

Also, laptop computers can use less than 10% of the energy consumed by desktop PCs. Take advantage of the energy-efficient potential of your equipment.

Manufacturers have begun producing power-management devices to retrofit existing computers. Some of these devices can control not only the computers but the monitors and printers, too. While this is good for everyone, it's especially important for those machines that are left on all of the time. Since these devices actually turn the equipment off and don't just put it into a sleep mode, there may be a brief lag time between switching the machine and peripherals on and having them ready for use.

Power commanders are a little more complex. They let you use a master switch or individual switches that are plugged into each device.

Some people seem concerned that turning any equipment off whenever it's not in use will shorten its life. However, most experts now agree that turning your equipment on and off more often won't decrease its life significantly. But, if it makes you feel better, you can check with the equipment manufacturers before retrofitting your equipment with power-management devices.

One easy way to cut back on your energy use is with a switch box. A switch box is an inexpensive strip outlet (about $10) that you can turn on and off to turn your equipment on and off.

Power commanders, surge protectors, and strip outlets can be great ways to dramatically cut your energy use. But be aware that they continue to draw power when they are turned on, something known as *phantom load*, even if the equipment plugged into them isn't being used.

If you might not remember to turn your equipment off, consider using timers, which are useful for power lines or dedicated circuits. Timers turn off computers and peripherals at the end of the day or whenever you set them to turn off. Be sure, though, that all of your work is saved before your timer turns the power off. Setting up alarms that go off a few minutes before the timer can provide a reminder to save your work before the equipment will be turned off.

Using a timer or other power-management device to turn off your lights, copier, PC, and fax machine just for one kilowatt/hour each day, you will save about $25 each year. Think of how much you'd save if you have 100 PCs, several copiers, printers, and other equipment.

If you don't turn off your computer when you're not using it, at least turn off the monitor, printer, and other peripherals. Some monitors use up to three times the power of the computers to which they are attached.

If your equipment is connected to a local area network (LAN), there are energy-saving steps you can take. LANs can range from printer-sharing to completely interoperable computers and printers. Increased PC connection to LANs could result in additional energy use. Network adapter cards use at least 10W per computer, and peer-to-peer networks may end up with everyone's equipment being on all of the time to allow constant access to all files and software programs.

While some computer setups will increase energy consumption, some may reduce consumption. For instance, 10 PCs use more energy than a file server with 10 "dumb" terminals.

Using the sun to power your PC and equipment is another way to save money and energy. Solar-powering PCs is not that difficult. Electricity that comes from power lines is alternating current, or ac, which is what your computer needs. Solar panels and other off-the-grid sources are direct current, or dc. Since your computer needs 110-120-volt ac, you'll need to get an inverter, which can power a desktop or recharge notebook batteries. However, be aware that experts recommend that you shouldn't directly power a notebook computer from solar panels. While some notebook PC battery rechargers can be plugged directly into a solar panel, some cannot. But many solar panels are made with a car-cigarette-lighter receptacle that your notebook's recharger can hook right into. Try to keep at least two batteries – one for recharging and the other for use.

Pocket-sized inverters can be used with your desktop PC as well. Inverters work with several types of ac power, including car batteries, windmills, and generators.

Solar panel battery chargers charge nearly all batteries for laptop and notebook computers as well as for mobile phones; the charger senses the voltage needed by the particular battery and automatically adjusts. Devices for powering notebooks and recharging batteries using solar energy can be found from such sources as Real Goods Trading Company. Apparently, requests for these devices are on the rise.

You can save money, energy, and paper by using electronic mail. Take advantage of the Internet or other computer networks to market your products and services, solicit or search for requests for proposals, keep up with the latest information in your industry, or even just catch up on the news. For just a few dollars per hour (and a monthly fee), the whole world is open through a variety of Internet providers.

COMBINATION EQUIPMENT

Although the machines filling our offices are useful, faxes, copiers, printers, scanners, and other equipment can add up your costs and can take up a lot of precious work space. These machines can use a great deal of electricity and other resources in their manufacture and use.

Fortunately, there is a trend toward integrating peripheral functions (faxing, copying, scanning, printing, etc.) into one piece of equipment. Machines that combine functions are known as multi-function machines and save desktop space and cut energy costs. The new printers with fax, scan, and copy options are just one example of this. Luckily, both the purchase price and the energy cost of one multi-function machine can be far below that of separate pieces of equipment.

In 1992, multi-function machines (scanning, printing, copying, faxing) made up $750 million in U.S. sales. In 1996, sales were projected to reach over $4 billion. These save energy by combining several functions into one machine (ACEEE, 1996, 63).

COPIERS

Copiers use more energy than any other piece of office equipment. Of course, energy use varies depending on the type of copier you have. Heat- and pressure-fusing copiers use heat and/or pressure to affix toner to the paper. Ink jet copiers are slower and more costly. Surface-fusing copiers are similar to the heat- and pressure-fusing ones except that the fusing rollers are smaller and require less energy to heat. These machines are best for small volumes, but the quality is not as good as that of heat- and pressure-fusing and ink jet copiers.

Another copier good for low-volume copying uses a liquid ink technology. It, too, affixes toner to paper through heat-fusing but has lower image quality than both heat- and pressure- fusing and ink jet copiers. Digital duplicators are intended for high-volume copying, but their printing quality is lower than that of conventional heat- and pressure-fusing machines.

The American Society for Testing and Materials (ASTM) developed a procedure to rate copiers on their energy consumption. This makes it easier to compare different copiers when you're thinking of purchasing one. The inclusion of copiers in the EPA and DOE's Energy Star program makes it easy for you to find copiers that have power-down features.

WHAT YOU CAN DO

Determine Your Needs

Choose a copier sized to your needs. After all, total energy use generally increases with price and increased volume capability.

Consider a non-heat- and pressure-fusing copier. It will use less energy than a heat- and pressure-fusing one. For high-volume needs that do not require high-quality copying, consider digital duplicators. For low-volume printing with decent quality, consider liquid ink copiers.

Power Management

When purchasing a copier, be sure that it has power-management features. Most heat- and pressure-fusing machines have an energy-saver feature. Some only turn off their panel lights, giving the appearance of low energy use, so check first before you buy. Many machines with an energy-saver feature cut energy use by over half compared to being on standby, significantly decreasing their lifetime costs.

Use Duplexing Features

Choose a copier with good duplexing capabilities. Most have a double-sided copying feature, which cuts back on paper use. It also reduces paper supply costs. Be sure, however, that your copier doesn't have a poor reputation for duplexing. If your duplexing feature works only sometimes, it may be taking more time, paper, and energy to get the double-sided copies that you want.

Copying on both sides of the paper is important from an efficiency perspective since paper manufacture is a very energy-intensive process. The embodied energy, or energy that it takes to produce each page of paper, is anywhere from 1-20 times greater than what it takes to make a one-page copy.

Turn It Off

By turning off your copier at night and on weekends (try a plug-in timer), you can reduce energy consumption by about 65% (EPRI, 6).

Use Power Management

Be sure to purchase copiers with power-down capabilities, and be sure that the power-down setting is enabled.

Copy Efficiently

When you have several copying jobs to do, try to do them all at once. If you're running in and out of the copy room and the machine sits at full power for a few minutes before going into sleep mode, you will use more energy than if you do your copies at once. Also, using an energy-saving feature can cut reduced energy use by another 25%.

Get Energy Ratings

Get the ASTM ratings for individual machines because machines with the same printing technology and copy volume capability can vary greatly in energy use.

FACSIMILE (FAX) MACHINES

Fax machines are a handy tool for many of us. As with printers and copiers, many technologies are used to send faxes. They include: laser, direct thermal, thermal transfer, ink jet, and fax cards installed in PCs. Since energy use varies among machines with similar capabilities, check individual machines.

Laser/light Emitting Diode (LED) fax machines fuse toner to the paper, creating high-quality images. To receive faxes, these machines can use plain paper, which is recyclable (thermal paper is not recyclable because of the clay coating on its surface, and the quality of faxes tends to decrease over time).

Thermal paper fax machines use heat-sensitive coated, or thermal, paper without using high-temperature fusers found in laser faxes. Thermal paper is hard to write on, has a short shelf life, is non-recyclable, and can be destroyed by heat (a hot coffee cup placed on fax paper, a fax set on a radiator, etc.). The direct, or up-front, cost of these machines is less than laser or LED machines, but the rolls of thermal paper are much more expensive and even out the cost difference in the long run.

Thermal transfer faxes melt pigment onto a ribbon that is then transferred to the paper. While some are heating mechanisms, they are not as high-powered as direct thermal fax machines. They generally use either coated or plain paper, and prices fall somewhere between laser/LED and direct thermal machines.

An ink jet fax machine uses a small, disposable printhead, its resolution varies. The energy use is low, and costs are about the same as thermal transfer machines.

Fax cards use a PC port to allow the transmission and receipt of messages. As with fax/laser printer combinations, using a PC fax card could lead to increased energy consumption if the computer is a desktop (rather than a laptop) and is left on all the time to receive messages. However, PC fax cards can save time that you or someone else would spend running to and from a separate fax machine. It also saves the time and the paper that it takes to print a document before faxing it.

Generally, laser and LED machines are the most energy-intensive. These are followed by direct thermal and thermal transfer fax machines and, finally, by ink jet, the most energy-efficient. Because of variations, however, check individual machines' energy ratings before making a decision.

Also, if you are in the market for a fax machine, take into account the lifetime cost of your machine – not just the purchase price. Through your machine's lifetime, the cost of ink or toner cartridges, paper, and other miscellaneous supplies can add up to more than you paid for the machine itself.

WHAT YOU CAN DO

Consider Fax Machine Alternatives

If you have an internal fax modem, your PC needs to be on to receive a fax. However, timers are available that turn PCs on and off whenever a fax comes in.

If you would like fax capabilities but don't want to invest in a fax machine, you can send electronic mail through an Internet provider or use an online fax service. All you will need are a modem and telecommunications software. Some fax services will send your file to the fax number of the receiving party.

Look for Energy-efficient Machines

While power levels may be comparatively low for fax machines, some people leave them on all the time. Also, turn them off when they are not in use. Buy a fax with a low standby energy rating. This is especially important if you will leave it on much of the time because most of the energy is used during standby. An efficient laser fax could use one-half the energy of a conventional laser fax.

Use a Plain Paper Fax Machine

Taking lifetime cost and paper recyclability into account, you may want to consider a plain paper fax machine. While the purchase price of the machine may be more, look at the costs that you'll incur over the lifetime of the machine. A plain paper fax machine may cost more up front than a thermal paper fax machine, but thermal paper costs a good deal more than the same amount of plain paper and is not recyclable. In less than one year, this difference, alone, can more than make up for the cost of buying an ink jet fax over an inexpensive thermal fax machine. In addition, thermal paper faxes often are copied onto plain paper, increasing the paper costs and energy consumption associated with their use.

Reuse Paper

Reuse paper in thermal transfer and ink jet fax machines. Paper's embodied energy far exceeds, by several times, the energy that it takes to print on it. Reusing fax paper is ideal since fax messages often are discarded. While laser and LED fax makers do not recommend reusing paper that has print on one side, you can find many uses for paper that has one blank side (note pads, scratch paper, memos, etc.)

Use Electronic Mail (e-mail)

Use electronic mail rather than faxing. It saves both energy and paper. E-mail can displace a fair amount of faxing, printing, and expensive overnight mailing and the associated energy use.

MODEMS

Modems send information in the form of pulses from a PC over phone wires, allowing you to send files or other information on your computer. They are inexpensive, and fax/modem combinations are readily available.

If you want to send sheets of paper or images that are not already in your computer – such as book pages, photos, or signed contracts – you may want to scan the images of your documents into your PC so that you can send them by modem. There are flatbed scanners that can scan single pages, business cards, books, and odd-sized papers. Smaller scanners can scan one page items (you cannot fit a book into them). Even some keyboards have small scanners built into the rear. Hand-held scanners are available, too.

If you decide that you don't want to purchase a scanner, there are some copy stores and other places that provide scanning services. If you have a lot to scan, you may want to buy a scanner of your own or purchase one and share it with a neighboring office if that's an option to save money. Be aware, however, that scanned images can use a large amount of disk space, and scanners may work better with additional memory.

WHAT YOU CAN DO

Take Advantage of Speed

Use a high-speed modem. The quicker your modem, the less time you will spend online. That means reduced energy use and lower on-line costs if you have an Internet provider that charges you by the minute.

Determine Your Needs

Save paper, postage, and labor and energy (for mail transport) by sending information over the wires instead of mailing hard copy. If the information would need to be retyped by the recipient, sending your document via electronic mail saves valuable labor, time, and money.

MONITORS

About one-half of a PC's energy consumption is due to its monitor. The Environmental Protection Agency estimates that computer users look at their monitors only about 20% of the time that they are on. This means that 80% of the time, the monitors are standing by, unused. While they can be a lot of fun to have as background, using screen savers can use 20% more energy than not using screen savers.

Color, size, and resolution help to determine a monitor's energy demands. Cathode ray tubes (CRTs) are the most common in desktop monitors. In 1992, color CRTs (rather than monochrome) made up 80% of CRT sales.

WHAT YOU CAN DO

As with your computer, there are a number of ways to prevent your monitor from using too much energy.

Keep It Clean

Keep it clean so you don't strain your eyes or have to increase your monitor's brightness, using more electricity. You can use vinegar or citrus-based glass cleaner to clean your monitor.

Use an Energy-efficient Monitor

There is a movement toward larger, higher resolution monitors. Unfortunately, energy consumption increases proportionately with the monitor's size and resolution.

In terms of energy efficiency, the liquid crystal display (LCD) monitors that laptops have used are much more energy-efficient than the cathode ray tubes (CRTs) commonly found in desktops. Because higher resolution and color images are energy-intensive, your best bet is to purchase a monitor suited to your needs and not necessarily the biggest and the highest resolution one.

If you are really looking for efficiency, you may want to consider a monochrome monitor. A monochrome backlit LCD uses only 2-5% of the energy of a color CRT. Or, consider a color, active matrix LCD monitor. They consume only 10-20% as much energy as the color CRT. Monochrome CRTs use approximately 0.4 Watts per square inch of display; VGA (Video Graphics Array) color CRTs use 0.6-0.7, and Super VGA use more. Color CRTs make up over 80% of CRT sales.

Color quality and the potential for eye strain in using monitors are influenced by ambient lighting. Having a monitor that suits your needs is important, but be sure that your lighting does not create glare or other problems that affect your vision or ability to work well.

Determine Your Needs

Buy a monitor only as large as you need; a 17" color one uses about one-third more energy than a 14" monitor.

Take Advantage of Power-down Capabilities

Buy an Energy Star monitor, which it could save 60-80% energy. And don't forget to enable the power-management features. Also, don't mistake screen savers as energy savers. They are not. Instead, you can set your screen saver to "Blank" to save energy.

Turn It Off

Remember to turn your monitor off before you leave work and during weekends. Better yet, turn it off whenever you leave the room. If it's left on all the time, a 75W CRT can use about $50 of energy each year. You can save about $30 by turning it off nights and weekends without negatively affecting its life.

Even when you are in your office, you can turn monitors off when you are not using them, or use retrofit devices can turn them off automatically after a set period of inactivity. This will save another $10-15 per year per monitor. If you only have one or a few computers, this may not seem like much, but it does add up. And why pay for energy that you didn't use? After all, it's just one push of a button, and it's too easy not to do.

Even if these monitors are power-managed (e.g., Energy Star), you will still save money by turning them off. As a matter of fact, Royce Green showed his company how much they could save simply by turning off their monitors when they weren't using them. Royce works at an auto parts firm that has 150 IBM workstations with InfoWindow displays. It seems he was the only one to turn off his computer monitor whenever he left his desk.

One day, his boss asked him to prove the prudence of this. After Green got information from IBM and the local electric utility, he showed that shutting off all monitors just overnight and on weekends would save over $17,000 each year in electric bills (Anzovin, 39). Of course, if employees turned them off whenever leaving their desks, the company would save even more.

PERSONAL COMPUTERS

While some personal computer (PC) parts may be recycled, unless we become really good at reusing materials, all of the world's existing computers will one day become billions of pounds of solid waste. This problem will increase since people upgrade to keep up with the latest software, computers, and components.

The Environmental Protection Agency estimates that 30-40% of computer users keep their computers on all of the time. This results in an enormous amount of costly waste. Computers use about half of the energy used by office equipment, and this is expected to rise.

Although the energy use of machines normally increases with increased capabilities, this is not always the case. Rest assured that the most efficient Pentium uses less power than the least efficient 386. As PC technology increases, efficiency probably will, too.

While it may be tough to determine the actual power consumption for your whole PC, you can look for some important, energy-saving features:

- Low-voltage machine
- Low-energy hard disk drives
- Good power management (EPRI, 15)

When you are looking for information on your computer's energy use, there is one thing to keep in mind. Although the power levels found on the computer's nameplate may say 300W, your PC probably only operates at 1/3-1/4 that capacity.

Energy Star and the new National Testing and Information Program should make PC purchasing easier. Right now, the most energy-efficient options are:

- Laptop, notebook, and hand-held computers
- Energy Star computers

WHAT YOU CAN DO

Keep It Clean

Keep your computer clean. It will it run longer, and save more energy. To keep the keyboard clean, you can put a thin plastic skin over it to protect it from food, coffee, and dust. And if you need a new keyboard, look for those that are comfortable to use and efficient in their use of resources. Keep your eyes open for keyboards made of recycled materials.

Use a pencil eraser to clean circuit board connectors of oxidation and particles. PC circuit fans draw in dust, which can limit the life of your PC by leading to the overheating of dust-covered chips. If you do not want to do it yourself, computers can be cleaned by any PC service center. You also can get a power surge-suppressing strip to protect your PC from being fried in an electrical storm. Many manufacturers guarantee to pay for any equipment damaged by power surges while using their surge suppresser strips.

Turn It Off

Of course, for easy savings, turn off your computer whenever you are not using it. Even if you use an old computer that gobbles up electricity, you still can minimize its energy use by turning off either just the monitor or the whole computer whenever it is not in use.

If possible, try turning your computers off

- during the day when inactive
- at night
- on weekends

One 75W computer left on all the time can use $50 of electricity each year. Turning it off at night and on weekends can lead to a $30 savings per computer every year. In addition, by turning off your computer during significant periods of inactivity (during meetings, lunch, etc.), each computer will cost you even less in operating costs.

If you don't want to turn off your computer by hand, you can use retrofit devices. Most experts say that turning your computer off whenever it is not in use will not significantly affect its life span. But if it makes you feel better, check with the manufacturer first.

According to *The Green PC*, if each computer user turned off his or her machine for just one more hour every week, one billion tons of coal (or 31.4 million gallons of fuel oil) would be conserved, keeping 2.46 billion pounds of CO_2 out of the air (Anzovin, 9). If you won't be using your machine for a few minutes but don't want to turn it off, just turn off your monitor until you need it again – it still will save electricity since monitors can use a considerable amount of power.

Update Your System

You also can do less obvious things, like deleting unnecessary files and upgrading your operating environment to the newest, quickest version – it can shorten computing time. Also, you can use a compression utility to compress your files, thereby saving room and operation time.

Use Small Disks

You can save a lot of energy by using smaller disks, too. The smaller the floppy disk, the less power it demands when in use.

Take Advantage of E-mail

Some companies watching their bottom lines have found that electronic mail is much less expensive than overnight mail and even faxes. As a result, they have broadened their electronic mail communications to include other organizations and the government, a cost-, energy-, and paper-saving step. Since notes and other documents are stored on disks rather than being printed on paper, you can save network space, energy (photocopying), and money by using electronic mail.

Use Laptops & Notebooks

Another way to save energy is by using laptop or notebook computers. When they first came out on the market, laptops and notebooks were the computers of choice only for those who could afford their high purchase prices. If you've been keeping an eye on them, though, you know how much the prices have dropped over the past few years.

While more expensive than their desktop equivalents, both laptop and notebook computers demand much less energy. Laptops have great power-management capabilities, using about 15W; however, desktops (including the monitors) can demand about 130W, particularly without any power-management capability. Therefore, using a laptop in place of a desktop can cut energy use by over 90%.

Other laptop benefits include:

- They use less desk space.
- The EMFs from the LCD monitor generally used with laptops is less than those found with desktops.
- There is no fan noise from the power supply.
- They allow easier telecommuting if you need to take work with you. And since information is already on your laptop's hard disk, you don't have to worry about copying it onto diskettes and possibly leaving important information on your computer at work or at home.
- They save home energy costs (EPRI, 18).

If you want a laptop machine for portability and a desktop for its easier-to-read screen, you may want to consider buying a laptop and a full-sized monitor and keyboard for office use rather than both a laptop and a desktop. Some laptops are not equipped to handle separate keyboard and monitor connections, so check first. Laptop docking stations also can allow you to link your PC and desk top computers.

PRINTERS

As with copiers, there are many technologies for printers, and energy consumption varies greatly.

IMPACT PRINTERS

Impact printers (dot matrix and daisy wheel) carried the printer market throughout the 1980s, but the drop in non-impact printer (laser, ink jet, bubble jet) costs, better quality, speed, and quiet printing have seen these printers take over.

Improvements in ink jet printers have seen an increase in their sales nearly equal to that of laser printers. Although the larger laser printers can print faster than ink jets, ink jet printers are less expensive to purchase and to operate. Higher end ink jets, however, can use about the same amount of energy as lower end laser printers.

NON-IMPACT PRINTERS

Ink jet, laser, and LED printers are known as non-impact printers and require more energy than do impact printers. Ink jets spray microscopic streams of ink onto the paper. Because they do not use a heat-fusing mechanism, they are much less energy-intensive than even the most efficient laser printers. In active mode, they can use as little as only 1% of the power that a laser printer uses while being much less costly to operate.

Both laser and LED printers affix toner to the paper using pressure-fusing and/or heat. Energy-efficient models can use one-third or less energy than do conventional laser printer models.

WHAT YOU CAN DO

Consider an Ink Jet

If you need great printing quality that isn't the absolute best, consider an ink jet. As with other computer peripherals, the technology is improving. So, if you haven't looked at printers lately, you may want to check them out. For most text and simple graphics uses, you cannot

distinguish much between an ink jet and a laser – except, perhaps, in desktop publishing.

Although ink jets are much less expensive than lasers, check the full life cycle costs of the equipment. This includes energy use, paper, toner, and maintenance. Be aware that some high-end color ink jets are not more energy-efficient than color lasers. Some color ink jets have heat lamps and fans to dry ink on the paper before it comes out. Because the heat lamp is kept on during standby, it adds to the machine's energy consumption.

Look for the Energy Star Rating

To work toward better efficiency, buy an Energy Star printer. Since the majority of printer energy use occurs while the printer is inactive, Energy Star models that power down during these periods are useful. Most ink jets, with the exception of some high-end color printers, should meet the Energy Star requirements. Low-power lasers and LEDs are available, as well.

Share a Printer

To further cut back on energy use and the costs of maintenance, you may want to share a printer. Since most office printers are inactive most of the time, the fewer there are, the more energy will be saved. While three networked printers may spend more time printing, energy will still be saved over 10 individual printers that sit inactive much of the time.

Power-management Accessories

Fortunately, there are a number of devices that can be used to network printers, including manual printer switches and printer buffers. A manual printer switch can route incoming signals from computers to a printer. While inexpensive, these switches are good for only a few computers. According to EPRI, several of the manual printer switch manufacturers have warned that voltage spikes to the printer can occur when one connection is made before the other is broken.

A printer buffer takes printing commands from the computer and transmits them to the printer or holds them until the printer is available. Although printer buffers have 64 ports, allowing them to be connected to many computers and printers, the cables are only so long, so make sure that you're covered. Buffers run just over $100 per port. Computer LANs generally allow for printer networking. They can be configured with a variety of software and hardware combinations, and prices vary.

Consider Double-sided Printing

If you're in the market for a printer, consider one that can do double-sided printing. A few printers have a double-sided printing option. Because there is a lot of energy embodied in paper (meaning it takes a lot of energy to make paper), cutting paper use in half by doing double-sided printing saves money otherwise spent on paper and is good for the environment. By some accounts, the energy it takes to make each page of paper is anywhere from 2-10 times higher than the energy that it takes to print one page of paper. Also, don't forget to enable your printer's power-management features.

Turn It Off

Turn printers off at night, on weekends, and whenever they are not in use. Pacific Gas and Electric did a study that showed over 10% of computer printers are left on all night. Also, try a plug-in timer that turns the printer off on nights and weekends. They can be overridden easily by those working during these times. They also can turn off when not used (e.g, during lunch).

Reuse Paper

In you have ink jet or dot-matrix printers, you can reuse paper if it's been printed on only one side. But don't try this with laser printers. Their manufacturers warn that this may jam and mess the fuser mechanism. (Also, don't use acetate or non-laser labels in your laser printers – they'll melt in your machine.) If you have a laser printer and a lot of paper with one blank side, have a your local printing company cut it and turn it into memo pads for you.

Use E-mail

Use electronic mail (e-mail) to cut the time, energy, and expenses of printing, copying, mailing, and faxing.

Keep It Clean

Clean your printer. You can use a foam swab and isopropyl alcohol to clean the head of your impact printer. Also, dust its inside using a damp cloth to wipe the toner cartridge area, and take out any paper you find around the tractor feed wheels. For more information on how to clean your printer, refer to your printer's manual for instructions.

REFRIGERATORS

If your workplace has a kitchen, chances are good that you have a refrigerator in it. The average, inefficient refrigerator of 15 or 20 years ago costs about three times more to run during its lifetime than it cost to buy. The best refrigerators on the market today use one-third less energy than those made 10 years ago and use no ozone-depleting chemicals.

For more than a decade, the federal government has required major appliance manufacturers to put energy labels on their products. These labels tell us how products compare in energy efficiency with other models of the same type.

New energy standards have been proposed for refrigerators. These standards would require refrigerators to reduce their annual kilowatt usage from 700 to about 500. Look at the Energy Efficiency Rating, EER, (5.5 is considered wasteful; 10 is better and uses much less energy than most) and the Operating Cost. The operating cost is always given in dollars per year. This will help you to calculate the real cost of your appliances.

VACUUMS

If you need a vacuum cleaner, look for an efficient model. You will find that the number of amps used by different vacuums generally is on box or the vacuum itself. Be careful, however, if you're comparing various cleaners; some manufacturers are advertising that their vacuums have a "cleaning effectiveness" of 17 amps, for instance. This does not mean that the vacuum actually uses 17 amps – it may only use 5 or 10 amps. You want to conserve energy, but don't buy such a weak machine that it does not do its job well.

For cleaner air, consider purchasing a vacuum with a HEPA filter system. Again, a word of caution. Many manufacturers are trying to capitalize on people's interest in removing dust, pollen, mites, and other microscopic organisms from their indoor air. Some are advertising that their machines use HEPA filters or HEPA bags that remove 98% of all particles down to 1 micron, for instance. This does not mean that the machine was designed to keep the dust out of the air; it only means that the bag was. Only a few companies' vacuums have been HEPA certified, and you will find that their vacuums cost a few hundred dollars more than most. The idea of HEPA is a great one; just don't fall into a marketing trap when you purchase your vacuum.

For small areas, consider a carpet sweeper over a vacuum cleaner since it uses no electricity.

HELPFUL RESOURCES

INFORMATION

American Council for an Energy-Efficient Economy (ACEEE)
1001 Connecticut Ave., NW
Suite 801
Washington, D.C. 20036
ph: 202-429-8873/ Fax: 202-429-2248

ACEEE
2140 Shattuck Avenue
Suite 202
Berkeley, CA 94704
510-549-9914
ACEEE publishes the *Guide to Energy-Efficient Office Equipment.* Regularly updated, it has useful information, tables, and figures that illustrate the savings of energy-efficient equipment over less efficient options. The *Guide* also has worksheets that allow you to calculate your office costs, from copier use to printer use.

Electric Power Research Institute (EPRI)
P.O. Box 10412
Palo Alto, CA 94303-8743
415-855-2411/ Fax: 415-855-2954

Rocky Mountain Institute
1739 Snowmass Creek Rd.
Snowmass, CO 81654-9199
303-927-3851/ Fax: 303-927-4178

U.S. Department of Energy Office of Conservation and Renewable Energy
1000 Independence Avenue, SW
Washington, D.C. 20585
202-586-5000/ Fax: 202-586-5049
Contact for a copy of their energy-efficient office equipment guide.

U.S. Environmental Protection Agency, Global Change Division
Mail Code 62025
401 M STreet SW
Washington, D.C. 20460
202-233-9190/ Fax: 202-233-9575
The EPA's Global Change Division is in charge of the Agency's Energy Star Program.

PRODUCTS

For addresses and phone numbers, refer to *Appendix A: Directory of Suppliers.*

Because Energy Star and energy-efficient office equipment is available from a variety of common sources (e.g. computer stores), only appliance (dishwasher, refrigerator, etc.) suppliers are listed below.

APPLIANCES
AEG, Andi-Co Appliances, Inc.
ASKO
Bosch
Electron Connection
Energy Concepts Co.
Frigidaire
Miele Appliances, Inc.
Norcold
Real Goods Trading Co.
Regency USA Appliances, Ltd.
Staber Industries, Inc.
Sunelco
Sun Frost
Traulsen & Co., Inc.
Whirlpool Corp.

Summary of Recommendations

Copiers

• Choose a copier sized to your needs.

• Consider a non-heat- and pressure-fusing copier, which is less energy-consuming than heat and pressure-fusing ones.

• When purchasing a copier, be certain it has power-management features. Most heat- and pressure-fusing machines have an energy-saver feature.

• Choose a copier with good duplexing capabilities. Most have a double-sided copying feature, which cuts back on paper use and the energy consumption that it takes to make it (embodied energy).

• Turn off your copier at night and weekends to reduce energy consumption about 65%.

• Enable power-management features.

• When you have a lot of copying jobs to do, try to do them all at once.

• Get the ASTM ratings for individual machines since machines with the same printing technology and copy -volume capability can vary greatly in energy use.

Fax (Facsimile) Machines

• If you have an internal fax modem, your PC needs to be on to receive a fax. However, timers can be purchased to turn PCs on and off when a fax comes in.

• If you decide not to get a machine of your own, you can use an online fax service.

• Fax attachments are available for laser printers. This way, images can be sent "directly from a computer to a fax machine or to another computer with a fax card."

• Turn machines off when not in use.

• Buy a fax with a low standby energy rating.

• Consider a plain paper fax.

• Reuse paper (for thermal transfer and ink jet fax machines).

• Use electronic mail rather than faxing. It saves both equipment energy and paper. E-mail can displace much faxing, printing, and expensive overnight mailing and associated energy use.

Modems

• Electronic Data Interchange (EDI) standard (known also as ANSI protocol X.12) lets organizations "exchange purchase orders, invoices, shipping notices, and more than 100 other forms of standard business information in a universal digital format.

• Use a high-speed modem. The quicker your modem, the less time you'll have to spend online.

MONITORS

• Keep it clean so you don't strain your eyes or have to increase the brightness, using more electricity.

• If you can, choose liquid crystal display (LCD) monitors.

• If you don't need the higher-resolution monitor, go with a more energy-efficient, lower-resolution monitor.

• Consider monochrome (it uses 50-65% as much energy as a color CRT). A monochrome backlit LCD uses only 2-5% of the energy of a color CRT.

• Consider a color, active-matrix LCD.

• Buy a monitor only as large as you need.

• Nanao (Japanese monitor maker) makes monitors that turn themselves off when the PC is idle.

• Buy an Energy Star monitor. It could save 60-80% energy.

• By all means, turn your monitor off at night and weekends.

• Turn off when not used during the day. Retrofit devices can turn monitors off automatically after a set period of inactivity.

• Enable power-management features.

PERSONAL COMPUTERS

• Purchase Energy Star-rated PCs.

• Turn your PC or at least the monitor off when it is not in use.

• Take advantage of portable computers to save on operating costs and allow more flexibility in where you work.

• Use an internal fax\modem to send faxes and electronic mail to send notes. This will save energy and money for paper and postage.

PRINTERS

• If you need great quality that isn't the absolute best, consider an ink jet.

• To work toward better efficiency, buy an Energy Star printer.

• To cut back further on energy use and the costs of maintenance, you may want to share a printer.

• A manual printer switch can route incoming signals from computers to a printer.

• A printer buffer takes printing commands from the computer and transmits them to the printer or holds them until the printer is available.

- If you're in the market for a printer, consider one that can do double-sided printing. A few printers have a double-sided printing option.

- Enable your printer's power-management features.

- Turn printers off at night, on weekends, and whenever they're not in use.

- Try a plug-in timer that turns the printer off during nights and weekends.

- In your ink jet or dot-matrix printers, reuse paper if it's only been printed on one side.

- Use electronic mail (e-mail).

- Clean your printers.

REFRIGERATORS

- Look at the Energy Efficiency Rating (EER) and the operating costs. Determine which refrigerators will be the most efficient and least expensive over their .

- Purchase a refrigerator that doesn't use CFCs, which contribute to the depletion of the ozone layer.

VACUUM CLEANERS

- Consider a carpet sweeper over a more traditional vacuum.

- When purchasing a vacuum, consider one with a HEPA micro-filter that holds particles that generally are blown back into the air by traditional vacuums.

CHAPTER 7

EFFICIENT BUILDING SYSTEMS

townsend, 1994

Structures like these cliff dwellings in Mesa Verde, CO, provide ancient examples of non-toxic, biodegradable buildings. Their materials absorbed the heat by day and released it at night, keeping their inhabitants warm.

A building can be a microcosm of nature or an artificial world with all of its alienating tendencies. Unfortunately, much of today's architecture reflects a separation from the natural world.

Although natural factors – wind direction, solar orientation, and weather – once were incorporated into design, construction, and lifestyle, these factors often are ignored in today's construction. Instead, artificial systems of lighting, heating, cooling, and ventilating are installed in buildings that are poorly sited and made of materials inappropriate to the climate and the needs of the building's end users.

If you do not take into account the specific characteristics of your building's location, you may make some very costly and inefficient decisions. For instance, if you don't pay attention to the sun and to the natural shelter of nearby trees and hills when you design and site your building, you may create the need to compensate with sophisticated heating, cooling, and lighting systems. In addition, you may choose building materials that must be transported from great distances, which demands a lot of energy and may not be appropriate to local needs or fit in with local aesthetics.

Unfortunately, many buildings are designed without regard for their local contexts. In other words, the same building may be built in Anchorage, Alaska, or Miami, Florida. That means that their heating and cooling systems may have to compensate for inappropriate building designs.

Of course, you probably will want to heat, cool, and light your building through smart design. That means taking advantage of the sun's warmth and light as well as the cooling provided by good design, outdoor shade trees, etc. Remember that the employees are the end users of your company's buildings and office equipment. Design according to their needs. After all, buildings are not created for architects and designers, they are built for the employees who work in them.

Amory Lovins, founder of the Rocky Mountain Institute, once said, "People don't want electricity or oil, they want 'comfortable rooms, light, vehicular motion...and other real things'" (Romm, 40). He and others have shown how to have far better lighting and comfort while reducing energy use by 50-90% – simply by meeting the end users' needs through efficiency.

With regard to mechanical heating and cooling, be sure that it is efficient. Because several types of equipment (e.g., appliances, furnaces, hot water heaters, and air conditioners) are rated according to their power demands and their power output, it will give you an indication of the lifetime costs of the equipment you choose.

Mechanical Heating & Cooling

Whether you're creating a new building or retrofitting an existing one, there are a number of things that you should know about mechanical heating and cooling.

Of course, a building's heating and cooling systems should be designed according to the uses and needs of the building's occupants. For example, the density of persons per square foot will affect the amount of cooling or heating that a space will need; a crowded theater may need less heating and more cooling than a hotel or a warehouse. Depending on the building materials and design, the extra body heat could call for higher cooling, particularly in the summer months, or less heating in the winter.

Mechanical Heating

There are four main types of mechanical heating sources. They are:

Boilers: Usually used in large buildings, boilers heat and distribute water or steam through pipes. They use fossil fuels (natural gas, fuel oil).

Electric resistance: Electric resistance is used in smaller buildings and in larger buildings' air ducts to reheat air prior to entering rooms. It heats local air for circulation within the room or wall and ceiling surfaces for radiation into the room. It also requires wiring for heat production and distribution.

Furnaces: Like boilers, furnaces typically are used in larger buildings and also use fossil fuels to generate heat. They heat and distribute air through ducts.

Heat pumps: Heat pumps tend to be used in medium-sized and small buildings. They heat the air and water using refrigeration techniques, taking heat from the out-

doors and using it to heat indoor air. They require less electricity for this process and a heat source (e.g., outdoor air, ground water).

Mechanical Cooling

Mechanical cooling uses refrigeration to remove heat. The heat is expelled, and cool air is circulated. There are two methods used to cool buildings:

Absorption: This method uses liquids (e.g., ammonia, lithium bromide) to absorb water. Absorption does not use compressor pumps or other moving parts as does vapor-compression refrigeration. It can be used with inexpensive heat sources and also with solar collectors.

Vapor compression: This method moves refrigerant through metal pipes; as the liquid passes from a high-pressure to a lower-pressure compartment, vaporizes, absorbing heat from the evaporator coil. With the release of heat, cooling occurs. Less expensive and used more often than absorption, vapor compression also can be used as a heat pump.

HVAC Systems

When heating, ventilation, and cooling systems are integrated, they are known as HVAC systems. They can be classified according to the substance that passes through them. They are:

All-air systems: These systems clean and heat/cool and humidify/dehumidify the air, moving it through ducts and circulating it within the space via mixing terminals or outlets. They can operate with up to 100% outdoor air, eliminating the need for mechanical cooling when outdoor temperatures go below 50-55 degrees Fahrenheit (Moore, 225).

Air-water systems: These systems respond quickly to fluctuating demands from various zones and provide centrally controlled humidity and forced-air ventilation. Because both air and water are sent to each space, one or both can be used to control the temperature. Air-water systems use about one-sixth the fan power of all-air systems to circulate the water. They offer the flexibility of air systems and the energy- and cost-efficiency of water systems. Unlike all-air systems, air-water systems can require refrigeration even when outdoor temperatures go below 50 degrees Fahrenheit (Moore, 225).

All-water systems: All-water systems cool and dehumidify the air by circulating chilled brine or water through coils. They are especially useful for smaller spaces (e.g., apartments, motels, small commercial buildings).

Unitary systems: Unlike the other systems described above, unitary systems use refrigerant and are decentralized. In other words, a building's cooling is not covered by one centralized system but by window air conditioners or by packaged terminal air conditioners (PTACs). While PTACs, or through-the-wall air conditioners, usually have a heating capability, window air conditioners do not. Other decentralized heating systems include forced-air, natural convection, and radiant units. These unit types are powered by electricity or gas.

CHOOSING A SYSTEM

Several factors influence a building's demand for heating and cooling and should be taken into account in a building's design. Fuller Moore, author of *Environmental Control Systems: Heating, Cooling, Lighting*, suggests that there are a number of things that should be taken into account in determining how much heating, cooling, lighting, and dehumidifying your building needs:

Air filtration: Filters generally are found at the air-return inlet of HVAC equipment to benefit the space being served and the equipment. For those places requiring especially good air quality (e.g., industrial "clean" rooms, critical care rooms), consider the following when choosing an air filtration system:

- Effectiveness
- Health benefits
- Initial cost
- Maintenance ease
- Quality
- Size/quantity of particles

There also are several types of filters, and Moore lists them from least to most expensive and effective:

- Disposable dry filters (fine mesh screens)
- Disposable viscous (sticky) filters
- Non-disposable filters (panels, roll mats, washable media filters)
- Electrostatic (eliminate smoke/pollen) (Moore, 235)

Climate
- How much does the building envelope insulate against the outdoor climate?
- How much outdoor ventilation air is required for the HVAC system? (The HVAC system may need to condition the outside air for temperature and humidity.)

Heat recovery: For larger buildings, the types of heat used include: thermal wheels, heat pipes, and run-around coils. In addition to using these systems for heat recovery, some systems can be used to cool machinery and lighting fixtures by recovering the heat emitted by them. Removing heat from lighting fixtures, alone, can raise their efficiency by 10-20% (Moore, 237).

Occupancy
- When is the building occupied?
- By how many people and for how long? (There may be some building zones with zero occupancy for extended periods of time, requiring a minimum of space conditioning.)
- What will the building's occupants be doing? (Lighting, machinery, and people all contribute to a building's heating load.)

Reducing peak loads
- When is your building's peak energy demand? (Commercial buildings pay not only for energy consumption but for demand based on the peak rate of use. This demand charge can be substantial.)
- What strategies will you use to reduce the demand charge? (e.g., conservation to cut heating/cooling loads, daylighting to cut lighting needs, using more energy during off-peak times)

Space Requirements
Of course, any equipment that you have for heating and cooling will take up space, and that dead space costs money. But how much space will it take? According to Moore, HVAC systems take up the most space in smaller buildings and the least in large ones. Here's the breakdown:

Small buildings/buildings requiring a good deal of cooling: 3-9%
Large buildings: 1-3%

Below are the general space requirements for the various types of HVAC systems:

All-air: 3-8%
Air-water: 3-6%
All-water: 1.5-5%
Dispersed, stand-alone units/roof-mounted units: 1-3% (Moore, 239-240)

System Selection
Moore examines several building types and offers some factors to consider when choosing appropriate systems.

Factories

• Most factories are one-story buildings with systems for heating and ventilation. Increasingly, they have cooling systems as well, which may increase employee comfort and productivity in the long run.
• Some factories, such as textile color printing factories, require some control over humidity and temperature for good-quality end products.
• Independent units probably can handle any separate thermal zones that may exist.
• Factories can use large self-contained air conditioners and central-chilled water plants with fan coils.

Hospitals

• Hospital systems are regulated heavily and have restrictions. Surgical suites often are required to ventilate odors and hazardous fumes with outdoor air.
• Areas near surgical suites often are the site of exhaust openings in order to trap heavy gases.
• Since discharges of static electricity are dangerous around flammable gases, humidity is closely controlled.
• Humidity and temperature are controlled, particularly in cardiac and intensive care areas, delivery rooms, and nurseries.
• Varied pressure is required throughout various hospital zones to prevent the migration of dangerous organisms. Isolation wards, in particular, generally are cooled and properly filtered by induction units or individual fan-coil units.
• Hospital cooling rarely uses fiberglass ductwork because ducts offer microorganisms a good place to breed.

Houses

• Most houses use a direct-expansion cooling coil with a forced-air furnace and air-cooled condensing unit.
• Large houses can be separated into sleeping and living area zones

Multi-residential buildings

• Apartment occupants want to control their own heating and cooling.
• One- to three-story apartment buildings can be cooled using a remote, air-cooled condenser on the roof and heated using forced-air furnaces in each apartment.
• Buildings using individual fan coils in each apartment also can use central-chilled water plants.
• Apartments also can use water-to-air heat pumps that have a circulating heat sink; individual heat pumps can accept or reject warmth from the heat sink.
• Housing high-rises use individual fan-coil units for each apartment and central water-chilling and water-heating plants. Water-to-air heat pumps also can be used.

Office buildings

• Include changes and variances in office space use into the system design.
• Create separate climate-control zones, making future zone changes easy as the building's occupancy changes.
• Use rooftop, packaged, air-cooled units in small one- or two-story offices. While not as flexible as other zoning systems, they are less expensive.
• Use double-duct or multi-zone systems for zoning and future zone change flexibility; these systems are popular for office buildings.
• Induction-type systems, which require minimum shaft space and relatively small ducts and pipes, can be used in high-rise buildings' perimeter zones while variable-volume or double-duct systems are appropriate for the core zone. This combination can be very flexible and has great zoning potential.
• Large office buildings also can use fan-coil units. Although these units are not as flexible as the induction or double-duct systems, the capital cost may be lower.

Schools

• Classrooms should be quiet and well ventilated.
• Classrooms require separate zoning; as a result, they generally use heat pumps or fan-coil units located beneath the windows or run by remote control.

Stores and shopping centers

• Central water-chilling and water-heating systems sometimes are used in large shopping malls.
• Smaller shopping centers and stand-alone stores generally are cooled using self-contained rooftop packages.
• For individual shops, fan-coil units are used with chilled and/or hot water.
• Since shoppers move about and are not as sensitive to drafts as would be persons in an office or hospital, air distribution is not as important.

Theaters

• Theaters need not be zoned for temperature.
• They must be quiet, well-ventilated, and low in humidity.
• Theaters often have single-zoned fan-coil units for air-conditioning, using chilled water or direct expansion refrigeration. Taking advantage of outside air for ventilation, the system is quiet and has a high capacity to dehumidify. This is important in spaces that have a high density of people (Moore, 241-242).

WHAT YOU CAN DO

Choose Efficient Equipment

Air Circulation
You may want to use ceiling fans to distribute warmer air in the winter and cooler air in the summer. Variable-speed models can conserve energy by allowing you to control how quickly or slowly you want the fan to rotate.

Air Conditioners
If you're in the market for an air conditioner, check the Energy Efficiency Rating (EER) and Seasonal EER (SEER) ratings to find the most efficient unit. Both measurements show a ratio of electrical input to cooling energy. High-efficiency units have EER and SEER ratings of 10 and higher. Anything below eight is considered wasteful.

Traditional cooling systems used chlorofluorocarbons (CFCs), which have been blamed for the degradation of Earth's protective ozone layer. A ban on CFC production by the Clean Air Act of 1996 mandates that alternative, CFC-free methods be used in such cooling systems as air conditioners and refrigeration systems.

Some building owners use cooling systems based on ice storage. These systems produce ice during the night, when utility rates are lowest, and are cooled in the daytime by chilled water from the melting ice.

Furnaces
If you're looking for a new furnace, be sure to look beyond purchase prices, and consider the furnace's lifetime costs.

New furnaces have yellow labels that rate their energy use. If you do not find a label in the upper right corner, ask the dealer for the Annual Fuel Utilization Efficiency (AFUE) rating. The AFUE is a rating system developed by the U.S. Department of Energy to help consumers know how efficiently different furnaces extract and use the heat from the fuel they burn. Higher AFUE ratings mean higher efficiency. This will help you to estimate a furnace's life cycle costs in advance and enable you to make the best decision.

If you are not convinced of the impact of taking small steps toward efficiency, consider this – by replacing just one furnace that is only 65% efficient with one that is 90% efficient, you can prevent the annual emission of an extra four tons of carbon dioxide from entering the atmosphere.

Water Heaters
The best water heaters are over 90% efficient, meaning that they heat water with almost all of the energy that they use. However, keep in mind that, just as with air conditioners, high ratings don't mean that there isn't energy lost on the other end. Power plants turn fuel into electricity at only about 35-40% efficiency. Since the total efficiency of electric heat is only about 35%, you may want to consider a gas heater, which has a real efficiency of about 60%. Of course, using renewable resources is the smartest choice of all.

NATURAL HEATING & COOLING

There are many things that you can do to cut your heating and cooling costs through both the exterior and interior design of your workplace and your choice of a heating and cooling system.

WHAT YOU CAN DO

Use Efficient Strategies in and around Your Building
There a many challenges to keeping the indoors comfortable. Below are some of them and some strategies that you can use to keep your building's temperature and humidity within a healthy range.

Challenges & Strategies

Heat Transmission
Heat transmission occurs when heat escapes from your building. There are several things that you can do to keep the indoor temperature indoors. You can design a compact building (it can have multiple stories) with well-insulated ceilings, floors, and walls. Of course, you will want to use insulated windows that have been installed properly (there should not be a breeze around the window frame) and use caulk and weatherstripping. Be sure that your building's least used spaces (e.g., closets) are located along the outside walls to insulate the more interior areas against outdoor temperature fluctuations. Finally, if you are designing more than one building, you can join them using common walls to provide additional insulation.

Heat Infiltration
Heat infiltration occurs when air enters your building. You may notice this when it is especially windy outdoors, or you may be able to feel breezes along windows, electrical sockets, underneath doors, and other areas. You can plant a wall of evergreens along the windward side

of your building, build a wall or use an exterior overhang to protect the building's entry from the wind, place buildings close together to protect one another from the wind, design the building so that less unoccupied areas (e.g., garage) are located on the windward side, create earth berms to move wind over and around the building, and design a sloping roof to aim wind quietly over the building.

Solar Heat Increase

To increase the sun's heat in your building, there are several things that you can do. You can design the building to face south to take advantage of solar heat throughout the year, put the most heavily used areas near the southern part of building, have your building's largest window surface area on the south side, create a sun space or other area with thermal mass to collect warmth during the day and release it at night, and be sure that your outdoor ground materials are light in color so that they reflect additional sun onto the south wall.

Solar Heat Decrease

To decrease the sun's heat in your building, you can place exterior shades or overhangs with louvers over south-facing windows to keep summer sun out while allowing breezes to cool the exterior, use shutters on the outside and shades on the inside of east and west windows to protect against morning and evening summer sun, ensure that roofs and walls are light in color to reflect the sun, steer clear of skylights as they are difficult to shade from the high summer sun, create a double roof with an air space to act as insulation for the spaces below. Of course, you will probably want to create shaded activity areas outdoors (i.e., on north side), where people can interact comfortably.

Indoor Temperature Swings

To minimize the effects of daily and annual changes in the outdoor temperature, there are several strategies that you can employ. You can build thick walls for added insulation, and cover the roof with sod or another protective material. In addition, you can take advantage of the stable underground temperatures by building partly or fully below ground. In this event, you may want to use open-loop ducts underground to moderate ventilation air and closed-loop ducts underground to cool indoor air that is being recirculated. Be certain that your underground ducts are sealed well to prevent radon gas from seeping in and to make cleaning easier.

Increased Ventilation

To increase your building's ventilation, you may want to design a narrow floor plan that will encourage cross-building circulation. In addition, consider using raised floors, attic vents, roof belvederes and open interiors,

clerestory windows on your building's leeward side, and designing a landscape that directs summer breezes toward your building.

Evaporative Cooling Increase

To increase evaporative cooling, consider using indoor greenhouses and pools, roof ponds, sprayed patios and fountains that air can blow across before entering the building, hybrid evaporative coolers rather than mechanical air conditioners, and wetted curtains (with a loose weave than allow evaporation). Also, you may want to spray roofs and walls with water.

Radiative Cooling Increase

To increase radiative cooling, you can use a roof pool (covered during the day with movable insulation and exposed at night) and use north-sloping louvers to expose roof to nighttime climate while guarding from solar gain (Moore, 89-90).

Shading

Just as you can take advantage of renewable resources to heat intelligently, you can cool smarter, too. For instance, shading softens the sun's heat on buildings and can be provided easily in hotter climates. Well-planned roof eaves and awnings can allow for the sun's winter rays to penetrate while keeping them from overheating your building in the summer's hotter months. Low-emissivity glass, insulating curtains, blinds, or shutters can serve to shade your office as well. Screens and lattices allow for ventilation while cutting down glare and heat. White walls can be used to repel the sun's light when shading is difficult. Trees, shrubs, creepers, and earth cover all can be used to shade and protect your building from the sun's heat. Planting trees near buildings can cut cooling needs up to 30%. Where appropriate, verandahs can be useful as well. In addition, using shades, drapes, and blinds can cut air conditioning costs by at least 20%. Awnings, overhangs, and shade trees are better since they keep the sun from reaching your windows and heating your office.

If you design a new building, don't forget to take advantage of solar benefits and landscaping. South-facing awnings can lower interior room temperatures by 8-15 degrees. Talk with architects and landscape planners who are familiar with smart office design. Also, contact your local utility for possible rebates, loans, and other economic incentives. Some states offer these incentives for improved energy efficiency.

Ventilation

Cross-ventilation is one traditional way to cool. Preferably, air enters at a lower level, and, because heat rises, warmer air is expelled at a higher level. In the

Middle East, wind scoop devices are used. These are placed on the roofs to catch cool breezes, sending the air down shafts into the living areas below. If necessary, incoming air can be moistened by having it pass over water or vegetation.

POWER SOURCES

Geothermal

Geothermal energy is one source of energy although it is less commonly used than other renewable resources. Geothermal power comes from harnessing the steam and extremely hot water that comes from within the earth. Pipes are laid three feet underground, where it is always between 40-70 degrees Fahrenheit, and pumps capture the heat from these pipes.

Some experts estimate that plants using the underground steam and hot water to create electricity will accommodate the energy needs of more than 1.8 million households. As the use of geothermal energy increases, this number is expected to increase by nearly 25%. Sites not yet tapped are expected to support the energy needs of about 17.5 million households. A number of utility companies as well as the Department of Energy have offered $100 to bolster geothermal sales.

Solar

The sun is a powerful source of energy. It has provided the earth with natural light for millions of years. It makes no sense that over three-quarters of the world's energy consumed comes from expensive, non-renewable resources (mainly oil, coal, and natural gas) when we could increase our dependence upon the sun's energy.

The amount of sunlight that falls on the United States is about 500 times more than the amount we use, and we could depend on the sun's constant output for lighting, heating, and powering equipment. If solar cells covered just 1% of the U.S. land area and ran at only 25% efficiency, they could accommodate all of the United States' energy needs. The U.S. Department of Energy has stated that large, photovoltaic (PV) "farms" designed for public use would use less land than do today's coal-burning plants. In addition, solar collectors can supply more than enough power without pipelines, oil spills, strip mining for coal, air pollution, nuclear waste, or contributing to global warming or acid rain. Whenever the sun shines on them, solar cells make electric current – with no noise or moving parts.

In building construction, there are two types of solar thermal energy – *passive* and *active (photovoltaic* or *PV)*. Some systems use a combination of the two. Hybrid solar systems are mostly passive but may use pumps and fans in helping to move the heat around.

Passive Solar

Taking advantage of the sun's energy can be free and easy, and the savings can be remarkable. *Passive solar* energy is created by collecting and distributing the sun's heat using a building's natural systems. For instance, a building may be designed so that the sun's rays pass through the windows and strike dark, heavy masonry walls and concrete floors, which absorb heat by day and release it at night. These walls can be covered with glass and allow stored heat to passively circulate through wall vents into living areas.

Many natural materials, including water and stone, collect and store the sun's heat by day and release it at night. These materials can be used in a building's walls and floors. For instance, there are two types of walls used to collect heat from the sun: Trombe walls and water-container walls. Trombe walls, named for Dr. Felix Trombe, are made of heavy masonry, such as stone, brick, earth, or block. They have a dark surface that absorbs the sun's heat. Water-container walls are clear, water-filled columns or drums that store heat.

Existing, lightweight walls can be covered with plaster or with thick, ceramic tiles to increase their thermal mass, and this increases their heat absorption capabilities. As weight is added, thermal stability increases; however, this doesn't necessarily result in added warmth.

If you're considering water container walls, be aware that while water is more efficient at heat storage than is masonry, water-filled columns are very heavy and need maintenance to combat leaks and algal growth.

One Illinois residential developer, the Bigelow Group, uses passive solar design features that don't raise the costs of their houses. The company guarantees customers in writing that their passive solar homes' annual heating costs will not exceed $200 of the 100 homes that the Bigelow Group has built each year since the mid-1980s, the company has had to pay only $470 in refunds to its customers.

Self-adhesive, foil-like products that can be applied to the exterior glass side of a thermal storage concrete wall. This material acts as a one-way solar sponge, absorbing sunlight during the day and giving it back slowly at night, leading to increased energy savings.

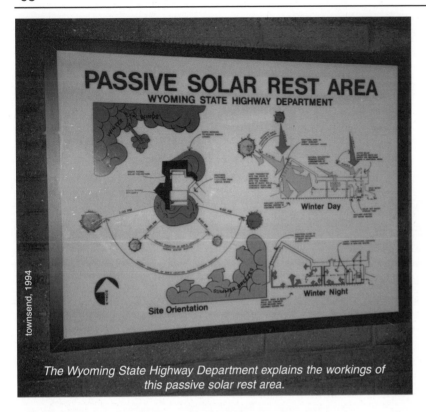

The Wyoming State Highway Department explains the workings of this passive solar rest area.

collected on site using solar water heaters, roofing tiles, and window-glazing with built-in solar cells.

Although the initial cost of photovoltaics is still more than that from the public utilities' electricity, the operation cost is minimal, and solar-powered systems can pay for themselves rapidly. Photovoltaics generate far more energy than they take to make. And once they are made, they do not harm the environment throughout their use as do fossil fuels and other non-renewable resources. Their manufacture is not as bad, either. They are constructed with silicon (which is made from sand) and such "safe" materials as boron and phosphorous.

There are several products available that enable us to take advantage of energy from the sun. Photovoltaics are available as integral parts of roofing panels, canopies, skylights, rain screens, shingles (United Solar in Troy, MI, is manufacturing these), and other exterior

Building for a Sustainable America

If you are a facilities manager struggling to incorporate information on solar power into your company's design, you may want to look into the Building for a Sustainable America (BSA) Education Campaign. The Campaign, developed by the Passive Solar Industries Council and the American Solar Energy Society, uses buildings to showcase the potential of solar design features, daylighting, and other renewable energy technologies. This program is aimed at facility managers and other corporate decision-makers who affect U.S. building retrofits and construction.

Water Heaters

Solar-water heaters can reduce your hot-water bill by 60-80%. A number of systems are available, including those in which solar-heated liquids (methanol-water antifreeze) pass through a system down to a heat exchanger under the hot-water tank and back up to the collector again.

Photovoltaics

Active solar power, or *photovoltaics (PV),* depends upon glass- or plastic-covered metal panels facing the sun. These panels collect the sun's heat, and a mechanical system distributes it. Either liquid or air is passed through these panels and fed into a thermal store, which can be a rock bed for an air system or a water tank for a liquid system. Then, heat is distributed on demand by water pipes or air ducts and assisted by fans or pumps. The little energy that efficient buildings use often can be

Individual solar panels at Real Goods Trading Company.

Today's photovoltaic panels are more efficient than their earlier counterparts. These supply power to the Real Goods Trading Company's Solar Living Center in Hopland, California.

housing materials. Sun spaces also can be used to house passive or active solar collectors.

Wind

Wind is often overlooked as a source of energy. However, with the deregulation of U.S. utilities, U.S. companies may be able to buy power from utilities that have wind power in their portfolios of electric power sources.

It is estimated that energy produced today could power nearly 300,000 households. And with the development of new projects, enough wind power could be produced that would accommodate another 540,000 households. It also has been estimated that the potential for wind power in the U.S. would supply nine times more than the country's current power needs.

These turbines in California take advantage of the local winds to produce energy.

INSULATION: KEEPING THE INDOORS COMFORTABLE

We cannot talk about heating and cooling without talking about insulation. After all, the purpose of insulation is to maintain indoor air temperatures. Minimizing the impact of outdoor temperatures occurs when air is trapped inside the insulation's tiny pockets and is unable to circulate. Believe it or not, the energy flowing through U.S. windows is about the same amount as that produced by the oil flowing through the Alaskan pipeline. Designing and working in an inefficient office building could be the most expensive and ecologically harmful thing you ever do.

For those of you with home offices, consider this: over 50 years, most houses use about 50,000 gallons of oil for heating, cooling, and lighting. But things are better than they used to be. If the U.S. had remained at its 1973 efficiency levels, by 1986, those of us in the U.S. would have put 50% more carbon dioxide into the atmosphere. Luckily, smart design, products, and energy use can cut energy bills by over 75% for most houses built today. This means saved money, reduced waste, and less pollution.

INSULATION BASICS

Any type of heating or cooling system, solar or otherwise, will not be nearly as effective if your building is not well insulated, or weatherproofed. Heat energy always migrates from warmer to cooler; ideally, insulation prevents this migration from happening.

A material's ability to insulate is measured by its resistance, or R value. The R value of fiberglass, for instance, represents the material's resistance to conducting heat. The higher the R value, the higher a material's ability to insulate. So, a one-inch thick wall with an R-55 value insulates much better than one rated R-10.

Fiberglass insulation requires 287 times the amount of electrical energy to produce per pound than does cellulose insulation.

Batt insulation, an alternative to fiberglass, is made of 95% post-industrial textile fibers (75% cotton/25% polyester).

Cellulose insulation is made mainly of recycled newspapers. It generally is thought to be non-toxic. Ammonium sulfate, borax, or boric acid are used as fire retardants in cellulose insulation. There is some concern over the corrosion of metal that comes in contact with cellulose insulation containing ammonium sulfate, so you may want to check with insulation installers about protection around pipes.

Expanded polystyrene (EPS), a recyclable product, is used to make foam insulation board. Rather than CFCs or HCFCs (hydrochlorofluorocarbons), it uses pentane as an expansion agent; most rigid foam boards contain HCFCs. Although pentane is an element of smog, it breaks down easily. Rigid foam insulation is treated with fire retardants and emits toxic fumes when it burns.

Mineral fiber insulation is inflammable, non-corrosive, odorless, and does not host the growth of bacteria or fungus. The two types of mineral fiber, or mineral wool, are rock wool (from natural rocks) and slag wool (from blast furnace slag).

The earthsheltering and heavy walls help keep this northwestern U.S. rest area warm at night.

Perlite and vermiculite are minerals used as loose-fill insulation in masonry wall cavities and in some rigid insulation boards. When they are used as loose-fill insulation, they are easy to recover and reuse.

Silicate foam ("air-krete") is a wet insulation sprayed into the cavities of concrete, masonry, and frame construction. This material is characterized by low toxicity.

According to the EPA, the procurement for insulation in federal building designs has the following minimum recycled content requirements:

Cellulose, loose and spray-on: 75% post-consumer paper, by weight

Fiberglass: 20-25% recovered glass cullet, by weight

Perlite composition board: 23% post-consumer paper, by weight

Rock wool: 75% recovered material, by weight

Rigid foam: 9% recovered material, by weight

Foam-in-place: 5% recovered material, by weight

Glass-fiber reinforced rigid foam: 6% recovered material, by weight

Phenolic rigid foam: 5% recovered material, by weight

WHAT YOU CAN DO

Air-to-air Heat Exchangers

By the way, insulating well does not mean that you have to give up fresher air and ventilation. Heat recovery ventilators (or air-to-air heat exchangers) force the air leaving your office to give its warmth or coolness to the air brought in. You can adjust it for the season so that warmed, exiting air heats cold, incoming air in winter, and cooler air cools the warm, incoming air in the summer. Good heat recovery ventilation can save 80% of the outgoing air's energy. These exchangers allow for ventilation without resulting in the energy loss you would experience by opening a window.

This rock art recollects a time when humans depended solely on natural materials for shelter and all other needs.

townsend, 1992

Cellulose

The insulation industry has changed markedly over the past several years as new materials are found to be effective at keeping temperatures indoors. One new material is cellulose insulation, which is creating competition with fiberglass in the insulation industry. Made of recycled newspaper and treated with fire retardant (nontoxic borax) to make it less flammable, cellulose insulation is more energy-efficient than fiberglass insulation.

Icynene is one type of cellulose insulation. It is a water-based, aerated cellulose spray that is installed before the walls are closed in with drywall (wallboard). Sprayed into the wall cavities, it sticks to the studs' sheathing and completely fills in the wall, including the areas all around wiring. Although messy to apply, it insulates to about R-3.5 per inch with almost no air passing through it. Be sure to use fully fire-rated cellulose.

Cotton

Cotton is used as insulation, too. It can be a good, natural alternative to fiberglass. One company makes a blue cotton denim insulation out of fabric scraps leftover from Lee and Levis blue jeans production.

Earthsheltering

Earth sheltered buildings can be partially or fully underground. If you are building from scratch, one method of insulation is "earthsheltering." Earthsheltering uses the earth's constant, underground warmth as an effective method of insulation against one or more of the building's walls. Even if the above-ground temperature is below zero degrees Fahrenheit, it is always about 32 degrees Fahrenheit just below the surface of the ground. The farther down you go, the warmer it gets. Three to four feet below ground is always above freezing, and six feet below the surface can be as warm as 60 degrees Fahrenheit in mid-winter.

Don't think that you have to sacrifice light for earthsheltering. Structures built fully or partially underground (if appropriate to their locations) do not have to give up windows, skylights, and sunshine. Even fully underground buildings can be solar-powered, kept relatively temperate by the earth, and full of light.

Fiberglass

Fiberglass insulation is made mostly of recycled glass. Although it currently controls about 95% of the insulation market, fiberglass' potentially negative effects on human health have been a cause for concern. Increasing public attention has been brought to fiberglass' apparent role as a skin irritant, as harmful to human lungs and eyes, and as a possible cause of cancer.

Fireplaces

If you're looking for innovative ways to add heat to certain areas in your workplace and are considering building a fireplace, be aware that fireplaces often are inefficient. Although they can add to the ambiance of restaurants, hotels, and other businesses, heat is lost through the damper. If you'll be using a fireplace, your best bet is to put it in the middle of the building, where the heat can radiate, and use a massive chimney.

"Russian fireplaces" and some wood stoves are more efficient alternatives to traditional fireplaces; however, they do release carbon dioxide from burning wood, contributing to global warming. The best way to create and retain heat in a building is through sunlight and good insulation.

Windows

In the past, windows have been a major source of temperature loss. With single-layer windows having an insulation capacity of only about R-1, heat is lost easily through the glass. That is why windows have been considered poor insulators.

Better Windows

Fortunately, the window industry has advanced enough to create windows with R values even higher than the brick walls into which they are installed. Window technology has changed, and those changes have included the availability of double-glazed (R-2) and triple-glazed (R-4) windows. Vast improvements over the windows of the past, some of the new windows are made with two layers of glass coated with low-emissivity (low-e) coatings, which do not allow much heat to escape through the glass. The space between the layers of glass is filled with argon gas, which conducts heat less than does air.

Although these windows may cost more, the energy savings often have them pay for themselves in a year or two and make standard, insulated windows (thermopanes) obsolete. The new windows allow more heat in than they allow to escape, even on the north side of a building on a cloudy day.

One window, the Hurd Insol-8, has an insulation rate of R-8. That means that each square foot loses only 1/8 the heat of that same area in a single pane of glass. This degree of insulation is achieved by the windows' two layers of glass and two low-e suspended plastic Heat Mirror® films. The three air spaces inside the window are filled with a low-conductivity gas mix. There also is an insulating edge spacer between plastic films. With sunlight coming through the glass, the InSol-8 saves more energy than an R-19, well-insulated wall.

Windows with insulating shutters also are available. The shutters direct sunlight in, out, or partly into a building. And when the aluminum-faced insulation panels are closed (they pivot inside fiberglass tubes that serve as windows), R values range from R10 – R-20.

Window Glazing

One of the things that makes today's windows so effective at keeping moderating heat and light is the glazing used. Glazing can affect several lighting and heating aspects of a building and should be considered early in the design.

Glazing can have an impact on: color, condensation, daylighting, energy use, glare heat gain/loss, privacy, shading/control of sunlight (including ultraviolet), sound control, thermal comfort, and view (Franta, Anstead, and Andor, 27, 1997).

Depending on whether or not your building is climate-load-dominated (most of its annual energy use is due to climatic conditions) or internal-load-dominated (most of its annual energy use is because of appliances/equipment, lighting, and people), the importance of a glazing strategy may vary.

Additional Tips

In addition to smarter windows, you may want to invest in insulating, roll-down window blinds. They more than double the R value of standard, double-glazed windows from R-2 to R-5.2. In addition, they will cut back on air infiltration through your windows and can be used to prevent unwanted heat gain. One insulates by holding air between its two layers and has a metal coating on one of the layers, boosting the total R value of a double-glazed window from about R-2 to R-4.2.

By the way, be sure to keep your windows sealed in cold weather. This is especially true for those windows near thermostats. Since cracks and drafts can trick thermostats into thinking it is colder indoors than it is, you may be getting more heat than you want and the increased bills that go with it. Remember that there are methods of ventilating your office other than windows.

For instance, you can take advantage of heat exchangers, which can warm incoming, cold winter air before it circulates throughout the building.

Positioning windows to capture the sun's warmth in the winter, along with insulation and airtight construction, can cut heating needs by more than 97%. Similar techniques can eliminate air conditioners in hot climates as well.

OTHER INSULATION METHODS

Air-krete is a non-toxic insulation made of magnesium. Although more expensive than most insulation materials, it is healthier since it has no chemicals that offgas. It is mixed with air and sprayed into wall cavities by licensed contractors. The resulting brittle foam is weak but insulates well once it is inside the walls. Air-krete is non-flammable.

Low-e insulation is a radiant barrier insulation. It is less costly than fiberglass and does not shed fibers as fiberglass insulation does. Like air-krete, it's fireproof, and it does not offgas. It has a high R value, too. Unlike most insulations, which depend on convection, this insulation operates by reflection. Used on NASA shuttles, it is useful especially in places without the thick walls required by the thicker, fiber insulation.

Pur Fill provides tight seals around window and door frames, wall holes, and cracks. Pur Fill was the first foam sealant introduced that doesn't contain CFCs, which means that it's ozone-friendly (others CFC-free insulation include Forno Products, air-krete, Polycell – from Grace Construction Products – and Touch 'n Foam from Convenience Foam Products). EDPM Construction Gaskets, made in Sweden, can be placed under window sills and wall plates and between drywall and studs or plates during construction. They act as temperature, air, and moisture seals. Foam rope backer rods can be used to seal wide cracks, spaces between logs in log homes, and as caulking backing. It is sold in rolls. Acorn vent spacers are stapled to sheathing. Batt insulation is installed against them. For roof ventilation, they are used to provide a continuous air flow channel under the roof sheathing in insulated cathedral ceilings.

RAINWATER COLLECTION

If your company owns its building space, you may really be able to maximize your efficiency by freely collecting another natural resource– rainwater. The architect Malcolm Wells once calculated that the entire city of Philadelphia receives nearly as much rainwater (122 billion gallons/year, which runs down the gutters, into the sewers, and back to the source before being processed and piped back), as it pipes in to use (125 billion gallons/year). If most of this water had been collected and used in the first place, the incredible amount of energy, expense, and resources wasted in treatment could have been avoided.

For those of you working from your homes, you may be interested to know that in the developed world, the average family of four uses between 10,000-40,000 gallons of water each year. Yet, rather than collecting and using it, most of us waste all of the rainwater that falls on our buildings. About 50 trillion gallons of rainwater become runoff from American lawns every year. This is about half of the U.S. water budget, including that for irrigation and industry. Rather than collect rainwater, most of us allow it to run down the streets and into the gutters. But large quantities of uncollected rainwater contribute to erosion and flash floods.

Using rain, treated wastewater, and smart landscaping techniques can cut municipal water reliance by two-thirds, resulting in a 90% drop in the wastewater headed for sewage treatment. This may be especially cost-effective in drier regions, where water is more expensive. Also, check with local authorities to be sure that your rainwater collection design will be approved.

WHAT YOU CAN DO

Collect Rainwater

It doesn't really make much sense to use drinking-quality water for landscaping and other outdoor activities when you have the facilities to collect rainwater. Rainwater can be stored in holding tanks, much like cisterns. Talk to an architect to find out if you can integrate a rainwater collection system into your building's plans.

One U.S. stadium, Coors Field, built a wetlands to manage storm water. The system can hold 330,000 gallons of run-off water in a cavern designed for this purpose. The wetlands, six in all, measure 700-by-30-feet. They have microbes that digest the standard baseball foods, including beer, popcorn, corn dogs, gum, and other miscellaneous food scraps that end up in the stadium's run-off (Hammer, October 12, 1994).

Water-efficient Landscaping

Hoses and sprinklers can use about 2.4 gallons of water every minute. If you like your landscaping but you want to reduce your water consumption, you can cover your soil with compost or mulch to reduce evaporation, eliminating the need for constant watering. Also, native plants are better acclimated to your local temperatures and rainfall, so you may want to replace your more water-hungry plants with better-acclimated, native ones.

Other Uses

You can use collected rainwater in swimming pools as well. But be sure to have the water tested on regularly. Also, you can create a sunken garden or a percolation bed to hold the water until it soaks in. Rainwater can be used in greenhouses, gardens, toilets, and washers, but to use it in pools and hot tubs, it may need some treatment. Water from roofs with lead flashings or valleys is not suitable for use.

Toilets & Waste Treatment

What should we do with human waste? It's not something most of us discuss too often. But think about it. When we came up with the idea of putting human waste into drinking-quality water, it was not one of our most shining moments. Yet, that's what we do in our toilets. Not only do our wastes go into toilets but the chemicals that we use to clean them do, too. It's the equivalent of opening up a pipe that leads to our drinking-water supply and throwing pollutants in. Although most places in the U.S. have some type of municipal water-treatment facilities, they are expensive and don't always work as well as they should.

Over half of the people living in developing countries have no access to safe water supplies, yet we threaten our own. Safe supplies are scarce and expensive in arid regions. Of course, in areas where water supply is low or erratic, flush toilets are inappropriate. The more water we use, the more energy it takes to collect and process it, pipe it into our homes, and clean it again afterwards.

What You Can Do

Smarter Toilet Paper

First, use plain, non-rebleached, 100% recycled fiber toilet paper. It degrades more quickly than colored, decorated papers do.

Smarter Ways to Handle Waste
Low-Flush Toilets

When it comes to toilets, there are smarter alternatives. Low-flush toilets use about 1.6 gallons of water for each

flush. They save 60-90% of the water used in a traditional system. The types of low-flush toilets are *compressed air* and *gravity* systems. Compressed air systems use air pumps to help move waste. Gravity systems use only gravity to move waste. Because their design is simple, they are less expensive than compressed-air toilets. Gravity ultra-low flow toilets (ULFs) also come with tapered water-rocket nozzles in the bowl to speed up the water as it leaves the tank.

No-Flush Toilets

Of course, the biggest water-savers are the no-flush toilets. These are dry, waterless toilets that can handle waste in a variety of ways. There are different ways that no-flush toilets handle their waste:

Burn It
Using electricity or propane, waste is burned and turned into sterilized ash. Although burning is somewhat energy-intensive, it can be used for sites without plumbing.

Compost It
Biological (composting) toilets change urine, feces, and toilet paper waste into a dry soil conditioner. They can reduce water use by at least 50% and treat waste on site while using hardly any energy. Small, vented tanks hold the waste and keep the area around them odor-free. Aerobic microbes (naturally occurring but more can be added), in the presence of oxygen and heat, turn waste into carbon dioxide, water, vapor, and soil-enriching humus. The humus is dry, safe, and portable.

Another way to handle human wastes is by using an aquatic system designed for this purpose. One such system, the solar aquatic system was developed in Massachusetts by John and Nancy Todd of Ecological Engineering Associates. This system moves human and organic kitchen wastes through a miniature ecosystem of plants whose roots filter out the impurities. Once treated, the water that comes out the other end is reusable for gardens and other gray-water uses. Several companies have them, including Ben & Jerry's Ice Cream in Vermont.

Before installing a special, on-site treatment facility, check with local authorities to make sure that these systems are acceptable for your local building codes. Some building codes have not been updated yet to accept newer, smarter technologies, and those wanting to try something new may require approval first.

Wrap It
The Swedish invented a way for toilets to wrap solid waste to be taken elsewhere for treatment; however, this has not caught on in the United States.

WATER WASTE & INEFFICIENCY

Every day, Americans use about 400 billion gallons of water. Of course, water use varies from workplace to workplace. You can lose 40-50% of your water through old, corroded, underground distribution pipes and 5-10% through faulty toilet tank valves and worn tap washers. A steady drip can lose 24 gallons each day, and one leaky toilet can waste over 50 gallons of water each day. A dripping kitchen faucet can waste 1,000 gallons of water per year. Hot water leaks are more expensive since they mean increased energy costs (Pearson, 92).

For those of you in home offices, toilets can account for half of your household's water use. Baths and showers use about one-third. For every flush, toilets can consume several gallons. Dishwashers use about 16 gallons of water per cycle. Washing machines use 29-58 gallons per load; front loaders use 40% less water than top loaders (Pearson, 92-93).

If it takes some time for your faucet's water to heat or cool to the desired temperature, you may want to use a bucket to collect it for watering plants, cleaning, or flushing toilets. Use gray water (without hazardous chemicals) for plants and gardens. Replace rubber washers on leaking water valves.

WHAT YOU CAN DO

Combat Leaks

Make water conservation a priority. Check for leaks regularly. To check for a leaky toilet, put a dozen drops of red or blue food coloring into the tank. Wait 15 minutes. If there is colored water in the bowl, there is a leak.

Minimize Flow

You can fit a check valve onto the incoming, main water supply. This will turn off your water flow if your desired amount is exceeded.

Generally, showers use about 5.3 gallons per minute. Flow restrictors, aerators, and sprayers can cut water consumption in half. Although sink flow generally ranges from 2.6-5.3 gallons per minute, for most uses, 0.8 gallons is adequate. You also can add flow control aerators (Pearson, 92).

New toilets use 1.6 gallons or even one gallon for each flush. But you can toilet-water use in older toilets by 30% simply by displacing that amount of water in the tank. Fill two to three bottles, weighted with stones, with water; put the bottles into the toilet tank.

Kitchens

If you are choosing a dishwasher, be sure that it conserves water. Also, remember to turn on the tap water whenever you need it rather than leaving it running.

Laundry

If your business is a hospital, hotel, prison, or gym, chances are you'll need a washing machine. Look for a front-loading machine. Also, choose one with an economical cycle to match the load sizes that will be used.

Purifying Water

Water can be treated with sand, gravel, and mechanical and biological filters. There are some water-sanitizing systems available that use ozone and ultra-violet (UV) light, making water safe. Of course, keeping toxic chemicals out of the water in the first place also will result in cleaner water.

Wastewater recycling (gray water) is appropriate for reuse from bath, shower, and bathroom sink water. Gray water can be treated and reused for many things, including industrial purposes, crop irrigation, and lawn care. The 1994 Uniform Plumbing Code has the gray-water guidelines for 22 western states.

It is best not to include kitchen sink, laundry, and toilet water (black water) because they contain certain types of food particles, grease, and detergent.

Water Heaters

If you are in the market for a hot water heater, you may want to consider a solar hot water system. Most other systems require a good deal of energy. Generally, water heaters are simply large tanks filled with water. The water is heated with gas or with an electric resistance coil. When the water reaches 110 degrees Fahrenheit, the heating stops, and when the water cools, the system heats it up again.

However, on-demand, tankless water heaters are available. Rather than heating large quantities of water before allowing it to cool and then starting over again, a propane or gas flame rapidly heats water as it passes through pipes when the hot water tap is turned on. When there is no demand, there is no heating, relieving a great waste of energy.

HELPFUL RESOURCES

INFORMATION

American Solar Energy Society, Inc.
2400 Central Avenue, G-1
Boulder, CO 80301
303-443-3130

Center for Renewable Energy and Sustainable
Technology
c/o SEREF
777 North Capitol Street, NE
Suite 805
Washington, D.C. 20002
202-289-5370/ Fax: 202-289-5354
Internet: solstice.crest.org
E-mail: info@crest.org
Gopher: gopher.crest.org
FTP: solstice.crest.org
The Center for Renewable Energy and Sustainable
Technology (CREST) is one great source of online infor-
mation.

Department of Energy
Energy Information Administration
National Energy Information Center
1000 Independence Avenue
Washington, DC 20585

Energy Center of Wisconsin
595 Science Drive
Madison, WI 53711-1060
608-238-4601/ Fax: 608-238-8733
Internet: www.ecw.org
E-mail: ecw@ecw.org
This organization supports and carries out research
toward the efficient use of energy. It works to educate
the public and energy providers about energy efficiency.

Energy-Efficient Building Associates.
1000 W. Campus Drive Wausau, WI 54401
715-675-6331

Energy Efficient Building Association (EEBA)
2950 Metro Drive
Suite 108
Minneapolis, MN 55425
612-851-9940/ Fax: 612-851-9507
E-mail: EEBANews@aol.com

Energy Star Buildings Program
U.S. EPA (6202J)
401 M Street, SW

Washington, DC 20460
888-STAR-YES
Fax (24-hour): 202-233-9659
Internet: www.epa.gov/docs/GCDOAR/EnergyStar.html

ENSAR Group
2305 Broadway
Boulder, CO 80304
303-449-5226/ Fax: 303-449-5276
ENSAR Group is working on a number of projects,
including EcoVillage in Loudon County, Virginia, a
resource-efficient, healthy community projected to be
finished in 1999. For more information, call EcoVillage
at 301-662-4646 or via e-mail at: ecovil@aol.com.

EREC
P.O. Box 3048
Merrifield, VA 22116
800-DOE-EREC (363-3732)
Fax (fax your request): 703-893-0400
Internet: www.eren.doe.gov
E-mail: energyinfo@delphi.com
TDD (for hearing impaired): 800-273-2957
The Energy Efficiency and Renewable Energy
Clearinghouse (EREC), run by the Department of
Energy, covers such topics as alternative fuels and
energy efficiency and speaks to commercial, industrial,
and residential needs. EREC provides answers to a
variety of questions on energy efficiency by phone, mail,
or electronically.

Home Energy Rating Systems Council (HERSC)
1511 K Street, NW
Suite 600
Washington, DC 20005
202-638-3700/ Fax: 202-393-5043
E-mail: HERSCDC@aol.com

North American Insulation Manufacturers Assoc.
44 Canal Center Plaza
Suite 310
Alexandria, VA 22314
703-684-0084

Passive Solar Industries Council (PSIC)
1511 K Street, NW
Suite 600
Washington, DC 20005
202-628-7400
This non-profit organization works to increase the energy performance of all U.S. buildings, making them more
affordable, comfortable, and environmentally sound.
Passive Solar & Energy-10 Software were designed to
create high-efficiency tools for designers and engineers.

Society of the Plastics Industry
1275 K Street, NW
Suite 400
Washington, DC 20005
800-951-2001

Solar Energy Industries Association
777 North Capitol Street NE, #805
Washington, DC 20002
202-408-0660

Solar Today magazine
American Solar Energy Society
2400 Central Avenue, Suite G-1
Boulder, CO 80301

Sonoma Energy Center Sonoma State University
Rohnert Park, CA 94928
707-664-2577

SUNELCO
The Sun Electric Co.
P.O. Box 1499 Hamilton, MT 59840 800-338-6844/ 406-363-6924

Woodburning Handbook
1991 California Air Resources Board
P.O. Box 2815
Sacramento, CA 95812
800-952-5588

Sustainable Design Group (SDG)
22923 Wildcat Road
Gaithersburg, MD 20882
301-428-1040/ Fax: 301-916-8786
SDG works with building owners, architects, developers, and others who are interested in designing ecologically responsible, energy-efficient buildings and communities. The company works on new and existing buildings.

Utilities and Rebate programs:
Potomac Electric Power Company
Commercial Energy Services
1900 Pennsylvania Ave., NW
Suite K-407
Washington, DC 20068-0001
202-872-2470/ Fax: 202-331-6710
The Potomac Electric Power Company (PEPCO) has a Custom Rebate Program for existing commercial buildings in Maryland. This program offers to rebates to building owners who use more efficient lighting as well as chillers, motors, air conditioners and heat pumps, HVAC equipment, refrigeration, water heating, and a building envelope.

HOME OFFICE HELP
For those of you with home offices, you can find additional helpful information on smarter buildings from the following sources:

ACEEE
1001 Connecticut Avenue NW
Suite 801
Washington, DC 20036
202-429-8873/ Fax: 202-429-2248

ACEEE
2140 Shattuck Avenue
Suite 202
Berkeley, CA 94704
510-549-9914/ Fax: 510-549-9984
The American Council for an Energy-Efficient Economy (ACEEE) works toward economic prosperity and environmental protection through energy efficiency and has several informative publications.

Building America Program
U.S. Department of Energy
1000 Independence Ave., SW
Washington, DC 20585
202-586-9472

Hickory Consortium
P.O. Box 249
West Wareham, MA 02576
508-291-7666/ Fax: 508-295-8105

Consortium for Advanced Residential Buildings
50 Washington Street
Norwalk, CT 06854
203-852-0110

IBACOS, Inc.
2214 Liberty Avenue
Pittsburgh, PA 15222
412-765-3664/ Fax: 412-765-3738

Building Science Consortium
68 Main Street
Westford, MA 01886
508-589-5100

NY-Star Builder's Field Guide
Northeast Sustainable Energy Association
50 Miles Street
Greenfield, MA 01301
413-774-6051/ Fax: 413-774-6053

Yestermorrow Design/Build School
RR 1, Box 97-5

Warren, VT 05674
802-496-5545/ Fax: 802-496-5540
Internet: www.yestermorrow.org
Founded in 1980, this non-profit organization offers seminars and hands-on courses that can last a weekend or a week. Courses include solar design, straw bale construction, ecological house design, landscape design, waste water treatment, and others that are geared toward residential and commercial buildings. The staff includes a host of visiting architects and others that are expert in their fields.

STATE ENERGY OFFICES
* The 800 numbers listed are for in-state callers only.

Alabama	800-452-5901/205-348-4523
Alaska	800-478-3744/907-563-6749
Arizona	800-352-5499/602-280-1402
Arkansas	501-682-1370
California	800-772-3300/916-654-5106
Colorado	800-632-6662/303-620-4292
Connecticut	203-566-5898
Delaware	800-282-8616/302-739-5644
District of Columbia	202-727-1800
Florida	904-488-6764
Georgia	404-656-5176
Hawaii	808-587-3800
Idaho	800-334-7283/208-327-7870
Illinois	800-252-8955/217-785-5222
Indiana	800-382-4631/317-232-8940
Iowa	515-281-4739
Kansas	800-752-4422/913-296-2686
Kentucky	800-282-0868/502-564-7192
Louisiana	504-342-1399
Maine	207-624-6800
Maryland	800-723-6374/410-974-3751
Massachussetts	617-727-4732
Michigan	517-334-6261
Minnesota	800-657-3710/612-296-5175
Mississippi	800-222-8311/601-359-6600
Missouri	800-334-6946/314-751-7056
Montana	406-444-6697
Nebraska	402-471-2867
Nevada	702-687-4909
New Hampshire	800-852-3466/603-271-2611
New Jersey	800-492-4242/201-648-7265
New Mexico	800-451-2541/505-827-5900
New York	800-423-7283/518-473-4377
North Carolina	800-662-7131/919-733-2230
North Dakota	701-238-2094
Ohio	800-848-1300/614-466-6797
Oklahoma	800-879-6552/405-843-9770
Oregon	800-221-8035/503-378-4040
Pennsylvania	800-692-7312/717-783-9981
Rhode Island	401-277-6920
South Carolina	800-851-8899/803-737-8030
South Dakota	800-872-6190/605-773-5032
Tennessee	800-342-1340/615-741-2994
Texas	512-463-1931
Utah	800-662-3633/801-538-8690
Vermont	800-828-4069/802-828-2393
Virginia	804-692-3220
Washington	800-962-9731/206-296-5640
West Virginia	304-293-2636
Wisconsin	608-266-8234
Wyoming	307-777-7284

PRODUCTS

For addresses and phone numbers, refer to *Appendix A: Directory of Suppliers.*

ENERGY CONSERVATION
E Source, Inc.
EPA Green Lights Program
Pacific Gas & Electric
Real Goods Trading Corp.
Rising Sun Enterprises
Rocky Mountain Institute
Zemos Technology

FAUCETS
Chatham Brass Company, Inc.
Energy Technology Labs, Inc.
Interbath, Inc.
Melard Mfg. Corporation
Moen Incorporated
Niagara Conservation Corp.
Chronomite Laboratories, Inc.
Pacific Environmental Marketing & Development Co.
Resources Conservation
Whedon Products, Inc.

GENERAL
Allied Thermal Systems
Command Aire
Geothermal Heating Systems
Delta T Corporation
Earth Systems International, Inc.
Tetco (Thermal Energy Transfer Corporation)
U.S. Power Climate Control, Inc.
Water Furnace International, Inc.

HEATING/VENTILATION
Aireox Research Corp.
Allermed Corp.
American Aides Ventilation Corp.
American Air Filter

Aptech Detectors
Asahi Electronics
Attic Technology Inc.
B.R. Enterprises
Centercore Inc.
Conservation Energy Systems
CYA Products, Inc.
Dietmeyer, Ward & Stroud, Inc.
Dwyer Instruments
E.L. Foust
Eneready Products
Environmental Purification Systems
Ford Technologies
Johnson Controls
Kachelofens Unlimited
Maxon Corp.
Mountain Energy and Resources, Inc.
N.E.E.D.S.
Nigra Enterprises
Pace Chemical Industries, Inc.
Pure Air Systems, Inc.
Quantum Group
Quantum Electronics Corp.
Research Products Corp.
Superior Fireplace Co.
Therma-Star Products Group, Inc.
Vanee Equipment
Vent-Aire

HYDRONIC HEATING
Baseboard Systems
Runtal North America

Radiant Floor Systems
Aztec International
Easy Heat, Inc.
ESWA STK Canada
Heatway
Maxon Corporation
Wirsbo Company
DK Heating Systems, Inc.

ICE/COLD WATER STORAGE SYSTEMS
Baltimore Aircoil Co.
THP/3, Phenix Heat Pump Systems

INDIRECT EVAPORATIVE AIR COOLERS
DePeri Manufacturing
Vari-Cool

INSULATION
Denny Sales Corp.
Dow Chemical USA
DuPont Company
Fiberiffic Energy System

Global Technology Systems
Perlite Institute
Reflectix
Rector Mineral Trading
Thoro System Products

Blankets/Batts
Environmentally Safe Products, Inc.
Greenwood Cotton Insulation Products, Inc.
Insulcot Cotton Insulation Products
Owens Corning
Schuller International, Inc.

Blown-In/Foamed-In
Air Krete, Inc.
Amoco Foam
Cellulose Insulation Manufacturing Association
Cotton Unlimited, Inc.
Georgia Pacific
Greenstone
GreenStone Industries
Green Thumb
Greenwood Cotton Insulation Products, Inc.
Insul-Tray
Louisiana-Pacific Corp.
Nordic Builders
Palmer Industries
Reprocell
Story Enterprises Co.
Thermoguard Insulation Co.

MASONRY HEATERS
Biofire, Inc.
Temp-Cast
TuliKivi Swedish Soapstone Heaters

RUMFORD FIREPLACES
Buckley Rumford Company
Superior Clay Corp.

SEWAGE TREATMENT
Ecological Engineering Associates
Dr. John Todd/Ocean Arks International

SOLAR
Solar Energy Systems
Advanced Photovoltaic Systems, Inc.
American Solar Network
American Solar Service and Sales
Atlantic Solar Products
Attic Technology, Inc.
B & E Energy Systems
Burns-Milwaukee Inc.
Copper Cricket
Energy Conservation Services of North Florida

New England Solar Electric
Inter-Island Supply
William Lamb Corp.
Photocomm
Photron, Inc.
Real Goods Trading Corp.
RMS Electric, Inc.
Siemens Fuller Solar Industries
Solar Design Associates
Solar Electric of Santa Barbara
Solar Electric Systems
Solar Energy Systems
Solec International, Inc.
Solar Works

Solar Hot Water Systems
Solar Energy Industries Association
Florida Solar Energy Center (FSEC)

TOILETS
American Standard
Artesian Industries
Bio-Sun Systems, Inc.
Briggs Plumbingware
Crane Plumbing
ECOS
Eljer Industries
Gerber Plumbing Fixtures Corporation
Kohler Co.
Living Technologies
Mansfield
Peerless Pottery
Porcher Inc.
Sancor Industries, Ltd.
Septic Care
Sun-Mar Corporation
Titon Industries
Universal Rundle Corporation
Western Pottery

WATER CONSERVATION
B.R Enterprises
Conservation Concepts
Dolphin Engineering
Environ Technologies Corp.
Nigra Enterprises
Planetary Solutions
Real Goods Trading Corp.
Resource for Conservation
Water Treatment Systems

VARIABLE AIR VOLUME COOLING SYSTEMS
Lennox Industries

WINDOWS
Andersen Windows
Architectural Openings, Inc.
Hope's
Hurd Millwork Company, Inc.
Owens Corning
Planetary Solutions
Resource Conservation Technology, Inc.
Southwall Technologies
Suntek, Inc.
Thermacore

WINDOW COVERINGS
Deerfield Woodworking
The Futon Shop
Unicel Inc.

WOOD-PELLET-BURNING STOVES
Emerald 2000
Guertin Brothers Industries, Inc.
Winrich International
Whitfield Advantage WP-2
Pyro Industries, Inc.

SUMMARY OF RECOMMENDATIONS

HEATING & COOLING

• Take advantage of the sun's light.

• Properly site your building, paying attention to the sun's orientation and obstructions.

• Look for potential sun spaces and gardens.

• Pay attention to the direction of prevailing winds and seasonal temperatures, trees that could shield, and the topography in cold climates.

• Insulate well.

• Be sure that windows have a high R value and are treated with shutters, blinds, or other materials to maintain indoor temperatures.

• Consider using heat-exchangers and allow for good ventilation while keeping indoor temperatures indoors.

WATER USE

• Consider collecting rainwater.

• Use native plants and other smart landscaping techniques to avoid using more water than necessary.

• Use plain, white toilet paper made of recycled content paper.

• Use waterless or low-flush toilets.

• Consider treating wastewater and reusing it for landscaping and other uses.

• Check for and fix plumbing leaks.

• Be sure that your appliances are efficient in their use of water.

• Think about using a solar hot-water system.

PART THREE

• • • • • • • • •

THE HEALTHY OFFICE

CHAPTER 8

THE COSTS OF AN UNHEALTHY WORKPLACE

"'Tis a sordid profit that's accompanied by the destruction of health....Many an artisan has looked at his craft as a means to support life and raise a family, but all he has got from it is some deadly disease."
Bernardo Ramazzini, 1705 (quoted in Rodes and Odell, 141)

townsend, 1987

These ancient Indian dwellings were carved from a stone hillside, taking advantage of natural materials while sheltering people from the hot sun.

Imagination is an extraordinary thing. And from it have come the ideas that have created the physical, human-built environments surrounding most of us.

Yet, with our wonderful minds that have engineered flying machines, global communications, and other once-unimaginable feats, we sell ourselves short. Somehow, the structures and communities that we have designed are unhealthy – culturally, biologically, and spiritually.

When most of today's office buildings were created, not many thought much about designing healthy buildings. Buildings, as we know them, disturb and often ruin the natural environment under and around them and harm their occupants. Composed of synthetic materials that are harmful to both inhabitants and the environment, buildings can be hazardous from their manufacture to the disposal of their components. Every line of an architect's blueprint can represent a degraded quality of life – from the destruction of forests full of birds, insects, plants, and other creatures to the systematic wreckage of scenic vistas and villages for marble quarrying.

Unfortunately, the ecology of architecture and health often is ignored in building design and construction. Frank Lloyd Wright's concept of organic architecture was a useful one, asserting that a building should be "integral to site, integral to environment and integral to the life of its inhabitants" (Pearson, 21). Instead, buildings often are created for their own sake, without regard for the people who will live or work within them and without regard for their physical and cultural context.

Certainly, it does not have to be that way. There is a movement within the architectural field to put buildings back into context again, to take advantage of the natural systems around buildings rather than ignore them. It moves away from the concept of a building in a bubble, separate from the natural systems around it. Taking advantage of nature in the orientation and construction of buildings also can mean saving money that would have been spent on fuel bills.

Of course, architects are not the only ones responsible. We all should be held accountable for what we create. After all, it is the responsibility of all of us to see that, when building or retrofitting, we make as little negative impact as possible.

It would be a challenge – albeit a worthwhile one – to try to give back more than we take, to be healthier and more resource-efficient, and to focus on regeneration rather than degeneration. Even if you lease your office space and cannot make physical changes to it (moving walls for daylighting, etc.), at least you can be sure that the products that you use and the energy that you consume create as little a negative impact as possible.

The idea of regenerative architecture and development – that is, doing more good than harm – is just coming into its own. This can be accomplished partly through retrofitting old buildings to be healthier and less resource-intensive and by regenerating degraded land into more natural habitat.

Responsible building rests upon one thing – the environments in which we design and build must be a part of our buildings' designs. These ecosystems are what all of us live from, and these must be intertwined with our built environments and our lives rather than separated from them.

Responsible building means using nature as our model. And nature uses the sun as its single source of energy. Nature creates no waste. Everything that exists gives life to something else, even in death or through its own decomposition. And we humans are as dependent upon these natural laws for our survival as our ancestors were 50,000 years ago.

So, we must be careful to imagine, design, and create in ways that are holistic and healthy for ourselves and the other species with which we share this unique planet. Of course we need shelter in which to live and work, but

We All Pay

Many people are somewhat aware of the environmental degradation that results from inefficiency and toxins. But how about the cost to us? You, whoever you are, will pay in some way.

- You, as a taxpayer, will pay because the costs of environmental degradation need to be absorbed by someone.

- You, as a worker, will pay if you have medical bills or have taken time off from your job as a result of working in an unhealthy environment.

- You, as a business, will pay if you are inadvertently using products that are making employees sick – the costs of insurance, sick days, and less than stellar performances by workers who may suffer from headaches, lethargy, and a host of other workplace-related symptoms.

this can be had in ways that do not dislocate us from our nature, roots, and identity. Ways that do not create isolation and stress.

Moving away from non-renewable resources, harmful materials, and non-life-giving synthetics is a first step. Using products that are resource-efficient and healthy to a building's inhabitants and appropriate to its natural context are important factors in creating a smart building.

If you stop and think about it, today's office products have not been around that long. When many of them were developed, the issues of indoor air pollution, sick workers, and environmental damage were not as widely known as they are today, although they did exist.

As you have seen throughout this book, the costs of an inefficient, unhealthy work environment are tremendous. The following sections provide further discussion of some of the health problems related to unhealthy work environments.

AIR POLLUTION

Breathing is such a natural thing that you may never think about it. But what and how you breathe help to determine your state of health. Every minute, adults breathe 20-40 times, averaging about 56,000 times per day (Pearson, 96, 1989). The average, resting adult requires 8,640 liters of fresh air every day (Matthews, 5).

Of course, oxygen is what feeds our brain and other cells, helping to keep us alive, thinking, and functioning. When you breathe shallowly, you take in only a small amount of oxygen. This keeps you from being as healthy and full of life as you could be. There are many reasons for breathing shallowly. Stress is one. When you are stressed or inactive for long periods, you may notice that your breathing becomes shallow. Poor posture also can cause shallow breathing. If you have a habit of slumping or have a chair that does not support upright posture, you may not be breathing fully. You can help to ensure that your breathing is more life-giving.

Aside from thinking of *how* you breathe, do you ever think about *what* you are breathing? Air quality is another important factor in your breathing.

Using filters that trap even the smallest particles are one way to keep breathing cleaner air.

townsend, 1996

synthetic environments. These artificial spaces often are full of unhealthy chemicals and electrical equipment.

Cars, for instance, are made of 100% synthetic materials with over 100 volatile organic compounds, all of which contribute to that "new car" smell. Combined with the exhaust sucked through the vents and into

When you are in a polluted place, you're taking dirty or poisoned air into your body. our cars, motor vehicles are one of the worst indoor air experiences available today.

Many substances contribute to poor air quality. These include ozone, radon, carbon monoxide, nitric oxide, sulphur dioxide, carbon dioxide, formaldehyde, organochlorines, phenol, asbestos, metals, and microorganisms (Pearson, 51, 1989). Indoor air pollution can be 10 times worse than that found outdoors. Long-term exposure can cause serious health problems, something with which many people are now having to come to terms. Over the past two decades, the use of synthetic building materials and furnishings, fabrics, and cleaning chemicals, as well as dust, bacteria, and fungi, have contributed to dangerous conditions for those who work or live in these environments.

Toxin-filled, sealed buildings with little or no fresh air exchange or ventilation cost businesses a lot of money. And while HVAC systems may circulate the air, if they only draw in more polluted air, you are not benefitting. The existence of toxins in the indoor environment and the lack of fresh air can lead to many health problems.

Since 85% of the per-square-foot office costs you pay goes toward employee expenses, just a 2% drop in productivity due to an unhealthy work environment could cost you an enormous amount. And this is money unnecessarily spent.

Between home and work, most of us in the U.S. spend up to 90% of our time indoors (Pearson, 99, 1989). While most of our waking hours are spent at work or at home, we also spend time in our cars, stores, and other

Modern chemicals aren't the only substances that contribute to indoor air pollution. Mold and mildew can cause problems when the relative humidity indoors is over 40%. With time, it can cause structural building failures as well.

Fibers can be another source of irritation and indoor air pollution. Mineral fibers come from such sources as fiberglass, which is often used in the thermal and acoustic insulation found in ventilation systems and ceilings.

WHAT YOU CAN DO

The best thing that you can do about air pollution is to prevent it. This will be discussed in detail throughout this chapter, but here are a few tips to get you started:

• Make clean, healthy air a priority in your workplace.
• Pinpoint your sources of air pollution.
• Find healthier alternatives to the toxic materials in your workplace. Keep impurities out of the air. After choosing the right furnace for your heating needs, you can follow the following eight steps:

1. Have your oil burner checked each year for efficiency. If the Annual Fuel Utilization Efficiency (AFUE) is below 70% and cannot be adjusted to get it up to 80%, you would probably do well to replace it.

2. Check your filter cleanliness every month by holding it up to the light. During heating season, replace or

clean it every two to three months. Dirty filters can add up to 10% to your heating and cooling bill.

3. Brush or vacuum your furnace blower every year. Even with a filter, dust and lint accumulate in the blower. You may want to oil the motor (check manufacturer instruction manual first). Remember to turn off your furnace power before opening any of its access doors.

4. Check your office ductwork for leaks. Feel for escaping air, and seal leaks with duct tape. Wrap ducts that run through cold spaces (attics, crawl spaces) with two-inch-thick duct insulation. Up to 40% of your furnace's or central air conditioner's output can be lost through a leaky, uninsulated distribution system in an unheated space.

5. Vacuum and clean your registers if you have an HVAC system. If you have a hot-water system, vacuum and clean the baseboards. Even a thin dust layer on baseboard heating coils can be strong insulation that keeps the heat from emanating.

6. Be sure that your system's dampers are balanced.

7. Remove indoor impurities with air cleaners. The best ones are those that you add to your heating system. While clean furnace filters help, they are not enough. Air cleaners can improve the effectiveness of your system and prevent dust and grease buildup in ducts and air-conditioning coils, making your indoor environment a healthier one.

8. Be certain that gas-fired appliances are installed and vented properly. Otherwise, combustion gases could be a problem. Carbon monoxide (CO) and other contaminants can leak indoors.

CHEMICAL SENSITIVITY (CS)

WHAT IS IT?

Chemical sensitivity, or CS, is an acquired, self-perpetuating disease in which the central nervous, immune, and/or endocrine systems are debilitated, and the person affected becomes extremely sensitive to one or more chemicals. Gastrointestinal, reproductive, respiratory, and other systems can be affected, too.

Chemical sensitivity can be traced back to the 19th century. Alfred B. Nobel (1833-1896) invented dynamite, and both he and his factory workers suffered from dynamite-induced headaches. Marcel Proust (1871-1922), the French author, isolated himself in a cork-lined room. His biographer noted that perfumes often made him ill, and he had to set his visitors' perfume-contaminated chairs outside to air.

In 1991, the National Academy of Sciences came up with a working definition of CS. They defined it as a condition in which:

• someone reacts to chemicals in amounts well below normal tolerance
• symptoms arise in one or more organ systems
• symptoms rise and fall depending on exposure.

Individual symptoms do vary. Some people are much more sensitive than others and are likely to respond more quickly or more severely.

For the chemically sensitive person, any of a number of unrelated chemicals, in doses that are so small as to be considered "safe" for most people, can trigger a multi-symptom reaction. Once someone has developed CS, the amount of the toxin needed to trigger reactions decreases. In other words, if someone develops a chemical sensitivity to formaldehyde after being exposed to formaldehyde-infused carpeting/wood, it will take lower and lower amounts of exposure to the substance for a reaction to occur. That person may become sensitized to other, unrelated chemical substances, something known as the spreading phenomenon.

CS has been defined as an "illness within an illness" or a "macro-disease" because many diseases can result from chemical sensitivity. For instance, some believe it may be linked to chronic fatigue syndrome. It is important to note that CS is not the same as sick building syndrome (SBS, discussed later in this chapter). While SBS, or chemical poisoning, may cause acute (self-quenching) illness that disappears with the end of exposure to the trigger chemical(s), chemical sensitivity is a self-perpetuating illness. In other words, it does not go away.

CAUSES

Chemical sensitivity is a breakdown of the integrity of the body's various systems due to toxic exposure. Over 37 million people in the United States, alone, are thought to have a heightened sensitivity to chemicals (Matthews, 38). One National Academy of Sciences report projected that by the year 2010, 60% of the U.S. population will suffer from chemical sensitivity.

One cause of CS is toxic exposure to one or more substances. This may be a one-time, acute exposure, such as inhalation of and skin contact with pesticides or inhalation of new carpet or paint fumes. Or, exposure to toxic substances may be chronic (prolonged), and symptoms can be persistent.

After either an acute or a chronic, low-level exposure, irritation or poisoning can occur. Irritation simply refers to discomfort that goes away shortly after contact without causing permanent damage to the body's normal functioning. An example of irritation can be dry skin resulting from sick building syndrome.

If the toxin reaches excessive levels, it can result in poisoning, when the body's normal functions are affected by the toxic substance. For instance, the effects of low levels of toxic substances (e.g., carpet glue, formaldehyde-treated wood particleboard) can accumulate in the body over time and cause permanent damage to the body's systems. In the case of CS, this damage will not disappear but can worsen over time with exposure to the trigger toxin(s).

Of course, air-pollution problems have been around for a long time, but they have increased considerably in today's sealed buildings that are filled with toxins. Toxins with volatile organic compounds (VOCs) and biological contaminants are commonplace in today's workplaces, and these things are trapped indoors with us.

Between 1965-1982, more than four million new chemical compounds were created, and this phenomenal growth in new compounds has not lessened. Up to 6,000 new compounds have been created every week since 1982. Common pollutants/chemicals include:

- Carbon monoxide (reduces the oxygen-carrying capacity of blood and weakens heart contractions)
- Particulate matter (injures the respiratory tract by itself or in conjunction with gas)
- Sulfur dioxide (constricts lung passages and is associated with respiratory disease and increased mortality rates)
- Lead (affects the blood-forming systems, nervous system, and kidneys)
- Nitrogen dioxide (causes respiratory disease) (Matthews, 60)

Many terms are associated with CS. Among them are:

- Multiple chemical sensitivity syndrome
- 20th century disease
- Total allergy syndrome
- Ecological or Environmental illness
- Universal reactors (patients)
- Chronic immune system activation

The National Institute of Occupational Safety and Health (NIOSH) has files on more than 100,000 of these chemical compounds. The EPA has files on about 65,000 toxic chemicals and receives requests to register about 1,500 new compounds every year (Matthews, 6). But that still leaves millions that have been created but for which there is no federally available information.

Currently, about 300 chemicals are added to food alone, 700 are found in drinking water, 400 are identified in human tissue, 500 are found under the sink and in the laundry room of the average home, and 100 pounds of hazardous waste are stored in the average U.S. basement or garage (Wilson, 1).

The National Cancer Institute has estimated that up to 98% of all cancers may be linked to chemical exposures (Wilson, 2). In addition, three out of 10 people in the U.S. can expect to contract some form of cancer in their (Wilson, 2).

For all known health hazards in the U.S. population associated with the EPA's 65,000 toxic chemicals, there should be at least 16,250,000 chemical injury victims with 375,000 new ones every year. NIOSH figures suggest that there are as many as 25 million victims (Matthews, 1-2).

Formaldehyde is a big indoor air-quality problem. It affects 10-20% of the population at any level of exposure. All told, it is capable of harming 25-50 million people (Wilson, 2). Unfortunately, it is found in newspaper, wood, cosmetics, food, carpets, and plastics, making it very hard to avoid. And formaldehyde is just one of the chemicals that we are in contact with regularly.

Carpets are a big source of formaldehyde and another, unintended compound known as 4-Phenylcyclohexane (4-PC). (For more information on carpets, turn to Chapter 10, "Smarter Carpets & Flooring"). All carpets using SB (styrene and butadiene) latex (about 95% of all U.S.-made carpets) give off some 4-PC. In addition to carpets, there are other SB latex-containing materials that can contain 4-PC. These include indoor paints, some outdoor paints, wallcoverings, carpets, mats, seals, tubing, shoes, rainwear, caulks and sealants, tires, and other rubber products.

Other plastic-based products also contain SB or SB latex. In 1988, NIOSH predicted that over 92,000 U.S. employees would be exposed to SB latex on the job, and this did not include those exposed through their office surroundings to carpets, wallpaper, and other materials. Exposure is through inhalation and/or skin absorption.

While many people expect protection by the Food and Drug Administration (FDA), the Occupational Safety and Health Administration (OSHA), and the EPA, these agencies are limited by law to what they can protect. While NIOSH has found 884 neurotoxic chemical compounds used in the cosmetic and perfume industries alone, there are no regulations that prohibit their use. In addition, the Federal Food, Drug, and Cosmetic Act does not require cosmetic ingredients to undergo pre-market toxicity testing. As a result, these industries are exempt from ingredients labeling laws (Wilson, 3).

When pesticide ingredients are listed on products, the manufacturers often are required only to list the active ingredient (the only one required to undergo toxicity testing), even when inert ingredients may be highly toxic and comprise between 50-99% of the product.

The Northwest Coalition for Alternatives to Pesticides (NCAP), in a Freedom of Information Act lawsuit, got a list of 1,400 of the 2,000 substances being used as inert ingredients. It turns out that those inert ingredients include hazardous waste, Chicago sludge, asbestos, and some illegal chemicals, including DDT (banned because of its severe toxicity to humans and the environment). Unfortunately, the Trade Secrets Act protects manufacturers so that they don't have to give away their complete ingredients lists, thereby overriding consumers' rights to know (Wilson, 4).

THE BODY'S RESPONSE

With our constant exposure to toxins, it's a wonder that our bodies tolerate what they do. When CS affects the central nervous system, the toxin can cause brain fog, similar to intoxication. Loss of concentration and irritability also are common. Unfortunately, because so few doctors are trained to recognize CS, many chemically sensitive individuals are diagnosed as having psychiatric or behavioral problems. Symptoms include but are not limited to:

• Asthma
• Menstrual problems
• Skin irritations
• Fainting
• Dizziness
• Inability to concentrate

• Nausea
• Insomnia
• Memory lapses
• Diarrhea
• Vomiting
• Upset stomach
• Nosebleeds
• Vision problems
• Fatigue
• Muscle aches and pains

Of course, the body was not designed to ward off man-made toxins. Some can bypass our natural defense mechanisms. When striking the central nervous system, chemical poisoning can lead to toxic encephalopathy, a form of brain damage known as organic brain syndrome. Most chemical exposure victims "have some form of brain damage impairing higher cognitive functions such as memory, reasoning, or the ability to acquire or process new information. This central nervous system damage is often accompanied by damage to the peripheral nervous system as well" (CEHH, x).

Unlike the body's other cells, brain cells do not regenerate. When harmed by chemical poisoning, the brain can be damaged, affecting the body's functions. This can result in a number of symptoms, such as tingling of hands and feet, tremors, difficulty in concentrating or reasoning, anxiety, paranoia, and depression.

Many doctors are stumped because, in a classic immune response, the body reacts strongly against irritants, or antigens (see below). CS victims, hypersensitive to various substances, are not given to normal immune responses. Most victims of toxic chemical exposure suffer from immune-system damage. Poisoning can lead to the development of an abnormal, active immune system that, eventually, will become suppressed.

Poisoning also can lead to the development of autoantibodies. Autoantibodies can cause a disease known as autoimmunity, in which a person's antibodies attack parts of the body rather than protecting it. Generally, attacks tend to be upon the stomach, intestines, kidneys, myelin sheathing, liver, and thyroid but are not always organ-specific (CEHH, x).

The immune system's purpose is to protect the body from invading substances, or antigens. These antigens include bacteria, fungi, viruses, and particulates (dust, pollen). To enter the body, they must bypass the body's first line of defense – the skin and the respiratory, gastrointestinal, and genitourinary tracts. Upon entering the body, an antigen sets off mast cells in the body's connective tissue (muscle, bone, mucous, fibrous, reticular, cartilage, or adipose). To protect the body and fight off the invaders, the mast cells wage chemical warfare against the antigens. This chemical warfare is fought by mediators (histamine, prostaglandins, leukotrienes, and heparin, which inhibits coagulation), chemicals released by the mast cells. The release of these chemicals affects several of the body's other systems.

If this first step in the body's defense mechanism is breached, another set of things happens:

1. acute phase reactants – After contracting an illness, these chemicals appear in the blood, making us feel the symptoms of our illness.

2. phagocytic cells – There are three types of phagocytic cells that feed on particulates (histiocytes), bacteria (microphages), and dead cells, tissue, and particulates (macrophages).

3. killer cells – Killer cells search for/ destroy cells affected by viruses and bacteria as well as cancer cells.

4. complements – These are proteins that enter the blood to burst and help phagocytize antigens.

If the phagocytes cannot grasp the antigen or if the antigen is not detected by the complement system, the second line of defense is breached. Then, the next line of defense is called in to play (the humoral immune response and the cellular immune response).

The humoral immune response is generated by the B lymphocytes, which produce antibodies, and begins in the lymph and bone marrow. The antibodies attach phagocyte to the invader, stimulate the complement system, and work to give immunity as long as you live by recognizing the invader.

There are five antibodies produced by the B lymphocytes. They are IgA (protects salivary glands and bowel against invasion), IgM (following chemical exposure, it is the first antibody produced and can stay in blood up to a year), IgG (it replaces IgM and stays in blood for several years), IgE (this antibody creates a classic allergic reaction), and IgD (unknown purpose).

The cellular immune response starts in the thymus before traveling through the blood and ending up in the lymph nodes and spleen. This occurs when a microphage captures an antigen and brings it to a T lymphocyte, or T helper cell. At this stage, the microphage releases interleukin 1, a chemical that stimulates the T helper cell to produce interleukin 2; interleukin 2 stimu-

lates the production of more T helper cells. In addition to producing interleukin 2, these T helper cells produce chemicals known as lymphokines. These lymphokines enable communication among lymphocytes, creating a full-blown immune response. Lymphokines cause B lymphocyte cells to turn into antibody-producing cells, the equivalent to calling in reinforcements. Some of the T lymphocytes are changed into cytotoxic T cells, which, with the help of the complement, attack the antigen. This attack continues until the T suppressor cell is activated and shuts down the immune response by inhibiting the macrophage-T helper cell reaction.

When chemical poisoning occurs, this full-blown immune response has been activated; this response, on a repeated basis, causes fatigue. Sometimes, however, it takes years for a chemical exposure to manifest itself in illness, making it difficult to diagnose. Because of the abnormal symptoms that may not be easily traceable to their source(s), conventional doctors usually refer their CS patients for psychiatric treatment. CS indicates that something has gone wrong in the functioning of the immune and/or central nervous system. Four hypersensitivity reactions to immune system failure at any of three stages have been documented medically.

DIAGNOSIS

CS can be hard to handle for many reasons. For the patient, it can be difficult because the number of chemicals manufactured is growing quickly. Another is the perception that CS is not only difficult to diagnose, but the wrong belief that it occurs infrequently and only to a small part of the population that is especially susceptible to toxic chemical effects. Therefore, CS is not a medical priority. The legal issues involved, as well as frequent failure of insurance to cover CS medical expenses, are additional disincentives to medical community involvement and prioritization.

In addition, according to the National Academy of Sciences' Institute of Medicine, many U.S. doctors have misdiagnosed it. Although over 40 chemicals cause depression, most doctors are not trained to look for environmental illness as a source of the problem. This is not surprising when considering some of the everyday symptoms. As a result, many chemically sensitive people have reported seeing over 30 doctors before being diagnosed correctly. Most were referred for psychiatric help because they are seen as hypochondriacs or mentally ill.

There is a prejudice that MCS victims were defective to begin with; however, there is no evidence of any genetic predisposition to MCS. MCS victims trace back to 1800s, and a large number emerged after World War II.

Regarding CS and chemical poisoning, Cynthia Wilson, publisher of *Our Toxic Times,* points out that chemicals cause a number of illnesses – not just CS. "On average, a toxic chemical can cause approximately 25 separate health problems and generally targets 2 to 4 separate organs and/or body systems." The question is not "Who is affected?" It is "How are people affected?" If one person develops MCS and another does not, what does the other person develop? Wilson asserts that what might take form as MCS in one person may show up as cancer, heart disease, or arthritis in another.

If you need medical help for CS, call prospective doctors and ask about their experiences with toxic exposure patients. A number of different tests, taken together, can help to determine if someone is suffering from CS. Blood tests showing chemical exposure as well as toxicological tests identifying poisons in blood or fat are helpful. When the chemical is unknown, antibody assays are useful as a general screen. Autoantibody profiles indicate the presence of autoantibodies and the resultant abnormal, activated immune system.

Physicians can look for high amounts of white blood cells, T helper cells, B lymphocytes, and interleukin 1 and 2, reflecting a full-blown immune response from chemical poisoning. Low amounts of T cells can indicate immunosuppression of CS. Be aware that a lack of evidence from the above tests does not mean that the person is not chemically sensitive. If someone is aware enough of trigger chemicals to avoid them, the indicators may not be there at the time of testing. According to Matthews, if a doctor knows what to look for, other useful tests can include magnetic resonance imaging (MRI), colonoscopy, electroencephalogram (EEG), inhalation challenge, abdominal ultrasound, and PET scan, to name a few (Matthews, 16).

WHAT YOU CAN DO

Currently, there is no cure for chemical sensitivity. The best treatment is avoidance. But those familiar with it point out that little literature about CS has been directed to primary care physicians, and CS victims often are viewed as problem patients. There has been little emphasis on relationships among nervous, immune, and endocrine systems when affected by toxic chemicals. Be certain to keep track of your chemical exposures and reactions.

Get Material Safety Data Sheets (MSDS), which focus on acute exposure to a substance, by calling or writing

to the product manufacturers. Although these often list only the active ingredients (which sometimes make up the smallest part) of products, they can be useful. They include:

- product information
- emergency and first aid
- toxicology and health information
- physical data
- fire and explosion data
- reactivity data
- special protection information
- special precautions
- spill, leak, and disposal procedures
- transportation information (Matthews, 111)

People often involved in chemical poisonings include, construction workers, painters, biocide applicators, manufacturing, workers in sick buildings, teachers/students in sick schools, people who often work with carbonless carbon paper, medical personnel, chemists, print shop operators in sick buildings, meat wrappers.

ELECTRO-MAGNETIC FIELDS (EMFs)

WHAT ARE THEY?

Electro-magnetic Fields (EMFs) are invisible waves that threaten human health. These waves come from electronic sources, including microwaves, computers, and cellular phones. They penetrate everything but iron. Each time someone gets close to these machines and appliances, he or she is exposed to EMFs. The Environmental Protection Agency has reported on the dangers of EMFs, which can emit fields high enough to cause cancer for those within very close proximity to appliances and machines.

Health problems associated with EMF exposure include leukemia, reproductive problems, breast and skin cancers, brain tumors, and mood disorders. Just look at some of the research findings:

- A Swedish study of nearly half a million Swedish people found that the leukemia rate for children living near power lines was about four times that of other children. Cancers were 1.5-3 times higher for adults living near power lines than for those who did not (Maryalice Yakutchik, January 3, 1993).
- Just a few years ago, a report in *The American Journal of Epidemiology* found that those living near transmis-

sion lines are twice as likely to suffer from depression as those who do not.

- In late 1992, a study by Battelle Pacific Laboratories (Richmond, WA) found a link between men using electric razors and adult leukemia.
- A 1988 report from Kaiser Permanente Health Group studied the impacts of video display terminals (VDTs) (computer monitors) upon 1,583 pregnant women. Women who used VDTs over 20 hours each week had nearly twice the miscarriage rate as those who do similar work without using computers (*East West*, 56).
- One study at the University of Texas (Russell Reiter) showed that the brain's pineal gland, which manufactures melatonin (a hormone that suppresses some cancers) is suppressed by EMFs. So, while EMFs may not cause cancer directly, they may inhibit cancer suppression.

While electric fields occur any time an appliance is plugged in, magnetic fields occur only when an appliance is running. Low EMFs "tickle" cells, whereas high-frequency EMFs from such devices as X-rays and microwaves rearrange the contents of cells and are known to be harmful.

How Do I Measure EMFs?

EMFs can be tested by gaussmeters, which measure units known as milligauss. Often, local utilities will test for EMFs. Also, you can buy an inexpensive gaussmeter and measure the milligauss level yourself.

For appliances emitting radio frequency (computers, stereos), you can measure EMFs by using a battery-operated AM radio, which is sensitive to the electrical interference caused by EMFs. To do this, stand in front of a computer monitor that is turned off. Turn on the AM radio, turn the dial until you find a spot where no channel is picked up, and then turn the volume up all the way. Then, holding the radio about one foot from the monitor, turn on the monitor. You should hear interference, or static. Back away from the monitor. When you reach the point where the sound stops, about 1 milligauss is being emitted (*East West*, 112).

Now, check different spots around the monitor to find at what points the field drops down to about 1 milligauss.

In most U.S. homes, the background, or ambient, EMF field measures about 0.5 milligauss. Some say that the tolerable limit is 2.0 milligauss. Apparently, the typical exposure from various appliances can be:

Electric blanket: 20
TV: 100
Power drill: 500
Blow dryer: 1,400
Electric shaver: 1,600
Can opener: 4,000

These numbers are not the only factors in determining the safety of an electric appliance. Another important factor is the dose rate, or the time that you are exposed to the appliance. Spending one minute every morning with an electric shaver against the skin may be less harmful than spending a full night under an electric blanket. A blow dryer beside the head may be more threatening than the power line across the street.

Standing directly below a distribution line (smaller neighborhood lines) can result in exposure ranging from less than 1 milligauss to 30. Usually, it is 5-10. The larger transmission lines emit 20-600 milligauss directly underneath but generally average about 100.

People's increased awareness has already cost some industries a great deal of money. The power-line construction delays and real-estate slowdowns due to a growing knowledge of the dangers of EMFs were projected to have cost over $1 billion dollars in 1993 (*USA Today*, 7).

While great for energy conservation, fluorescent lighting emits far more EMFs than does incandescent. Fluorescent lighting is created by causing the chemical coating inside the glass tube to glow by a high-voltage discharge in the tube. Unlike incandescent bulbs, the light created by fluorescent bulbs covers only a small area of the spectrum, making it less like sunlight.

Two inches from a 60-watt incandescent bulb finds the 60-Hz field at 0.3 milligauss. Six inches away, the field is 0.05 milligauss, and one foot away, a measurement cannot be detected. The fluorescent bulb is another story. Two inches from a 10-watt tube finds 6 milligauss. Six inches away is 2 milligauss, and one foot away is 1 milligauss. Fluorescent ceiling fixtures with several 20-watt bulbs create a field greater than 1 milligauss over the heads of office workers. Task lighting can create high EMFs as well. This is partly a function of the wattage. Be sure to have your work areas tested.

A baseboard electric heater that is four feet long produce 23 milligauss at six inches, 8 milligauss at one foot, and 1 milligauss at three feet. Portable, electric, plug-in heaters produce about the same intensities but are more dangerous, potentially, because they can be moved close to the body. Electric heat cables installed in ceilings create average fields of 10 milligauss for an entire room. Electric stoves can create 50 milligauss fields 18 inches above a 12-inch burner.

Although there remains some argument over how much EMF exposure is acceptable, there is some government regulation in place. A Federal Consumer Commission (FCC) rule limited the amount of radiation computers could produce in post-1982 models when strong, broad-band radiation caused interference with airport control-tower operations from workplaces adjacent to airports. Although post-1982 model computers produce less-intensive EMFs, it is still wise to take precautions. Keeping three feet from your monitor by using a detachable keyboard should keep your head's exposure down to about 1 milligauss. Again, check the area around your PC. The EMFs emitted vary from computer to computer.

Microwave ovens, like computers, have been limited since 1983 on the amount of radiation they can leak. If you have a microwave oven at work, check the gasket material once each year. If the door gasket is damaged, don't use the oven until it is repaired. Although there are leakage detectors on the market, they are not regulated. So, have a qualified person check it out; their meters usually are well calibrated.

By the way, magnetic field standards of 150-200 milligauss have been set in both New York and Florida for power lines. While these are much higher than the 2 milligauss standards Sweden may set for its new power lines, it's a start.

WHAT YOU CAN DO

When building new, be careful when locating your workplace. Avoid being near power lines; high-voltage power lines and telecommunication transmitters should be taken into account. Radon and zoning problems should figure in as well.

Of course, other factors also should be taken into account, including sources of pollution and noise from power stations, factories, incinerators, flight paths, highways, railways, and parking lots.

If possible, limit the time you spend exposed to EMFs.

Use a computer keyboard with a long cord so that you can sit farther from your computer. Three feet away from appliances is a good rule of thumb.

Don't use a cellular phone if a hard-wired one is handy.

Battery-powered things are virtually harmless. Choose them, when possible, over electrical things. Of course, use rechargeable batteries whenever possible.

ERGONOMICS

Ergonomics studies the relationship of humans with their environments. At the office, an ergonomic workspace is one that is comfortable, non-stressful, and promotes the well-being of those working there.

WHAT YOU CAN DO

Making your computing environment more comfortable may require a few, simple changes. When working at your computer, be sure that you are comfortable.

You should feel comfortable and without physical strain. Your chair's height and angle should be adjustable, with the ability to tilt back about 15 degrees. It should support the center of your back, allowing you to sit upright without back strain. The seat should support your thighs completely, curving down in front so that it doesn't cut off your circulation when you lean forward. It should swivel and roll. While such a chair may cost a little extra money, it sure beats paying more than that for doctor visits.

Your computer and peripherals should be easy to reach. A good height for desks on which you'll be typing or working with a computer is about 26-28 inches rather than the usual 30 inches.

Having to reach up or down for the keyboard can cause carpal tunnel syndrome, or CTS. This is an inflammation of the wrist's transverse carpal ligament. This ligament squeezes the arm's median nerve, which runs into the hand through a bunch of nerves and tendons known as the carpal tunnel. OSHA reports that CTS accounts for about half of all U.S. workplace illnesses. Many companies, including Apple, AT&T, Digital Equipment Corporation, and IBM, have been sued by their employees who have ended up with work-related CTS.

Your PC's monitor and keyboard are the major ergonomic components of computing. Be sure to use a keyboard that is comfortable and has legs so that it can be raised or lowered. Keyboards come in a variety of sizes and shapes, including some made specifically with ergonomics in mind. Try them out at a PC store to find what is comfortable for you.

You need a good relation between the line of sight of your monitor and your keyboard height. This relationship will be different for everybody, but the monitor and keyboard heights should be adjustable, each independent of the other. Older, one-piece data entry terminals don't allow this, so you should consider upgrading them to modular units for the health of your employees. Also, use a copy stand when referring to documents.

Having a keyboard you can swing out of the way when you need space for reading or writing on paper can help, too, so you don't have to twist around to find room somewhere else. However, the correct height for working on your keyboard is not the same as it is for manual writing and reading. Having an adjustable height desk with a rounded edge that does not cut into your wrists is ideal. Resting your wrists on a foam pad (available through many PC product catalogues) placed in front of your keyboard may help as well.

ERGONOMIC NEEDS FOR EMPLOYEES WITH DISABILITIES

If you have special needs in your work space, there are several alternatives available. Particularly if you spend your workday in a wheelchair, you probably have different ergonomic needs than those who don't. Handicapped-accessible workstations are required by the 1990 Americans with Disabilities Act (ADA) for workers with disabilities such as "sight, hearing, speech, access, and mobility" (Anzovin, 127).

What You Can Do

To make computer workstations accessible, the ADA requires the following:

- Provide better access to PC cubicles by widening doorways and paths.
- Use height-adjustable work tables for PCs. These tables must roll away or swing away to allow access.
- Use trackballs or other non-moving pointing devices.
- Provide special hardware as needed (e.g., voice recognition).
- Provide helpful software as needed (e.g., typing aids) (Anzovin, 127).

Check with the ADA periodically to find out if there are new requirements for employers.

EYE STRAIN/VISION PROBLEMS

Eye strain and vision problems resulting from poorly designed lighting and computers are common in the workplace. Computers may require us to focus our eyes on a short-range object (the monitor), but our eyes were made to see medium- and long-range complex patterns and motions, too. Eye strain, headaches, and blurry vision are just a few of the problems that can result. In addition, people tend to move their bodies to see better, which can lead to poor posture.

A 1982 Canadian Labor Board study found that users of VDTs "changed their glasses prescriptions twice as often as other workers as they tried to compensate for the stress on their visual systems" (Anzovin, 128).

WHAT YOU CAN DO

Your monitor should be at least at arm's length, or 20 inches, and farther if possible. If you can't make out the characters, make them bigger if possible. But don't move the screen closer. The farther away you sit, the less dust will build up on your corneas from static charge, and the less low-frequency radiation you'll be exposed to.

You can get a tilt-and-swivel monitor stand to accommodate your needs.

Focus, screen flatness, and refresh rate have the biggest immediate impact on your vision. Some monitors are flat, causing less distortion at the edges. Be sure your screen doesn't flicker. It shouldn't be under 60 Hz (60 flickers every second), which creates eye fatigue. Instead, it should be above 70 Hz (Anzovin, 130).

No area of work space should be in deep shadow or bright light. Be sure overheads and desk lamps aren't more than three times brighter than the computer screen. Your screen should be less than three times brighter than the ambient light level. You can check this with a light meter.

If there is glare, swivel your monitor or move lights as necessary. Be sure that there are no windows behind you that reflect onto your monitor. Monitor glare guards can help but may also reduce the screen contrast, impairing your ability to make out the images on the screen. Many of the new monitors have antiglare coatings on them already.

Radon

What is It?

Radon is a naturally occurring, radioactive element from decaying uranium that emanates from the soil and from rocks. Although it normally is dispersed by outdoor air, radon can become trapped and build up in tightly sealed buildings. It can be the source of more radiation exposure than all other sources combined.

The primary concern with radon exposure is its link to lung cancer. In the U.S., alone, 5,000-20,000 people die every year of lung cancer attributable to radon exposure. Fortunately, there are inexpensive radon test kits that can be purchased in supermarkets or hardware stores. These kits contain small canisters filled with charcoal, which absorbs radon particles over time. There are kits that measure radon over a season and kits that measure it in one to 12 months. When the measurement period is over, you send your kit to a lab where the absorbed particles will be measured.

Measuring Radon

Radon Kits

Instructions are included with the kit, but it generally goes like this – the kit is put into the lowest level of the building (away from walls and drafts) since radon concentrations are highest near the ground. Meanwhile, all windows, outside doors, and vents to the outside are kept closed. (You can leave on your HVAC system.) After the specified amount of time, reseal the radon kit canister, and send it as soon as possible to the test lab, where each canister is placed in a radon sensor. This detector measures the amount of radon in the canister, and the results should be mailed back to you within a few weeks. Real Goods sells one radon detector that monitors air continuously and doesn't require lab tests.

Understanding the Results

Radon is measured in picocuries per liter, or pCi/l. According to EPA guidelines, if you are exposed to under four pCi/l throughout your life, you have less than a 5% risk of getting lung cancer. But the risk of lung cancer with exposure to 200 pCi/l is the equivalent of smoking four packs of cigarettes each day. If you smoke, the lung cancer risk is even higher. Keep in mind that dangers from radon are worsened by nicotine, a co-carcinogen. With exposure to radon, those who smoke

cigarettes have twice the chance of getting lung cancer as those who don't (Taplin and Foraker, 1989).

According to an Environmental Protection Agency video on radon, if your radon measurement comes to:

<4 pCi/l	do a periodic retest
4-20 pCi/l	do further tests
20-200 pCi/l	take action within months
>200 pCi/l	take action immediately

Be aware that fireplaces can draw radon up from the ground since the air drawn up the chimney (particularly with the windows closed) creates a pressure vacuum indoors.

What You Can Do

To decrease your exposure to radon, you can either prevent or remove the presence of radon in your building.

Prevention

The first thing you'll need to do is to seal openings in the floors and walls of your building's lowest levels. With caulk or some similar material.

First, remove loose particles from the area to be sealed. Grind away a small area so that the caulk holds better (DON'T FORGET TO WEAR GOGGLES IF YOU DO THIS YOURSELF). You can apply a non-toxic, urethane-based caulk or similar material. Then, work it into the opening with your finger, and seal the whole area. Also, remember to seal the spaces around the pipes that come up through the floor, even if there are not large gaps. Radon gas slips through the smallest crevices. Inactive sump pumps can be covered and sealed with Plexiglas® covers. Then, you can caulk around the cover.

Urethane foam can be used to fill in wall holes and cracks. After allowing a few days for the old radon to dissipate, test again for radon. Remember that old cracks can reopen, and new ones can form, so inspect your walls and floors periodically.

Radon Removal

If sealing the floor and walls does not stop radon penetration, you can have the gas removed. Ventilation through open windows allows some gas to escape but can result in higher utility bills and compromise your building's security. You may want to consider forced ventilation, fans pulling fresh air through the vents and blowing it into the building. The air can circulate around the room, leaving through vents on opposite or adjacent walls (this won't work if the vents are on the same wall). If this is not done properly, it can create an uneven pressure that will draw even more radon into the building.

If the radon level is high, you can set up a subslab ventilation system. With this type of system, a hole is drilled into the floor, and a pipe is run from it through the room to the outside of the building. A blower uses suction to draw radon gas up (through pipes that run from your basement level to the outside) before it has a chance to seep into the building. This works best where there is a layer of crushed rock beneath the building's foundation. This method may cost over $1,000 for homes (for those of you with home offices) and may remove up to 98% of the radon. In other words, a radon measure of 200 pCi/l can be reduced to less than 4 pCi/l (EPA radon video).

In buildings with basement walls made of cinder block, which is often hollow, radon can be drawn into the blocks through outside cracks and up into the building. When this happens, a system can be devised to suction radon from the walls, rather than the floors, and vent it outside.

Test for radon if you own a building or if your office is on or below the second floor. Start with a short-term test. If radon measures over 4 pCi/l, do a long-term test to get the annual measure. If it measures between 4 and 20 pCi/l, either prevent it from coming in, open windows, or use vents. If the measure is over 20 pCi/l, try forced ventilation or a suction/piping system of some kind (Taplin and Foraker, 1989).

Both the EPA and some states certify contractors and builders for radon remediation. For a listing of EPA-approved laboratories, contact:

National Institute for Standards and Technology
Laboratory Accreditation Administration
Building 411
Room A-162
Gaithersburg, MD 20899
301-975-4016

Sick Building Syndrome (SBS)

What Is It?

Sick Building Syndrome (SBS), is a temporary, or "self-quenching," sensitivity to chemicals. "Self-quenching" means that symptoms disappear when the immune system is no longer active against chemical exposure.

Symptoms include irritation of the eyes, nasal passages, and mucous membranes, dry skin, lethargy, difficulty concentrating, headaches, dizziness, and nausea.

Causes

SBS has been studied since World War I, with the first report coming out in England in 1948. It is a reaction against indoor air pollution, against working and living in sealed, polluted buildings that have dulled our senses.

The EPA has ranked indoor air pollution as the fourth largest of 31 environmental concerns. But in 1991, less than 4% of the EPA's air program budget was spent on this problem because it was not one of Congress's priorities. In an American Lung Association of Washington, D.C., survey, 24% of U.S. office workers experienced air-quality problems in their offices, and 20% said that their work quality was negatively affected by indoor air pollution. Some employees have quit their jobs and filed lawsuits against their employers or building owners because of permanent, physical impairment left by indoor pollutants.

Toxic materials are major culprits in creating a sick building. A few examples of their use are:

• Cleansers used in bathrooms (sinks, toilets, tile, mirrors), kitchens (floors, counters, sinks, and dishwashers), and on walls and carpets.
• Chemicals used in manufacturing or other processes.
• Furnishings, such as carpets (content, chemicals, glues), furniture (fiberboard and plastic offgassing), insulation, paints, and plastics.
• Perfumes (Some airlines actually deny rides to overly perfumed customers).
• Pesticides used indoors (rodenticides, spraying for cockroaches, etc.) and on indoor plants (insecticides).

A recent Cornell University study suggested that SBS also may be caused by tiny mineral fibers that originate from ceiling tiles and the insulation found within ventilation systems. Inhaling these fibers can irritate the mucous membranes and throat as well as causing headaches, respiratory problems, and other symptoms.

What You Can Do

Heating, ventilation, and air conditioning systems heat, cool, and ventilate a building. Sometimes, the road to better air quality requires an HVAC upgrade. First, though, find out the following:

1. Is the ventilation adequate?

2. Is the air drawn from the roof (which does not contain as much pollution as street-level air) or the loading dock area (which may contain vehicle exhaust and other pollutants)?

3. What types of filters are used to keep the air relatively clean?

4. How often is the air exchanged?

To avoid Sick Building Syndrome, be sure that office supplies, carpets, and other materials are non-toxic or have very low toxicity. Ensure that your ventilation system is working well and that the cleanest air possible is being drawn in from outside to replace stale, indoor air. Use heat exchangers if necessary to increase ventilation while maintaining the indoor temperature.

If you do a lot of traveling, you may want to stay at a smarter hotel. If you are sensitive to particular chemicals, call ahead to find out what the hotel uses. One hotel, Alexandria's Embassy Suites Hotel, in New Jersey, claims to receive requests from potential guests who want to avoid many of the chemicals typically used in room cleaning, laundering, and in the complimentary body care products often left in the rooms.

Upon receiving a request for an environmentally clean room, the hotel needs two days' notice to prepare a room. It shampoos carpets with distilled water, runs an air purifier, and washes linens in a hypo-allergenic detergent. Then, these rooms should be free of any harmful chemical cleaners and have a balcony or window that can be opened for fresher air if necessary. Contact the "Green" Hotels Association for more information.

STRESS

Even small levels of negative stress on a daily basis can lead to physical problems including ulcers, gastrointestinal dysfunction, heart disease, high blood pressure, and emotional and psychological problems. While stress affects people differently, studies have shown that working in a highly competitive office can create problems, particularly in sedentary working conditions.

A 1992 National Institute for Occupational Safety and Health (NIOSH) report showed that at U.S. West, 22% of 593 video operators had stress-related injuries, despite the company's efforts to create an ergonomic workplace. Psychological stress factors seemed to be a

large part of the problem as high productivity was demanded, workers were monitored closely, and job security was a concern (Anzovin, 134-135).

And while the Macintosh development team's T-shirt bragged "Working 90 hours a week and loving it," many suffered stress and strain, including carpal tunnel syndrome, chronic exhaustion, and depression.

WHAT YOU CAN DO

Stress can be a disabling and very costly work-related health problem. However, there are several things that you can do in working to overcome these problems.

Be sure that any ergonomic problems or pain that you have are taken care of immediately.

Take regular breaks to avoid eye strain and repetitive stress injuries, such as carpal tunnel syndrome. Some experts suggest that data entry or computer work be limited to four hours per day and that the remainder of the work day be mingled with other tasks.

Do a variety of tasks so that your mind is fresher and different muscles are used.

Use software programs with online ergonomic recommendations and diagrams of helpful exercises.

Work toward getting better software if yours is difficult to use or if it requires that one hand do more keystrokes than the other, resulting in strain.

Try to avoid working long hours. Also, avoid working in situations in which you are micro-managed and monitored at all times. This can create unnecessary stress and interfere with your job performance rather than enhance it.

If you work in an isolated area, be sure that you take occasional breaks to socialize with others. Also, don't be embarrassed or afraid to seek medical help in the event of severe stress or depression.

WATER POLLUTION

Most of us probably don't think twice about the water we drink at work. However, according to the EPA, disease-carrying organisms (including giardia) have been found in over 100 large water systems, including such cities as San Francisco and Boston. One General Accounting Office study showed about 80% of the drinking water surveys required of states found contaminated wastewater and sewage leakage to be present in drinking water.

The major threat to water is pollution from industrial, agricultural, municipal, and household wastes. The EPA has identified over 700 pollutants that are found regularly in drinking water. Of these, 20 are known carcinogens. In addition, hundreds of these pollutants contain carbon and are synthetic organic compounds (SOCs), and some are volatile organic compounds (VOCs) (Pearson, 88, 1989). At room temperature, VOCs from bath, sink, and shower water form gases that can be inhaled and put your body at risk. In addition, these toxins can enter your body through your skin.

Trihalomethanes (THMs) are found commonly in drinking water that has been disinfected with chlorine. These are formed when natural, organic material (dead leaves, soil, humus) combines with chlorine, which often is used to kill bacteria. Using ozone in place of chlorine, as some bottled waters do, does not result in THMs. The most common THM is chloroform, a carcinogen affecting the colon, rectum, and bladder (Pearson, 88, 1989).

Benzene and trichloroethylene are other suspected carcinogens commonly found in water. Pesticides such as chlordane – a mutagen and carcinogen – can be present as well (Pearson, 88, 1989).

Nitrates come from chemical fertilizers and leach into rivers. Especially harmful to children, high nitrate concentrations are found in both urban- and rural-area waters. They lower the blood oxygen level and are thought to cause "blue baby syndrome." They also may cause stomach cancer in adults (Pearson, 88, 1989).

Metals are found in drinking water as well. Lead in old pipes and solder from copper pipes are particularly bad for young children and in soft-water areas, where lead is easily leached. Soft water is found in areas with lower amounts of calcium and magnesium in the water. There is a higher incidence of deaths associated with heart disease in soft-water areas (Pearson, 88, 1989).

Aluminum is used in water treatment. It causes discoloration and is thought to be associated with Alzheimer's disease (senile dementia). Sulphuric and nitric acids form in the atmosphere and come to earth as acid rain. They soak into the soil and groundwater and corrode metal pipes, causing the metals (cadmium, lead, aluminum, mercury, copper) to leach into drinking water. And while fluoride, added to water to prevent tooth decay, may increase bone strength, it is linked to premature aging, crib deaths, and increased incidences of cancer (Pearson, 1989, 88-89).

Radon is a natural, radioactive element that sometimes is present in groundwater. It can be hazardous when released into the air and can be inhaled when water is heated (producing steam) or sprayed in a fine mist in showers. Exposure to organic compounds through baths, showers, hot tubs, spas, and pools may be higher than from exposure from drinking water (Pearson, 89, 1989).

Chloroform gas, a byproduct of chlorinated water, can be inhaled just as radon gas. In addition, plastic bottles also can leach byproducts into your water.

WHAT YOU CAN DO

Have It Tested
Some states are taking things into their own hands. For instance, while the EPA allows drinking water to be contaminated with arsenic at 50 parts per million (1:100), California wants to lower its arsenic level standard to two parts per trillion (1:1,000,000).

Have your water tested regularly for pollutants by an independent professional who does not sell water purification devices. Each state, following standards set by the EPA, certifies water-testing laboratories. Check with your state or with the EPA regarding water-testing laboratories.

Bottled Waters
For drinking water, if you choose to use bottled water, ask the company for a water analysis report giving the water's source and the treatments used. Also, look for independent consumer reports for additional, unbiased information.

Water-purification Systems
If you are looking for a water-purification system, you have three types from which to choose: activated carbon, osmosis, and distillation. Check into each of these types to find which is best suited for your needs. For information on certified water filters, contact:

National Sanitation Foundation
Drinking Water Treatment Units
P.O. Box 130140
Ann Arbor, MI 48113-0140

Tap into Cool Water
If you want to drink hot water, don't get it from the tap. Turning the faucet on to "hot" can leach harmful metals from your pipes and into the water you'll consume.

Instead, take cold water from the tap, and heat it on the stove or in the microwave.

HELPFUL RESOURCES

INFORMATION

CHEMICAL SENSITIVITY

For more information on CS, read Bonnye Matthews' book *Chemical Sensitivity: A Guide to Coping with Hypersensitivity Syndrome, Sick Building Syndrome and Other Environmental Illnesses.*

Contact the Association of Occupational and Environmental Clinics 202-347-4976. Doctors there treat chemical exposure regularly; most do not "recognize MCS as a valid diagnosis, but they can help you sort out what might be triggering your reactions" (*Health*, "Allergic to the 20th Century," Stephen S. Hall, May/June 1993, 76).

Carpet/4-Phenylcyclohexane Toxicity: The EPA Headquarters Case, by J. William Hirzy and Rufus Morison. In *The Analysis, Communication, and Perception of Risk*. B.J. Garrick and W.C. Gekler, eds. Plenum Press, NY: 1991.

The Chemical Injury Information Network, P.O. Box 301, White Sulphur Springs, MT 59645. Contact: Cynthia Wilson, Executive Director, 406-547-2255. Monthly publication *Our Toxic Times.*

The Green Chemistry Challenge
U.S. Environmental Protection Agency
Toxic Substance Control Act Assistance Information Servi ce
202-554-1404
TDD: 202-554-0551
EPA's Industrial Chemistry Branch: 202-260-2659
The Green Chemistry Challenge is a voluntary alliance between the EPA and chemical industry that works toward pollution prevention and industrial ecology.

The Human Ecologist, published by the Human Ecology Action League, Inc., P.O. Box 49126, Atlanta, GA 30359-1126. 404-248-1898.

National Center for Environmental Health Strategies, 1100 Rural Avenue, Voorhees, NJ 08043, 609-429-5358. Send a self-addressed, stamped envelope for a free information packet on MCS.

Rachel's Hazardous Waste News, published weekly by Environmental Research Foundation, P.O. Box 5036, Annapolis, MD 21403-7036
410-263-1584/ Fax: 410-263-8944
Internet: erf@igc.apc.org.

Toxic Carpet Information Exchange, P.O. Box 39344, Cincinnati, Ohio 45239.

The following titles are available from Lewis Publishers, 2000 Corporate Blvd., NW, Boca Raton, FL 33431, 407-994-0555:

Definitions, Conversions, and Calculations for Occupational Safety and Health Professionals, Edward W. Finucane, 1993.

Ecological Risk Estimation, Steven M. Bartell et al, 1992.

Environmental Risk: Identification and Management, Albert R. Wilson, 1991.

Environmental Risk and Insurance, Chester A. Zagaski, 1991.

"Fundamental Toxicology and Risk Assessment" software program, Ann Anderson and Michael Dailey, 1991.

Risk Management of Chemicals, conference proceedings from "Risk Management of Chemicals – Can Chemicals Be Used Safely?" meeting held in the U.K. July 1991. M.L. Richardson, editor.

EMFs

Cross Currents, by Robert Becker, Jeremy P. Tarcher, 1990.

Currents of Death, by Paul Brodeur, Simon and Schuster, 1989.

"Measuring Power Frequency Fields" and "What Do We Know About Possible Health Risks?" are both available from the Department of Engineering and Public Policy, Carnegie Mellon University, Pittsburgh, PA 15213.

Microwave News, P.O. Box 1799, Grand Central Station, New York, NY 10163. Send $1.00 and a self-addressed, stamped envelope for a list of gaussmeter distributors. You can subscribe to the publication.

Warning: The Electricity Around You May Be Hazardous to Your Health, Ellen Sugarman, Fireside Books, 1992.

INDOOR AIR QUALITY

"Green" Hotels Association
P.O. Box 420212
Houston, TX 77242
713-789-8889
For a few dollars, this association sells travel kits. These kits contain a letter to hotel management requesting that guests be allowed to decide when sheets and towels need to be washed. The kit's cards (intended for the maids) are illustrated on one side and translated into four languages on the reverse side.

The EPA published *Managing Indoor Air Quality: A Guide to Maintaining the Indoor Air Quality of Commercial Buildings,* a pamphlet, in January 1994. It was prepared by the Rhode Island Lung Association and the Rhode Island Department of Health. Another publication is titled *Secondhand Smoke: What You Can Do About Secondhand Smoke As Parents, Decisionmakers, and Building Occupants.*

Occupational Safety & Health Administration
200 Constitution Avenue, NW
Washington, D.C. 20210
202-219-8021

RADON

"Radon – A Homeowner's Guide" videotape by Philip Taplin and Richard Foraker. Produced by NUS Training Corp., 1989.

For a listing of EPA-approved laboratories that measure radon, contact the National Institute for Standards and Technology.

U.S. Radon Hotline
800-SOS-RADON (767-7236)
Request the *Citizen's Guide to Radon* and information about your state.

U.S. Radon Helpline
800-55-RADON (557-2366)/202-293-2270
Call if you have specific questions about radon.

WATER

U.S. Environmental Protection Agency's Drinking Water Hotline: 800-426-4791

PRODUCTS

For addresses and phone numbers, refer to *Appendix A: Directory of Suppliers.*

AIR FILTERS/PURIFIERS

American Air Filter
American Environmental Health Foundation
Dasun Company
Enviroclean
Environmental Health Shopper

COMPUTER ANTI-GLARE

Optical Coating Laboratory, Inc.

EMF-RELATED PRODUCTS

Clarus Technologies
EcoVision, Blackhawk Computers
Fairfield Engineering
Health Magnetix, Inc.
Holaday Industries
Integrity Electronics and Research
Mitchell Instrument Co.
Monitor Detection Systems
Narda Microwave Products
Real Goods Trading Corp.
Safe Environments
Safe Technologies
Sigma Designs

HEALTH-RELATED PRODUCTS

ALLERX
American Environmental Health Foundation
Coastline Products
Dasun Company
Enviroclean
Environmental Health Shopper
Non-toxic Environments, Inc.

VENTILATION

Airxchange, Inc.
American Aldes Ventilation
Bard Manufacturing
ClimateMaster
United Technology Carrier
Command-Aire
Environmental Air Ltd.
DesChamps Labs
Honeywell, Inc.
Research Products Corp.
Kooltronic
VanEE
Venmar Ventilation
Engineering Development, Inc.

WATER FILTERS/PURIFIERS

Absolute Environmental's Allergy Products & Services
Culligan International
Environmental Purification Systems
FILTRX Corporation

General Ecology, Inc.
Global Environmental Technologies
Hach Company
Kentrel Corporation
Lowry Aeration Systems
Multi-Pure Drinking Water Systems
National Testing Labs
N.E.E.D.S.
Nigra Enterprises
Pacific Environmental Marketing & Development
Pure Water Place
Real Goods Trading Corp.
Waterforms, Inc.
Water Treatment Systems

SUMMARY OF RECOMMENDATIONS

AIR POLLUTION

• Check your oil burner every year.

• Use air cleaners to remove impurities from indoor air, and be sure that your air filters are clean.

• Brush/vacuum your furnace blower annually. If you have an HVAC system, keep your registers clean.

• Use HEPA filters on vacuums.

• Be sure that dampers are balanced.

• Check your office ducts for leaks.

• Ensure that gas-fired appliances are installed and vented properly.

CHEMICAL SENSITIVITY & SICK BUILDING SYNDROME

• Avoid toxic products

• If you have used toxic products that offgas, consider using one of the sealers (for carpets, etc.) to help prevent off-gassing.

• Have your indoor air quality tested.

ELECTRO-MAGNETIC FIELDS (EMFS)

• Limit your exposure to EMFs by cutting back on the time you use cellular phones and other equipment.

• Sit farther from the computer. Use a longer computer keyboard cord if necessary.

• Use (recyclable) battery-powered equipment rather than equipment that plugs into a socket.

ERGONOMICS

• Position your body correctly.

• Be sure to use a chair with an adjustable height and angle.

• Your computer and peripherals should be within easy reach.

• Use a keyboard that's comfortable – such as those that are ergonomically designed. Keep a good relation between your line of sight for your monitor and your keyboard's height.

• Use a copy stand when referring to documents.

• If physically challenged, look for specially designed equipment.

EYE STRAIN/VISION PROBLEMS

• Be certain that your lighting is adequate and well designed.

• Stay a good distance from your monitor.

• Use a monitor stand to change the angle as needed.

• Consider using a flat-screened monitor to reduce distortion at the edges.

• Avoid screens with flicker.

• Your screen should be less than three times brighter than the ambient light level.

• If possible, be sure that there is no window behind you to avoid glare from your monitor.

RADON

• Prevent radon.

• Fix radon leaks.

• Remove radon.

• Call your state's radon hotline for additional information.

STRESS

• Fix ergonomic problems.

• Take breaks regularly.

• Alternate tasks.

• Find medical help for stress.

• Reduce isolation working.

• If possible, limit data entry to four hours each day.

WATER POLLUTION

• Test your water regularly.

• Get a water analysis report for information on the your bottled water's source and how it is treated.

• Don't use the hot water tap for water you'll consume as it can leach metals from your water pipes.

CHAPTER 9

SMARTER BUILDING MATERIALS

The smartest materials are those that are non-toxic, don't require much transportation or processing, are used efficiently, and are renewable, recyclable, or both.

Some manufacturers are beginning to create healthier alternatives to today's toxic and inefficiently made products. A number of issues have inspired this positive change – mainly, a concern over indoor toxins, the inefficient use of finite resources, and waste. Construction waste, alone, makes up nearly 20-26% of landfill trash. Each year, approximately 40% (by weight) of the raw materials entering the global economy are used in buildings. Buildings also are responsible for using between 36-45% of the United States' energy output.

Some architects, engineers, and others believe that the future of architecture and design will revolve around buildings that can be regularly disassembled and their parts reused. In Portland, Oregon, a whole house was taken apart by hand so that the parts could be recycled rather than having it destroyed by equipment. Lumber, metal, concrete, bricks, doors, windows, and a tub could be reused, and the manual dismantling was done at a price competitive with mechanical demolition that would have destroyed everything in the process.

The buildings in which we work and live can contribute greatly to pollution, deforestation, water shortages, global climate change, and acid rain. According to the Worldwatch report *A Building Revolution: How Ecological and Health Concerns Are Transforming Construction*:

- Construction accounts for 55% of non-fuel wood use.
- Worldwide, buildings account for 40% of energy and materials use.
- Sick building syndrome is a problem in 30% of new and newly renovated buildings.

WHAT TO LOOK FOR IN BUILDING MATERIALS

If you're moving into an existing building, there are several factors that you should examine. First, look into the building's chemical history. Find out about insulation, mildew control, and the treatment of the lumber used. Also, find out what fuels are used and what the building's annual fuel and electric consumption are.

Look at the materials used on both the interior and exterior. Signs of a good building include thick walls and floors, wallboard, doors, and cupboards made of solid wood. In the flooring, check for brick, ceramic tile, cork, stone, or terrazzo. Try to avoid composite boards, hollow-core doors, and thin stud walls. Also, stay away from asbestos, vinyl tiles, plastic surfaces, and foam-backed synthetic carpets.

If you are building a new office or retrofitting an existing one, do a life-cycle assessment of the health and efficiency of any materials that you are thinking of using. Consider the raw-material sources, the energy used and pollutants produced in manufacturing, and the reuse. Be aware that comparing different materials may be difficult. While one material may pollute the air throughout its lifetime, another might contaminate water as long as it's used, and another might require a great deal of energy and water in its manufacture and transport.

When you consider the collection of raw materials and the manufacture and transportation of building materials, the energy that goes into creating a building can be enormous. According to one article, "a steel and glass building, for example, might require about three gallons of oil per square foot to make, while a concrete and glass building requires only about two." Compared to a wood-framed structure requiring 0.4 gallons, "for a 100,000-square-foot building the differences can mean as much as 260,000 gallons of oil. That represents a lot of CO_2 we don't have to be putting into the air" *(Interiors,* "Visionary Architect," March 1993, 58).

Choosing the best building materials is not always easy. But it helps to research your options, looking for materials that have not been transported great distances, that have not been heavily processed, and that do not create much pollution in their manufacture, use, and disposal.

To determine which material selections are more crucial ecologically, designers should consider the quantities of materials used in the building, their life spans, and their environmental impact. Regarding quantity, buildings use some materials, such as concrete and steel, in large quantities, and these deserve special attention. As for life span, roofing and interior finishes are replaced frequently during the useful life of a building. It's important to know the impacts of materials since their extraction, use, and disposal can result in intense, extensive, and enduring damage.

Those of you building or retrofitting commercial buildings should check into local and federal government programs and with your local utility for helpful information on building and design issues. Those of you with home offices should rest assured that there are home rating and certification programs. They include the Colorado Green Program, City of Austin's Green Builder Program, Edison Electric Institute's E Seal, and Southern Electric International's Good Cents Environmental Homes program. One Canadian program, formed by the Greater Toronto Home Builders' Association, is known as Build Green, Inc. This program assesses building finishes, furnishings, materials, and specialty products that show an efficient use of renewable resources or are made with recycled materials.

Using non-sustainably harvested wood for construction contributes to deforestation, the loss of habitat, and the additional release of carbon dioxide into the atmosphere (worsening global warming). It is also costly in terms of erosion and road construction. For instance, the U.S. Forest Service spends a considerable amount of money building roads just so that logging companies can access uncut areas for timber.
(This photo was taken inside Lassen National Forest, California.)

SMART MATERIALS RESOURCES

A number of computer databases have been designed to help architects, engineers, and others choose from smarter building materials. One such database is the Resources for Environmental Design Index, or the REDI Guide. The REDI Guide, created by Eugene, Oregon's, Iris Communications, allows the user to search over 1,000 building products. Searches can be done on the manufacturer name, product name, keywords, geographical distribution region, and four environmental categories – natural, low-toxicity, recycled content, or sustainably harvested woods. See Chapter 20, "Surfing the Internet," for information on how to access the REDI Guide on line.

The National Park Service (NPS) also has a database of information on over 700 environmentally responsible building materials. The materials included are based on the manufacturers' claims. In addition to the material information, there is a list of over 2,000 North American companies that recycle construction waste. The database is available to anyone with Internet access and can be downloaded for free. See Chapter 20, "Surfing the Internet," for information on how to access the database.

Environmental Construction Outfitters (ECO) is a building-materials store in New York City. The materials sold there meet recyclable, renewable, and non-toxic criteria. ECO also sells water- and energy-efficient appliances, energy-efficient lighting, and non-toxic building maintenance supplies.

Turner Corporation, one of the larger construction companies in the U.S. wants to be one of the "greenest." To reach its goal, it has implemented construction-site recycling, encouraged sensitivity to construction-site environments, and used low-toxicity and recycled products.

Another company, Stafford-Harris, Inc., has designed a computer database of environmentally responsible building materials. The database, with over 1,500 recycled-content building materials, includes sources for insulation, wood products, plastic products, paints, and wallboard.

Other sources for smarter building materials are mail order catalogues and the manufacturers themselves, many of which are listed in this book.

Finally, for more information, try the American Institute for Architects (AIA) in Washington, D.C. and the U.S. Green Building Council.

ACOUSTIC CEILING PANELS

One source for smart acoustic ceiling panels is Wilhelmi Acoustic Ceilings and Walls, in Roswell, Georgia. These panels have high sound absorption, are easily washable, and have no mineral fiber backing.

BRICK

In brick production, generally oil is added; however, some brick manufacturers now use soils already contaminated with oil rather than adding oil to clean soils. Machine-made, unbaked earthen bricks compete in dollar terms with kiln-fired clay bricks, but their environmental cost is 500 times lower.

CARPENTRY

Many types of woods can be used in construction. Unfortunately, not all are created equally, so you may want to do a little research into the source and processing of wood products prior to making a purchase. (See the section on "Wood" later in this chapter.)

Many of the old trees once used to produce beautiful wood products are gone, and there has been a steady decline in wood quality over the years. As a result, the wood industry has changed significantly.

"Engineered" woods, or composites, have been developed to take the place of the lumber that comes directly from trees. Engineered woods use wood scraps from lumber milling or from smaller, faster-growing trees. The scraps are glued together and pressed into shape, resulting in particleboard, oriented strand board (OSB), plywood, and other products.

Aside from the toxicity of the glues that offgas from engineered wood products, lamination of the wood can cause health problems, too. If you're searching for smarter wood products, find out what types of adhesives are used. Generally, laminated products use an adhesive containing formaldehyde. There are different kinds of formaldehyde, so find out if your products contain urea or phenol formaldehyde. Urea formaldehyde, found in inferior grades of plywood and other wood products, is more toxic than is phenol formaldehyde. Of course, using screws or nails to avoid adhesives altogether is the best course.

Of course, if the wood is new wood – that is, if it's not recycled or "engineered" wood – it should come from a sustainably managed forest. Look under "Wood" in this chapter for more information.

CONCRETE

The gathering of resources and production of concrete are usually done near the job site, requiring less transportation than is generally needed when other building materials are used. The production of portland cement, on the other hand, requires more energy and may require transportation over longer distances.

Autoclaved cellular concrete (ACC) is one lightweight concrete now being produced. ACC uses small amounts of aluminum in the concrete mix, creating hydrogen bubbles that cause the concrete mass to expand. Unfortunately, the production process is energy-intensive, as are the mining and production of aluminum.

Both fly ash and granulated, ground blast-furnace slag have been used in the standard concrete or ACC mixes in place of portland cement. Waste ash, resulting from incineration, has been found to make a paste that can be poured and shaped like concrete yet is twice as strong. The EPA's guidelines for federal agencies' procurement of concrete require cement and concrete purchases to contain ground, granulated blast-furnace slag and coal fly ash.

Some concrete producers are using plastic, wood chips, or crushed glass, too. The end product of these recycled aggregates generally holds more water than the natural, virgin aggregates and is more durable when bound in concrete than are the natural aggregates. Of course, using recycled aggregates and fly ash results in a product with a much higher recycled content. In addition, rather than using form-release agents in the production process, mineral oil can be used as a non-toxic substitute. Sulphur, taken from the petroleum industry, can be used instead of concrete block, brick, and other masonry materials.

DOORS

Fiberglass doors are manufactured using petroleum, a non-renewable resource. In addition, they often have foam cores and other materials that are not easily recyclable.

Although metal doors may be insulated, the type of foam insulation often used is not recyclable and may contain CFCs. The production of aluminum requires a great deal of energy, but aluminum recycling uses only a small fraction of the energy that it takes to produce virgin aluminum. So, if you're looking for an aluminum door, try to find one with recycled materials.

Wood doors are becoming more expensive due to the decreasing quality of wood, a result of poorly planned and managed forestry practices. In response to the severe shortage of good quality wood, a number of products are available that use recycled wood or ground wood. For example, medium-density fiberboard and paper honeycomb are used as substitutes for traditional plywood door cores. Unfortunately, these substitutes are laminated and may offgas toxic fumes from the adhesives. Finger-jointed products are available as well.

You may want to check with local salvage companies for used doors. Or, look for doors made with wood from sustainably managed forests. For more information on various wood products and sources, see "Wood" later in this chapter.

DRYWALL

As far as drywall goes, you can find gypsum board that contains recycled gypsum and/or newsprint. In addition, you can substitute drywall clips for wood blocking at the inside corners and use mechanical fasteners rather than adhesives. When choosing joint compounds, be aware that some contain stabilizers and biocides. These toxins can be problems to those working around them, particularly those individuals who are chemically sensitive. Fortunately, there are less-toxic joint compounds available with fewer additives.

EARTH STRUCTURES

Some builders are returning to tried and true, natural materials. Adobe, rammed-earth, and straw (not hay) bale technologies all rely on thick, load-bearing walls made of non-toxic, natural materials for insulation. In the past, these have tended to be used more in parts of the western U.S., where the weather generally is characterized by clear skies and not much rain. However, some

Everything we use and do impacts the world around us. The cuts into this mountain face in the desert of Eastern California can be found near the Mitsubishi Cement Corporation.

of these less costly and lower impact technologies are making their way across the U.S. and abroad.

ADOBE

The thickness of adobe walls slows the heat transfer between indoors and outdoors, giving it a high R value. Most adobe used today is stabilized with either portland cement or emulsified asphalt. Adobe is fireproof, insect-proof, and energy-efficient.

BLOCKS

Earth blocks, similar to adobe, can be produced using a variety of soils, which can be collected on site. While these blocks may be labor-intensive to create, the soil used to make them may cost nothing if taken from the building's excavation site. Because these blocks can be made on site, transportation costs are eliminated.

RAMMED EARTH

Otherwise known as soil cement, rammed earth is made by compressing a mixture of soil and cement. Rammed-earth walls are fireproof and termite-proof and can be both inexpensive and energy-efficient. For new construction, soil from the building's site can be used.

STRAW BALE

Straw-bale walls are made of well-cured, dry, tightly formed straw bales (straw is what's left over after grain is separated from its stalk). They can be made of straw bales or of a straw and clay mixture. The best straws to use come from barley, flax, oats, rice, rye, or wheat; avoid hay and straw taken from alfalfa and native grasses.

Contrary to what you may think, straw-bale construction is insect-resistant. In addition, a 24-inch-thick wall has an R value of about 55. Straw-bale walls can be used for both loadbearing and non-loadbearing walls. Check your building codes to find out if they approve the use of straw bales in construction.

METALS

When building with metals, be sure that composite assemblies can be easily disassembled for later recy-

cling. You should know that the process of galvanizing is energy-intensive and creates severe pollution.

Making virgin aluminum from bauxite is the most energy-intensive process in the entire construction industry. Recycled aluminum production uses less than 10% of the energy used to make virgin aluminum and produces only 5% of the air pollution.

Eighty-five to ninety percent of the bauxite used in U.S. aluminum production comes from the Caribbean and South America. The remaining 10-15% is open-pit-mined in Arkansas. Aluminum plants are found mainly along the Gulf of Mexico coast, the lower Mississippi River, and in central Arkansas.

The average recycled content of American steel is about 46%. Light-gauge steel framing is increasingly popular over wood framing. Its prices, quality, and insect resistance are more stable, and it's generally better tolerated by people with chemical sensitivity. Its main drawback is its thermal performance.

PAVEMENT

One problem with much of today's pavement is that it can cause runoff, flooding, and erosion. A rainstorm that delivers an inch of rain can repel 26,000 gallons of fresh water from an acre of land. If it were not for non-porous pavement, this water could soak into the ground and go into nearby waterways.

To avoid the problem of runoff, one of the least expensive options is to use crushed stone. Unfortunately, it is dusty and needs constant regrading. Porous paving blocks are a better way to go, and some are made of recycled materials. You also can drain paved areas into retention basins, sunken gardens, and percolation beds rather than having water go into the storm sewers.

Some companies have found a new way to reuse old jars and bottles by turning them into glass bricks for use in paving, concrete work, and decorative edging. Other companies are finding ways to reuse glass for paving and drainage as well. Glass blocks are being used for driveways and paths. Recycled, clear-glass "stones" can even be used with lighting underneath to create an illuminated walkway.

One product worth mentioning is recycled playground pavers. These rubber, interlocking blocks, made of shredded truck tires, are available in a variety of thicknesses.

PLASTIC WOOD

When using plastics, consider their advantages and disadvantages. While using recycled plastic can be a great reuse of a persistent material, it also helps to support the continued use of these non-renewable, petroleum-based products. In addition, the colors of recycled plastics are not always consistent unless the producer controls the source of the plastics. Be aware that a warping of recycled plastics, particularly in the direct sun, can be a problem.

There are two types of plastic "wood." They are co-mingled and low-density polypropalene (from high-density polypropalene, or HDPE). Co-mingled plastics warp less than HDPE but tend to be less consistent in both weight and color. On the other hand, polypropalene has a lower melting point than co-mingled plastic, making it more susceptible to warping. As a result, structures that will be carrying any weight need steel frames underneath the plastic for support.

Recycled plastics can expand and contract up to 1/32" per linear foot under different outdoor weather conditions. In addition, plastic wood with a smooth texture can be slippery, which is a concern when it's being used for decking and other outdoor surfaces. Because plastic wood has different structural qualities than real wood, joists need to be spaced closer together. Try to create a design that allows plastic components to be changed easily if necessary.

Although plastic lumber may cost more than wood initially, its durability can outweigh those costs over its life cycle.

As a resource, consider contacting the Plastic Lumber Trade Association. It was formed in 1993 to help coordinate the recycled plastic lumber industry and help the ASTM develop testing and labeling standards. Also, according to the National Park Service database, Dr. Tom Nosker of Rutgers University's Center for Plastic Recycling Research is one of the top researchers in the plastic wood field.

Recycled rubber can be made into pavement, playground tiles, and other materials.

ROOFING

Fiberglass asphalt shingles rarely contain recycled glass content, but organic asphalt shingles often contain some recycled waste paper. Some also use mineral slag. Asphalt shingles last 20-30 years but are not easily recycled.

In areas that need a lot of cooling, you may want to use light-colored or white shingles. Asphalt shingles aren't as reflective as other light-colored roofing materials, but they do reflect about 25% of the solar radiation. Using light-colored shingles can reduce a building's cooling costs from 10-40%.

Cedar is generally the wood used to manufacture wood shingles and shakes. Unfortunately, cedar is a slow-growing, threatened species. Although treated roofing has a 30 year warranty, the untreated shakes last between 10 and 15 years in moist climates and 25-30 years in dry climates. Shakes are available in slow-growing oak and can last as long as 50 years. They're also made from faster growing pine, such as the Southern Yellow Pine often grown on tree farms.

One alternative to using wood, "plastic lumber" can be used for a number of products, including benches.

Alternatives to wood shakes and shingles include fiber-cement or plastic mock shingles or shakes as well as hardboard shakes. These can be more durable than wood, more successfully resisting damage from hail. Consider installing a layer of sheathing between the roofing membrane and the roof insulation so that the insulation can be reused when the roof is redone.

Slate is a limited natural resource but is durable as a roofing material. The quarrying and production associated with slate doesn't create the degree of pollution associated with some synthetic roofing materials. Its primary detriment is the pit associated with slate-quarrying. Fortunately, slate can be reused, and salvaged slate usually is less expensive than new slate.

Tiles made of clay are natural, and the materials are easy to get. Be aware that tiles with high water absorption can be damaged in the freezing and thawing process and should be used in warmer climates.

Fiber-cement tiles are made of wood fiber, sand, and cement. These tiles last up to 50-60 years and are fireproof. Be aware that the autoclaved tiles are more brittle than the air-cured tiles. In addition, fiber-cement tiles are more susceptible to freeze/thaw damage than are clay tiles. When no longer used as roof tiles, the fiber-cement tiles can be crushed and used as mineral dust.

Metal roofing tiles are lightweight. Of course, the production of virgin metals is highly energy-intensive and polluting. Luckily, 100% recycled-content roofing tiles are available and can be recycled when their use as roofing tiles is over. United Solar (Troy, MI) has designed photovoltaic roofing shingles, which generate power and serve the basic function of shingles. They have been used already at the Southface Energy and Environmental Resource Center in Atlanta, Georgia.

SIDING

Fiber-cement siding can last longer and be more fire-resistant than wood siding. Metal siding that contains a high recycled content also is available.

WATERPROOFING & WOOD TREATMENT

For a healthier alternative to solvent-based waterproofing, use water-based waterproofing products. Using

solvent-based products poses a health risk to those manufacturing, applying, and working around them.

As far as wood treatment is concerned, borax-based wood treatments are the safest available.

WINDOW-GLAZING

Window-glazing is one way to increase a building's insulation. One glazing method is a Heat Mirror®, a polyester film coated with microscopic dots of many precious metals, mainly silver. This heat mirror is installed in the air space inside insulated glass and reflects heat and ultraviolet radiation while allowing visible light through. It is available in many coating weights, so one building may contain windows with varied heat mirror weights as needed.

Reflective glass reflects out both heat and visible light; as a result, cooling loads are cut, but lighting needs increase. Because green glass contains a lot of iron, it performs somewhat like a heat mirror since it also is reflective.

WOOD

Wood has long been used in building construction. Heavy timber structures built from large old trees can withstand fires that would warp steel. Unfortunately, many of these old trees are gone, and clear-cut forests have been replaced by faster-growing, genetically engineered tree strains. This has compromised not only biological and genetic diversity but the strength of the trees. Higher-priced and lower-quality wood has resulted. Today's wood studs are susceptible to warping, and it would take 12 2"x4" planks to equal the strength of one old 8"x8" post (Manning, 105-106).

Oriented strand board (OSB) is a product made of weak trees that are ground and glued together to make them strong. Glue technology has advanced greatly; the liquid resin used to make OSB goes into the tiny spaces between the wood particles, and wafer boards are made. Unfortunately, the glues used in most OSBs contain phenol-formaldehyde or isocyanates, substances that have poisoned mill workers. Urea-formaldehyde, the glue used in particleboard, is highly toxic and offgasses volatile fumes, contributing to sick building syndrome and chemical sensitivity.

OSB does offer an alternative to the big beams that come from old-growth trees. The best OSB comes from aspen, which is not old growth at all. Aspen trees take about 20 years to grow to maturity; Douglas firs take about 200. However, the method of cutting trees for OSB does not promote a selective cutting of trees; instead, it promotes clear cutting using a feller-buncher, a driveable machine with a giant pair of scissors on the front that cut every tree in its path.

Several wood products are made with recycled or sustainably harvested woods and non-toxic finishes.

Although it's true that wood is expensive and the quality has suffered, there are some alternatives. International Wood Products, Inc., the first company to be certified by Scientific Certification Systems for its 100% post-consumer content, recycled wood. International Wood Products uses this recycled wood, from 19th century building beams, in its flooring products. The Queen Anne, Maryland, company also reclaims federally protected species such as heart pine. Georgia-Pacific Corporation is working to create engineered woods, including medium-density fiberboard made from sawdust, waste, and wood scrap, to reduce pressure on old-growth and tropical species.

More companies are using salvaged wood – from barns, urban buildings, and other structures – in building construction. One such company is Big Timberworks, Inc. Salvaged, good quality wood is taken from retired buildings, including warehouses, bridges, and factories. After resawing and planing, the salvaged lumber is about 25% more expensive than similar grade, new green timber, but salvaged lumber doesn't shrink.

Aged Woods is another company that uses older wood for a number of purposes, including flooring, paneling, molding, and millwork.

Once, before railway transport, logs were floated down rivers to their destinations, but some never made it. Now, timber salvagers are taking sunken logs out of rivers and using them to make furniture and flooring. Some salvagers in Northern California are getting between $2,000-6,000 for each log they find in the Big River. The Knoll Group, a New York furniture manufac-turer, makes veneers from salvaged logs for its Cactus and Propeller table collections.

When it's not being dredged and salvaged, wood is such a hot commodity that some people are trying to make "wood" out of plastic. While great for docks, porches, and decks, it is not strong enough for interior, structural applications. But it is insect-proof, rot-proof, and waterproof. Trex lumber is manufactured using recycled plastic grocery bags, industrial stretch film, sawdust from furniture factories, and used wood pallets. It can be drilled, sanded, and painted just like wood. However, it is not as strong as wood.

Another company makes "woods" from recycled photo film. While this company began recycling film to get the silver from it, it decided to use the remainder of the film "waste" for something useful and came up with the idea for wood. Yet another company makes "wood" from recycled carpeting.

W.H. Porter, Inc., manufactures FiberBond®, which is a wood panel insulated with foam.

If you do use virgin (non-reused) lumber, go for native spruce or pine over more expensive cedar or redwood cut from the few remaining virgin forests in the U.S. If there are no moisture problems in your walls, spruce should last nearly as long as cedar or redwood. Pine is good, too, but it has to dry for several months (to let its pores open) before it can be finished.

WHO'S DEVELOPING SMART WOOD STANDARDS?

The organizations listed below have developed good wood standards. Look for the good wood stamp from the following certification and monitoring organizations:

EcoForestry Institute
Located in Victoria, B.C. (Canada), this company has affiliates in the U.S. Pacific Northwest as well. The EcoForestry Institute trains people in sustainable forestry practices and helps to set up model forestry

operations. It also works to develop certification standards and publishes the quarterly *Ecoforestry Report,* which reports on North American forestry.

Institute for Sustainable Forestry (ISF)

Pacific Certified Ecological Forests Products (PCEEP) is a community-based organization. Founded in 1991, this organization is working in Northern California's Redwood areas to create a rural economic development strategy that would benefit the region's forest and human communities.

The ISF's certification is based on its Ten Elements of Sustainability:

"1. Forest practices will maintain and/or restore the aesthetics, vitality, structure, and functioning of the natural processes, including fire, of the forest ecosystem and its components.

2. Forest practices will maintain and/or restore surface and groundwater quality and quantity, including aquatic and riparian habitat.

3. Forest practices will maintain and/or restore natural processes of soil fertility, productivity, and stability.

4. Forest practices will maintain and/or restore a natural balance and diversity of native species of the area, including flora, fauna, fungi, and microbes, for purposes of the long-term health of ecosystems.

5. Forest practices will encourage a natural regeneration of native species to protect valuable native gene pools.

6. Forest practices will not include the use of artificial chemical fertilizers or synthetic chemical pesticides.

7. Forest practitioners will address the need for local employment and community stability and will respect workers' rights, including occupational safety, fair compensation, and the right of workers to bargain collectively.

8. Sites of archaeological, cultural and historical significance will be protected and will receive special consideration.

9. Forest practices executed under a certified Forest Management Plan will be of the appropriate size, scale, time frame, and technology for the parcel, and adopt the appropriate monitoring program, not only in order to avoid negative cumulative impacts, but also to promote beneficial cumulative effects on the forest.

10. Ancient forests will be subject to a moratorium on commercial logging during which time the Institute will participate in research on the ramifications of management in these areas."

The Rainforest Alliance's Smart Wood Program

The Rainforest Alliance, a New York City non-profit organization, started its Smart Wood Program in 1990. This forestry certification program, which evaluates timber sources and forest products, is the largest and oldest. It evaluates companies from around the world that sell smart wood-certified products exclusively as well as those that sell both certified and uncertified products.

I should mention that any company can apply for certification; this is a voluntary program. However, the Rainforest Alliance hopes that Smart Wood certification will be sought increasingly by consumers and will encourage forest managers to manage their forests sustainably and seek out certification.

According to the Alliance, Smart Wood operations follow a number of principles:

• Long-term forest security (i.e., it will not be cleared in the foreseeable future
• Maintenance of environmental functions, including watershed stability and biological conservation
• Sustained-yield forestry production
• Positive impact on local communities
• The existence of suitable forest management plans.

While Smart Wood does not support converting forests into tree plantations, the program will certify plantations that have been planted on lands deforested previously to help prevent erosion, protect watersheds, cut pressures on natural forests, and restore tree cover.

Scientific Certification Systems' (SCS)

SCS, an Oakland, California, non-profit organization, has worked to create a certification system for environmental products. Its certification symbol is a Green Cross. The Green Cross wood certification program's primary goals are to:

• "Identify and catalogue effective sustainable forest management systems currently in place throughout the world.
• Identify consumer and industrial products produced from materials obtained from forests managed under certified sustainable forest management systems
• Establish clear guidelines for competing companies who wish to be recognized for their sustainable management efforts.
• Provide an economic incentive for producers of forest

products to develop and adopt sustainable forest management systems.
- Collect data and stimulate additional research to identify

1. specific species that are being threatened

2. areas of concentrated biodiversity

3. specific regions requiring exceptional preservation steps

4. new sustainable forest management practices.

- Provide retailers with a uniform certification system to help their customers identify environmental achievements with respect to products throughout their stores.
- Give consumers the power to make clear, informed choices in the marketplace, backed by sound scientific documentation."

MORE SMART WOOD
INFORMATION

Check with any of the certification organizations mentioned above or with the following organizations for information about smarter woods and furniture sources.

EcoForestry Institute
Publishes the quarterly *Ecoforestry Report*. For more information, contact

The Ecoforestry Institute
785 Barton Road
Glendale, OR 97442
phone/ Fax: 503-832-2785
Internet:
envirolink.org/orgs/ef/
index.html

Forest Partnership
P.O. Box 426
431 Pine Street
Burlington, VT 05402
800-858-6230 (US & Canada) or
802-863-6789/ Fax: 802-863-4344
E-mail: wow@together.net
Internet: www.together.net/~wow
The Forest Partnership, a non-profit, educational organization, publishes *Initiatives* monthly. A "sister" organization of Tree Talk (below), the Forest Partnership maintains a Sustainable Forests Directory.

Forest Stewardship Council (FSC)
The Forest Stewardship Council is developing comprehensive, global guidelines for sustainable forestry (tropical, temperate, and boreal) to keep wood certifiers (there are 10 wood certification companies worldwide) together instead of splitting off, each with its own idea of sustainable forestry. This should help both the wood industry and consumers. For more information, contact:

Forest Stewardship Council
Avenida Hidalgo 502
68000 Oaxaca
Oaxaca
Mexico
Phone/ Fax: +52 (951) 621-10
E-mail: fscoax@antequera.antequera.com

Good Wood Alliance
289 College Street
Burlington, VT

Tree Talk, Inc.
P.O. Box 426
431 Pine Street
Burlington, VT 05402
800-858-6230 (U.S. & Canada)/802-863-6789
Fax: 802-863-4344
E-mail: wow@together.net
Internet: www.together.net

One of the ways to work toward sustainable forestry is to reduce the demand on such popular species as mahogany and rosewood by using lesser-known tree species. Thousands of species with potential market value are not used, partly out of habit. In addition, many people are not aware of different species and their characteristics.

To help fill the information gap on various tree species, the Woods of the World database was created. This database was designed to help environmentally concerned professionals specify wood. The database provides physical, mechanical, environmental, and woodworking characteristics on 750 common and lesser-known tropical and temperate wood species and on composite and structural wood products. It includes engineering characteristics and information on where the wood's geographic origins and methods of logging. The database is designed to help locate alternative species whose use will be less ecologically damaging.

Woods of the World helps designers make quick decisions on using any of thousands of species. It offers information on the qualities of various woods. Users can go into 20-25 different files on such information as a tree's habitat(s), hardness, methods of harvest, and where it is found. Using this database, for example, you can ask for the wood that most closely resembles such endangered species as rosewood or sapele.

Woods of the World was developed for both Apple and IBM-compatible systems, with a choice of floppy disks or a CD-ROM. The database will be updated and administered by Philadelphia's Academy of Natural Sciences.

CD-ROM and multimedia integration will allow you to see actual logging operations for particular species, providing valuable information for you and for conscientious lumber yards and sawmills. It also has scanned images of species with common and botanical names. You can see a demo or get more information about the database on the Internet: www.woodweb.com/~treetalk/home.html

After this rustic Wyoming homestead has served its purpose, the wood can be used again or it can be allowed to return to the soil over time.

Woodworkers' Alliance for Rainforest Protection (WARP)
WARP publishes *Understory* quarterly. This publication covers new initiatives on forestry in the tropics and is geared toward environmentally conscious woodworkers.

Internet Resources
See "Chapter 20: Surfing the Internet" for some great forestry and wood resources available on the Internet.

SMARTER BUILDINGS THAT ARE PAYING OFF

Worldwide, people are recognizing the advantages and practicality of smart design. Combining old technologies and new technologies, we can meet our needs at work while working in more efficient, healthier, more productive buildings. Below are just a few examples of what different companies have done to design better buildings.

Homes in California & Texas
For those of you with home offices, you may be happy to know that smarter housing is increasingly popular. A subdivision of homes in California was built incorporating solar heating and bike paths. Now, those houses are worth 12% more than the nearby, conventional homes. In Texas, one affordable housing development was designed with efficient appliances and solar heating. Although these homes' mortgages cost $13 more each month, the household utility bills have been reduced by $450 a year simply through efficiency.

Southern California Gas
The Southern California Gas Company's Energy Resource Center is located in Downey, CA. The building used digital lighting sensors and super-insulated windows. It also incorporated about 400 tons of recycled and reused materials, most of which were taken from a dismantled gas company office building. Other materials include:

• Flooring made of posts and beams from an old warehouse
• Reception desk made from recycled glass
• Reinforcing bars made of weapons and submarine metal
• Parking lot coating made from melted tires (Hammer, August 31, 1994).

Washington's Department of Ecology

The state of Washington's Department of Ecology designed a smart building that includes renewable construction materials, sediment ponds and filtration vaults to collect and purify storm water, and daylighting to reduce cooling and lighting loads.

California State

California State Polytechnic's Center for Regenerative Studies' has some impressive facilities. Located 40 miles south of Los Angeles, the Center's facilities include a 16-acre experimental prototype with solar energy, water reclamation, soil fertility, food cultivation free of pesticides or chemical fertilizers, waste recycling, and shelter compatible with the land (Hammer, January 4, 1995).

NRDC – Washington, D.C.

Following in the footsteps of its successful predecessors, NRDC's Washington, D.C. branch created a smarter building in 1996. It's new smart office features:

- Cabinets/shelving made of agricultural waste and compressed straw doors rather than wood
- Ceiling tiles made of 25% recycled cellulose (no mineral fibers)
- Desks and work surfaces made of recycled newspaper and soybeans ("works like wood, looks like marble and feels like plastic")
- Energy-efficient appliances (including a Sun Frost, "the most efficient refrigerator ever made")
- Energy-efficient lighting (uses 75% less energy than convention lighting)
- Energy Star office equipment
- Furniture made of certified. sustainably harvested wood.
- Low-toxicity, no-VOC paints
- Natural linoleum floors
- Operable windows
- Recycled nylon carpets applied with non-toxic adhesives (the carpet manufacturer will recycle the carpet when NRDC is done with it)
- Recycled rubber wall trim
- Recycled carpet (manufacturer guarantees that it will be recycled after it is finished = cradle-to-cradle)
- Recycled floor tiles with 70% recycled glass content
- Walls made of compressed straw and power plant waste (synthetic gypsum).

For tours and information, contact NRDC at:
NRDC
1200 New York Ave., NW
Suite 400
Washington, D.C. 20005
202-289-6868

University of British Columbia

The University of British Columbia's Institute for Asian Research was designed as a smart building. The materials used in its construction will have at least 50% recycled content. And while an old-growth post-and-beam frame will be used, the wood will be salvaged from a local, demolished building. Rather than being connected to the sewage system, the Institute will use waterless composting toilets and a subsurface constructed wetland to recycle gray water. Rainwater will be collected and either absorbed on site or used for irrigation.

The Pentagon

The Pentagon is working toward smarter offices, too. Energy-efficient lighting, double-pane windows, and energy-efficient computers will be used to increase efficiency and make it a more comfortable place in which to work. The smart materials used must pay off in three years or less (Hammer, March 1, 1995).

Real Goods Trading Co.

Real Goods Trading Corporation created its new store, the Solar Living Center, on 12 acres of land. Located in Hopland, California, the Center is not only a great source for smarter products, but it also was built using sustainable principles. It takes advantage of solar power, collects rainwater, uses daylighting, and has a landscape of natural vegetation.

Smart Vacations

The Harmony and Maho Bay resorts in the U.S. Virgin Islands (St. John) give a whole, new meaning to ecotourism. Low-impact construction techniques were used, such as elevated walkways connecting the 118 tent cottages at Maho Bay to keep people from walking on the rare vegetation. Harmony resort is powered by solar and wind only and was made using recycled building materials. Rainwater is collected in cisterns for irrigation (Hammer, September 14, 1994).

Internationale Nederlanden (ING) Bank

Amsterdam's Internationale Nederlanden (ING) Bank headquarters' design has saved the company millions. The new building consumes about 10% of the energy of its previous building, and worker absenteeism has been reduced by 15%. These two factors, alone, have saved ING $3.4 million each year. The building's smart designs were developed when architects, engineers, future occupants, and scientists got together to communicate their needs and created ways to meet them.

In addition to the savings, ING created a more pleasant work environment. Each of ING's towers has a glass-roofed atrium. No desk is more than 23 feet from a window, and window louvers throw light deep into the building. That way, all workers have access to sunlight.

Sweden
In 1995, Sweden's largest housing bank announced it will loan money only to those who are building environmentally responsible buildings.

Germany
Stores in most major German cities sell smart building materials.

Thailand
In Thailand, the government has ordered a building that will be 25 stories tall and consume only 20% of the energy of similar buildings in Bangkok.

U.S. Materials Engineering Firm
In the U.S., the country's biggest architectural/engineering company examines the environmental and health impacts of the materials that it specifies.

Real Estate Perks for British
Worldwide, people are recognizing the advantages and practicality of smart design. Many countries have industry or government groups voluntarily working to establish rating systems to rank buildings. Nearly one-quarter of Great Britain's commercial properties are being rated. High scores for smart buildings are being touted by real estate agents.

Go, Brazil!
The city of Curtiba, Brazil, with its population of 1.6 million, had an unusual mayor. Jaime Lerner (now the governor) is also an architect. During his time as mayor, he had "planted 1.5 million tree seedlings in neighborhoods, solved the city's flood problems, and converted the downtown shopping district into a pedestrian zone." The city recycles two-thirds of its garbage and has a good system of transportation (Hammer, May 24, 1995).

Southwestern Suburbs
Village Homes in Davis, California, and Woodlands in Houston, Texas, were two of the original ecoburbs – ecologically sensitive, suburban areas – built in the early 1970s. Now, two ecoburbs are being developed near Chicago – Prairie Crossing and Tyron Farm. These will take into account the natural drainage features of the land, site buildings in response to the sun, and encourage compact living and less car use (Hammer, June 21, 1995).

The Netherlands
Holland's Ecolonia community is made up of 101 private homes. Each uses smart architectural strategies such as sod roofs, solar collectors, and a wastewater treatment pond (Hammer, September 19, 1994).

Arizona's Environmental Showcase Home
Arizona Public Service, the state's largest utility, designed a house known as the Environmental Showcase Home. Designed by Jones Studio, Inc. (Phoenix) and built by Homes and Son Contractors, Inc. (Phoenix), this home was designed with energy-efficient, environmentally responsible technologies and materials. Its design also took into account the comfort of people living in the Phoenix area; in other words, it was designed for its particular site and region, with no preconceived notions of how it should appear.

While competitively priced with other homes in the area, the house was designed to be about 60% more energy-efficient than most current energy-efficient homes. It also uses 60% less water. In addition, it has the following features:

- "Passive solar design
- High-efficiency triple function heat pump
- Stand-alone heat pump and solar water heating
- Photovoltaic panels turning sunlight into energy
- Highly insulative glazing in the windows
- Unique, energy-efficient concrete block walls filled with Super Green polyurethane insulating foam
- Cellulose insulation in other exterior walls and the vaulted ceilings
- Cementitious foam insulation in the garage roof
- Energy-efficient lighting and appliances
- Naturally daylit interior with light on two sides of every space
- Xeriscape landscaping with sub-surface irrigation system and computerized controller
- Greywater recycling system and rainwater harvesting system to provide all landscape watering needs
- Almost every building material has recycled content or is especially resource-efficient
- Indoor paints and finishes selected to reduce indoor air pollution
- Carefully selected environmentally sensitive furnishings and accessories with organic fabrics, non-offgassing and recyclable materials
- Environmentally responsible swimming pool" (EcoNet, *Environmental Building News*).

For more information contact Tom Hahn at Jones Studio (602) 264-2941 or at the Sol Source (602) 257-9635, or contact APS for media kits or tours at (602) 250-2340. Tom Hahn also can be reached by e-mail at tomhahn@igc.apc.org. The house is located at:

15241 N. 60th St
Phoenix, Arizona

Eugene's Eco-House

Eugene, Oregon's Eco-House recently received an environmental certification from the Rogue Institute for Ecology and Economy (Ashland, OR). After framing the Eco-House with selectively cut, second-growth Douglas fir, the builders made double-wide walls filled with cellulose insulation and a concrete floor with heating tubes running through it. These heating tubes keep the room warm by carrying water heated by a rooftop solar water heater. The materials used in construction were either low- or non-toxic (Hammer, February 1, 1995).

Real Goods' Tour of Independent Homes

Every year, the Real Goods Trading Company, the largest seller of renewable energy materials, helps to organize the National Tour of Independent Homes. This tour is hosted by those willing to open their homes to outsiders to show off their solar, wind, and other-powered homes. For a list of the homes nearest you and directions on how to get there, contact Real Goods.

If you are building from scratch or retrofitting an existing structure, build with as little negative impact as possible and as much positive impact as possible. If you're building a new office, make a commitment to regenerate degraded land by building on already ruined land. Whenever you can, leave it better than you found it.

Wooden structures such as this old Washington State cabin are just what some salvage companies are seeking out.

HELPFUL RESOURCES

INFORMATION

American Institute for Architects
1735 New York Ave., NW
Washington, DC 20006
202-626-7300
Internet: 199.170.0.130/homepage.htm

BJ Harris
Stafford-Harris, Inc.
1916 Pike Place # 705
Seattle, WA 98101-1056
206-688-4042/ Fax: 206-447-1670

Canadian Portland Cement Association
1500 Don Mills Road, Suite 703
Toronto, Ontario M3B 3K4
416-449-3708/ Fax: 416-449-9755

Certification
Two other wood certification organizations are the British SGS Forestry and Canada's Silva Foundation. Their addresses are listed below:

SGS Forestry
Oxford Centre for Innovation
Mill Street

Oxford, OX2 OJX
United Kingdom
+44 (0) 1865-202345
Fax: +44 (0) 1865-790441
Internet:
www.sgs.co.uk/forestry.htm

Silva Forest Foundation
Box 9
Slocan Park
British Columbia
V0G 2E0
604-226-7222/ Fax: 604-226-7446

EcoTimber International
350 Treat Avenue
San Francisco, CA 94110
415-864-4900/ Fax: 415-864-1011
This organization trades only with socially and environmentally responsible, community-based tropical forestry operations. It also has developed a good wood list available to anyone interested. The list includes sources of recycled, salvaged, and ecologically harvest-

ed forest products and names of smart wood organizations.

Environmental Construction Outfitters
44 Crosby Street (near Soho)
New York, NY 10012
212-334-9659/ 800-238-5008

Environmental Home Center (materials for home and office)
1724 4th Avenue South
Seattle, WA 98134
800-281-9785/206-682-7332

Lead information hotline:
800-262-5323

Menominee Tribal Enterprise
P.O. Box 10
Neopit, WI 54150
The Menominee living on their reservation in Wisconsin have been practicing a sustainable forestry program since the 1850s. They have worked carefully to maintain the health of their 220,000-acre stretch of forest and have received certification for their sustainable-forestry-use practices. Not only are they a source of smarter wood, but they are a great source of information.

National Safety Council
Lead information hotline (in English or Spanish):
800-532-3394
Out On Bale (Un)Limited
1037 East Linden Street
Tucson, AZ 85719
602-624-1673
You can subscribe to their straw bale construction newsletter.

Rammed Earth Construction
Two books on rammed earth construction are available from Real Goods Trading Company. They are *Adobe and Rammed Earth Buildings* (Paul Graham McHenry) and *The Rammed Earth House* (David Easton). For online information on rammed earth construction, visit: www.hypersol.com/ecoearth.html

Structural Insulated Panel Association
1511 K Street, NW

townsend, 1996

Real Goods Trading Company's Solar Living Center in Hopland, California, displays smarter building design and is a good source for everything from solar panels to tree-free writing papers and books on smart design.

Washington, D.C. 20005-1401
202-347-7800

Timber Grading
Timber Products Inspection
503-254-0204
Grades salvaged lumber.

West Coast Lumber Inspection Bureau
503-639-0651
Grades salvaged lumber.

U.S. Green Building Council
1615 L Street, NW
Suite 1200
Washington, D.C. 20036-5601
202-778-0760/ Fax: 202-463-0678

or: 505 Sansome Street, 6th Floor
San Francisco, CA 94111-2790
415-398-3900/ Fax: 415-398-3980

Yestermorrow Design/ Build School
RR 1, Box 97-5
Warren, VT 05674
802-496-5545/ Fax: 802-496-5540

PRODUCTS

For addresses and phone numbers, refer to *Appendix A: Directory of Suppliers.*

BOARDS
Advanced Wood Resources
Boise Cascade Timber and Wood Products
Domtar
Environmental Construction Outfitters
Evanite Fiber Corp.
Homasote Co.
Louisiana-Pacific Corp.
Meadowood Industries, Inc.
Medite Corp.
Rodman Industries
Trendway
Wood Recycling, Inc.

BRICKS/BLOCKS
Rastra Building Systems, Inc.

CABINETS
Becker Zeyko
Canac Cabinets
Crystal Cabinet Works
The Masters Corporation
Millbrook Custom Kitchens
Neff Kitchens
Quality Custom Cabinetry
St. Charles Manufacturing Co.
Woodmode

CONCRETE PRODUCTS
Lite-Form, Inc.
North American Cellular Concrete

DOMESTIC WOOD
Aged Woods, Inc.
Almquist Lumber
Andy Johanneson
The Brightwork Oat and Lumber Company
Caldwell Building Wreckers
Collins Pine Co.
Duluth Timber Co.
Evenson, Michael
Forest Trust Wood Products Brokerage
Goodwind Heartpine Co.
Into the Woods
Jefferson Recycled Woodworks
The Joinery Co.
Mack, Steve P. and Associates
Menominee Tribal Enterprises
Mountain Lumber

Pittsford Lumber
Southern Humboldt Builders Supply
Super Tech Wood
Tosten Brothers Saw Mill
Trade Winds HCR
Under the Canopy
Urban Ore
Wesco Used Lumber
Wild Iris Forestry

ENGINEERED WOOD
AFM Corporation
Agriboard Industries, L.C.
Bellcomb Technologies
Gridcore Systems International
Homasote Company
Integrid Building Systems
MacMillan-Bloedel
Trus-Joist MacMillan
Mansion Industries, Inc.
Master Builder Technologies
Mobil Chemical Co.
Composite Products Division
Phenix Biocomposites

Fiberboard
Gridcore Systems International
Homasote
Medite
Natural Fiber Boards, LC
Phenix Biocomposites
Rodman Industries

FINISHES
Wood Siding Finishes
<u>Natural Finishes</u>
Auro, Sinan Co.
Eco Design
Low-VOC Finishes
Kaupert Chemical & Consulting, Inc.

Floor Finishes
<u>Natural Finishes</u>
Auro, Sinan Co.
Eco Design

<u>Natural Varnishes</u>
Auro, Sinan Co.
Eco Design

<u>Low-VOC Finishes</u>
AFM Enterprises, Inc.
Henry Flack International
Marc's Furniture Restoration
Skanvahr Coatings

Water Tech Finishes

Furniture & Woodwork
Natural Finishes
Auro, Sinan Co.
Eco Design
William Zinsser & Co.

Low-VOC Finishes
AFM Enterprises, Inc.
Henry Flack International
Marc's Furniture Restoration
Skanvahr Coatings
Water Tech Finishes

GROUTS
AFM Enterprises, Inc.
American Olean Tile
Auro, Sinan Co.
Bostik
C-Cure Chemical Co.
H. B. Fuller Company
North American Adhesives

INSULATED PANELS
W.H. Porter, Inc.

JOINT COMPOUND
AFM Enterprises, Inc.
M-100 HiPO Joint Compound
Murco Wall Products

KITCHEN/BATH
Allmilmo Corp.
American Council for an Energy-Efficient Economy
Avonite, Inc.
Becker Zyko Kitchens
Bosch Custom Kitchens
Frigidaire Co.
Planetary Solutions
Real Goods Trading Corp.
Santana, Inc.
Sunfrost Refrigerator
Syndesis
Whirlpool Fulfillment
Appliance Information Service

METALS
American Iron and Steel Institute
Angeles Metal Systems
Clean Way Co. (Lead Alert kits)
Copper Development
Association, Inc.
Hybrivet Systems, Inc.
Maze Nails

Pace Environs, Inc.
Safer Home Test Kit

OTHER MATERIALS
Avonite, Inc.
Domtar
Re-Source Building Products Ltd.
Resource Conservation Technology, Inc.
Syndesis

PANELS
Advanced Wood Resources
AFM Corporation
AgriBoard Industries
Architectural Forest Enterprises
Bellcomb Technologies
Eternit, Inc.
Evanite Fiber Corporation
Fibrelam
Homasote Company
Louisiana-Pacific
Mansion Industries
Meadowood Industries
Medite Corporation
PanTerre American, Inc.
Sea-Star Trading Co.
Simplex Products
Weyerhaeuser

PAVEMENT
Pavestone Company
Uni-Group USA

PLASTIC LUMBER
Aeolian Enterprises, Inc.
AERT
Aldan Lane Company
American Recreational Products
Bedford Industries, Inc.
TW Industries, Inc.
Carrysafe
Coon Manufacturing
Custom Materials
Duratech Industries
Eaglebrook Products
Earth Care Products
Earth Safe
Eco-Tech LP
Environmental Recovery Systems
Environmental Recycling, Inc.
Envirowood Corp.
Hammer's Plastic Recycling
International Plastics
Iowa Plastics, Inc.
Mobil Oil Corporation

NEW Plastics Corp.
Plastic Lumber Co.
Plastic Pilings, Inc.
Recycled Plastics Industries, Inc.
Recycled Polymer Associates
St. Jude Polymer Corp.
Superwood of Alabama
Trimax of Long Island
United Sanitation
U.S. Plastic Lumber Corp.
Westmont Building Products

PLASTIC PROCESSING EQUIPMENT
International Plastics Equipment Ltd.
(formerly Humphrey Plastic Machinery)

PLUMBING
Englehard Corp.
21st Century Water Systems
Vital Systems

PLYWOOD
Molding and Millwork
Bainings Community-Based Ecoforestry Project
Chinquapin Mountain Designs
Colonial Craft
A. E. Sampson & Son

PRESSURE-TREATED LUMBER
AFM
Auro/Sinan Co.
The Bio-Integral Resource Center
Eco Design
Etex Ltd.
JH Baxter
Live Oak Structural
Perma-Chink Systems
Tallon Termite
Watershed Sales Corp.

RECYCLED STEEL
American Stud Co.
Angeles Metal Systems
Approved Equal
California Building Systems
CEMCO
John W. Hancock, Jr.
Knorr Steel Framing Systems
Steeler
U.S. Posco
Vulcraft
Western Metal Lath

ROOFING/SIDING
Abitibi-Price Corp.

AFM
Auro/Sinan Co.
Eternit, Inc.
G.E. Plastics Roofing Systems
G.E.S. Roofing
Homasote Co.
James Hardie Building Products
Maxi Tile
Metal Sales Manufacturing
Resource Conservation Technology, Inc.
Thermo Products

SEALANT
Natural Sealants
Auro Sinan Co.
Eco Design

Low-VOC Sealants
AFM Enterprises
Environmental Construction Outfitters
Gloucester Company
W. F. Taylor

Foundation Sealers
AFM Enterprises, Inc.

Masonry Sealers
Low-VOC Sealers
AFM Enterprises, Inc.
Kaupert Chemical & Consulting, Inc.
Skanvahr Coatings

Foam Tape Gaskets
Denarco, Inc.
Will-Seal, Illbruck/USA

SHINGLES
Industries Maibec, Inc.

TILES
Hot Stuff Glass Works

TROPICAL WOODS
Architectural Forest Enterprises
Crosscut Hardwoods
John Curtis
Cut & Dried Hardwoods
Ecological Trading Co., Ltd.
Ecotimber International
Edensaw Woods
Gilmer Wood
Handloggers Hardwood Lumber
I & J Construction
Northern Hardwood Lumber
Pittsford Lumber

Rio Rivuma
Uniquely Australian
Wildwoods Co.
Wilson Woodworks
Wise Woods
Woodcastle Forest Products
Wooden Workbench
Woodworkers Source

WALLBOARD

Agriboard Industries
Domtar Gypsum
Eternit, Inc.
G-P Gypsum Corporation
Homasote Company
Louisiana-Pacific
Meadowood Industries
Niagara Fiberboard, Inc.
US Gypsum

WALL COMPONENTS

Ener-Grid
Faswall Building Systems
K&B Associates

WINDOWS/DOORS

Architectural Openings, Inc.
Southwall Technologies

SUMMARY OF RECOMMENDATIONS

MATERIALS

• When retrofitting existing buildings, recycle as much of the discarded materials as possible.

• Use non-toxic, recycled materials.

SITING

• In locating your business, look for positive aspects, such as public transportation, recycling programs, bicycle access, and sources of organic foods.

• Be sure to properly site the building, taking advantage of its natural surroundings.

• Learn about and support the area's plants, animals, soil type, and groundwater.

• Be aware of the local air and water quality.

• If you can, undo some of the damage of those who came before you.

CHAPTER 10

SMARTER CARPETS & FLOORING

"The nation's largest cancer research laboratory is the American workplace."
Susan Q. Stranahan, *Philadelphia Inquirer*, 15 March 1975 (quoted in Rodes and Odell, 141)

As you are well aware by now, the materials that fill your office can be a big problem to you and your employees. Contemporary furniture and carpeting can cause both health problems associated with indoor air pollution and pollution throughout their life cycles, from their manufacturing to their discard. They often contain volatile organic compounds (VOCs), which are toxic compounds found in carpets, glues, wallcoverings, furniture, and other products.

You might think that once furniture is made or once paint dries, the VOCs are no longer harmful. Unfortunately, they can continue to offgas, meaning that they are emitted into the air in a gaseous state. We breathe them in, and they settle on exposed areas of skin. VOCs are a main contributor to indoor air pollution. In some cases, the offgassing from formaldehyde in furniture has been known to increase over time rather than decrease.

Prolonged exposure to VOCs can make people ill (the length of time varies from individual to individual), and many companies have had employees become sick from VOC exposure. Depending on the individual, physical reactions can be almost immediate or may take years to develop. The problems resulting from exposure to VOCs can include cancer, immune system problems, and fetal development defects. For more information about VOCs, toxic environments, and resulting health problems, turn to Chapter 8, "The Costs of an Unhealthy Workplace."

CARPETS

PROBLEM CARPETS

Now, Americans spend an estimated $8.5 billion each year on carpeting, and a large part of this is used to furnish offices. Less than 200 years ago, if floors had any covering, it was generally canvas or grass mats. Then, about 150 years ago, the U.S. carpet industry began to grow, making carpets of only cotton, wool, and other natural fibers.

Now, synthetic carpets make up the majority of U.S. carpeting, with about 80% of carpet fibers being made of nylon and about 20% made of plastics. Although carpets using these synthetic fibers are durable and fairly inexpensive, they often are one of the biggest sources of toxins contributing to Sick Building Syndrome and poor indoor air quality.

In 1987, the Environmental Protection Agency decided to re-carpet its Washington, D.C., headquarters. Afterward, about 10% of the employees had medical

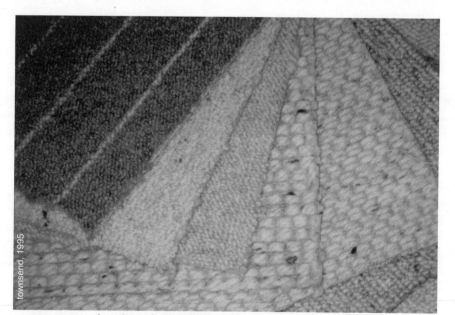
townsend, 1995

A variety of natural, non-toxic carpeting is available.

complaints, ranging from an inability to concentrate to blurred or double vision, depression, coughs, chest tightness, fever, burning eyes, nausea, and numbness. Some had reactions so severe as to warrant hospitalization, and some never went back to work in the building again. This has been one of the most publicized carpet stories to date, it is far from being the only one. For information on how some chemicals can affect human health, see Chapter 8, "The Costs of An Unhealthy Office."

Toxic materials are common in carpets. Chemicals are used for many reasons, from stain resistance, dye retention, and mildew and mold prevention to fire retardants. These chemicals include formaldehyde, pesticides used for mothproofing wool carpets, and plastics (acrylonitrile, latex, nylon, polyester, polyurethane, polyvinyl chloride (PVC), and vinyl chloride). In addition, synthetic, wall-to-wall carpeting is often glued to the flooring beneath it. Generally, the glues are highly toxic and off-gas, making those installing carpets and those working around them more susceptible to health problems.

Additionally, the backing found on synthetic carpeting usually includes polyester finished with formaldehyde, a chemical to which many are sensitive. Carpets also can contain 4-Phenylcyclohexane (4-PC), a compound found to be problematic in the EPA's carpet installation. Unfortunately, this compound has been hard to test for. It is so unstable that it sometimes breaks down into styrene and butadiene fragments during testing. It took some time before analysts realized that these fragments were from 4-PC decomposition. Instead, they thought that the victims' medical problems arose from styrene.

The existence of 4-PC in carpets is unintended by manufacturers. When a carboxylated styrene-butadiene (SB) latex is applied as the carpet's backing to hold its fibers together, a chemical reaction occurs between the styrene and butadiene to create the polymer that holds the carpet together. Simultaneously, some of these two chemicals form 4-PC.

All carpets using SB latex (about 95% of all U.S.-made carpet) give off some 4-PC. Resulting symptoms from exposure can include headaches, dizziness, fatigue, irritability, anxiety, feeling cold, dermatitis, vertigo, insomnia, thirst, and even hallucinations. Chemically, 4-PC is similar in composition to 1-phenylcyclohexane (1-PC), which is formed when PCP ("angel dust") is heated. It is possible that 4-PC causes psychological activity like 1-PC does.

In addition to the health problems associated with chemical-laden carpets, another concern with carpeting is the large amount of water consumed during carpet manufacture. One square yard of carpet takes about 15 gallons of water to produce.

Since about 1.1 billion square yards of carpet were manufactured in the U.S. in 1990, you can estimate that about 16 billion gallons of water were used in the process. Carpets that are batch-dyed can use three to four times that water during the dyeing process.

Synthetic carpets and those impregnated with chemicals also contribute to air pollution, ozone depletion, disposal problems, and our demand for petroleum (although some plastic carpets now are being recycled).

SMARTER CARPET ALTERNATIVES

If you have been working around a synthetic carpet that is over five years old, it probably has finished offgassing. Otherwise, untreated, natural carpeting and flooring is the smartest way to go. You can find carpeting made of 100% cotton, wool, or natural plant fibers (some are made as soft as regular carpeting, and some are stiffer and feel more like dried, woven grass).

Some of the healthier, durable alternatives include carpeting that is made out of 100% wool. These are available dyed, undyed, or without added chemicals. They can be custom-made to suit your workspace size. While some may run about $2-3 more per square yard than synthetic carpets, wool carpets last much longer, are naturally fireproof, and, without added chemicals, are much healthier to work around. Some wool carpets are available with fire retardant – probably more to adhere to carpeting standards than anything else. However, I'm told that wool does not burn well – it only chars.

For a healthier wool carpet, consider one with a backing made of jute, a natural fiber. You can tack carpets to the floor instead of gluing them to avoid the toxins that off-

Cork is just one of many smarter flooring materials available.

townsend, 1995

These carpets are made of recycled materials.

SMARTER FLOORING ALTERNATIVES

If you are in the market for a new type of flooring, there are many healthier alternatives available today. For example, cork and cork-based linoleum (a common flooring material originating in Europe) are natural, non-toxic products. Coir, seagrass, and sisal are other smarter flooring options. Rubber flooring can be made of recycled tires or virgin, petroleum-based material. Plain, sanded wood floors with non-toxic varnish are another alternative to carpeting.

gas from the glue. Also, consider using cotton and wool area rugs. One company, Hendricksen Naturlich, is a great source for chemical-free carpets and flooring. As far as carpet pads go, you may want to consider one made of jute or other natural fibers. Some products (e.g., Carpet Guard) can be sprayed onto synthetic carpets to minimize their offgassing for a while. Consider using an odor-free, dye-free shampoo.

There is another option that is becoming increasingly popular. Since carpets can wear out in five years, many companies lease them. That means that the carpet companies are responsible for maintaining the carpet during its lifetime and then taking it back when its life is over. Carpet tiles, small squares of carpet, are making one-piece carpets obsolete. Worn or soiled tiles can be replaced easily and save users from having to replace entire carpets because of a few bad spots.

FLOORING

COSTLY FLOORING

Like carpets, synthetic floor tiles have been known to cause problems. The culprits may not be just the tiles themselves but also the glues holding them down. Many contain VOCs and are highly toxic. If you work in a building with poor air quality and little ventilation, you could be at risk especially when new flooring is installed.

Synthetic floor polishes can offgas toxins, too. Most aerosol floor and furniture polishes contain silicone (plastic). They make wood shine but don't nourish it or allow moisture to evaporate. Additionally, some aerosols contain ozone-layer-damaging CFC propellants.

Ceramic tiles can be a good choice for flooring. To avoid toxic dyes and glazes, you can use natural, unglazed tiles. Fortunately, most ceramic tile producers incorporate recycled glass into their tiles for a better depth of color and recycle their waste tiles into their new tiles. As far as laying tiles goes, mortars and thinset mortars are better and less toxic in both their manufacture and their use than are resin adhesives.

One new flooring product is called plyboo. Imported from China, plyboo is made from bamboo and is tougher than most hardwood floors, including teak, cherry, and walnut. It's priced competitively with red oak, which is one of the hardwood floor sources most often used.

Plyboo is more environmentally friendly than wood from trees. This is because its source, bamboo, is a fast-growing grass that can be cut every four years. Mature stands of bamboo grow to 40 feet high with stalks six inches across. (And, when the bamboo is cut, it doesn't need to be replanted as do trees but grows back, preventing erosion that is associated with deforestation.) Of course, using the fast-growing bamboo wood makes more sense than using much slower-growing trees.

Stone is a durable flooring material. Because it is so heavy, transportation costs can be quite high, and it is fragile in transport. In addition, most stones, with the exception of granite and a few other very hard materials, need to be sealed against stains. When using stone, be sure that it does not come from a site with much radon. One drawback of using virgin stone is the environmental degradation in and around the quarry site.

Here are a few other flooring alternatives:
• Armourtile is a linoleum tile made of natural materials.
• Marmoleum, made by Forbo Industries, is one smarter flooring product that is available in tiles or linoleum. It

townsend, 1995

townsend, 1995

Flooring made of recycled materials, from crushed lightbulbs to old tires, is available in a variety of colors, designs, and textures.

is made of natural products such as linseed oil, cork, wood flour, and rosin binders. Dry pigments are mixed in as well, and the linoleum is put onto natural jute backing. The tiles are put onto a polyglass backing.
• Chicago Art Glass makes ceramic tiles.
• Mai'bec Corporation's wood flooring is made of 100% recycled (pre-consumer) wood that is left over from the manufacture of wood furniture.
• Prominence Tile is made by GTE Products Corporation. This glass-based ceramic tile is made using recycled GTE lightbulbs. Although it is more expensive than some tiles, it is known for its durability and does not chip easily. So, it should not need to be replaced as often.

• Syndecrete Studio's tile is made of fly ash, portland cement, and aggregate.
• Terra-Green Technologies' Traffic Tiles are ceramic tiles made from over 70% recycled glass. The pigment is mixed in.
• Rubber flooring also is available from Endura. It comes in solids, with flecks, and is textured.

Another type of flooring that may be of interest to you is the Silent Floor. Its manufacture requires about one-third less wood than most floors. It is made of wood scraps but does contain a lot of glue. Apparently, it off-gasses formaldehyde, and its use would call for sealing it to cut down on the indoor air pollution. This is one good reminder that just because a product is recycled or all natural doesn't mean that it was manufactured to be non-toxic, too. Always check first.

The EPA's government procurement requirement for floor tiles in heavy-duty, commercial applications is for recycled rubber with 90-100% recycled content and recycled plastic with 90-100% recovered content.

HELPFUL RESOURCES

INFORMATION

Air Quality Sciences
404-933-0638
Environmental Bamboo Foundation
www.kauai.net/bambooweb/whybamboo.html

Carpet & Rug Institute
310 Holiday Dr.
Dalton, GA 30220
800-882-8846/ 706-278-3176

Consumer Product Safety Commission
800-638-2772

EPA Employees
202-260-2383

National Center for Environmental Health Strategies
1100 Rural Avenue

Vorhees, NJ 08043
609-429-5358

Wool Bureau, Inc.
240 Peachtree Street, NW
Atlanta, GA 30303
404-524-0512/ Fax: 404-659-6974

PRODUCTS

For addresses and phone numbers, refer to *Appendix A: Directory of Suppliers.*

CARPETS
Carpet Tile Leasing
Interface Flooring Systems

Low-Emission Synthetic Carpets
Collins & Aikman
Floor Coverings Div.
Sutherland Carpet Mills
Talisman Mills
Wellman, Inc.

Natural Fiber (Wool/Plant)
Allegro Rug Weaving
Allure Rug Studio
Bellbridge, Inc.
Bremworth Carpets
Carousel Carpets
Carter Carpets
CDC Carpets & Interiors
Colin Campbell & Sons
Corniche Carpet Mills
Dellinger, Inc.
Design Materials, Inc.
Desso Carpets
Eco-Container Corp.
Environmental Construction Outfitters
Floorworks
Foreign Accent
Harbinger
Helios Carpets
Jack Lenor Larsen
Merida Meridian
Naturlich
Prestige Mills
Gordon T. Sands
Alison T. Seymour
Spectra, Inc.
Vanbesuw

Natural or Recycled Synthetic Underlayment
Chris Craft Industrial Products, Inc.
Dodge-Regupol
Dura Undercushion
Homasote Company
R.B. Rubber Products
Gordon T. Sands
Sutherland Carpet Mills

Products (Sealants, etc.)
AFM
Bentley Mills
Collins and Aikman, Floor Coverings Division
Du Pont Flooring Systems
Envirowise
Harbinger Company
Helios
Horizon
Interface Research
Tack Fast
United Recycled, Inc.
US Axminster, Inc.

Recycled Content Carpets
BASF
Carpet Cushion Associates
Chris Craft Industrial Products, Inc.
Hoechst-Celanese
Homasote Co.
Image Industries

FLOORING & PRODUCTS
Ceramic/Glass Tiles
AFM
Bedrock Industries
Crossville Ceramics
Master Builder Technologies, Inc.
Metropolitan Ceramics
Summitville Tile
Syndesis
Terra-Green Technologies

Cork/Linoleum
Bangor Cork Co.
Corticeira Amorim
Dodge-Regupol, Inc.
Environmental Flooring Products
EX
Forbo Industries, Inc.
Gerbert Limited
Global Technology Systems
Naturlich
Non-Toxic Environments

Low-VOC Adhesives
AFM Enterprises, Inc.
Earthbond 7000
Franklin International
Environmental Construction Outfitters
North American Adhesives
W. F. Taylor Co., Inc.

Natural Adhesives
Auro, Sinan Co.

Related Products
AFM
Auro/Sinan
Bomanite Corporation
Chicago Adhesive Products Co.
Flecto
Gloucester Company
Roberts Consolidated Industries
Syndesis
United Recycling, Inc.
W.F. Taylor Co.

Rubber/Recycled Rubber
Carlisle Tire & Rubber
Mat Factory, Inc.
RB Rubber Products
Tarkett, Inc.
Yemm & Hart

Wood
AFM
Aged Woods
Amati bambu (bamboo)
Basic Coatings
Bonakemi USA, Inc.
Eco Design
EcoTimber International
G.R. Plume Company
Jefferson Recycled Woodworks
Junckers Danish Beech Flooring
Mai'bec Corporation
The Roof Tile & Slate Company
Smith & Fong Company (bamboo)
Texas Kiln Products

SUMMARY OF RECOMMENDATIONS

INSTALLATION

• Tack flooring down rather than gluing it.

• Consider scoring and/or staining concrete floors (particularly if they have access to the sun) to look like tiles to save money on special flooring and take advantage of their ability to collect warmth during the day and release it at night.

MATERIALS

• Go for carpets and flooring that contain no (or few) toxins and are made of renewable/natural or recycled materials.

• Take advantage of carpet tiles or area rugs that can be replaced in high traffic areas rather than buying a one-piece carpet.

• Avoid carpets and flooring containing formaldehyde and other toxic chemicals.

• Use non-toxic carpet and floor cleaners.

• Seal carpets and flooring that contain chemicals that may offgas.

CHAPTER 11

SMARTER PAINTS & WALLCOVERINGS

"While we plan and decorate with meticulous care, we often then proceed to fill [buildings] with unnoticed chemical vapours and electrical pollution, leaving ourselves disoriented, confused, and frustrated."
Pearson, 62

PAINTS

Unfortunately, paints and wallcoverings often are sources of indoor air pollution. Most paints are made with petrochemicals, which are non-renewable and toxic. Exposure to them for prolonged periods can be unhealthy. In addition, paints also contain pigments that can be toxic. For instance, the pigment for white used to come from lead. Now, it generally comes from titanium dioxide. Aside from being a pigment, lead also acts as a drying agent. Due to its toxicity, it has been removed from most paints, but other products have taken its place. Now, cadmium, another toxic element, is often used as an alternative drying agent to lead.

Oil-based (gloss) paints can be highly toxic. They tend to have much larger amounts of solvents, which make paint flow smoothly, than do water-based, (latex) paints. They also contain alkyds, synthetic, resinous binders that allow pigment dispersion. Alkyds are created when oil (usually soya oil) combines with chemical additives to form polymers (chemical chains). One British study showed 93% of the professional painters studied exhibited symptoms of solvent poisoning.

For flexibility and durability, plastics such as acrylic, vinyl, and polyvinyl chloride (PVC) also are added to paints. Unfortunately, these plastics don't allow wood to "breathe" or for any moisture to evaporate. Fungicides and preservatives are added as well. Exterior, masonry, and wood paints also contain mold inhibitors (espe-

Kurfees is one manufacturer of smarter paints.

townsend, 1995

cially dodecyclamine, a known irritant), solvents, and fungicides.

Even if you recycle your paint leftovers, be aware that much of the paint that is collected with other hazardous waste ends up incinerated or put into a landfill. As for paint removal, conventional paint stripper is one of the most toxic things that you can use in a building. One solvent used in paint strippers is dichloromethane (methylene chloride). This substance creates toxic fumes, burns skin, and, if the fumes are near an ignition source, a toxic phosgene gas is created. Sodium hydroxide, a toxic substance, is another ingredient found in paint strippers.

Just as with synthetic paints and paint strippers, paint thinners can cause health problems. Although turpentine (distilled from pine resin) was once the paint thinner of popularity, synthetics made from petrochemicals (e.g., turpentine substitute, white spirit) have become competitive forces in the market. However, white spirit, with prolonged exposure, is related to both severe dermatitis and severe nervous-system damage. If you have to use these products, open the windows for plenty of fresh air, don't inhale much, and keep these substances off of your skin.

SMARTER PAINT ALTERNATIVES

A number of paint companies have begun making better, non-synthetic paints. Natural paints, for example, are made with citrus-oil solvents rather than petrochemicals. They get their colors from minerals and clays, not the heavy metals like cadmium that other paints contain. They also don't have the toxic fungicides, mildewcides, and preservatives that the synthetic paints contain.

Two German companies, Auro and Eco Design (formerly Livos), are good sources of natural paints. Eco Design uses natural ingredients to make everything from oil- and water-based paints and varnishes to wood stains, shellacs, glues, soaps, cleansers, and products for furniture and leather care.

If you don't want chemicals or plastics in your paint, you also can go for a casein (milk enzyme) emulsion and limewash or distemper. There is something you should know about natural paints. They contain different ingredients than their synthetic counterparts and may have different application needs. Be certain to read the directions before using them.

Also, be careful when you're shopping for paints. Some paints may say that they are low-odor, but they may not be free of toxic solvents. Even though a paint says that it's made out of natural products, read the

Milk Paint is one alternative to conventional paints.

ingredients. Although it uses natural oils and ingredients, one European company's paints have high VOCs and odor. (It's not listed in the "Helpful Resources" section of this chapter.)

Kurfees, one U.S. company, makes a popular hypo-allergenic, latex paint. It has almost no VOCs, nearly no odor, and has a high scrubability. Safecoat also makes a good paint; while more expensive, it is considered one of the best for those with high chemical sensitivity.

A few paint companies, including the Green Paint Company, Rasmussen Paints, Major Paint Company, and E Coat use discarded paints to make various shades of whites, browns, grays, and other colors.

Skanvahr, a company based in Washington State, makes wood floor and cabinet varnishes. These varnishes have a low VOC content and little odor, rapidly offgas, and are said to be of high quality.

If you need to use paint stripper, be sure that you find one made without dichloromethane, or caustic soda, and that is low-VOC. One brand, Citrus Strip, is synthetic, but it has no methyl chlorides.

As far as paint thinners go, pure turpentine is safer than many other types. Thinners made with citrus oils tend to be good since they can be produced without pesticides and tend to dry more quickly than other alternatives; they clean brushes, too. Citrus paint thinners are good alternatives for those sensitive to turpentine.

WALLCOVERINGS

Wallpaper can be another source of indoor pollution at work. For instance, wallpapers made of vinyl – while easy to keep clean – offgas and are sources of indoor pollution as well as pollution created during their manufacture. In addition, wallpaper glues offgas and can contribute to indoor air quality problems.

Rather than using conventional wallpaper, you may want to consider using faux finishes, non-toxic paints, or stencilling with non-toxic colors. Otherwise, there is a variety of better wallpapers to choose from – they're made from everything from plant fibers and cork to linen.

Several paint products are available that are made of non-toxic or natural materials.

HELPFUL RESOURCES

PRODUCTS

For addresses and phone numbers, refer to *Appendix A: Directory of Suppliers.*

Exterior Cleaning Products
Armor All

PAINTS
Low-Biocide/Low-VOC Paints
AFM Enterprises
Benjamin Moore Paints
Best Paint Co.
Bonakemi USA, Inc.
Chem-Safe Products
Ecos Paint
Ecowise
Environmental Technology
The Glidden Co.
Kurfees Paints
Miller Paint Co.
Murco Wall Products
Nigra Enterprises
Pace Chem
Sherwin Williams
Weather Bos
William Zinsser Co

Natural Paints
Auro, Sinan Co.
Eco Design
Old Fashioned Milk Paint Co.
Sun Frog Products
Tulip (Authentic Milk Paint)
Weather-Bos Stains and Paint

Paint Strippers
AFM Enterprises
Auro, Sinan Co.
Eco Design
Dumond Chemicals
Klean Strip
Savogran
Specialty Environmental Technologies, Inc.

Recycled Paints
Kelly-Moore Paint Co.

Whitewash Paints
Auro Natural Chalk Water Paint
Eco Design Albion White Wash Paint

SEALANTS
Encapsulation Technologies Corp.
Kaupert Chemical & Consulting, Inc.
Pace Chemical Industries
Palmer Industries, Inc.
Safer Home Test Kit

WALLCOVERINGS
Alteschuler Wallpapers
Crown Corporation, NA
Design Materials, Inc.
Euro-Tap
Ex
Fabritex, Inc.
Flexi Wall Systems
Roman Adhesives, Inc.
Maya Romanoff Corp.
Swede-Tech

NATURAL/LOW-VOC ADHESIVES
AMF Enterprises, Inc.
Auro, Sinan Co.
Eco Design
ICI
Roman Adhesives, Inc.

Summary of Recommendations

PAINTS

• Use paints made of non-toxic, natural ingredients.

• Avoid paints containing heavy metals, formaldehyde, and other toxins that can create physical harm to those who apply it and to those who work near it.

• Consider using non-toxic products for stenciling and to create faux finishes.

• When in the market for paint strippers, try to avoid those containing methyl chlorides (e.g., dichloromethane) and that have high VOCs.

• Go for paint thinners made of citrus oil rather than synthetics and petroleum products.

WALLCOVERINGS

• Avoid plastic wallcoverings, which rely on non-renewable products for their manufacture, can offgas, and are non-recyclable.

• When applying wallcoverings, look for non-toxic adhesives. You also may want to consider tacking them into place.

• Consider using natural fiber wallcoverings that will add texture without creating indoor air quality problems.

CHAPTER 12

SMARTER FURNITURE

> *"In the future, we want to change the expression "Knock on wood" to "Knock on bamboo."*
> Dean Sanaee, Amati Bambu

FURNITURE

Furniture can be expensive. Not only do you have to pay the direct cost, or purchase price, when you buy your furniture, but somebody, possibly you, may have to incur the indirect costs of your furniture – the maintenance costs and the potential costs of employee health problems and environmental degradation.

For instance, much of today's furniture is impregnated with volatile organic compounds. These compounds include such poisonous solvents as toluene, benzene, and xylene. The pressed wood found in some furniture

Trees are great sinks for carbon dioxide, helping to prevent global warming.

and wallboard contains these VOCs. If you do decide to purchase something made of pressed wood, check into the toxicity of the glues used. You may want to look for healthier alternatives instead.

Aside from health risks, there are other things that should be taken into consideration when purchasing furniture and other wood products. You may want to ask the following questions:

Is this product made from recycled wood or virgin timber? If it's from virgin timber, how was the wood harvested?

It is important to find out if the timber-harvesting was done in a way that would support the continuation of a healthy forest. In other words, were the trees clear-cut, or were they selectively cut? Clear-cutting leaves no habitat for resident animals, insects, and other plants dependent upon the trees' shade and ability to hold moisture with their roots; it also causes erosion and the resulting loss of topsoil that is necessary for the healthy growth of new trees or other plants. If the trees were carefully and selectively cut, taking some and leaving some in a way that supports the health of the forest, then forest regeneration has a better chance of occurring. There are an increasing number of forests that are certified as having only sustainably harvested wood – Wisconsin's Menominee Tribal Enterprise is one.

Did the wood come from threatened or endangered tree species?

Find out about your wood product's origin. Some furniture dealers may not know or may not tell you if you are purchasing furniture from an endangered species or one whose harvesting practices are ecologically detrimental. Check with one of the smart wood organizations listed below before you buy. If you buy furniture made of a threatened or endangered tree species, you're helping to create a market demand for the extinction of rare species. Some scientists have estimated that one species' extinction results in the extinction of over 40 other species dependent upon it for their survival, so it's vital that we all tread as lightly as possible.

From where (geographically) did the wood come?

Be aware of the source of your furniture. The long-distance transportation of exotic woods requires more fuel and labor than that of more local species. Also, in some regions around the world, there are disputes over land ownership and rights to the forests and other resources. Poor working conditions are, unfortunately, still an issue. Try to check with one of the smart wood organizations to be sure that you're not supporting unhealthy logging and furniture manufacturing operations.

Many factors need to be taken into account when deciding which woods to use. Taking down trees often has economic, environmental, social, and legal ramifications for communities living in or around the logging regions. Irresponsible forestry practices can lead to the loss of cultural integrity, biological diversity, and topsoil upon which peoples' livelihoods and the health of the forest depend.

SOME SMARTER FURNITURE EXAMPLES

The wooden desk and chairs on Jay Leno's Tonight Show set were made using sustainably harvested hardwood from EcoTimber International. When the National Audubon Society retrofitted its building, it also was very careful in choosing its new furnishings. Their non-toxic furnishings included:

- Aluminum/steel chairs with low-toxic fabric and toluene-free foam padding made without CFCs
- Rubberized components in place of PVC plastic ones
- Recycled steel workstation shelving
- Recycled PET plastic bathroom countertops
- Sustainably grown North American cherry and tropical rainforest mahogany (purchased through the Rainforest Alliance's Smart Wood program) furniture. This was for environmentally responsible reasons and to support the market for sustainable forestry.

townsend, 1994

Office furniture made of recycled materials comes in many styles.

Some furniture companies have made smart changes in their raw-material acquisition, manufacturing, packaging, and refurbishing methods. Those using environmentally responsible woods include Haworth, Herman Miller, Kimball, Knoll, and Steelcase. Since 1988, Haworth also has shipped its furniture in blanketing, thereby cutting its packaging waste by 24 million pounds. Herman Miller has cut back on its VOC emissions simply by burning the VOCs and using the steam generated as heat. The company also purchases and refurbishes its own used office panels, reselling them at considerably lower costs.

In 1990, architect William McDonough, Dean of the University of Virginia's School of Architecture, worked with the Herman Miller furniture company to find sustainably grown and harvested sources of wood. This means that the trees have been grown in an environmentally friendly manner and that their harvest has left their habitat intact. At first, the Herman Miller company believed that the quantity of veneer needed for corporate projects could not be obtained sustainably. However, the company is now fully committed to using only sustainably harvested woods.

McDonough began working to design "furniture using enzymes and agricultural waste and reforming them under heat." As McDonough said, "Forget plastics. When you get rid of something you'll be able to throw it in the garden and it can decay. Wonderful. And there's nothing to kill you" (*Interiors*, "Visionary Architect," March 93, 57).

As mentioned earlier, the offgassing of toxic chemicals from furniture has become an important issue in indoor air quality. Steelcase, a furniture manufacturer, had help from Air Quality Services, Inc., to develop guidelines to rank the emissions of its office furniture lines. Its results were enough of an incentive for it to change the materials and processes it uses to cut back on emissions.

Amati Bambu is making bamboo furniture and flooring as well. Bamboo is a tropical grass characterized by strength, flexibility, and fast growth. It can be stained to match other wood types (e.g., cherry). The varnish is water-based. According to Amati Bambu, there are several advantages to using bamboo. It is:

- "The fastest growing plant on this planet....It grows one-third faster than the fastest growing tree. Some species can grow up to 1 meter per day.
- An enduring natural resource....Bamboo can be easily selectively harvested annually....It can be harvested 3-5 years versus 10-20 years for most softwoods. Bamboo tolerates extremes of precipitation, from 30-250 inches of annual rainfall.
- Bamboo's tensile strength is 28,000 per square inch compared with 23,000 for steel.
- Versatile with a short growth cycle
- An essential structural material in earthquake architecture....In Limon, Costa Rica, only the bamboo houses from the National Bamboo Project stood after their violent earthquake in 1992. Flexible and lightweight bamboo enables structures to endure earthquakes.
- A renewable resource for agroforestry products
- Over 1,000 species of bamboo currently grow on the earth.
- A natural controllable barrier....bamboo provides shade, wind break, acoustical barriers and aesthetic beauty.
- A critical element of the economy....Bamboo and its related industries already provide income, food and housing to over 2.2 billion people worldwide. There is a 3-5 year return on investment for a new bamboo plantation versus 8-10 years for rattan.
- A viable replacement for wood
- A critical element in the balance of oxygen and carbon dioxide in the atmosphere....Bamboo is the fastest growing canopy for the re-greening of degraded reas

A close look at bamboo shows the strong, beautiful grain.

Townsend, 1987

and generates more oxygen than equivalent stand of trees. It lowers light intensity and protects against ultraviolet rays and is an atmospheric and soil purifier" (Amati Bambu fact sheet, 1997).

Fortunately, aside from antiques and secondhand furniture, which take you out of the demand-for-new-resources loop, there is a growing number of sources for smarter furniture.

A FEW WORDS ON UPHOLSTERY

If you're looking for healthier furniture, don't overlook the upholstery. You can go with recycled fiber, looking for chairs covered with recycled PET bottles. Or, you can look for natural fibers.

As far as natural fibers go, try to stay with the organically grown fibers. Cotton is natural, but it is the most pesticide-intensive crop grown in the United States. Obviously, the pesticides impact our water, microorganisms that determine the health of the soil, and human health.

Organically grown cotton, hemp, and other fibers are available as fabric and on already-upholstered furniture. One company, Furnature, was begun as a spinoff from one family's old furniture company after requests from chemically sensitive clients to make something non-toxic.

One cotton, Fox Fibre (Natural Cotton Colors), is grown with the colors in the cotton. In other words, the pale browns, greens, and other colors that come in their cotton are natural tints in the fiber. Using fibers that are naturally tinted avoids the issue of having to use dyes and determining which are healthier than others.

HELPFUL RESOURCES

INFORMATION

Ida Grae has written books on natural dyes, yarns, and weaving, including *Nature's Colors: Dyes from Plants* and *Dressing the Loom*. She has a studio in California, and students that come from around the world. You can contact her at:

Ida Grae
424 LaVerne Avenue
Mill Valley, CA 94941
415-388-6101

Patagonia Public Affairs
Box 150
Ventura, CA 93002
Contact for information on organic cotton.

Pesticide Action Network North America
116 New Montgomery Street
Suite 810
San Francisco, CA 94105
415-541-9140
Contact for information on organic cotton.

PRODUCTS

For addresses and phone numbers, refer to *Appendix A: Directory of Suppliers.*

FABRIC/BEDDING

The Cotton Place
Coyuchi
Crown Bedding Sleep Shops
Deepa Textiles
Designers Fiber Protection
Dona Designs
Ecosport
Exotic Gifts
Fieldcrest Cannon, Inc.
Garnet Hill
Guardian Protection Products, Inc.
Guilford of Maine Textile Resources
Heart of Vermont
Homespun Fabrics & Draperies
Inchcape Laboratories
Interface Research Corp.
Jack Lenor Larsen
The Janice Corp.
J.P. Stevens & Co.
Maharam
The Natural Bedroom
Natural Cotton Colours
Natural Resources
Network/Allergy
Royal-Pedic Mattress
Sunrise Habitat
Sureway Trading
Testfabrics
Thai Silks
West Point Pepperell
Winter Silks

OFFICE FURNITURE

Brayton Int.
Bronx 2000
Contour Paper Products
Eldon Rubbermaid
Executive Office Concepts
Falcon Products
Furnature
Golden Rabbit
Hardware Designs
Haworth, Inc.
Herman Miller
Kimball International
The Knoll Group
Latitude 16 Designs
The Lowenstein Furniture Group
Meridian
MicroCentre
Miller SQA, Inc.
Monel
Nada-Chair
The Naturalist
Pegelli Forest
Dyfed, Wales, England
Contact: Dyfed Wildlife Trust
Poly-Wood
Roche-Bobois
Smith & Hawken
Steelcase, Inc.
Terra Verde
Trendway
Ultracel
Victorian Reproductions
Yemm & Hart

RESIDENTIAL FURNITURE

Agnes Bourne Studios
American Forests
Barlowe Tyrie, Inc.
Cooperative Business International (Indonesia)
Donghia Furniture
Heart of Vermont
Kingsley-Bates, Ltd.
Latitude 16 Designs
Lister
The Natural Bedroom
Nathenson Fine Furnishings
The Plow and Hearth
Pompanoosuc Mills
Ron Fisher
Shaker Shop West
Shaker Workshops
Smith & Hawken
Structural Plastics Corp.
Summit Furniture

Thomas Moser Cabinets
Union Carbide Corp.
Vermont Country Store
Victorian Reproductions
Wambold Furniture
Willsboro Wood Products

NOT EXCLUSIVELY RAINFOREST ALLIANCE-CERTIFIED SMART WOOD PRODUCTS

(Check on the certification of the wood before you buy.)
Michael Elkan Studio
The Libra Company
Summit Furniture, Inc.

UNTREATED/SMARTER UPHOLSTERY FABRIC AND BATTING

Canvasmaker, Inc.
The Cotton Place
Crocodile Tiers
Deepa Textiles
Home Couture, Natural Fabrics
Homespun Fabrics & Draperies
Ida Grae (hand weaving design/instruction)
Janice Corporation
Karen's Non-toxic Products
Jack Lenor Larsen
The Natural Bedroom
Natural Cotton Colours
Quaker Jobbing
Rainbow Organic Fiber Mill
Ruby & Coco
Utex Trading Enterprises
Vermont Country Store

SUMMARY OF RECOMMENDATIONS

DISPOSAL

• When disposing of older furniture, consider donating it to schools, non-profit organizations, homeless shelters, or churches. Or, look for someone who can recycle it.

• Use non-toxic, natural products to clean, polish, and maintain wood and other furniture.

MATERIALS

• Be sure that your furniture will not offgas VOCs, such as formaldehyde, which can make those around it sick.

• Look for furnishings made of recycled products or of all-natural, sustainably harvested wood and other materials.

UPHOLSTERY

• Look for fabrics colored with natural, non-toxic dyes.

• For chairs, sofas, curtains, and other upholstered items, try to find furniture with untreated fabrics that are made of natural fibers. In addition, try to ensure that the fibers were grown without use of toxic pesticides and fertilizers. (For example, unless it's organically grown, cotton is the most pesticide-intensive crop grown in the U.S.)

CHAPTER 13

SMARTER OFFICE SUPPLIES

About 200 square miles of forest are cut every year to make computer printer paper.

Maybe you haven't noticed, but this is a very exciting time in manufacturing. You'll probably tell me that I need to get away more often, but I can't think of too many things that are more exhilarating than learning about smarter office materials. Why? Because smarter office supplies are often like the ones you already use, but they're sporting a new twist – they're recycled and/or less toxic versions of their older counterparts. Smarter office materials are so exciting because they represent some of humankind's best qualities – an enterprising, creative spirit and the desire to make things better than what's already around.

STANDARDS FOR SMARTER PRODUCTS

The degradation of environmental and human health as a result of our technologies and behaviors is very real. Knowing that there are much healthier and, in the long run, less costly alternatives out there is reassuring and can save us all the headache – literally – of working in an unhealthy place.

Often, the basic office supplies that we use are toxic and can add to the overall air quality and health problems in our work environments. Healthier alternatives are available and affordable.

One organization, World Wildlife Fund (WWF) – U.S., created a Green Task Force to examine, among other things, its own purchasing decisions and look for better alternatives to typical office products. As a non-profit, environmental organization, environmental health was a large priority for WWF. But, as a business, the organization was concerned with the bottom line before changing its purchasing decisions. After carrying out an environmental audit and researching its options, WWF found that there were some immediate changes regarding office products that it could make to work toward a healthier office and better environment.

For one, WWF replaced its individual-serving coffee packages (made of mylar and plastic) with bulk coffee measured with scoops. This may seem like a small thing, but when you think of the purchasing power of a large company, it can make a big impact environmentally. Second, purchasing smart also can make it clear to your office-supplies distributors that becoming smart is a high priority for you. Third, buying smart helps to support and establish companies that make smarter products.

And, understanding the high toxicity of chlorine compounds, WWF switched from strictly chlorine-bleached coffee filters to oxygen-bleached ones. In addition, it also uses unbleached paper towels.

One of the strongest bleaching agents used for paper is chlorine (it bleaches fibers very white). Unfortunately, chlorine can mix with the organic compounds found in paper pulp and create organochlorines. Dioxin (2,3,7,8-tetrachlorodibenzo-p-dioxin, or TCDD) is of great concern due to its high toxicity.

These are just a few examples of small purchasing decisions that can make a positive difference. You're not sacrificing and doing without – you're just doing it smarter.

A number of smarter alternatives to the old stand-bys are available. They include 100% recycled, non-rebleached copy paper and legal pads, recycled-paper corrugated shipping boxes, biodegradable sealing tapes, non-toxic, water-based correction fluid, pens made of recycled materials, non-toxic markers, and vegetable-oil-based ink printing in lieu of petroleum-based inks – soy inks rub off less, are environmentally better (cleaner) to make and dispose of, are easier to clean off presses, and are safer for press operators to use. The list is almost endless.

PAPER

We'll begin with paper since it is one of the most heavily used materials in many businesses. In the U.S.,

townsend, 1994

The above is an example of an old deforested area in Washington.

manufacture of virgin paper, one of the most polluting industries around.

In addition, it takes about 10-20 Watt-hours to make one page of plain paper, depending on the mill. It takes about 5 Watt-hours to print on one page using a laser printer and about 2 Watt-hours using an ink jet printer. The energy costs of making paper by conventional methods are high, helping to result in the high purchase price of paper.

It also takes about 7,000 gallons of water to make just one ton of paper. This water, polluted with chemicals such as chlorine (often used in the bleaching process), is then discarded, often into nearby streams and other bodies of water (unless, of course, the chemicals are reused).

alone, so much paper is discarded every year that a 12-foot-high paper wall could be built stretching from New York to Los Angeles.

PAPER COSTS

The costs of paper are tremendous. They include the energy, environmental, and human health costs associated with deforestation (erosion, lost biodiversity, reforestation), transporting timber, processing trees, packaging, storage, transportation of the finished paper to its destination, its use (the energy it takes to print, photocopy, and fax), and recycling/disposal costs (e.g., transport, remanufacture).

Paper is the major "consumable," or product, used in computing and in many businesses. Depending on the industry, annual paper use at work can be as much as 80 pounds per employee, or 8,000 letter-sized (8.5" x 11") sheets reaching almost three feet in height. This only includes printing and writing papers, not thermal (fax), packaging, or other papers (ACEEE, 1996, 69).

Nearly half of all U.S. solid waste is made of paper. Although recycling programs have grown considerably, some studies show that only about 20% of virgin, high-grade paper is recycled from commercial offices (ACEEE, 1996, 70). The EPA has estimated that paper is the main component in domestic landfills, half of which are expected to be filled and require closure by some time in 1997. The tree fiber used goes into the

Dioxin, a by-product of the chlorine-bleaching process that makes paper very white, is highly carcinogenic. It bioaccumulates, meaning that it is stored in the tissue of organisms. If one organism is polluted with dioxin (such as a mollusk or fish) and another organism eats the first, dioxins will settle in its tissues. The more polluted creatures it eats, the more polluted it becomes. Rather than being eliminated, this pollution accumulates in the organism and is stored in its cells.

Fish and other creatures living downstream from pulp and paper mills that use chlorine have been terribly affected. Females have developed physical characteristics of males and vice versa. In British Columbia, great blue herons nesting near pulp and paper mills have given birth to baby herons with half or no brain. Exposure to dioxins has also affected human reproductive systems. For example, human male sperm counts have dropped considerably, male impotence has risen, and women's reproductive systems have been affected.

One company, Louisiana-Pacific, decided in 1992 to eliminate chlorine from its paper-manufacturing process, making it the first bleached-kraft pulp mill in the U.S. to do so. Louisiana-Pacific proposed switching to a totally chlorine-free (TCF) process within three years after being brought up on 40,000 Clean Water Act violations.

Instead of using chlorine, it would use hydrogen peroxide and oxygen, and it asked for the flexibility to make the change over three years to develop new markets for slightly less-bright white pulp.

In addition to creating pollution, paper manufacture uses a considerable amount of energy. Depending on the paper mill, one sheet of paper takes 10-20 Watt-hours to make. Add that to the approximately 10Wh per page to use a laser printer and 2Wh per page for an ink jet, and that's a lot of energy associated with that paper's manufacture and use. Now, consider that annual office paper use has been measured to be upward of 80 pounds per employee per year. This is equivalent to about 8,000 sheets, a stack almost three feet tall, and includes only medium- and high-quality paper – not thermal paper, packaging, and other special and low-grade papers.

PRINTING

We cannot talk about paper without touching briefly on printing. Many of the inks used in pens and in printing presses are petroleum-based and contain heavy metals. They are toxic, and they don't biodegrade.

Fortunately, soy-based inks are available and are increasingly popular. While many still contain toxic heavy metals, they do degrade better and are easier to clean off printing presses. Some printers prefer working with soy-based inks over the petroleum-based ones. One Silver Spring, Maryland-based printing company, Ecoprint, actually developed a soy-based ink that does not contain heavy metals.

WHAT YOU CAN DO

Smart Paper Use

Whatever happened to the paperless office? That's a good question. With the wonder of today's technology, we have the capacity to contain whole filing cabinets of information on just one CD-ROM. Look at what the following can hold:

1. One floppy disk: 750 sheets, about a five-inch stack of typed pages
2. 100Mb hard disk: contents of a four-drawer filing cabinet
3. CD-ROM: entire roomful of paper

townsend, 1995

Fish depend on clean water but often have to live in waters poisoned by chlorine and other industrial wastes.

Saving paper can mean fewer file cabinets, which can reduce your office space needs dramatically. It's estimated to cost over $2,000 each year to maintain a filing cabinet and about $25,000 to fill it. These costs include the labor and paper costs. One estimate even states that about 3% of your filing cabinet documents will become misplaced, and it will cost about $120 in labor to find each one. On the other hand, storing files on disk or CD-ROM is much less expensive in human time and in storage space (Anzovin, 58).

While relying less on paper has many advantages, be aware of possible disadvantages:

- Your office may use more energy if computers, faxes, or other equipment are left on longer with higher demand.
- Increased health risks can arise due to eye strain, low-frequency radiation, carpal tunnel syndrome, non-ergonomic workstations, etc.

Corporate Examples
Boeing knows one real-life benefit of using computer disks for storage rather than paper. Its 50,000-page 727 maintenance manuals, full of text and images, can be put onto one CD-ROM disk and read on a PC with a CD-ROM player. This saves storage space and paper and is cost-effective. Major business software is found increasingly on CD-ROM.

Another company that understands the benefits of efficiency is IBM, which increasingly publishes its documentation on CD-ROM. You don't have to be a large company to publish on CD-ROM, though. Anybody can do it. If you create newsletters, magazines, or any other publications, CD-ROMs are not your only paperless option. You can transmit these publications electronically by posting them on the Internet or via electronic mail. This, is increasingly common and can ensure you a much larger readership than your present system.

Fax Paper
There are a number of things that you can do to work toward smarter paper use. If you're shopping for a fax machine, you can buy a plain-paper fax machine. Thermally treated paper, which is three to five times more expensive than plain paper, cannot be recycled under current recycling regulations and must be thrown away unless you use it for scratch paper. Thermal paper also cannot be faxed and must be copied to be faxed to another person. On the other hand, the installation of plain-paper fax machines will:

1. Reduce the amount of chemicals in the environment needed to produce thermal paper.

2. Be able to fax to another recipient without using the photocopier (saving energy, time, and the cost of the support staff expected to perform this duty).

3. Increase the amount of recyclable paper.

In addition, you can buy recycled paper for your fax machine. You also can reuse fax paper for scratch paper and eliminate fax cover sheets.

Using Copiers
Buy copiers with good automatic duplexing capabilities. According to EPRI, "A copier making 200 single-sided copies per day would result in an annual paper use of 50,000 sheets, accounting for:

- approximately $900 in direct paper costs
- about 7500 kWh in embodied energy in the paper
- approximately 17 linear feet of file space

If 100 of the 200 copies per day were double-sided, all these numbers would drop by 25%" (EPRI, 64).

You may want to post signs above copy machines to remind everyone to do double-sided copying.

Reuse & Recycle
Reuse paper for ink jet faxes and for printers when possible.

Remember to recycle. It takes about 1/3 less gross energy to make one sheet of recycled paper than it takes to make one sheet of virgin paper. The precise number varies from mill to mill; however, the manufacture of one sheet of virgin paper takes about 15Wh of energy, far more than the energy it takes to copy, print, or fax on it (EPRI, 10). It's important to recycle not just for energy savings but for solid waste reduction, too. Over 40% of typical office solid waste is paper. Recycling bins can be placed in central locations or under each desk.

Buy Smarter Paper Products
Paper is made from plant cellulose. Historically, paper was made from cotton, hemp, grasses, and other fibers. Yet, today, half of the trees cut in the U.S. are for paper. While most of us probably don't think much about paper production, trees are not the most efficient source of cellulose for making paper. In fact, trees contain only about 30% cellulose. A few alternate paper fibers are discussed below:

Agri-pulp

Agri-pulp, made by Arbokem, is one of the smartest papers available. Not only is agri-pulp made of 45% agricultural waste, 43% post-consumer waste paper, and 12% calcium carbonate filler, but it is acid-free, totally chlorine-free processing, totally effluent-free agri-pulp manufacturing. Considering the terrible pollution created at most pulp and paper mills, agri-pulp is impressive.

Price-wise, agri-pulp is competitive. Although it is more expensive to process it using the effluent-free and chlorine-free technologies, the agricultural waste used in manufacture costs about one-third that of wood chips. Contact Arbokem at: 604-322-1317
Internet: www.agripulp.com

Papers made of tree fiber are gaining in popularity. The above are made using such fibers as hemp, cotton denim, and jute.

Bamboo

Other fibers can be used for making paper, too. Bamboo is one. Because of its speedy growth, it is a great replacement for using trees for paper and goes much easier on the environment.

Hemp

Throughout history, hemp has been a popular fiber for paper, textiles, and other uses. As early as the first century BC, hemp was used in China's Western Han dynasty to make paper. It was milled in Spain by the Moors in the 12th century AD, in Italy one hundred years later, and in England beginning in the 15th century. In the United States, it was the fiber of choice for drafting the Declaration of Independence and the Constitution. It was harvested as a major crop not only for paper but also for boat sails, soldiers' uniforms, anchor cables, and rope until the 1930s. Then, it became confused with marijuana because of their similar appearances and was banned in the United States.

Now, hemp paper is available from a few manufacturers although the hemp is still grown outside the U.S. One company makes Tree Free EcoPaper, manufactured from 50% hemp and 50% cereal straw. Its shelf life is over 1,500 years as opposed to wood-fiber paper's 75 years.

Tree Free EcoPaper is acid-free and uses hydrogen peroxide, rather than chlorine, to whiten the fibers. Since no chlorine is used in the bleaching process, toxic dioxins are not produced. Because the fibers are relatively short and weak, paper from trees can be recycled only a few times; however, hemp paper can be recycled up to 20 times. Hemp also produces about four times more fiber per acre than do trees. Its fiber can be used to make other fiber products such as rope and fabric. The fabric can be woven into a variety of textures similar to canvas, denim, linen, and others.

Kenaf

Another fiber gaining popularity for paper-making is kenaf (*Hibiscus cannabinus L.*). A relative of the cotton plant, kenaf originated in southern Africa and can grow six meters in just one season. This makes it a quick-growing source of fiber.

India was the first known country to use kenaf for making paper a century ago. Like trees, kenaf contains a material called lignin, which binds together the individual plant fibers. When the lignin is left in the fiber, the paper yellows over time and with exposure to light. Then, the fibers are separated manually or chemically and made into paper.

As with tree fibers, kenaf fibers are bleached. If it is bleached without chlorine, kenaf can be a less-toxic and more environmentally better alternative to paper made from trees.

OTHER OFFICE SUPPLIES

There are a number of paper products on the market right now that win hands down over the conventional alternatives. For example, various types of writing papers are available. Index cards, steno notebooks, legal pads, and "while you were out" pads made of 100% recycled content paper are available. Computer, shipping, and file-folder labels also are on the market. Envelopes, adding rolls, self-stick notes, computer paper, calendars, desk pads, file folders, monthly and daily planning books, file pockets, tab labels, easels, desk files, expanding wallet folders, brief covers, and pocket portfolios are available in recycled paper, too.

Don't forget to go for unbleached paper products in your kitchen and restrooms at work, also. Napkins, paper towels, coffee filters, and toilet paper are all available. Unbleached, gold mesh (Krups), and cotton coffee filters (Co-op America) are all alternatives to the bleached, white, disposable coffee filters with which many of us are familiar. Below are some smarter versions of non-paper office supplies, too.

Binders

Several smarter binders are made. One is made of old computer hardware and recycled plastics. Another is made of 100% post-consumer-content plastics from two-liter soda bottles. (One testament to the fact that your household and office recycling efforts can be used to make smarter products!)

Computer Diskettes

GreenDisks are reformatted, prelabeled, pretested diskettes retrieved from software publishers who often update their software packages.

Correction Fluids

Some non-toxic correction fluids are made without CFCs; these products will not add noxious odors to your office environment or contribute to indoor air pollution.

Glues

Use white or yellow commercial glues since they tend to be safer than others. Whenever possible, substitute paper clips or rubber bands for glues.

Highlighters

Non-toxic highlighters can write on all sorts of papers without bleeding through, including fax, copy, writing, and recycled papers. These markers are refillable with water-based pigment.

Mailers

Bubble plastic mailers made with post-consumer content plastic waste are available. Also containing post-consumer waste are corrugated mailing boxes, diskette mailers, video mailing boxes, 100% recycled tube mailers, and recycled paper photo mailers.

Markers

Luckily, non-toxic, colored markers are easy to find. Non-toxic, chisel and bullet tip markers, and both dry erase (wipeable) and wet erase (semi-permanent–wipe with water) are made for writing on white boards. Low-odor, non-toxic, permanent markers with various tip and barrel sizes can write on a variety of materials, including plastic, glass, metal, and paper. There are low-odor, water-based markers for overhead projectors, too. These come in a variety of colors and point sizes.

Packing Materials

As for packaging materials, check with your office supply distributors to have them take back your non-recyclable packing materials. Use padded envelopes, or "jiffy bags," which can be put in the recycling bag with your old newspapers. Try to reuse cardboard boxes as much as possible.

If your company uses packaging materials, it may help to develop some purchasing guidelines. Here are a few.

Cardboard boxes:

- Be sure they're made of unbleached (brown) recycled fiber and is unlaminated (no waxy coatings).
- Use a box not much bigger than what you're shipping, eliminating the need for a lot of packaging.
- Be sure the box has both recycling symbols on it: the first, "may be recycled" symbol (three arrows chasing each other around a triangle) and the other, "made from recycled materials" symbols (three arrows on a dark circular background).

Other packaging materials:

- Find alternatives to foam peanuts. Instead, use recycled tissue paper, shredded paper, or cardboard
- If you must use plastic film wrapping, look for biodegradable poly bags or shrink wrap.
- Be sure they are not red or yellow (those colors generally contain cadmium, a toxic heavy metal).

Paper Clips & Staplers

There are alternatives to using conventional paper clips and staplers. For instance, some clips contain recycled material and come in recycled-content packaging. The Stapleless Stapler is another useful product. It is just a few inches long and is perfect for letters, memos, and other brief documents under five or six pages. To use, just fold the corner of your documents to be attached, squeeze the stapler over the fold, to puncture the paper, and then unfold. The small, partial cutouts made by the "stapler" actually hold the papers together.

Pens & Pencils

Smarter pens and pencils are on the market, too. You can find non-toxic, unpainted or painted pencils that are made of sustainably harvested wood or recycled cardboard. For example, American Ecowriter pencils by Eberhard Faber are made from 100% recycled cardboard and newspaper fiber. You also can find long-lasting pencils made of recycled plastic that use graphite refills. Smarter pens include those made of recycled plastic and filled with soy-based ink. One pen is even made of corn cellulose!

Planners

Use wipe-off planners (weekly, monthly) made of 100% post-consumer, two-liter pop bottles. And don't forget to recycle them when you're done.

Toilet Paper

Consider using recycled, non-rebleached toilet paper. To avoid waste, you may want to find out what your company does with partially used rolls of toilet paper. In World Wildlife Fund's environmental audit, it discovered that partially used rolls of toilet paper were thrown away every evening by the cleaning crew. Now, the facilities manager donates the partially used rolls to a homeless shelter.

All of the information regarding what's healthy and what's not may seem overwhelming. But, if you have any doubts about what's healthy and what's not, remember this one simple rule: Avoid inhaling anything that doesn't smell like clean air.

PERSONAL-CARE PRODUCTS

Companies that provide a gym for their employees often stock their gym restrooms with shampoos, conditioners, and other personal-care products. Even without a gym, office restrooms provide soap, lotions, and other products for employee use. Of course, many of today's personal-care products are full of artificial colors, fragrances, and other chemicals that aren't good for skin. You can replace artificial chemical soaps, hand lotions, and other body-care products with healthier, all-natural ones. Avoid products that are pearlescent or bright white, as they probably are not natural. Look for vegetable-based rather than petroleum-based products.

Even products labeled as gentle or for sensitive skin can contain harsh detergents. It is a good indication of how unhealthy many everyday products are when over 58,000 cosmetologists studies were found to get multiple myeloma (cancer) four times more often than the rest of the population (Anderson, 1990, 58).

GO CRUELTY-FREE

To increase your companies' sensitivity rating, choose products labeled as cruelty-free. This means that dogs, cats, rabbits, and other animals are not subjected to often excruciating or fatal tests that many companies making unnatural body-care products use. One such test is the LD-50 test, in which animals are exposed to certain products until 50% are dead so that the manufacturers know how much of something a group of animals needs to be exposed to before half are killed. Generally, over 200 animals are used in each test. Their responses during testing can include: bleeding from the eyes and mouth, bodily discharges, convulsions, diarrhea. The animals that do not die during testing are killed afterward.

The Draize Eye Irritancy Test also is used by many companies. Nearly all cleaners, bleaches, industrial chemicals, cosmetics, and other products are put into rabbits' eyes to determine how irritating they may be. If you have ever gotten even shampoo in your eyes, you'll know how painful this can be. The Draize test was developed by toxicologist Dr. John Draize of the U.S. Food and Drug Administration in the 1940s to test substances being developed as chemical warfare agents. Generally, 6-9 restrained rabbits are used in each test. Rabbits are used because their eyes do not tear. The substance is sprayed or dropped into the lower eyelid of one eye of each rabbit, with the other eye left alone for comparison. Not only do these tests create stress and pain, but they also can blind the animals.

Aside from discourse over the inhumane nature of the tests, there has been a great deal of debate over their usefulness. Many researchers have concluded that animal responses do not accurately reflect human responses to various products due to anatomical differences. In addition, using technologies such as chemical assay tests, cell and organ cultures, cloned human skin cell tests, tissue culture systems, human skin patches, human volunteers, and using ingredients already proven safe make animal testing obsolete.

If your product packaging does not say that it is cruelty-free, assume that it is not. Companies will state that their products are cruelty-free or will have a small rabbit symbol with a line across it somewhere on the packaging, indicating that animals are not used in the testing or to find the lethal doses of products.

SOME PRODUCTS TO AVOID

Petrochemicals: non-renewable, nonbiodegradable, mutagenic and carcinogenic to humans, pollutants.

Formaldehyde (a preservative sometimes called Quaternium-15): toxic to humans and wildlife.

Talcum powder (found in body powders): irritates lungs and eyes, often contaminated by cancer-causing asbestos, can endanger babies, and poses a health hazard to talc miners.

Artificial colors: contain irritating, dangerous chemical dyes, carcinogenic in animal testing, non-renewable, and non-biodegradable.

Fluoride (found in toothpaste): poses serious health threats (believed to be carcinogenic) and is banned as a water additive in 10 European countries.

Mineral oil (lubricant): suspected human carcinogen, prevents skin from breathing, dissolves skin's germ-fighting sebum, interferes with vitamin absorption, is phototoxic (becomes an irritant in sunlight), and is non-biodegradable.

HELPFUL RESOURCES

INFORMATION

National Anti-vivisection Society
Department 530-0110W
P.O. Box 94020
Palatine, Illinois 60094-4020
800-888-NAVS/ Fax: 312-427-6524
Cruelty-free product information

PETA
501 Front Street
Norfolk, VA 23510
757-622-PETA (7382)
Contact for *Caring Consumers,* a book of cruelty-free personal-care products.

Ecoprint
9335 Fraser Avenue
Silver Spring, MD 20910
301-585-7077/ Fax: 301-585-4899

Unlike some printers that use mixtures of soy-based inks with petroleum-based inks, this company uses 100% soy-based inks. And, unlike most soy-based inks, their Eco Inks contain no heavy metals.

Recycled Papers: The Essential Guide
The MIT Press
Cambridge, MA
800-356-0343/ 617-625-8569

PRODUCTS

For addresses and phone numbers, refer to *Appendix A: Directory of Suppliers.*

OFFICE SUPPLIES
Alte Schule USA
Atlantic Recycled Paper Co.
Be Earthlike
Blackfeet Indian Writing Co.
Earth Care
Eco Specialties
EcoTech Recycled Products
Environmentally Responsible Envelope System
Goodkind Pen Co., Inc.
Green Earth Office Supply
GreenCo Products
GreenDisk
The Green Office
KP Products, Inc.
Living Tree Tradition Bond Paper Products
New York Recycled Paper, Inc.
Recycled Office Products, Inc.
Signature Marketing
Summit Solutions
Treecycle Recycled Paper
Tree Free Ecopaper

PACKING MATERIALS
American Excelsior
Free-Flow Packaging Corp.
Tharco

PAPER
Arbochem
Atlantic Recycled Paper
Conservatree Paper Co.
Earth Care Paper
Hammermill
James River Corporation
Paperdirect, Inc.
Real Goods Trading
Techrite
Tree Free Ecopaper

RECYCLED/RECYCLABLE VIDEOCASSETTES
Global Zero, Inc.

PERSONAL CARE
Abkit, Inc.
Aubrey Organics, Inc.
Autumn Harp, Inc.
The Aveda Corporation
Boston Jojoba Company
Brookside Soap Co.
Crabtree & Evelyn
GreenCo Products
Natural Way Natural Body Care
Rachel Perry, Inc.
Terressentials
Tom's of Maine
Zia Cosmetics

SUMMARY OF RECOMMENDATIONS

OFFICE SUPPLIES

• Take advantage of the plethora of non-/low-toxic, recycled office supplies available. These range from non-toxic, refillable highlighters to recycled, non-re-bleached toilet paper.

PAPER

• Buy 100% recycled, non-bleached paper.

• Consider using papers made of alternative sources of fiber, such as hemp or kenaf.

• Choose a plain-paper fax machine over a thermal paper machine.

• Buy copiers with good automatic duplexing capabilities, and post signs above the machines to remind everyone to do double-sided copying.

• Reuse paper within the office, including fax paper – use it for scratch paper. Eliminate fax cover sheets whenever possible.

• Recycle. It takes about 1/3 less gross energy to make one sheet of recycled paper than one sheet of virgin paper.

• Don't print drafts unless you have to.

• Use unbleached, recycled-fiber paper towels, napkins, and coffee filters in your office pantries.

• Use computer diskettes to store your documents. Buy documentation (tutorials, etc.) on CD-ROM.

• Post publications online.

PERSONAL-CARE PRODUCTS

• Use healthy, all-natural, cruelty-free soaps, lotions, and other body-care products in office restrooms.

• Purchase products that come in recycled/recyclable content packaging.

• If your company won't switch to healthier soaps, lotions, and other products, you can bring your own to work and keep them in your desk.

Chapter 14

Smarter Cleaners & Pest Control

"...for a prudent toxicological policy, a chemical should be considered guilty until proven innocent." Umberto Saffiotti, May 1976 Canadian Research Conference (quoted in Rodes and Odell, 23)

Cleaners

What's In Your Cleaners?

Most cleaners are made of several toxic chemicals. Inhalation, skin contact, and consumption of these poisons can endanger your health. When they are flushed down the drain or the toilet, they enter the rivers, lakes, soils, and drinking water.

When using any of these compounds, wear gloves and use in well-ventilated areas. Also, check the ingredients on your cleaning products. Many contain the following:

Artificial dyes: Many cleaners contain toxic artificial dyes, which are hazardous to health.

Chlorine bleach: When emptied into waterways, chlorine combines with other chemicals to create toxic compounds, including carcinogens, that are stored in the cells of organisms (including humans and whales). These compounds can cause genetic mutations. Chlorine also kills the bacteria that many sewage treatment systems depend on to break down waste.

NOTE: NEVER MIX CHLORINE BLEACH WITH AMMONIA. IT RESULTS IN A DEADLY GAS.

Detergents: These can be made with petroleum, which contains toxic impurities that are difficult to break down.

EDTA/NTA: These toxic substances sometimes replace phosphates in cleaners. Both of these compounds stimulate heavy metals. NTA is a possible carcinogen.

Enzymes: Used in laundry detergent to get rid of stains, enzymes can cause skin and respiratory allergies.

Optical brighteners/whiteners: Used in laundry detergent to make clothes appear brighter and whiter, they can cause skin allergies. They also bioaccumulate (build up in organisms) in fish and plant root tissues.

Phosphates: While they boost the cleaning power of powdered detergents, phosphates end up in water and fertilize algae blooms. The algae consume oxygen in the water, suffocating fish and other aquatic life.

Washing soda (sodium carbonate): It cleans and strengthens the power of other cleaners, but it is moderately toxic and can irritate mucous membranes.

What You Can Do

There are alternatives to toxic cleaners. You can look for them at natural food stores, green stores, natural product mail order catalogues, and a growing number of grocery stores. Also, check with your cleaning supply distributor for smarter cleaners.

Use Alternative Ingredients

Some common, safer ingredients that you can use include:

Ammonia
Cleans carpets, copper, enamel, appliances, linoleum.

Baking soda
Cleans/deodorizes

Borax
Cleans, disinfects, removes stains, and softens water, strengthening the cleaning power of other products.

Vinegar
Cuts through mildew, stains, and wax buildup.

Make Your Own

Air freshener
Set out an open box of baking soda or a bottle of vanilla extract, simmer cinnamon and cloves in water, or put out a dish of warm vinegar.

Bleach
Mix borax or baking soda & water.

Brass
Worcestershire sauce or lemon juice

Carpet cleaner
Use club soda or baking soda. Or sprinkle a 2:1 of cornmeal to borax on the carpet, leave on one hour, and vacuum.

Chrome
Apple cider vinegar

Cleaners
Abrasive: Mix baking soda, soap, and salt.

Non-abrasive: Rub with one-half lemon dipped in borax, and rinse dry.

Coffee cup stain remover
Moist salt

Coffee pot stains
Put ice cubes and vinegar or lemon juice into the carafe, and swirl around until the stains are gone.

Copper
Lemon juice and salt

Dishes/grease cutter
Mix your usual amount of dish soap with baking soda.

Drain
Use a plunger or snake. Or pour one-half cup baking soda, one-half cup salt, and one-quarter cup vinegar down the drain, in that order. Close the drain until the fizzing stops, and then flush it with boiling water.

Glass
Mix two tablespoons white vinegar or lemon juice with one quart warm water, or use baking soda on a wet rag. Then, dry the glass with newspaper.

Grease
Use a damp cloth with borax.

Hand cleaner
Use baby oil or vegetable oil.

Ink spot remover
Mix cold water, one tablespoon cream of tartar, and one tablespoon lemon juice.

Laundry
Use basic soap, or add borax to your laundry.

Linoleum or vinyl tile floors
Use one cup white vinegar for every two gallons of water.

Mildew remover
Mix equal parts vinegar and salt.

Mosquitoes
Use citronella oil or citronella candles.

Moth repellent
Use cedar chips, and keep them in a cotton sachet. Or mix one-half pound mint, one-quarter pound thyme, and two tablespoons cloves, and hang the mixture in a cheesecloth bag. Or mix cedar chips, dried tobacco, mint, peppercorns, rosemary, and cedar oil.

Oil stains
Rub white chalk into the oil stain; launder.

Oven
Mix two tablespoons borax, two tablespoons liquid soap, and warm water.

Perspiration stains
Mix white vinegar with water.

Porcelain stains
Use baking soda.

Rust (on clothing)
Lemon juice, salt, and sunlight

Rusted bolts/nuts
Carbonated soda or other carbonated beverage

Silver
Use baking soda or toothpaste. Or use one quart of warm water, one tablespoon baking soda, one piece of aluminum foil, and one tablespoon salt.

Spray starch
Mix two tablespoons cornstarch with one pint of cold water. Put the mixture into a spray bottle and use.

Toilet
Mix borax and lemon juice.

Tub/tile
Combine one-quarter cup baking soda, one-half cup white vinegar, and warm water.

Upholstery spots
Club soda

Water marks
Toothpaste

Water softener
One-quarter cup vinegar per wash

White water spots (wood furniture)
Use toothpaste, cooking oil, nut meat, or mayonnaise, and scrub with a toothbrush.

Windows
Put two tablespoons of vinegar into one quart of warm water, and wash.

Wine stains
Rub with salt.

Wood furniture/floor polish
Put one teaspoon lemon oil into one pint of vegetable or mineral oil. Or use one teaspoon washing soda with one gallon of hot water. Apply beeswax after getting a glossy finish.

Pest Control

If you're a do-it-yourselfer, you may want to make your own pest controls, too. Of course, to keep pests from entering in the first place, seal cracks and pest-entry areas, fix plumbing leaks, and dry moist areas.

Ants
Create a barrier using salt or red chili pepper at the point of entry (doors, window sills). You can also try Drax, made with mint apple jelly and boric acid.

Fly repellents
Wipe a vinegar/water solution on counters, or use clove or citrus oil. Well-watered basil plants also repel flies.

Insects on plants
Wash leaves with soapy water, and then rinse.

Roach repellent
Chopped bay leaves/cucumber skins

Roaches/silverfishes
Put a beer-soaked rag (or one-half baking soda/one-half powdered sugar mix) in a shallow dish overnight.

Rodents
Make "rodent rocks." Use porous lava rocks soaked in an herbal mix that includes garlic and onions. The pungent odor will repel rodents.

Slugs/snails
Onion or marigold plants

Termites
Create a sand barrier around a building's foundation.

Helpful Resources

Information

Contact the following companies for information on less toxic pest control.

Bio Integral Resource Center
P.O. Box 7414
Berkeley, CA 94707
415-524-2567

Etex Ltd.
800-543-5651

The Natural Garden Book by Peter Harper, 1994. New York: Fireside Books.

Slug Bread & Beheaded Thistles: Amusing & Useful Techniques for Nontoxic Gardening & Housekeeping by Ellen Sandbeck, 1995. Duluth, MN: De la Terre Press.

Products

For addresses and phone numbers, refer to *Appendix A: Directory of Suppliers*.

CLEANERS
Cleaners and Polishes
AFM Enterprises, Inc.
Allen's Naturally
Auro, Sinan Co.
Cloverdale, Inc.
Dasun Company
Earth Rite
Earth Wise
Eco Design
Ecover
Enjo
Granny's Old Fashioned
Healthy Kleaner
Life Tree
Mia Rose
Natural Chemistry, Inc.
Seventh Generation

Laundry & Dishwashing Products
Allen's Naturally
Auro, Sinan Co.
Earth Rite
Earth Wise
Eco Design
Ecover
Life Tree
Seventh Generation

POOL AND SPA CLEANERS
Natural Chemistry, Inc.

PESTICIDES
Gardens Alive!
Gemplers
Harmony Farm Supply
Integrated Fertility Management
Lotus Brands
Mellinger's, Inc.
Mia Rose
Natural Gardening Co.
Nature's Control
Necessary Trading Co.
Ringer Corporation

Flea Control
Natural Animal, Inc.
Ringer Corporation
Sandoz Agro, Inc.

Less Toxic Termite Control
BioLogic Natural Pest Control
N-Viro Products, Ltd.
Tallon Termite and Pest Control

Roach Control
Copper Brite, Inc.
Organic Control, Inc.
R Value West

Rodent Control
Allen Special Products

Summary of Recommendations

Cleaners

• Look for cleaners that are labeled non-toxic, chlorine-free, and phosphate-free.

• Use cleaners that are made without petroleum products, optical whiteners, or artificial dyes.

• Buy cleaners made without NTA or EDTA.

• Use cleaners that biodegrade rapidly.

• Look for cleaners that are concentrated, requiring less packaging for more cleaning power.

• Never empty chlorinated swimming pool water into ponds, streams, or oceans (small amounts of chlorine kill fish). If you have to use chlorine detergent instead of soap, get liquid detergent in recycled and/or recyclable containers.

Pesticides

• Seal off areas where unwanted creatures enter so that you don't have to worry about using pesticides.

• Avoid toxic pesticides. Instead, use healthier alternatives.

• Fix leaks, and put an end to moisture in any areas around the office.

CHAPTER 15

SMARTER DAYCARE & CHILD CARE

"We are left to choose whether protecting our carpet from our children is more important than protecting our children from potentially toxic carpet fumes."
Wilson, 10

This book wouldn't be complete without something said on child care. If you run a daycare center or work for a company that provides child care for your children, you may want to look into some of the smarter products available.

THE CHALLENGE

ENVIRONMENTAL TOXINS

There are three ways that chemicals can enter the body: absorption (via skin contact), ingestion (eating, drinking), and inhalation (breathing vapors). Children's bodies tend to be more sensitive to their physical surroundings than adults'. That's because children take in more air, metabolizing larger amounts of whatever they inhale at faster rates. As a result, toxins in the environment – from lead, which can cause developmental problems, to pesticides, radon, and offgassing carpets and paints – can pose real health risks to kids.

Radon poisoning has contributed to childhood leukemia, adding to the 21.5% increase in cancer for children (0-14 years old) in the years from 1950-1986. Electro-magnetic fields are believed to be another cause of the increase in childhood cancer. Of course, other types of pollution are problems, too. Nitrate in water has sickened almost only children. And in Los Angeles, children have 10-15% lower lung capacities than do those children living in less polluted areas. While all of these health problems are real and severe, they don't compare with lead, which appears to be the biggest problem to children's health. It seems that between three and four million kids in the U.S., alone, already have enough lead in their bodies to damage their nerves and kidneys while decreasing their IQs and their learning abilities.

Clearing the Air

Some of these health dangers are difficult to avoid, and others are simple. For instance, if your child care or daycare center has many small children or infants, you may be tempted to use air fresheners. Be careful what you choose. Air fresheners don't really freshen a room but interfere with people's abilities to smell. This is done by coating the nasal passages with an oil film or by using nerve-deadening agents.

townsend, 1993

Children are especially susceptible to environmental toxins.

FOOD

Fruits & Vegetables

Unless specified "organic," you can assume that the produce you buy has withstood a number of chemical applications. Although washing may remove some pesticide residue, it often is ineffective. That is because many pesticides are systemic, traveling throughout a plant from its roots to its fruits. See the table below to get an idea of how many chemicals are used on various types of non-organic produce.

Fruit/Vegetable	Number of Chemicals
Carrots, lettuce	50-60
Cucumbers	75
Tomatoes	>100
(Natural Choices, 4-2)	

In addition, many fruits and vegetables are waxed; this wax can seal pesticides on the surface of produce, but it also can contain fungicides.

Waxed fruits and vegetables can include: apples, avocados, bell peppers, cantaloupes, cucumbers, eggplants, grapefruits, lemons, limes, melons, oranges, parsnips, passion fruits, peaches, pineapples, pumpkins, rutabagas, squashes, sweet potatoes, tomatoes, and turnips. (Natural Choices, 4-6).

Note that "pesticide-free" does not necessarily mean that something has been grown without pesticides – it may only mean that residues could not be detected on a random sample that was tested after harvest. Always ask.

Meat

Once considered a healthy source of protein and other nutrients, meat has fallen from grace over the past several years. Aside from its link to heart diseases, cancers, high cholesterol, and countless diseases, there are other health reasons that have prompted many people to reduce their meat intake or shun it altogether and avoid feeding it to their children.

Not only does meat contain approximately 14 times more pesticide residue than fruits and vegetables, but most dairy and meat animals are given growth hormones and antibiotics regularly. The use of growth hormones, alone, has caused alarm in some regions, where young girls have begun developing breasts and reaching puberty quite early, and boys have begun to develop female genitalia. In these areas, families have

eaten animal products containing high amounts of a growth hormone that the human body recognizes as estrogen.

Not long ago, the Surgeon General estimated that over 90% of all commercial chickens are infected with leukosis, a viral cancer peculiar to chickens. Before going to market, the tumors are cut off, and artificial colors are used to make the chickens appear healthy. Salmonella poisoning is common in the United States, too. It's not surprising that just a decade ago, the European Community banned imports of animal products to the Common Market by 11 major U.S. meat producers.

Everyone, especially children, should have easy access to healthy foods that haven't been tainted with toxic pesticides and other chemicals.

Milk

Milk also contains pesticide residues – five-and-a-half times as much as produce – because most cows are not fed organic feed. Growth hormones and antibiotics fed to cattle also taint their milk.

Even human breast milk is contaminated. For example, DDT, banned in the 1970s for its toxicity, is used today as an "inert" ingredient in U.S. pesticides. To protect

townsend, 1996

Real Goods Trading Company is just one source of healthier bedding.

their trade secrets, the pesticide companies are not required to report inert ingredients they use. As a result of nursing mothers non-organic diets, the average American infant ingests many toxic substances, including about 10 times the Food and Drug Administration's maximum allowable intake of toxic polychlorinated biphenyls (PCBs). PCBs are highly toxic compounds that can produce a wide array of symptoms in those exposed to them. They are found in such common products as inks, pesticides, adhesives, carbonless paper, transformers, asphalt, lubricants, waxes, rubber, and waterproofing. On the other hand, studies have indicated that nursing, vegetarian women have only 1-2% as much pesticide residue in their breast milk than non-vegetarian women.

Toys

Plastic toys and other children's products that offgas can be unhealthy. This is true especially when children put toys into their mouths and suck their thumbs after they've been playing with toxic toys.

Some toys contain polyvinyl chloride (PVC) and vinyl plastic (e.g., polyvinylpyrrolidone, or PVP). PVP was banned by NASA for use in space capsules due to its toxicity (it's been linked with cancer and lung disease). PVC has been associated with birth defects, mutations, and cancer (Natural Choices, 2-12).

CREATING A HEALTHY INTERIOR

First and foremost, be certain that the physical environment is healthy. It's important that the paints, floor coverings, furniture, upholstery, and other supplies found in childrens" areas don't rob children of their health. Refer to the chapters on those topics for further information on products and their sources.

Next, be sure that foods, toys, clothing, diapers, and other children's products are healthy. There are non-toxic products that have been designed especially with children in mind – from natural, chemical-free clothing to clays and toys. For instance, forego toys containing polyvinyl chloride and vinyl plastic in favor of healthier alternatives.

The typical American baby spends about 20,000 hours in diapers, many of which are plastic disposables containing toxic chemicals such as chlorine. Minimize babies' exposures to chemicals by using non-plastic disposable diapers or cloth diapers with a cleaning service that launders them with non-toxic soap.

Also, avoid unnatural, toxic air fresheners. For diaper pails, use non-toxic air fresheners that contain a mineral known as zeolite. Zeolite absorbs bacteria and some indoor air contaminants.

TEACHING CHILDREN TO BE SMARTER

Several programs exist to help educate young people about the importance of living healthy, more resource-efficient lives. Most of these are taught through ecology lessons. Schools interested or daycare centers interested in these lessons can contact a number of organizations and state agencies that have created curricula for teaching children to be more eco-friendly.

Steve Trash uses magic to teach children the importance of being smarter.

Many programs aim at trying to be entertaining and educational. One person that has taken that to an extreme is Steve "Trash," a magician with a message. Steve gives magic shows and lectures on the importance of being a responsible person, and being ecologically responsible is part of his message.

Steve's book *The Magic of Ecology* focuses on teaching valuable life lessons to children through the medium of garbage. It includes 22 magic tricks, each demonstrating an ecological idea or principle. "Kids learn how to respect themselves, other people, and the environment."

HELPFUL RESOURCES

INFORMATION

Diaper Services
To find the diaper service nearest you, call 800-462-6237.

Mothers and Others
888-326-4636

The Nontoxic Baby: Reducing Chemicals from Your Baby's Life by Natural Choices. Published by Natural Choices in 1991 and distributed by Lotus Light Publications, Box 325, Twin Lakes, WI 53181, 414-889-8561.

Steve Trash
For information, contact:
Steve "Trash"
975 Old Dirt Road
Spruce Pine, AL 35585
205-740-9797

For booking information contact:
G.G. Greg (colleges): 216-692-1193
Dean Short (fairs): 402-553-3502

Products

For addresses and phone numbers, refer to *Appendix A: Directory of Suppliers*.

AIR FRESHENERS
Lotus Brands
The Living Source
Swanstar

ART & CRAFT SUPPLIES
Eco Design
HearthSong
Karen's Nontoxic Products
Krafty Kids, Inc.
Pastorini Spielzeug of Zurich

BABY CARE
The Blue Earth

BABY POWDER (TALC-FREE)
Autumn Harp
Natural Lifestyle Supplies

BABY WIPES
Seventh Generation

BEDDING
The Cotton Place
Heart of Vermont

BLEACH
Ecover
Sunrise Lane

CLOTHING
After the Stork
Hanna Anderson
Biobottoms
Eco Design Co.
Motherwear
The Natural Baby
Seventh Generation

DIAPERS/DIAPER COVERS
Baby Bunz and Company
Biobottoms
i play
Motherwear

FOOD
Gold Mine Natural Food Co.
Green Earth Natural Foods
Mountain Ark Trading Co.
Walnut Acres

Baby Food, Organic
Earth's Best, Inc.
Gold Mine Natural Food Co.
Green Earth Natural Foods
Mountain Ark Trading Co.
Walnut Acres

FURNITURE
Cedar Works
The Children's Furniture Co.
Heart of Vermont
Heartsong Store
The Masters Corp.
Natural Baby
The Natural Bedroom

GAMES & TOYS
Baby Bunz and Company
Heart of Vermont
Hugg -A-Planet
Northern Lights
Papa Don's Toys
Pastorini Spielzeug of Zurich
Real Goods Trading Co.
Seventh Generation

LAUNDRY DETERGENT
Eco Source
Ecos
Ecover
Granny's Old Fashioned Products
Sunrise Lane

NURSERY
Terra Verde
Waterforms, Inc.

PETROLEUM-FREE JELLY
Autumn Harp
Lotus Brands
Motherwear

SHAMPOO
Aubrey Organics
Autumn Harp
Lotus Brands
Seventh Generation

SOAP
Desert Essence
Dr. Bronner's
Lotus Brands
Weleda

UPHOLSTERY
The Cotton Place
The Janice Corporation
Winter Silks

SUMMARY OF RECOMMENDATIONS

FOOD

• Use organic baby and other foods since children are especially vulnerable to the effects of toxic pesticide and other materials.

• Use non-chlorine-bleached napkins, paper towels, and other paper products.

• Be sure that drinking water does not contain contaminants.

• Avoid feeding children non-organic foods.

• Avoid giving children meat (including eggs) and milk. If they do ingest, these, be sure that they are organic, from animals that have been fed organic grains and have not been given hormones and antibiotics.

FURNITURE

• Consider using untreated bedding made of natural fibers.

• Use non-toxic furniture, such as that made of sustainably harvested wood without toxic stains, varnishes, and upholstery.

INDOOR ENVIRONMENT

• Be certain to provide plenty of fresh, clean air, and good ventilation.

• Use non-toxic paints, flooring, and building materials.

TOYS

• Avoid products made of plastics and other materials that offgas.

• Use paints and pencils that don't contain heavy metals and other toxins.

PART FOUR

· · · · · · · ·

SETTING UP
SMART PROGRAMS

CHAPTER 16

SMART OFFICE RECYCLING

"In the end, no matter what the substance, the rule is the same: If we don't buy it, if we don't use it, or if we recycle it, it won't be manufactured and it won't become trash. It's that simple."
Anderson, 1990, 38

STARTING AN OFFICE RECYCLING PROGRAM

Setting up a recycling program is a great way to reuse office waste positively. But since most office recycling programs don't start at the top with the CEOs, it helps to have someone – or a group of people – diplomatically pushing for one. If you're trying to start a program, pitch recycling as great for saving money, great for the company image, and great for the environment.

The market for recycled products is growing. There are companies that make nylon carpeting from PET bottles, crude oil from used tires, pavement and asphalt from used glass bottles, scratch-resistant windows from car headlight lenses, paper out of blue jeans, carpet underlay and industrial rags from old clothing, and tennis balls of scrap nylon.

Carpet Waste
Northeast Georgia's landfills see a lot of carpet waste, since this area is home to much of the U.S. carpet industry. The $30 per ton that is paid to landfills to dispose of carpet waste is one incentive for efficient production and waste reuse.

Collins & Aikman, one carpet producer, recently started something known as the Infinity Initiative. The company takes in both used carpet tile and vinyl-backed carpet, chops and granulates it, mixes it with recycled plastic, melts it down, and turns it into parking lot bumpers and other products.

Domtar
Domtar Gypsum spent a lot of money throwing away its manufacturing waste. Each month, the company paid $80,000 - 100,000 just to discard its 1,000 tons of scrap gypsum, but not anymore. Now, New West Gypsum (in Fife, Washington) remanufactures gypsum using scraps from Domtar Gypsum, Westroc Industries, and construction sites.

Deja Shoe
One company, Deja Shoe, used only recycled products in its shoe line. It made insoles from factory-reject file folders and coffee filters and makes uppers from textile scraps. It can pay to be creative! You can save money by being proactive and seeking positive change rather than resisting it. It's one way to keep your company on the cutting edge.

By the way, it is important that you set a good example in your recycling efforts. People can keep you in mind as their office recycling idol each time they begin to slip a piece of paper into the trash can. On the other hand, be aware that, as the recycling evangelist, you will be in the spotlight and under great scrutiny.

Deja Shoe made footwear from recycled materials.

WHAT YOU CAN DO

- Find/nominate someone to be in charge of recycling. If you can't find someone, volunteer.
- Enlist management backing.
- Define the extent of your recycling ambitions (paper, plastics, composting lunch scraps, etc.).
- Decide the type and quantity of recyclable waste.
- Find a buyer for your paper and other recyclable items. Then, include in your contract what quantities of which materials the buyer will accept. Check your local Yellow Pages under Recycling, Waste, Salvage, or Scrap. Call around for the best price per load.
- Research the best pick-up options.
- Set up a consistent, convenient, sanitary collection method. For instance, have employees keep their recyclables in a desktop container or folder (if it's paper) until the end of the day. Then, they can put their recyclables into a container at a centralized location, and cleaning and maintenance personnel can take it from there to the area where the recyclers empty the bins.
- Educate everyone in the office about the importance of recycling before you begin the program. Keep everyone involved at every step.
- Keep coworkers informed – start a recycling message center via electronic mail. Let them know how their recycling efforts are going, and ask them for their ideas on how to creatively reuse waste that isn't yet recyclable.
- Coordinate recycling programs with other businesses in your building.

Join EPA's WasteWi$e Program

As you have seen throughout this book, the federal government has several voluntary programs that help businesses become less toxic, more efficient, and save money. One is the Environmental Protection Agency's WasteWi$e Program. This comprehensive program focuses on three main areas:

- waste prevention
- buying recycled products
- recycling

The program has a number of goals for each area and works with members to develop and achieve their own goals. So far, over 400 companies have signed on to become WasteWi$e members. Not only do member companies work with the EPA to cut their waste, but members also get a *Recycled Products Guide*, containing over 4,000 listings of recovered-materials manufacturers, distributors, and merchants, and a special rate for RecycleLine, an online network for information on recycled products and markets.

WasteWi$e also developed an information exchange program that matches companies with similar goals so that they can share information and tips about what works for them. WasteWi$e's corporate partners include 3M, American Airlines, Lockheed-Martin, Martin Marietta, Nike, Quaker State, and Radio Flyer.

Contact a Waste Exchange

Also, there are a number of waste exchanges that try to match sources of waste with users of waste. The National Materials Exchange Network (NMEN) is a national computerized waste exchange catalog system. It was created by the U.S. Environmental Protection Agency and now is overseen by Earthcycle.

NMEN has over 10,000 listings (domestic and international). It allows state waste exchanges and industrial and consumer users to list items or search for items (e.g., scrap/precious metals, gems, textiles, auto/boat equipment, paper products) at no expense. In addition, its Recycling and Environmental Services Database is an extensive directory. For more information call 509-466-1532 or send an e-mail to nmen@eznet.com.

The rest of this chapter talks about common office products and some alternatives to throwing them away.

ALUMINUM

Because aluminum is easily recyclable, it is a good choice over plastic and glass. If you purchase drinks in aluminum cans, try to buy them in paperboard or cardboard packaging rather than in plastic rings, which don't biodegrade. To increase the success of your aluminum recycling program, put recycling bins beside vending machines as a reminder to everyone to recycle.

CARPETS

Have you ever wondered what you can do with an old carpet? Some companies do a great deal. Monsanto turns old nylon carpets into pellets used by injection molders for such things as auto parts. Anyone interested in buying DuPont's Antron carpet can give their old carpet to the company. The used carpet is made into Ford Company auto parts, a gypsum and wood substitute for use in marine environments, and other products. Collins & Aikman collects used carpet, grinds it, and mixes it with recycled plastics, turning it into marine bulkheads, sound barriers for freeways, flooring, and parking lot bumpers. Other companies have similar programs (Makower, October 1995, 7).

CD-ROMs

While many CD-ROMs contain quickly outdated information such as directories and mailing lists, they cannot be written over, and most people throw them away. However, some CD-ROM distributors are not using the "jewel box" containers they once used. Some computer companies sell their CD-ROMs in a recycled cardboard sleeve, packaged in a recycled plastic holder. Other companies use CD-ROM parts to make jewelry, clock faces, and other items. If you won't be reusing your old CD-ROMs, you may want to find someone who will.

COMPUTER BATTERIES

Nickel-cadmium, or "ni-cad," batteries contain toxic cadmium. These are the batteries most often used in notebook computers. They are good for about 1,000 charges, or two years, but they are the largest source of toxic cadmium in the waste stream.

The healthiest alternatives are nickel-metal-hydride (NMH) batteries. Although more expensive, some notebook computers use NMH batteries. Consider these if you have a choice.

PCs also use lithium batteries to back up their system setup memory. However, some companies are replacing them with flash memory instead, a chip that doesn't require constant power to hold information.

When recharging PC batteries, be sure that they are fully discharged first, or they will not be able to hold a full charge. If the full capacity to recharge is lost, run the batteries through a cycle of 10 or more full discharges, and they will recover their full recharge ability. Some companies actually drain batteries fully for you. However, if you recharge batteries only when they are powerless, you will make them last much longer.

Apple Computer recycles its customers' computer batteries. Through its service center or headquarters, it takes back used lead-acid batteries from Macintosh Portables and ni-cads from Mac Powerbooks. Check with your computer's manufacturer to find out if it does this, too.

COMPUTERS

Once upon a time, computer casings were made mostly of steel. But today, most of these casings are made of plastics. McDonald's even uses shingles made from old computer casings for the roofs of its restaurants.

There is a trend toward designing computers for easy disassembly, you can take apart your own PC when you're done with it to recycle many of its plastic parts.

However, grouping similar plastics together can be difficult for those who are not plastics experts. Since resins are often used, telling the plastics apart can be confusing. Unless you know how to tell these plastics apart, it might be better if you recycle the unit intact rather than stripping one or two PCs for their plastic parts. Be careful, though, not to take apart your monitor, which can hold a dangerous electrical charge.

Both Germany and Japan are leaders in PC recycling. In Germany, a 1992 law made electronics manufacturers responsible for the disposal of all their products and packaging, including PCs. NEC, one of Japan's hot electronics companies, has a plant that separates PC parts for recycling, including the gold and other elements from used electronics. IBM does this in the U.K. And one of Russia's Ural Mountains plants strips chips from circuit boards.

So far, the only U.S. manufacturer to accept large quantities of its used equipment is Hewlett Packard. Obsolete HP laser printers and PCs and trade-ins can be returned to the company's Roseville, California, facility, and HP will cover the mailing costs. It's likely, however, that more and more manufacturers will find it cost-effective to take back their parts rather than relying solely on virgin materials.

If you need a computer but don't need the latest model, you may want to buy a used, overstocked, close-out PC for much less than the original price. If you have a computer and you're ready to move on to another, here are two suggestions on what you can do with your used computer:

- Disassemble your computer, or return it whole if you've found someone willing to recycle it.
- If your PC still works but you're in the market for an upgrade, consider donating it to a charity. For instance, the East-West Foundation finds homes for used PCs that still have some life left in them. After refurbishing them, they give half to U.S. charities and half to overseas charities, largely in Eastern Europe.

Most schools need computers, as well, and if your machine is under five years old, you may be able to take the donation as a tax deduction.

Construction Site Recycling

The National Park Service's Sustainable Design database offers a number of options for recycling materials leftover from construction. The database also suggests contacting Habitat for Humanity and other such groups that may love to get construction leftovers. Also, look into donating to industrial art classes, community theaters, and others.

Look under these headings in your local phone directory for more recycling outlets:

Appliances: "Scrap Metal"
Asphalt: "Paving Contractors," "Aggregates," or "Sand & Gravel"
Brick: "Brick"
Concrete: "Concrete Contractors," "Aggregates," or "Sand & Gravel"
Metal: "Scrap Metal"
Salvaged Building Parts: "Salvage" or "Wrecking Companies"
Tree Trimmings and Brush: "Landscaping" or "Tree Services"
Wood: "Landscaping" or "Tree Services"

Floppy Disks

Whenever floppy disks develop bad sectors from dust or other contaminants, try resectoring them. After using a disk repair utility, reformat your disks.

If write-protect tabs have been broken or are missing on 3.5-inch floppies, pry out the rest of the tab, and replace it with a small piece of thin cardboard.

In addition, compress files to save space, which can be compressed to 25% of their original size.

Some companies sell reconditioned floppies. Be sure that they've been demagnetized (degaussed) and relabeled. Then, if you don't want your old disks, you can reformat them and donate them to schools and charitable organizations.

Glass

Although glass is a better choice than plastic, aluminum is still the best for its recyclability (although the manufacture of virgin aluminum has severe, negative impacts). Only glass that has held food or drinks can be recycled. Don't try to include drinking glasses, lightbulbs, eyeglasses, mirrors, or other types of glass in your recycling bin.

Hazardous Waste

Over 500 million pounds of hazardous chemical wastes are improperly disposed of every year. Some of this gets into our drinking-water sources. If your company has a manufacturing process that creates hazardous waste, look for a market for your waste. For example, some unrelated companies are beginning to work together to purchase waste from one another; some are able to strip certain components from others' waste and use them in their own manufacturing processes. In this way, a closed loop system can be established, keeping waste out of the environment.

If you find that no one can reuse your waste or certain components of it and you need to dispose of it, remember never to put it into unlabeled containers or into containers with a shape that would allow anyone, particularly children, to think that it may be safe or edible. Also, don't mix hazardous waste products. Work with a local community center or public works department to develop a waste-disposal program that is as safe as possible in your area. Of course, always try to reduce your use of hazardous waste products in the first place.

Holiday Cards

If you're wondering what to do with the cards that your company gets during the holidays, rest assured that you don't have to throw them away. There's an organization that helps troubled youth earn money by having them cut the covers off used holiday cards and paste them onto new card stock for sale. So, when you're cleaning up after the holidays and don't know what to do with the cards, just send the whole cards or just the covers to:

Card Recycling
100 St. Jude St.
Post Office Box 60100
Boulder City, NV 89006

LIGHT BALLASTS

Ballasts made before 1979 and some after contain PCBs. As a result, their disposal may be regulated at the local or state level. Ballasts leaking fluids from the outer case cannot be recycled and must be discarded as hazardous waste. Contact your state or local government for information on disposing of ballasts safely.

PACKING MATERIALS

Polystyrene and polyurethane packing foams are used often in the computer industry. Because they do not biodegrade and their manufacturing processes are ecologically detrimental, you can save or reuse the foam inserts, even if you have to cut them to size for packing other things.

Some recycling centers take foam packaging, and office-product distributors will agree to take your foam packaging back. The Association of Foam Packaging Recyclers operates over 45 foam-recycling plants in the United States. Mailboxes, Etc., a national shipping and mailing chain, also reuses unwanted foam "peanuts."

For a better packaging alternative, you can try crumpled or shredded wastepaper or biodegradable cornstarch packaging.   One company, PC Connection/ MacConnection, has found its own way to deal with wastepaper. Two local mills recycle it into biodegradable tissue that's great for packaging and is lighter than foam.

The European Community may be setting the standards for many of us. The European Community Commission developed an ambitious plan to reduce 90% of packaging material through recycling, composting, and incineration to create energy. The plan, implemented in 1992, set a 10-year deadline for EC countries to meet. Recycling efforts, alone, are expected to take care of 60% of the waste. Of course, it will take major re-thinking about what types of packaging should be used for products, and manufacturers will be forced to re-think the whole packaging life cycle, from production to use, reuse, and disposal. It's clear that a manufacturer's product responsibility does not end with the products' sale anymore.

PAPER

In 1990, American businesses recycled only about 15% of the approximately 11 million tons of paper used. By 1994, about 23% of U.S. office paper was being recycled. For more information on what your company can do to recycle paper, contact:

National Office Paper Recycling Project
c/o The United States Conference of Mayors
1620 Eye Street, NW
Washington, D.C. 20006
202-223-3089

Find a waste-paper buyer. Over 500 pounds of paper is probably enough to interest a waste-paper buyer, but check around to find out what the minimums are. The average office paper use is about 1/2 pound per person per day.

There are several things that you can do to encourage a successful paper recycling program. Keep a box for recycled papers by your desk, and encourage others to do the same. Generally, you'll get a better price for well-sorted paper. In descending value, it goes like this:

1. Plain white office paper (letterhead, memos, copier and laser printer paper, and tractor-feed computer paper)

2. Data-processing paper with blue or green stripes

3. Corrugated cardboard

4. Magazines

5. Newspapers

6. Mixed papers (folders, card stock, and brown paper products)

7. Nonrecyclable products (some envelopes, thermal fax paper, self-stick notes, express-service packs, dark-colored paper, and mixed shredded paper)

Check with local paper mills to find out if they take mixed paper. Most recyclers will accept the clay-coated (glossy) magazine paper now, but check first. If your recycler does not take magazines, you may want to consider giving the magazines to a local nursing home, hospital, or other facility.

If you just can't find anyone to pick up your used paper, and you don't mind boxing up your junk mail, you can send it to Sessile Paper Company. Sessile reuses all kinds of paper, even magazines and envelopes with plastic windows, and makes cards and other papers out of it. They will take any kind of paper but newspaper.

There are other options for recycling your used paper. You can make memo pads from discarded white paper with one blank side. Simply cut it to size, and staple it together, or put it in small boxes, and use it as note paper. The Natural Resources Defense Council in New York sends its used paper to the printer, who cuts it to size, binds it with glue along one edge, and sends it back to NRDC for use as memo pads.

If you have office paper that contains confidential information, consider shredding it and using it as packaging.

When possible, reuse brown mailing envelopes. You can even get a stamp that says something like, "Please use this envelope again," and stamp the envelope.

Try to limit your use of self-stick notes. While there are self-stick notes available that are made from recycled paper, the glues on them make them non-recyclable. Unfortunately, despite their convenience and charm, colored and sticky papers are difficult to recycle.

Ask your company and urge others (including utilities) to stop using envelopes with plastic windows; they cannot be recycled with most high-grade recycling programs.

To reduce the amount you have to recycle, request that companies don't include your name on mailing lists they sell and that they take your name off their lists. Whenever you get postage-paid envelopes in the mail, or when you place orders, you can write a message on them requesting that they remove your name from their list. You also can reduce the amount of junk mail you receive by contacting the Mail Preference Service.

Let the Mail Preference Service know the many ways that your name and address are printed on mailing labels, or send the labels themselves. Do this every few months as necessary. The organization claims as high as a 75% reduction in junk mail through this action.

Share memos and subscriptions to cut back on the demand for paper.

For your information, it seems as though there may soon be an improvement in the paper recycling industry. Two promising technologies, the recent focus of a United Nations expert team, would allow paper recycling without the use of water. They would allow the recovery of all chemicals, fillers, fiber, and ink. This would be especially useful in areas where water shortages occur.

PLASTIC

Because it is lightweight, permanent, waterproof, and nearly indestructible, plastic has been useful for innovations in medicine and other fields. However, it often is not the best material for packaging, where the desired characteristics are convenience and a brief life span.

Plastic is a non-renewable resource. It creates hazardous waste when manufactured and incinerated, often offgasses toxic fumes when used, and is dangerous to transport (spillage), and continues America's dependence on volatile foreign markets.

Some plastics are touted as biodegradable, but this is not the case. Although plastic molecules may be bound together by organic, biodegradable molecules, the plastic molecules, themselves, do not degrade. In addition, today's landfills do not allow for much to biodegrade because the garbage is packed together with little or no exposure to sunlight, rain, and the bacteria that could decompose some of it under different circumstances.

And remember that plastic recycling goes far beyond industrial recycling. Consider reusing your plastic lunch forks and other utensils, and wash and reuse your styrofoam and plastic lunch and salad containers (or, better yet, bring your own). These containers will outlast us all, and some of the plastics used to make these containers are not collected for recycling in all areas.

TYPES OF PLASTIC

When you look at the bottom of a plastic container, do you ever wonder what the numbers inside the three triangular arrows mean? Does the bottom of your flower pots or yogurt container have three arrows chasing each other with a 6 inside? If so, the plastic is polystyrene. See the list below for others:

1 Polyethylene terephthalate (PETE)
2 High-density polyethylene (HDPE)
3 Vinyl/Polyvinyl chloride (V/PVC)
4 Low-Density polyethylene (LDPE)
5 Polypropylene (PP)
6 Polystyrene (PS)
7 Other

PRINTER CONSUMABLES

When printing documents, print in draft mode if possible. Also, use a light-density printer setting. Re-ink your ribbon and use it again when possible.

RE-INKING PRINTER RIBBONS

Keep the ribbons well-inked, since it lubricates the printer head and may increase the printer's lifetime. If you need to re-ink ribbons at least six times each month, a tabletop re-inking machine can pay for itself in a year. Mylar ribbons, however, cannot be re-inked.

REFILLING INKJET CARTRIDGES

You can save money, waste, and packaging by refilling your ink jet cartridge. Refill the ink jet cartridge through a tiny pinhole at the top using a syringe (available at a surgical supply store), apron (it can be messy), and vegetable-based ink or Schaeffer or Scripto ink (available at a stationer's) (Anzovin, 85-86).

Refilling with vegetable-based inks, such as soy-based inks, is the less-toxic alternative over refilling with petroleum-based inks. Unfortunately, the pigments in both vegetable-based and petroleum-based inks generally contain heavy metals, although at least one company, Ecoprint (in Silver Spring, Maryland), uses soy-based inks without heavy metals. In addition, vegetable inks often produce cleaner, brighter colors. Many presses use vegetable inks for printing everything from business cards to company letterheads. Ask around next time you need to have something printed.

Unfortunately, while there are no printer ribbons loaded with vegetable-based inks, you may be able to use vegetable-based inks in re-inking machines or ink jet refills. To find out, contact your printer manufacturer. Also, you can call the American Soybean Association for more information on soy-based inks.

TONER CARTRIDGES

Some estimate at least 28 million new toner cartridges are made in the U.S. annually. With cartridge materials that can last 1,500 years without deteriorating, that's a lot of waste! Fortunately, it's easy to get your toner cartridges refurbished; yet, one study has shown that only 20% of U.S. corporations recycle their toner cartridges or sell them to remanufacturing outfits (Anzovin, 85).

You can recycle your laser printers' toner cartridges. Many companies will refurbish, refill, and return your cartridges at a cost far lower than that of a new one. While new toner cartridges cost about $70-100, recycled cartridges can cost 30-50% less. Companies that recycle toner cartridges will probably even pay the costs to return the cartridges to them. Hewlitt-Packard does – whenever you buy a new printer cartridge, the box includes an address label to mail back the old one at no charge. The United Postal Service (UPS) will take these cartridges as will some companies like Mailboxes, Etc.

You can find toner-cartridge refurbishers through your local stationer's or computer store. To find a good one, look for refurbishers that belong to the International Cartridge Recyclers Association (ICRA). ICRA sets professional standards for refurbishing that go beyond simply drilling a hole in the cartridge and refilling it with toner. While most laser-printer manufacturers take back used toner cartridges and reuse the parts, they don't refurbish entire cartridges like remanufacturers do. Since cartridges can be refurbished and refilled up to six times before wearing out, keep track of yours by putting a notch on it each time it's refilled. That way, you will know that you're getting back the same one you sent.

Most cartridges are supposed to last about 3,500 pages. If you are near the end of your cartridge's life and the pages streak, you may be able to get 500 more pages out of your cartridge. Simply take out the cartridge, hold it horizontally, and gently rock it back and forth a few times. Then, put it back into your printer, and give it a try.

PRINT DRUM

When the coating on the print drum in your laser printer wears out, it can be recoated one or two more times with a new, photosensitive material. New drums are coated with a hard coating that lasts up to 10 times longer than the old coating. Check with toner-cartridge remanufacturers to find out if they provide this service, too.

SHOES

If you have shoes that you need to give up, consider donating them to the One Shoe Crew. This group maintains a shoe bank of single and size-mismatched shoes. They keep a list of adults who only need one shoe or have different size needs for their feet. So, if you break a heel at work or your dog uses one of your favorite business shoes as a toy, don't throw the good one away!

SOFTWARE

If you have some software that you don't want anymore but still is in good condition, you may be able to donate it. Check with the manufacturer first. There may be some legal issues involved when recycling or donating commercial software. The end-user agreement that comes with software restricts your right to donate, copy, or resell the program and its documentation.

However, you can write a letter to the recipients of the software turning all rights over to them. In addition, you may be able to deduct the cost as a donation. Simply give the letter to the software recipient with the end-user agreement, floppy disks, and other materials. Then, erase all other copies of the software on your PC. WordPerfect Corporation has a formal method of donating software; you can fill out a copy supplied by the company, and mail it in. They'll send a new copy of the end-user agreement for the new recipient.

If your company has bought software under a site-license agreement, you have restrictions to be concerned about and should check with the software manufacturer before donating. You may not be able to give away older versions of the software. You may be better off just reformatting the old disks and putting the software manuals into your recycling bins.

TRAVEL

Airlines consume an enormous number of cups, cans, and other "disposables." When you consider the fact that there are about 25,000 flights every day, you will begin to get some idea of the mounds of garbage that can accumulate. Thankfully, a number of airlines are going out of their way these days to recycle. One flight attendant at American Airlines saw the enormous waste created by disposables used during flights. She spearheaded the airline's recycling program, getting fellow attendants, the caterer, and the ground crew involved. The program grew until it became nationwide. Used products were recycled, and the airline donated $250,000 of the money it made by recycling to the Nature Conservancy for land to protect an endangered coneflower species (*Co-op America Quarterly*, Summer 1996, 9).

A trash boat heaped with waste sits anchored near a cruise ship, Bahamas.

If you spend a good deal of time on airlines, consider helping them out. Take your own cup and plastic utensils. Find out what's recycled, and keep it separate from the rest (don't put garbage in aluminum cans, etc.). If the airline does not already recycle everything it can, consider letting one of the flight attendants know, it is important or write a letter to the airline and airport authorities. Some airlines have done environmental audits and reports; some have developed buffet-type food services, thereby eliminating a lot of the packaging. British Airways, American, Swissair, and Northwest are considered to be in the lead as far as the airlines go (*Co-op America Quarterly*, Winter 1994,7).

Finally, rather than travel, you may want to consider conference calls or video conferencing. According to one source, coast-to-coast teleconferencing can cost as little as $150 per site while travel can cost $1000-2000 per person (*Connections*, Summer 1996, 2). Additionally, one ton of carbon dioxide (a greenhouse gas that contributes to global warming) is emitted every 4,000 passenger miles. Whatever you do, try to fly less. It will save you time and money.

HELPFUL RESOURCES

INFORMATION

CARPET RECYCLING
BASF
800-477-8147

Collins & Aikman
P.O. Box 1447
Dalton, GA 30722
800-248-2878/706-259-9711
Fax: 706-259-2179

DuPont, Carpet Reclamations Manager
403 Holiday Avenue
Dalton, GA 30720
706-275-7791/ Fax: 706-275-7752

Earthwise Ennovations
Milliken Carpet
201 Lukken Industrial Drive W.
LeGrange, GA 30240
706-880-5739/ Fax: 706-880-5530

Carpet Recycle Team Leader
Monsanto Company
Technical Center
P.O. Box 97
Gonzalez, FL 32560
904-968-8190/ Fax: 904-968-8732

OTHER INFORMATION
3M
Commercial Office Supply Division
3M Center, Building 225-3S-05
St. Paul, MN 55144
800-395-1223
Contact for "30 Ways to Use Less Paper."

American Recycling Market (ARM)
P.O. Box 577
Ogdensburg, NY 13669
800-267-0707

American Soybean Association
World Headquarters
540 Maryville Centre Dr.
Suite 390
P.O. Box 419200
St. Louis, MO 63141
314-576-1770/ Fax: 314-576-2786
www.oilseeds.org/asa/index.htm

Environmental Protection Agency
For information on the EPA's WasteWi$e program, call: 800-EPA-WISE. Also, there are several EPA publications available free of charge. To get a current listing, call the EPA RCRA/Superfund Hotline: 800-424-9346

Mail Preference Service
c/o Direct Marketing Association

11 W. 42nd Street
P.O. Box 3861
New York, NY 10163
212-689-4977

National Materials Exchange
1521 N. Washington St.
Suite 202
Spokane, WA 99201
509-325-0507
Contact for information on office paper recycling.

Office Paper Recycling
Recycling Information Center
503-224-5555

Sessile Paper Company
125 Lincoln Avenue
Bronx, NY 10454-4432
718-401-0483

WMX Technologies Recycling Services
18500 Von Karmen Ave
Irvine, CA 92715
714-474-2311/ Fax: 714-757-2508

Your Office Paper Recycling Guide
San Francisco Recycling Program
415-554-6193

COMPUTER DONATIONS
Boston Computer Society
101 1st Avenue
Waltham, MA 02154-1160
617-290-5700

or:
9 Newman Avenue
East Providence, RI 02900
401-434-2395

CompuMentor
89 Stillman Street
San Francisco, CA 94107
415-512-7784

* Computer Recycling Center
Development and Technical Assistance Center
555 Weddell Drive
Sunnyvale, CA 94089
408-734-5030/ Fax: 408-734-5099

Nonprofit Computer Consultants Program
70 Audubon Street
New Haven, CT 06510

203-772-1345/ Fax: 203-777-1614

* East-West Education Development Foundation
49 Temple Place
Boston, MA 02111
617-542-1234/ Fax: 617-542-3333

National Cristina Foundation
591 West Putname Avenue
Greenwich, CT 06830
800-274-7846/ Fax: 203-622-6270

Nonprofit Computing
40 Wall Street
Suite 2124
New York, NY 10005
212-759-2368

MicroMenders
ShareWare Project
410 Townsend Street
Suite 408
San Francisco, CA 94107
415-543-0500/ Fax: 415-543-3845

Nonprofit Computer Connection
30 Federal Street
Boston, MA 02110
617-728-9138/ Fax: 617-728-9138

*These companies repair/refurbish donated equipment.
(Taken from *Inc. 1994 Guide to Office Technology*, 37)

RECYCLING
General
*Expanded Polystyrene (EPS) Packaging Recycling
Collection Sites* (November 1994)
Association of Foam Packaging Recyclers
1275 K Street NW, Suite 400
Washington, DC 20005
202-974-5254

Lighting Waste Disposal, Lighting Upgrade Manual
(April 1994)
EPA Green Lights Program

Partnership for Carpet Reclamation DuPont Flooring
Systems
403 Holiday Ave.
Dalton, GA 30720-3755
800-438-7668/302-996-1352

Recycled Plastic Products Source Book (free)
American Plastics Council
800-243-5790

By State
ALABAMA
Alabama Recycling List (January 1994)
Alabama Department of Environmental Management
Solid Waste Branch
P.O. Box 301463
Montgomery, AL 36130-1463

ALASKA
Alaska Department of Environmental Conservation
Pollution Prevention Office
3601 C Street, Suite 1334
Anchorage, AK 99503

ARIZONA
Top 25 Recyclers in the Valley (newspaper article,
December 23,1994)
The Business Journal
Phoenix, AZ

CALIFORNIA
California Integrated Waste Management Board
8800 Cal Center Drive
Sacramento, CA 95826
916-255-2296/800-553-2962
Internet: www.ciwmb.ca.gov

City & County of San Fransisco
Solid Waste Management Program
1145 Market St., Suite 401
San Fransisco, CA 94103
415-554-3400
Internet: www.sfrecycle.org

Los Angeles Integrated Solid Waste Management
Office
200 North Main St.
Room 580 City Hall East
Los Angeles, CA 90012
213-237-1444

COLORADO
RecycleNet Computer Markets Directory
303-620-4096 (modem only)

CONNECTICUT
Connecticut Department of Environmental Protection
Recycling Program
79 Elm St.
Hartford, CT 06106
203-424-3365

DELAWARE
Department of Natural Resources and Environmental
Control

89 Kings Highway
P.O. Box 1401
Dover, DE 19903

FLORIDA
Department of Environmental Protection
Twin Towers Office Building
2600 Blairstone Rd.
Tallahassee, FL 32399-2400
904-488-0300

GEORGIA
Georgia Department of Community Affairs
1200 Equitable Building
100 Peachtree St.
Atlanta, GA 30303
404-679-4950

HAWAII
Hawaii Department of Health
Solid and Hazardous Waste Branch
919 Ala Moana Blvd.
Honolulu, HI 96814

IDAHO
Idaho Department of Health and Welfare Division of
Environmental Quality
1410 North Hilton St.
Boise, ID 83706-1255
208-334-5860

ILLINOIS
Illinois Department of Energy and Natural Resources
Office of Recycling and Waste Reduction
325 West Adams, Room 300
Springfield, IL 62704-1892
217-785-0310

INDIANA
Indiana Recyclable Materials Market Directory (April
1994)
Recycling Market Development Information
Clearinghouse
Indiana Department of Commerce, Energy Policy
Division
1 North Capitol Ave., Suite 700
Indianapolis, IN 46204
317-232-8940

IOWA
Iowa Department of Natural Resources
Wallace State Office Building
Des Moines, IA 50319
515-281-5145

KANSAS
Kansas Business and Industry Recycling Program
2933 SW Woodside Dr.
Suite C
Topeka, KS 66614
913-273-6808

KENTUCKY
Resource Conservation and Local Assistance Branch
Division of Waste Management
Department for Environmental Protection
14 Reilly Road
Frankfort, KY 40601

LOUISIANA
Department of Environmental Quality
Solid Waste Division
Recycling and Waste Minimization Section
P.O. Box 82178
Baton Rouge, LA 70884-2178
504-765-0249

MAINE
Maine Waste Management and Recycling Program
Maine State Planning Office
38 State House Station
Augusta, ME 04333
207-287-5300

MARYLAND
Maryland Environmental Service
2011 Commerce Park Drive
Annapolis, MD 21401
410-974-7282

MASSACHUSETTS
Massachusetts Executive Office of Environmental
Affairs
Department of Environmental Protection
Division of Solid Waste Management
1 Winter Street, 4th floor
Boston, MA 02108
617-338-2255

MICHIGAN
State of Michigan
Departments of Commerce and Natural Resources
Steven T. Mason Building
P.O. Box 30028
Lansing, MI 48909-7528
800-662-9278

MINNESOTA
Minnesota Office of Environmental Assistance
520 Lafayette Rd. North, 2nd Floor

St. Paul, MN 55155-4100
612-296-3417

MISSISSIPPI
MISSTAP/MSSWRAP
P.O. Drawer CN
Mississippi State, MS 39762
601-325-2171

MISSOURI
Missouri Environmental Improvement & Energy
Resources Authority
The Missouri Market Development Program
P.O. Box 744
Jefferson City, MO 65102
314-526-5555

MONTANA
Keep Montana Clean & Beautiful
P.O. Box 5925
Helena, MT 59604

Solid and Hazardous Waste Bureau
Montana Department of Environmental Quality
836 Front St.
Helena, MT 59620
406-444-1430

NEBRASKA
Nebraska Department of Environmental Quality
1200 N Street, Suite 400
P.O. Box 98922
Lincoln, NE 68509-8922
402-471-4210

NEVADA
Nevada Environmental Protection Agency
Capitol Complex/Solid Waste
333 West Nye Lane
Room 119
Carson City, NV 89710
702-687-4670

NEW HAMPSHIRE
New Hampshire Governor's Recycling Program
2 1/2 Beacon St.
Concord, NH 03301
603-271-1098

SOUTH DAKOTA
South Dakota Department of Environment & Natural
Resources
Office of Waste Management
523 East Capitol Ave.
Pierre, SD 57501-3181

605-773-3153
Internet: www.state.fd.us/
state/executive/denr/denr.html

TENNESSEE
Tennessee Department of Environment and
Conservation
Division of Solid Waste Assistance
14th Floor, L & C Tower
401 Church St.
Nashville, TN 37243-0455
615-532-0082

UTAH
The Salt Lake Valley Recycling Information Office
6030 West 1300 S.
Salt Lake City, UT 84104
801-974-6902

VERMONT
Vermont Agency of Natural Resources – Waste
Management Division
Department of Environmental Conservation
103 South Main St.
Waterbury, VT 05671-0407
802-241-3444

WASHINGTON
Washington State Department of Ecology
Solid Waste and Financial Assistance Program
206-649-7048

WEST VIRGINIA
West Virginia Development Office
Energy Efficiency Program
Building 6
Room 553
State Capitol Complex
Charleston, WV 25305
304-558-4010

WISCONSIN
Wisconsin Bureau of Waste Management
P.O. Box 7921
Madison, WI 53707-7921
608-267-7566

WYOMING
Wyoming Department of Environmental Quality
Solid and Hazardous Waste Division
250 Lincoln St.
Lander, WY 82520
307-332-6924

SHOES
For more information, send a self-addressed, stamped envelope to One Shoe Crew. Contact:

The One Shoe Crew
86 Clavela Avenue
Sacramento, CA 95828

TRAVEL
Co-op America Travel Links
120 Beacon Street
Somerville, MA 02143
617-497-8163/800-648-2667
E-mail: mj@tvlcoll.com
Specializes in environmentally responsible travel.

"Green" Hotels Association
P.O. Box 420212
Houston, TX 77242-0212
713-789-8889
Internet: www.greenhotels.com

WASTE EXCHANGES
Alberta Waste Materials Exchange
P.O. Box 8330
Edmonton, Alberta
Canada
403-450-5050

Arizona Resource Exchange
AERE Recycling Office, Bldg 49
Facilities Management
University of Arizona
Tucson, AZ
520-626-1266/ Fax: 520-621-6086

Arkansas Manufacturing Exchange
Arkansas Industrial Development Comm.
#1 Capitol Hill
Little Rock, AR
501-682-7322

Bourse Quebecoise des Matieres Secondaires
Quebec Material Exchange
14 Place Du Comm.
Bureau 350
Les-Des-Soeure, PQ
Canada
514-762-9012

British Columbia IC & I. Materials Exchange
201-225 Smithe Street
Vancouver, BC
Canada
604-683-6009/604-732-9252

CAL Materials Exchange
c/o CIWMB
8800 Cal Center Drive
Sacramento, CA

Canadian Waste Materials Exchange
2395 Speakman Drive
c/o ORTECH
Mississauga, ON
Canada
905-822-4111, ext. 266

Canadian Chemical Exchange
900 Blondin
Ste-Adele, PQ
Canada
800-561-6511

Department Of Toxic Substances Control
P.O. Box 806
Sacramento, CA

Hawaii Materials Exchange
P.O. Box 121
Wailuku, HI
808-667-7744

IMEX Industrial Materials Exchange
506 2nd Avenue, Room 201
Seattle, WA
1-888-TRYIMEX

Indiana Materials Exchange
P.O. Box 454
Carmel, IN
In state: 800-968-8765
317-574-6505

Diane Millenger
c/o Recycler's Trade Network, Inc.
800-968-8764

Industrial Materials Exchange Svr.
P.O. Box 19276
2200 Churchill Road #34
Springfield, IL
217-782-0450

Iowa Waste Bi-Products & Waste Search Service
75 BRC-University of Northern Iowa
Cedar Falls, IA
319-273-2079/ 800-422-3109

Minnesota Materials Exchange
Minnesota Technical Assistance Program

1313 Fifth Street, S.E.
Suite 207
Minneapolis, MN
612-627-4555

MISSTAP Waste Exchange
P.O. Box 9595
Mississippi State, MS
601-325-8454

Montana Material Exchange
MSU Extension Service
Taylor Hall
Bozeman, MT 59717
Internet: www.montana.edu/wwwated

National Materials Exchange
P.O. Box 152
Hutchinson, KS
316-662-0551
E-mail: nmen@eznet.com

New Hampshire Waste Exchange
122 N. Main Street
Concord, NH
603-224-5388

Northeast Industrial Waste Exchange, Inc.
P. O. Box 2171
Annapolis, MD
E-mail: niwe@aol.com

Olmsted County Materials Exchange
Olmsted County Public Works
Campus Drive, SE
Rochester, MN
507-285-8231

Ontario Waste Exchange
2395 Speakman Drive
Mississauga, ON
Canada
905-822-4111, ext., 656

Portland Chemical Consortium
Portland State University
P.O. Box 751
Portland, OR
503-725-3893

Resource Conversion Manitoba
70 Albert Street/ Suite #2
Winnipeg, MB
Canada

Resource Exchange Network For Eliminating Waste (RENEW)
P.O. Box TNRCC-MC112
Austin, TX
512-239-3171

SEMREX
171 W. Third Street
Winona, MN
507-457-6460

Southeast Waste Exchange
Urban Institute – UNC Charlotte
Charlotte, NC
E-mail: milmay@unccvm.uncc.edu

Southern Waste Information Exchange
P.O. Box 960
Tallahassee, FL
800-441-7949
E-mail: swix@mailer.fsu.edu

Tennessee Materials Exchange (TME)
226 Capital Blvd
Suite 606
The University of Tennessee Center for Industrial Services
Nashville, TN
615-532-8881

Transcontinental Materials Exchange
Civil & Environmental Engineering
Louisiana State University
Baton Rouge, LA
504-388-4594

Vermont Business Materials Exchange
P.O. Box 935
Battleboro, VT
802-257-7505.

WasteLink
140 Wooster Pike
Milford, OH
513-248-0012

PRODUCTS

For addresses and phone numbers, refer to *Appendix A: Directory of Suppliers.*

OFFICE SUPPLIES
A-1 Products Corp.
Action Packaging Systems

CECOR, Inc.
Eldon/Rubbermaid Office Products
Environmental Plastics
Feeny Manufacturing
Hold Everything
Real Goods Trading
Safeco Products Co.
United Receptacle , Inc.
United Recycling, Inc.
Urban Ore
WMX Technologies Recycling Services

HOLIDAY CARDS
Card Recycling

PACKAGING
Association of Foam Packaging Recyclers

PAPER
Sessile Paper Company

Summary of Recommendations

Aluminum

• Use aluminum over glass or plastic because it is easier to recycle and can be used over and over.

Carpets

• Find a company or organization that will recycle or reuse your carpets.

CD-ROMS

• Some are even using CD-ROM parts to make jewelry, clock faces, and other items. Be creative! If you don't want to be, find someone who is and offer them your CDs.

Computer Batteries

• The newest, healthiest alternative is a nickel-metal-hydride (NMH) battery.

• When recharging PC batteries, be sure they're fully discharged first, or they won't hold a full charge again.

• Send batteries back to your computer company if they recycle them (Apple Computer does).

Computers

• Disassemble your computer or return it whole if you've found someone willing to recycle it.

• If your PC still works but you're in the market for an upgrade, consider donating it.

Construction Site Recycling

• If you're renovating, try to use as much waste as possible in your new design. If you're building new, look around for local sources of used building materials.

Floppy Disks

• Whenever floppy disks develop bad sectors from dust or other contaminants, try resectoring them. After using a disk repair utility, reformat your disks.

• If write-protect tabs have been broken or are missing on 3.5-inch floppies, pry out the rest of tab, and replace it with a small piece of thin cardboard.

• Compress files to save space – they can often be compressed to 25% of size.

• By recycled diskettes.

GLASS

• Ensure that your glass for recycling is acceptable to your local recycling company. Generally, only glass that has contained food or beverages is allowed. Lightbulbs, broken eyeglasses, and other sources of glass may be of use to some companies (in making paving blocks, etc.), so check around.

HAZARDOUS WASTE

• Locate a waste exchange, or contact local authorities to find out how to safely dispose of hazardous waste.

HOLIDAY CARDS

• Find a recycling company that will accept mixed papers.

• Send your cards to an organization that will reuse them (youth groups, schools, etc.)

LIGHT BALLASTS

• Contact your local authorities to find out how to dispose of light ballasts.

PACKING MATERIALS

• Save or reuse the polystyrene and polyurethane packing foams used in the computer industry. Their manufacturing process is not an environmentally friendly one, and they don't biodegrade. Some recycling centers and office-supply distributors accept/reuse foam packaging. The Association of Foam Packaging Recyclers runs over 45 foam-recycling plants in the U.S., so you can call them for the plant nearest you.

• Try crumpled or shredded waste paper or biodegradable cornstarch packaging in place of styrofoam.

PAPER

• Use white paper over colored since its easier to recycle.

PRINTER CONSUMABLES

• When printing documents, print in draft mode if possible, and use a light-density printer setting.

• Re-ink your printer ribbon, and use it again. Also, refill ink jet cartridges with vegetable-based inks when possible.

• Recycle your laser printers' toner cartridges. Cartridges can be refurbished and refilled up to six times before wearing out, keep track of yours by putting a notch on it each time it's refilled.

• When you're near the end of your toner cartridge and the pages streak, you may be able to get 500 more pages. Simply take out the cartridge, hold it horizontally, and gently seesaw it a few times.

• When the coating on the print drum in your laser printer wears out, it can be recoated one or two more times with a new, photosensitive material.

SHOES

• Rather than throw your shoes away, donate them to a person or organization that may be able to use them.

SOFTWARE

• If you have some software that you don't want anymore, but it's still in good condition, you may be able to donate it. Check with the manufacturer first.

• Reformat old software and use it to store your own files.

TRAVEL

• When traveling, encourage your airline to recycle its aluminum, plastics, and paper waste if it doesn't already.

• Take and use your own utensils on flights and train rides.

CHAPTER 17

SMARTER OFFICE LAWN CARE & LANDSCAPING

"The degradable point is largely moot. Landfills are technologically engineered tombs that will not allow anything to degrade, including grass clippings." Edward J. Stana, exec. director of the Council on Plastics and Packaging in the Environment, Anderson, 1990, 36

If you're lucky, you work in an office surrounded by trees, grasses, and other greenery. Not only do outdoor plants provide people with a sense of greater peace and a connection to the outside world, but they also can protect your building from cold winds, traffic noise, and pollution.

Unfortunately, lawns, as we know them, have been strongly influenced by the model golf course. Rather than consisting of native plants, which are best suited for their own natural climates, today's lawns often are made of non-native grass species. The introduction of non-native grasses for their various aesthetic properties has led to the displacement of many native plants. In addition, they are sometimes poorly suited to the climates in which they are planted, and they can require additional water and special care. Native species, on the other hand, often are viewed as weeds when they pop up in their natural habitats rather than allowed to flourish.

In creating a healthy landscape, there are many things to consider. Following is a discussion of some of the primary issues.

CHEMICAL FERTILIZERS & PESTICIDES

Artificial, chemical fertilizers and biocides (chemicals that kill life – insects, rodents, other plants) throw off the natural balance within the soil and plants. They affect plant metabolism and kill beneficial creatures. They get into our food, drinking water, and streams and rivers.

In addition, chemicals and mineral-salt fertilizers make brutal environments for the beneficial, life-sustaining organisms that live in soil. As these organisms are killed, the soil loses vitality, and plants are increasingly vulnerable to insects and disease.

Synthetic fertilizers work for short periods, generally supplying only a narrow range of nutrients (mainly nitrogen, potassium, and phosphorous). Such a narrow diet is not healthy. Some experts say that chemical fertilizers even alter both the protein and vitamin content of plants, thereby affecting their nutritional value. In addition, these fertilizers give offgasses and can leach through the ground soil into the water.

townsend, 1995

Building with nature rather than plowing it under can create a more peaceful and pleasant place in which to work.

Some biocides (pesticides, herbicides, fungicides, etc.) often are carcinogenic. When something kills unwelcome plants or creatures, it may also impact what you're growing, breathing, and eating.

In addition, lawn care chemicals can be harmful to humans and other animals. According to the National Coalition Against the Misuse of Pesticides, "Of the 34 chemicals encompassing 95 percent of lawn pesticides, 10 are carcinogens, 12 cause birth defects, 20 are neurotoxic, 7 alter the reproductive process, 13 cause liver and kidney damage and 29 are sensitizers or irritants" (Lloyd, 1991, D5).

GRASSCYCLING

"Grasscycling" is grass recycling, a process by which you recycle your grass clippings back into the lawn when you mow. Grasscycling improves the appearance and health of your office lawn.

Because grass contains a high amount of water, nitrogen, phosphorous, potassium, and other nutrients, it acts as a good fertilizer. The clippings from the lawn filter down to the soil's surface and can decompose anywhere from a few days to about one week. As the cuttings decompose and release nutrients, micro-organisms and earthworms take these nutrients down to the roots of the grass, thereby feeding your lawn.

Grasscycling offers many benefits. According to the Montgomery County, Maryland, Department of Environmental Protection's *Grasscycle* video, grasscycling

- "Makes herbicides and pesticides unhealthy
- Prevents groundwater contamination and run-off
- Improves soil ecology
- Returns nutrients to the soil
- Encourages deep root growth
- Prevents soil compaction
- Conserves soil moisture
- Puts less stress on your grass
- Inhibits weeds and disease"

With proper fertilization, watering, and aeration methods, grasscycling can give you beautiful office grounds without the use of chemicals.

Grasscycling eliminates the time someone would spend emptying, raking, and bagging grass clippings, activities that account for about half the time spent "mowing." It also saves the money that you might otherwise spend

on fertilizers. The average American suburban lawn, for instance, contains about 40 pounds of nitrogen in its grass. This is more than that found in most synthetic fertilizers, and many fertilizers don't contain the other nutrients found in grass clippings. So, by letting these clippings remain on the lawn to decompose, you are feeding your grass better than you could with most synthetic fertilizers.

Grass clippings make up as much as 10% of municipal solid waste. This number has been known to skyrocket to 50% of all household waste during the spring and summer months. Even when grass clippings are taken to large composting facilities, it takes a lot of money and energy for their collection, transport, and processing.

In the past, many people did not leave grass clippings on their lawns or office grounds because they believed that it wasn't good for the grass. Some feared thatch buildup or believed that leaving grass clippings on the ground would be unattractive. Fortunately, this isn't true. Excessive thatch buildup comes not from grasscycling but from poor watering methods and excessive fertilizing.

Poor watering methods (e.g., surface watering with a hose) can result in the grass roots growing toward the ground surface to get to the moist, top layer of soil. Excessive fertilizing can lead to the development of lazy roots, which don't need to dig down for nutrients since their nutrients come from the fertilizer on top of the soil. The roots can become weak and grow upward for more water or nutrients, where they are vulnerable to drying out when hot weather strikes.

Grasscycling is great for office grounds and lawns. And, if you keep the grass clippings short (one inch or less) so that they can filter down to the soil surface, they are not readily apparent. Even if your clippings are longer than the suggested one inch, you can double-mow (mow twice) to shorten them. Simply mow once, then mow perpendicular to the first cut. Also, to keep your grass in maximum health, try not to cut more than one-third of your grass' length in one cutting.

Fortunately, grasscycling doesn't require any special equipment. You don't even need a mulching mower. Any mower will do; just remove the bag to allow the grass to remain on the lawn. For rear discharge mowers, be sure that the chute is closed. And remember to keep the mower's blades sharp. A dull cut can be bad for the grass and encourage disease. Sharpen your mower blades at least once every year.

For a good lawn, aeration is also important. This means poking holes in the soil and pulling out two- or three-inch-deep plugs of soil. Leave these plugs on the surface, which will fertilize the grass. Aeration encourages microbes, breaks up thatch, and allows oxygen to reach the grass roots. It's recommended that you aerate your grounds once every two or three years. Aeration machines can be rented, or you can hire a lawn service to do this.

If, for some reason, you decide to fertilize with something other than your grass clippings, use a slow-release, organic fertilizer. It will keep your grass from growing too quickly, and you'll have to cut less often than you would with something other than a slow-release variety. Also, fertilize only in the fall before the first frost.

Smart Lawn Stories

Islip Town, located on Long Island in New York, was the first town to institute a "Don't Bag It" program for recycling grass clippings. Since then, programs have sprung up throughout the country.

In 1990, Montgomery County, Ohio, discovered just how smart grasscycling was. Its educational campaign promoting grass recycling averaged about $1.30 per ton, whereas its centralized composting of grass averaged about $40 per ton (*Grasscycling* video).

Lawn Mowers

There are alternatives to gasoline- and electric-powered lawn mowers. The manual, push mowers have made a comeback. They are sold in a variety of sizes for various lawn-care needs and don't create any pollution or demand for energy – except that of the person pushing it. They tend to be lighter in weight than engine mowers and cut the grass more quietly, without causing the noise pollution that engine mowers do.

Rechargeable electric mowers, while dependent on non-renewable resources for their energy, are less energy-intensive than their gasoline-powered counterparts. They also are quieter, create less pollution, and require little maintenance.

A less common mower is an automatic, solar-powered one sold by Real Goods Trading Company, based in Ukiah, California. This mower doesn't need anyone to push it; it runs by itself, sensing when to turn to avoid flower gardens and other, slightly taller areas.

Smart Watering

An enormous amount of water is used on office grounds and lawns every year. During the primary growing season, homeowners, for instance, put 10,000 gallons of water on each 1,000 square feet of lawn. That's a lot of water. Unfortunately, conventional watering methods don't always ensure that the water is put to good use. Whenever your grounds are watered with sprinklers and above-ground hoses, much of the water evaporates. You may want to consider using an underground watering system to conserve water. Here are a few suggestions for smarter watering:

- Consider an underground watering system that waters only as needed.
- Don't water your lawn by hand. Light watering only encourages the roots to keep close to the surface, where they are more vulnerable to heat and drought.
- Water deeply and only when needed. About an inch of water each week encourages deep root systems to develop. A one-quarter or half-inch hose generally takes about three hours to put out one inch of water, but you can put a bowl or can within range of your sprinkler to measure. For healthy plants, water needs to go deep into the soil; otherwise, the roots rise to the surface looking for water, making them less stable and more vulnerable to heat and droughts.
- If you see runoff, stop watering until the water soaks in.
- Only water in the morning so that your grass can dry out during the day. When it's watered later and left damp, it's more susceptible to disease.
- Try arranging plants with similar water, lighting, and soil needs together to make your watering easier.

Xeriscaping

Xeriscaping® is a trademarked term first coined by the Denver, Colorado, Water Department. It hails from the Greek term "xeros," which means "dry," and refers to landscaping using water conservation measures. It's particularly useful in areas that don't get much rainfall. Since the 1980s, the idea of xeriscaping has become increasingly common throughout the U.S. Southwest, California, Florida, and other areas.

Xeriscape landscaping, or xeriscaping, has many benefits. You can reduce water use, create less yard waste (grass clippings), lower your landscaping maintenance costs, create more wildlife habitat, minimize runoff of irrigation water and storm water, keep topsoil in place, reduce heating and cooling bills through properly placed trees and shrubs, and create healthier soil.

Xeriscaping can cut water use by 25%-75%. While it requires no extra work, it does require good planning. For xeriscaping, the lawn or office grounds are divided into various zones. One, the oasis zone, is located nearest the building. This is the zone that requires the most care and watering and, in the overall landscape, is the smallest. The next, the drought-tolerant zone, is located a little farther out and is comprised of plants that need watering only every 7-10 days. Beyond that is the natural zone, made up of native plants, which, once they're established, won't need any water other than rainfall.

Grass can be used as an accent and not as the main cover. Instead, ground cover or mulched beds make up the majority of a xeriscaped landscape. Mulching keeps the ground warmer in the winter and cooler in the summer. It also helps to increase moisture absorption in dry soils and holds moisture while preventing soil erosion. Of course, compost can be used for healthier fertilizing. Native plants, adapted to the rigors of their local environments, generally can protect themselves better against insects and disease than can exotic plants.

Good planning and design are basic elements of xeriscaping. Choosing the right plants for the site is important, too. Native plants can result in a landscape that requires little maintenance and is self-perpetuating. Good irrigation is an important component of smart landscaping, too. Unfortunately, a great deal of irrigation water can be lost through runoff (when lawns are watered too quickly and the water doesn't have a chance to sink in, for instance) and through evaporation.

HELPFUL RESOURCES

INFORMATION

Backyard Composting
Harmonious Press
P.O. Box 1865-100
Ojai, CA 93024
800-345-0096/ 805-646-8030/ Fax: 805-696-7404

Beneficial Organisms Booklet
Department of Pesticide Regulation
P.O. Box 94287
Sacramento, CA 94271-0001
916-654-1141

Bio-Dynamic Farming and Gardening Association
P.O. Box 550
Kimberton, PA 19442
215-935-7797/ Fax: 215-983-3196

Drip Irrigation for Every Landscape and All Climates and *Gray Water Use in the Landscape* by Robert Kourik
The Drip Irrigation Project
P.O. Box 1841
Santa Rosa, CA 95402
707-874-2606

International Alliance for Sustainable Agriculture
Newman Center, University of Minnesota
1701 University Avenue, SE
Minneapolis, MN 55414
612-331-1099/ Fax: 612-379-1527

Oasis Greywater Information (by Art Ludwig)
Oasis Biocompatible Products
1020 Veronica Springs
Santa Barbara, CA 93105
805-682-3449

Organic Gardening magazine
800-666-2206

Pesticide Action Network
116 New Montgomery
Suite 810
San Francisco, CA 94105
415-541-9140/ Fax: 415-541-9253

The Rapid Composting Method publication
6701 San Pablo Avenue
Oakland, CA 94608

Rodale Institute
222 Main Street, Box KS
Emmaus, PA 18098
215-683-6383/ Fax: 215-683-8548

Seeds of Change
P.O. Box 15700
Santa Fe, NM 87506-5700
505-438-8080/ Fax: 505-438-7052
Ask for *The Seeds of Change Catalogue* and *The Deep Diversity Catalogue*.

Seeds of Change: The Living Treasure by Kenny Ausubel, Harper San Francisco, 1994.

Soil Remineralization, A Network Newsletter
152 South Street
Northampton, MA 01060

Xeriscape: Quality Landscaping That Conserves Water and Protects the Environment
The Lower Colorado River Authority
Water Efficiency Department
P.O. Box 220
Austin, TX 78767
800-776-5272

PRODUCTS

For addresses and phone numbers, refer to *Appendix A: Directory of Suppliers*.

COMPOSTING
A-1 Products Corp.
Barclay Recycling, Inc.
Eco-Corporation
Environmental Applied Products
Gardener's Eden
Harmonious Technologies
Presto Products
Russell Wold
Smith & Hawken, Ltd.
Wastenot
Yemm & Hart
Zoo Doo Co.

LANDSCAPING
American Soil Products
BTW Industries, Inc.
Biofac Incorporated
Biological Urban Gardening Services
Carrysafe, Inc.
Carsonite International
Chicagoland Processing
Eco Enterprises
Environmental Applied Products
Environmental Plastics
Environmental Specialty Products
Florida Playground & Steel Co.
Gardens Alive
Garden City Seeds
Gardener's Supply
Integrated Fertility Management
Jervert Enterprises, Inc.
Native Seed/SEARCH
The Natural Gardening
Necessary Trading Co.
Outwater Plastic Lumber
Peaceful Valley Farm Supply
Planet Natural
The Plastic Lumber Co.
Positive Growth
Presto Products

Re-Source Building Products, Ltd.
Rincon Vitova Insectaries
Ringer Corp.
Scientific Developments, Inc.
Seeds of Change
Seed Savers Exchange
Smith & Hawken
Whole Earth Landscape Design, Inc.
Wood Recycling, Inc.
Yemm & Hart

REEL MOWER
Great States Corporation

WATERING
Agwa Systems
Aquapore Moisture Systems

Summary of Recommendations

Biological Diversity

• Plant with native plants that require less water and help to restore the ecology of the area.

Chemicals

• Avoid using chemical fertilizers and biocides (herbicides, pesticides, rodenticides, etc.).

• Use non-toxic lawn-care products and pest control methods.

Composting

• Be certain to compost organic materials to create healthier soil.

• Leave grass clippings on the lawn.

Energy

• Use manual or solar-powered lawn mowers.

Water

• Use xeriscaping methods.

• Focus on efficient water use.

"On an individual level, we may not feel powerful enough to take on the transnationals, but we can grow a garden." (*GreenMoney Journal's* Internet home page)

CHAPTER 18

SMARTER TRANSPORTATION & TELECOMMUTING

"Our national flower is the concrete cloverleaf."
Lewis Mumford, *The Culture of Cities*, 1938

TRANSPORTATION

In the short time since the car was invented, we've come to depend on it enormously. In the U.S., our dependence on the automobile is higher than in any other country in the world.

According to the U.S. Department of Transportation, there are 140 million cars in the U.S. These cars are fueled by over 200 million gallons of gasoline each day, or about 55 barrels each second (Anzovin, 106).

Each gallon of gasoline burned results in the release of 20 pounds of CO_2 into the atmosphere. As a result, over 7 million tons of nitrogen oxide are emitted annually, contributing to acid rain. Hydrocarbon emissions create "ozone smog," and gas and oil leaks pollute the air and water. Millions of barrels of crude oil, from which gasoline is made, are spilled into the ocean's each year. In addition, every year 40,000 people are killed in motor vehicle accidents in the U.S. alone (Anzovin, 106).

Using public transportation is one way to get around many of the problems associated with cars. When you need to get someplace, you may have several options. Trains are one of the most efficient ways of moving large numbers of people and goods. Some companies have creative, cooperative agreements with public transportation companies to get employees to and from work at a

townsend, 1995

A seemingly endless network of roads that disappears into the smog is a scene all too familiar to many commuters and city dwellers.

reduced rate. In addition, some companies offer incentives to employees who carpool, bike, walk, or take public transportation to work. The Monterey Aquarium even has a "green" transportation coordinator and a successful program.

There can be a downside to public transportation. For instance, buses often pollute the air, and their schedules and stops are sometimes inconvenient. Current bus and subway systems are not always good at providing transport between anything other than major hubs. Safety issues also can deter people from taking public transportation when bus stops are not well lit or are unguarded.

Italy and other European countries are considering making their urban areas car-free. Voters in Amsterdam, Zurich, and Bologna already approved a system restricting auto traffic within cities. Of course, living closer to work can greatly reduce the need for transportation.

There is no doubt that driving can be expensive, particularly in urban areas where parking is at a premium. One European Community report estimated that the cost of building transportation infrastructures in car-packed urban areas might be two to five times higher than they would be in car-free cities due simply to the fact that the costs of buying, insuring, and parking cars are quite high.

While many people in China, Denmark, and other countries often use bicycles to commute to work, in many U.S. suburban and urban areas, many people cannot safely bike to work. If you live in a bicycle-friendly area or a place with a great public transportation system, you're lucky. Many live in areas with poor public transportation and no bicycle-safe routes or travel lanes, so it's not surprising why cars are so common.

Unfortunately, if you drive a typical vehicle powered by fossil fuels, commuting causes damage to the environment and our health and takes valuable time from people's lives, families, and other activities. If you commute for two hours every day, for example, in 40 years you will have spent 2.3 years commuting (Anzovin, 106).

I'm sure that you can think of better things to do with your life. The only thing more depressing is to realize that 1) some people's commutes are even longer than yours, and 2) with the world's population growing, traffic problems are going to worsen.

MAKE THE SWITCH

When you have to get out, consider public transportation or carpooling. Or, if possible, walk or bike to your destination. It's not only good for your health but may help you to better connect with your community.

How Some Fuels Compare

If you have to drive, consider switching to natural gas. If you're firmly committed and able, consider purchasing or retrofitting a vehicle that uses a cleaner, more renewable fuel.

California's Energy Commission recently agreed to create an alcohol-fueled vehicle with ultra-low emissions. The engine used will be a medium-duty diesel engine with the ability to be powered by either methanol or ethanol. Both of these are renewable fuels that are much cleaner than the fossil fuels most of us use now.

Energy Content

	Gasoline	LPG	CNG
Btu/gallon	115400	82450	19760
% of Gas	100	71.4	17.1

Price Per Gallon of Natural Gasoline Versus Alternative Fuels

Location	Gasoline	LPG (liquid propane)	CNG (compressed natural gas)
Atlanta, GA	$.96	$1.11	$.75
Boston, Mass.	1.12	1.95	.68
Chicago, Ill.	1.23	1.30	.93
Denver, Colo.	1.16	1.04	.85
Houston, Tex.	1.03	1.11	.70
Los Angeles, Calif.	1.26	1.23	.73
Milwaukee, Wis.	1.12	1.15	.71
New York, N.Y.	1.18	1.46	.85
Philadelphia, PA	1.06	1.75	.72
Washington, D.C.	1.17	1.24	N/A
TOTAL AVERAGE	1.13	1.33	.74

(Taken from *Consumer's Digest*, September/October 1993)

For more information on cleaner, renewable fuels, contact an organization such as the Rocky Mountain Institute (Snowmass, Colorado). Also, check your bookstore for books on transportation, or do some research on the Internet.

EPA's Transportation Partners

Fortunately, the Environmental Protection Agency created a program to encourage the use of smarter transportation alternatives and telecommuting. EPA's Transportation Partners is a voluntary program intended to support public/private initiatives to reduce the negative, environmental impacts of transportation.

One of the program's goals is to use new technologies to encourage better transportation alternatives. These include telecommuting by working from telecenters or from home. Teleservices, such as getting financial advice and other professional services via computer, could make the telecommuting lifestyle easier. So could "interactive transit kiosks," which would offer information to commuters about their simplest route and the next scheduled public transportation pick-up times.

Hypercars: Building A Better Automobile

How would you like to drive a car that gets 150-300 miles per gallon? It will never happen, you may say, but it is already in progress.

The Difference
These cars will differ in many ways from conventional automobiles. For one thing, they will be 2-3 times lighter, 1-3 times less polluting, many times more aerodynamic, safer, better, and cost-competitive. They will use about 10% of the steel, 10-25% as much fuel, and 50% of the total polymer. Many of the systems present in today's cars will be downsized or eliminated.

The Fuel
These will not be battery-operated cars. Instead, they will run on gas or hydrogen. Fuel cells attached to the wheels actually create power as the vehicle is driven.

The Reality
In 1994-1995, about $1 billion was dedicated to creating ultralight-hybrid automobiles, and about 25 firms, including the big automakers, are competing for their shares in the market.

The Research
The idea for hypercars has been nurtured at the Rocky Mountain Institute's Hypercar Center. Expertise has been drawn from hundreds of automakers, research centers, government agencies, and others to determine the methods, feasibility, costs, and economics of this total car retrofit.

For more information, contact the Rocky Mountain Institute for brief publications on hypercars. If you are very interested, you can buy RMI's book *Hypercars: Materials, Manufacturing, and Policy Implications* for U.S. $10,000 (postage paid).

Telecommuting

Telecommuting saves workers from having to commute to the office every day while cutting down on traffic and pollution. Put simply, telecommuting means working from a location other than your company's office, usually from home. With today's technological capabilities, workers have a certain freedom that didn't exist just one or two decades ago. And many workers are taking advantage of this.

Telecommuting has the potential to change current ideas of the workplace altogether. Thanks to telecommuting and the establishment of satellite centers and televillages, all workers may not have to report to work at a centralized location five days each week. Instead, those who aren't needed at their workplaces all of the time can work from home or at a satellite center nearer their homes. This can save hours in commuting, help to increase worker productivity and quality of life, and cut down on office expenses, traffic, and pollution.

Telecommuting also has the power to change society and demographics. By decreasing or completely eliminating commuting time, workers may have more time to spend with their families or pursuing other interests. Of course, this could lead to happier, more fulfilled lives. They also could choose to live further from work without worrying about the driving time, distance, and expense of commuting.

Some Telecommuting Options

There are many ways to telecommute. Telecommuting can be informal and either part-time, full-time, or temporary. Employees can come into the office several times each week and take work home with them to do on their PCs. Or, they can work from home all of the time, coming in only for meetings, reviews, or whenever necessary. Telecommuting also can be done on a temporary, as-needed basis.

Some companies have formal telecommuting programs, including Apple, AT&T, Control Data Corporation, DEC, Hewlitt-Packard, IBM, and UMI/Data Courier.

Hewlett Packard set up a telecommuting program for its western region sales people and hoped to recruit half of these sales people into the telecommuting program. In 1991, Los Angeles county hired over 1,200 telecommuters. Not only did it save $30,000 monthly through higher productivity and lower costs, but it also helped the environment by keeping those cars off the streets (Anzovin, 108). Another method of telecommuting is working through satellite centers. These are computing centers established in places near employees' homes.

Several companies in Los Angeles (e.g., Disney, IBM, Pacific Bell, Southern California Edison, and Xerox) already take advantage of telecommuting. They lease office space from a building in suburban Riverside, 60 miles from the city. These companies save on rent, which is far less in Riverside than it is in Los Angeles. And employees of these companies that live in or near Riverside can drive or bike to work at the satellite center, taking advantage of the PCs, network connections, phones, faxes, and modems. Having these centers allows employees to skip the two-hour commute into the city, and go, instead, to their nearby satellite center.

Although televillages are similar to satellite centers in concept, they are residential. These are communities that are established with residents' telecommuting in mind. They are wired with advanced telecommunication systems and can offer work opportunities in isolated and rural areas. Examples of televillages are found north of Toronto, in Amelia Park (on Florida's Amelia Island) and in Wales in an enclave of cottages in Crickhowell (built by Acorn Televillages, Ltd.).

Who Should Telecommute?

All sorts of jobs may be perfect for telecommuting. Good telecommuting jobs are those that:

"• Can be performed outside the office and on a flexible schedule.
• Don't depend on a central, non-portable physical resource.
• Don't require constant supervision.
• Can be performed with the aid of a computer and telecommunications equipment" (Anzovin, 109).

The most successful telecommuters generally have certain characteristics in common:

• "they're self-motivated.
• they're hard workers who enjoy their work.
• they're flexible-minded, creative problem solvers.
• they work best without close supervision.
• they're comfortable with computers, networks, and other technologies.
• they have a personal stake in the success of the telecommuting programs in their organizations" (Anzovin, 109).

Of course, telecommuting is much better for the environment, too. According to EPA estimates, 10 million workers drive an average of 75 miles round-trip to work in cars that get an average of 25 miles per gallon. If these people telecommuted, 30 million gallons of gas would be saved every single working day, keeping 600 million pounds of carbon dioxide out of the atmosphere. And the more telecommuters there are and the more often they telecommute, the more traffic is reduced.

People who telecommute tend to be more conscientious about their use of paper and energy, particularly if they have to pay for these resources. Not only can there be higher morale on the part of employees, but employee expenses may decrease while productivity increases. In addition, as part of an overall, positive employee program, the flexibility allowed by telecommuting can help you find and retain good employees. In addition, employees may not feel that they are living such splintered lives as they would if they had to commute.

Telecommuting Caution

Just as there are advantages to telecommuting, there also can be some disadvantages of which you should be aware.

• If you thrive in an environment in which you're surrounded by others, you may not enjoy working alone. You may be able to get more accomplished during long hours of isolation, but it may drive you crazy.
• If you're in a position in which you need to report often or supervise employees regularly, you may find it easier to work at the office full-time.
• If you're working on a new project or just learning something, you may choose to spend some time at the office so that you can meet with people or ask questions if simply calling isn't enough. Although e-mail and telephoning are great tools, they don't allow eye contact and body language to be part of the working relationship; as a result, misunderstandings and client dissatisfaction can result if communication isn't frequent and well done.
• Now that you're telecommuting and are anticipating working only 40 hours every week without commuting, you have more time to yourself. Be sure that your

employer doesn't try to take advantage of the extra time you thought was your own by loading you down with extra work. Apparently, this happens most frequently to telecommuting women with low-paying jobs.

• Now that you have all of this excess time, what will you do with yourself? Be careful not to become a workaholic. This self-imposed slavery is a habit easy to get into and seems to be more common than employer-imposed slavery.

• Be sure that your benefits will not disappear once you work at home. Check to find out about insurance coverage and worker's compensation.

How to Start Telecommuting

If you're an employee interested in telecommuting, there are several steps that you should take. After you've looked over both the advantages and the disadvantages, you'll need to make a plan.

Your employer will probably be most interested in monetary savings and increases in your productivity, so keep this in mind when drawing out a plan. There are several issues that your employer will probably be interested in. They include:

1. Determine the best employees for telecommuting.

2. Ensure that you are using your time efficiently (e.g., that you're not goofing off).

3. Who supplies your PC and other office materials?

4. How will you record and be reimbursed for phone calls, couriers, postage, and other business-related expenses?

5. Insurance, workers' compensation, etc.

6. Red tape

If your employer is uncertain, offer to telecommute on a temporary or part-time basis to give it a trial run. Then, set up a resource-efficient, healthy home office, and get started! If your experience is successful, it may provide an incentive for your company to create a formal telecommuting program and help you decide if telecommuting is for you.

A BETTER CAB

If you need to take a cab, look for an innovative company like Clean Air Cab Company, a Washington, D.C.-based business with several cabs that run on natural gas. While natural gas is a fossil fuel, it burns a lot cleaner than gasoline. By using natural gas, sulfur and lead are not emitted into the air, and nitrogen oxides and carbon monoxides are kept to a minimum.

HELPFUL RESOURCES

INFORMATION

CABS
Clean Air Cab Company
1630 14th Street, NW
2nd Floor
Washington D.C. 20009
202-667-7000/800-999-8910

EPA'S TRANSPORTATION PARTNERS
If you would like to learn more about the program, contact the following:

U.S. EPA
401 M Street, SW
Mailcode 2126
Washington, DC 20460
Waterside Mall, Room 3202
202-260-3729/ 202-260-6123/ 202-260-6915

INSTITUTE FOR LOCAL SELF-RELIANCE
This organization has published several books and monographs on alternative fuels for transportation.

Institute for Local Self-Reliance
2425 18th Street NW
Washington, DC 20009
202-232-4108/ Fax: 202-332-0463

PEDICABS
Pedicabs
202-332-1732
Pedicabs also has offices in Atlanta, Burlington, Denver, Key West, New York, Phoenix, and San Diego.

SUMMARY OF RECOMMENDATIONS

LIFESTYLE

• Consider living closer to work.

• Telecommute full-time or part-time, or use a telecenter.

PROGRAMS

• Subsidize employees to encourage public transport (bus, subway, etc.)

• Become an EPA Transportation Partner.

TRANSPORTATION

• Ride your bike.

• Take public transportation.

• Carpool.

• If you're buying a car, consider fuel-efficient models.

• Switch to a cleaner fuel.

• Take advantage of companies like the Clean Air Cab Company that offer cleaner transportation alternatives.

PART FIVE

• • • • • • • •

ADDITIONAL

INFORMATION

CHAPTER 19

SMART INVESTING

"What's the use of investing for the future if it's not worth living in?"
Working Assets Advertisement

WHAT IS SMART INVESTING?

It takes the same amount of capital and time to invest in smart companies as it does for any other companies. If you are reading this book, you're interested in creating a smart office – one that is healthy and efficient and increases the comfort and productivity of everyone who works there. As a result, you are probably more likely to invest in other companies who, like yourself, are working toward becoming smarter. By investing in these companies, by buying not only their products but their stocks, you are helping to provide the capital for their expansion. You also are sending a signal to the market that you are interested in smart development, and encouraging other companies to create better products. Ultimately, this will help to drive down the prices of those smarter products that you purchase as competition among smart products and technologies increases.

Be it money market or mutual funds, stocks, or bonds, it's important that you invest your money into something that will not only pay off for you but will reflect your intelligence at the same time. After all, why support smarter technologies with your purchases while investing in technologies and processes counter to that? By investing in other smart companies, you'll be investing in a large and quickly growing market.

According to *Fortune* magazine, business executives and investment bankers look carefully for any trends that may affect the international flow of money since this money is what pays for new products, ventures, and expansions. As smart company actions and products become more of an interest in the mind of the global consumer, industries will turn increasingly in that direction to meet the demand. Investing in companies based on social criteria has become increasingly common, reflecting a growing interest of investors not only in making money but in making money wisely.

INCREASINGLY POPULAR

The business magazine *Bloomberg Personal* estimated that each year over $600 billion is invested according to social criteria. Socially response investing (SRI) has risen to about 10% of all investing from nearly nothing just a decade ago (Buss, 102, March/April 1997).

In addition, one *GreenMoney Journal* poll indicated that:

- "78% of all consumers are currently avoiding or refusing to buy from businesses because of negative perceptions of them. These include both organized boycotts and individual refusals to buy. Of that number, 48% said that unethical or unlawful business practices play a significant role in determining their decisions.
- 47% indicated they would be much more likely to buy from a company that is socially responsible and a good corporate citizen if the quality, service, and price were equal to that of competitors.
- A growing group – 16% – said they actively seek information about a company's business practices before purchasing" (in "The Renaissance of Values," *GreenMoney Journal*, Winter 94/95).

INVESTING WISELY

When investing in smarter technologies, products, and services, be as thoughtful as you would be in any other investment. While investing smart is important and helps to support technologies and the development of products that will benefit all of us, use your investment sense. As always, diversify and proceed with caution. Be aware that the optimism over smart technologies may inflate the prices of certain stocks. If you're waiting for government regulations to drive your stock prices up, remember that government can work slowly at times.
Be cautious about investments with "environmental" claims. Do your research. Although some companies

may deal with the environment, for instance, it doesn't mean that they're helping to improve it. Just as with any other investment, carefully examine company portfolios, and check to be sure they suit your needs.

Remember to set realistic goals, develop a comprehensive plan, choose advisors and invest carefully, and periodically review and adjust your strategy as needed. That way, you'll be making intelligent financial investments instead of sacrificing your money for well-intended but poorly spent investing.

If you're a shareholder, ask the company to print annual reports, brochures, catalogues, and proxies on recycled paper with soy-based ink. RCA, Texaco, Coca-Cola, Consolidated Edison, AT&T, and others already use recycled papers. Ask that they report on their environmental progress and other smart contributions as well.

SOME USEFUL INVESTMENT CRITERIA

When investing, consider some basic principles. First, keep your money out of inefficient, inhumane, or otherwise destructive companies. Second, invest in companies that better the community or the world. Third, consider investing small amounts in irresponsible companies (as a shareholder, you can be active in trying to get companies to create smarter goals, policies, and actions). Fourth, invest in companies whose actions are consistent with their stated goals. For example, any company can say that it has developed a set of smart policies, but take the time to find out if it lives by smart actions.

You can use a number of key criteria for choosing where to invest your money. For instance, if you are looking for a mutual fund, you want to be sure that your investment is in a successful, smart mutual fund. Don't invest in something just because it is altruistic; be sure that it's a well-managed, solid investment, too. Below are some criteria that you may want to consider before investing.

WHAT TO LOOK FOR

Look for positive characteristics. Invest in companies that benefit the environment and workers and that offer beneficial products or services. Look into the following issues:

- Labor relations
- Equal opportunity for women and minorities
- Human rights record
- Employment practices
- Family benefits
- Affordable housing
- Education
- Health care
- Child care
- Elderly care
- Community relations

WHAT TO AVOID

You may want to steer away from companies that have poor environmental and labor records and those that don't contribute something positive to their communities and the rest of the world. According to the *GreenMoney Journal* and Co-op America, avoid the following:

- Alcohol, tobacco, or gambling industries
- Animal testing
- Defense and weapons contractors
- Discrimination – gender, skin tone, ethnicity....
- Junk bonds
- Nuclear power
- Poor environmental records/EPA violations
- Poor human rights record
- Repressive government

SOCIALLY RESPONSIBLE COMPANIES

The *GreenMoney Journal* reports that about half of the largest 1,000 publicly owned U.S. firms live up to most socially responsible screening criteria. Socially responsible investing provides benefits and does not show any sacrifice in performance.

The Domini 400 Social Index (DSI) was created in 1990 to follow 400 companies that had passed screening on the basis of social criteria. The DSI continues to screen these companies for their social responsibility. It contains 250 companies that are found also on the S&P 500.

From May 1990 through December 1994, DSI's investment returns were over 70%; Standard & Poor's (S&P) 500 were just over 60%. For other years, The Domini 400 Social Index Fund has shown returns competitive with the S&P 500. While I'm not suggesting that you invest in any particular company, below are a few examples of three very different companies, each with smart attributes, that have done well for their shareholders.

HOME DEPOT

Background

Atlanta, Georgia's, Home Depot is the world's largest home improvement retailer and one of the largest retailers in the country. Its focus on customer service and local community involvement have helped make it a successful company. In 1996, *Fortune* magazine named Home Depot America's most admired retailer for the third year in a row. The company went public in 1981.

Sales: $15,470,358,000 (FY 1995)
$12,476,697,000 (FY 1994)
$9,238,763,000 (FY 1993)

Stock: HD (NYSE)

Community Contributions

Home Depot has won a number of awards for its commitment to improving the communities served by its stores. Its 1996 philanthropic budget is $8.5 million. In 1995, it spent $7 million funding non-profit programs. Its contributions include: affordable housing, at-risk youth, environment, United Way, and contributions through its Matching Gift Program (in which Home Depot employees decide where some of the company's contributions should go). In 1992, the company created a volunteer program through which employees have done everything from helping to build Habitat for Humanity homes to tutoring inner-city youth to searching for victims of the Oklahoma City bombing. Home Depot also promotes smart building design, recycling, resource efficiency, and product labeling.

STARBUCKS COFFEE: A CASE STUDY

Background

Headquartered in Seattle, Washington, Starbucks Coffee Company is North America's top roaster and seller of gourmet coffees. It has hundreds of retail stores in North America, and it also sells its coffee via direct mail and to restaurants, stores, and airlines.

Sales: $285 million (1994)

Stock: NASDAQ (SBUX). In 1994, the stock price rose 24%.

Mission Statement

"Establish Starbucks as the premier purveyor of the finest coffee in the world while maintaining our uncompromising principles as we grow. The following five guiding principles will help us measure the appropriateness of our decisions:

1. Provide a great work environment and treat each other with respect and dignity.

2. Apply the highest standards of excellence to the purchasing, roasting and fresh delivery of our coffee.

3. Develop enthusiastically satisfied customers all of the time.

4. Contribute positively to our communities and our environment.

5. Recognize that profitability is essential to our future success."

Environmental Mission Statement: "Starbucks is committed to a role of environmental leadership in all facets of our business. We will fulfill this mission by a commitment to:

Understanding of environmental issues and sharing information with our partners (employees).

Developing innovative and flexible solutions to bring about change.

Striving to buy, sell and use environmentally friendly products.

Recognizing that fiscal responsibility is essential to our environmental future.

Instilling environmental responsibility as a corporate value.

Measuring and monitoring our progress for each project.

Encouraging all partners to share in our mission" (*The GreenMoney Journal*, Spring/Summer 1995 issue).

Special Features

All stores have a water purification system to keep contaminants out of the coffee. Starbucks sells water filters and encourages brewing methods that avoid the use of disposable, often chlorine-bleached, paper coffee filters.

Paper bags, boxes, catalogs, brochures, letterhead, and publications are made of recycled paper; paper filters and cups are made of paper whitened by oxygen rather than chlorine, avoiding the emission of dioxins.

Discounts are given for the reuse of both the thermal cups sold at the stores and the coffee bags. In addition, store-wide recycling programs for used coffee grounds, paper products, and milk containers are being researched. Post-dated coffee is donated to hospices and homeless shelters.

Starbucks is the largest corporate sponsor of CARE, an organization that works toward education and literacy programs, reducing malnutrition, and decreasing children's mortality rates around the world. The company also supports other service organizations and is involved in a variety of community events.

WHOLE FOODS MARKETS, INC.

Background
Headquartered in Austin, Texas, Whole Foods Markets is the country's largest natural foods grocery chain.

Sales: $892,098,000 (FY 1996)
$709,935,000 (FY 1995)

Stock: WFMI (NASDAQ)

Smart New Headquarters
When Whole Foods built its new headquarters in Austin, Texas, it focused on creating an efficient, healthy building. As a matter of fact, it was one of Austin's first smart, commercial buildings.

The company used limestone from local quarries, reducing the time and cost associated with transportation. Rather than using black asphalt in the Texas climate, concrete with recycled fly ash was used in the parking lot to keep the surrounding area cooler. The roof was fastened in place to eliminate the need for tar.

There was a heavy reliance on daylighting through the use of skylights and windows on the interior walls of offices. T-8 lights with parabolic reflectors were used.

Rather than using adhesives, wool carpet was stretched and tacked in place. Sisal, a Mexican species of the agave plant, was used as wall treatment, and non-toxic

linoleum, made of jute, linseed oil, and cork, was used. The millwork, done locally, was finished with non-toxic products. The joists were made of remilled tongue and groove flooring. Paints with low volatile organic compound (VOC) contents were used since zero-VOC paints were not available at the time. Greenwood Cotton insulation (made from blue jean scraps) was used; Whole Foods was one of its first commercial applications in the United States.

As far as furnishings go, the company focused on healthier alternatives. Herman Miller's As New, low-VOC fabric chairs were used, and much of the furnishings were brought from the previous headquarters building. University of Texas drafting tables were used as well.

In the kitchen, efficient ASKO dishwashers were installed, and to provide healthier water, the water fountains and two of the kitchen sinks use water filters. Aluminum and glass are recycled.

In the restrooms, ceramic tile flooring was used, and the stall dividers are made by COMTEC out of recycled plastic. The shipping room floor is made of concrete but is colored and scored to look like tile. The store's flooring was made of quarry tile and stained, scored concrete.

Bike racks were installed to encourage employees to bicycle to work, and the restrooms have showers for the same reason. The oil used in the elevators is a vegetable-based, hydraulic oil made by Mobil Oil Company. Xeriscape landscaping is used, and there is an option to collect rainwater in the future.

HELPFUL RESOURCES

INFORMATION

Books
The 100 Best Companies to Work for in America (Moskowitz, Doubleday, 1992)

Best Business Practices for Socially Responsible Companies (Alan Reder)

The Better World Investment Guide, available from the Council on Economic Priorities. (Myra Alperson, Alice Tepper Marlin, Jonathon Schorsch, and Rosalyn Will) 800-822-6435

The E Factor: The Bottom-Line Approach to Environmentally Responsible Business
(Joel Makower, Tilden Press/Time Books, 1993)

The Ecology of Commerce: A Declaration of Sustainability (Paul Hawken, Harper Business, 1993)

Eco Management: The Elmwood Guide to Ecological Auditing & Sustainable Business
(Callenbach, Capra, & others, Berrett-Koehler, 1993)

Employee Ownership in America
(Corey Rosen, Katherine J. Klein, Karen M. Young).

The Healthy Company
(Robert H. Rosen)

In Pursuit of Principle and Profit
(Alan Reder)

The Soul of a Business: Managing for Profit and the Common Good
(Tom Chappell of Tom's of Maine, Bantam, 1993)

Magazines/Newsletters

Business Ethics
612-962-4702

Business
612-962-4700

Business & the Environment: Global News and Analysis
800-929-2929

Corporate Examiner (ICCR): Policies & Practices of U.S. Companies
212-870-2293

The GreenBusiness Letter: The Hands-on Journal for Environmentally Conscious Companies
800-955-4733

Green Market Alert: Analyzing the Business Impacts of Green Consumerism
203-266-7209

Healthy Companies: Leadership for the New Workplace
202-234-9288

In Business: The Magazine for Environmental Entrepreneuring
610-967-4135

BSR Update
Business for Social Responsibility

415-865-2500

National Green Pages
202-872-5307

Research Reports (CEP): Evaluating Companies & Current Issues
800-729-4237

"Investing for the Earth," a monthly SRI investment column, written by Jack A. Brill and Hal Brill, found in *In Business* magazine.

"You, Your Money, & the World" is published by Co-op America. It lists other smart investment resources, too. For more information, contact:
Co-op America
1612 K Street, NW, #600
Washington, DC 20006

Other Resources

Businesses for Social Responsibility has over 700 members, including:

Aveda Corporation, Ben & Jerry, Calvert Group, Co-op America, Levi Strauss, Lotus Development, Nike, Patagonia, Reebok, Starbucks Coffee Co., The Body Shop, *The GreenMoney Journal*, Timberland, Working Assets Common Holdings, and Working Assets Long Distance. For information, call: 202-842-5400

Council on Economic Priorities
New York, NY

Interfaith Council on Corporate Responsibility
New York, NY

The Investor Responsibility Center
Washington, D.C.

Kinder, Lydenberg & Domini (KLD), Domini 400 Social Index (DSI)
617-547-7479

National Center for Employee Ownership
510-272-9461

Smart Mutual Funds

Below is a list of socially responsible mutual funds.

EQUITY

Ariel Appreciation	800-725-0140
Ariel Growth	800-725-0140
Bridgeway	800-661-3550
Calvert Capital Accumulation	800-368-2748
Calvert Social Equity	800-368-2748
Calvert Strategic Growth	800-368-2748
Calvert Emerging Growth	800-223-7010
Citizens Index Fund	800-223-7010
Domini Social Equity Fund	800-762-6814
Dreyfus Third Century	800-645-6561
MMA Praxis: Growth	800-977-2947
Neuberger & Berman	800-877-9700
Neuberger & Berman S.R.	800-877-9700
New Alternatives Fund	800-423-8383
Parnassus Fund	800-999-3505
Righttime Social Awareness	800-242-1421
Women's Equity Mutual Fund	800-385-7003

INTERNATIONAL/GLOBAL

Calvert World Values International	800-368-2748
Citizens Global Equity	800-223-7010

FIXED INCOME

Calvert Social Bond	800-368-2748
Citizens Income	800-233-7010
Eclipse Ultra Short Term	800-872-2710
Muir CA Tax-Free	800-648-3448
Parnassus Fixed Income	800-999-3505
Parnassus CA Tax-Free	800-999-3505

BALANCED

Calvert Managed Growth	800-368-2748
Green Century Funds	800-934-7336
Parnassus Balanced	800-999-3505
Pax World Fund	800-767-1729
Money Market	
Calvert Social MM	800-368-2748
Working Assets Money Fund	800-223-7010

(Taken from Co-op America's *Connections*, Fall 1996)

SUMMARY OF RECOMMENDATIONS

• Invest in strong companies that are efficient and responsible.

• Invest in companies that make beneficial products and technologies using smart techniques.

• Don't invest in any company just because it's socially responsible. Be sure that it is a well-managed and capitalized company with a bright future.

• Look for companies that are known to be responsible in their relationship with their workers, the communities around them, and the environment in general.

• Stay away from companies that manufacture or promote products or technologies that cause a great deal of harm to the health of us and our environment.

CHAPTER 20

SURFING THE INTERNET

"The smart ones are going green, the dumb ones are not, and the foolish ones are pretending."
David Krentz, on corporate environmental policy, 1990 (quoted in Rodes and Odell, 73)

Checking out the best sites on the Internet, a.k.a. "surfing the Net," has become an increasingly popular and efficient way of getting information on nearly any topic without leaving your chair.

If you haven't yet spent time on the Internet, I encourage you to do so. There's a wealth of information available at the tip of your fingers – information about which you may be unaware if you haven't done a little surfing. For example, Enviroene's home page and has detailed information on several Environmental Protection Agency programs, including Green Lights (for energy efficiency) and Golden Carrot (for smart refrigerators). Within the span of about 20 minutes, you downloaded details of over 20 programs onto your hard drive. If you were to search for that type of information without the aid of the Internet, you could count on spending half the day on the telephone, in the library, and waiting for the the EPA to mail the appropriate information to you. The Internet is an invaluable tool that saves time as well as the costs associated with transportation (e.g., driving to the library), research, phone calls, and mailings.

Because such a wealth of information is available over the Internet, it can appear overwhelming at first glance. Luckily, the Internet is a pretty friendly place. Many people devote some space on their home pages to listing or creating links to some of their favorite home pages on the Internet. For example, if you find an organization that offers information on energy efficiency, chances are they will have links to other companies with information on energy efficiency. So, even if you have only a few home pages to visit in the very beginning, you may have a hefty list after one sitting.

By the way, you're probably aware of this, but it never hurts to say it again. Be careful about giving out personal information over the Internet. Security is not, well, secure yet, so ordering by credit card or passing on social security or other personal numbers could be risky. With that said, below is a list of some home pages with helpful information. Some belong to non-profits, some to corporations, and some have been created by gov-

ernment agencies to provide helpful information. Take your time and explore. And most of all, have fun.

You can access our smart office home page at the following address:

http://www.smartoffice.com

CASE STUDIES

Carnegie Mellon
http://www.ce.cmu.edu/GreenDesign/
Just one of the universities that has made a commitment to becoming smarter.

George Washington University
http://www.gwu.edu/~greenu/
Another institution's commitment to being "green" and some details of the process.

The White House
http://www.solstice.crest.org/environment/gotwh/

CONSTRUCTION

Agri-Business Assistant
http://www.trace-sc.com/agri/forestry.htm
This site offers a variety of information, from animal husbandry issues to forestry.

Center for Maximum Potential Building Systems
http://www.maxpot.com/maxpot/
A home page dedicated to sustainable building.

Energy Efficient Building Assoc., Inc.
http://www.ix.netcom.com
This is a great source for information on smart buildings.

GreenClips
http://www.crest.org/sustainable/greenclips/

This publication offers information about the latest smart building products, green buildings, government regulations, and more.

IRIS Forest Products Industry Directory
http://www.cdc.net/~primus/IRIS/irisfp.html
IRIS offers a wealth of information on forestry and forest products.

National Park Service (NPS)
http://www.nps.gov/dsc/dsgncnstr
The National Park Service created this free Sustainable Design database as a guide in design and construction. Providing a wide array of information, you can download this database onto your hard drive and use it as needed.

Oikos
http://www.oikos.com/irisinfo
A great site for construction products.

Plan it Earth! Marketplace
http://www.numenet.com/planit/pe_market.html
If you're looking for information on smarter building products, this is a great resource. Type in your search word, and you'll see a list of products and the addresses of their manufacturers.

SmartForest
http://imlab9.landarch.uiuc.edu/SF/SF.html
This site allows you to practice being a forester. It's an interactive, 3-D program that gives information on tree types, vigor, etc.

Solstice
http://solstice.crest.org/efficiency/straw_insulation/eip/StrawDE.gif
This site contains photos of buildings made with straw bales.

Woods of the World Database
http://www.woodweb.com/~treetalk/wowhome.html
This Wood of the Week page offers detailed information on the characteristics of a different wood each week. You also can access information on the interactive Woods of the World CD-ROM.

CRUELTY-FREE INFORMATION

People for the Ethical Treatment of Animals (PETA)
http://envirolink.org/arrs/peta/index.html

PETA is an organization that works to eliminate cruelty to animals. Use this Web page for more information on animal testing and sources for cruelty-free products.

DESIGN

Center for Building Science
http://eande.lbl.gov/CBS/CBS.html
This home page offers quite an array of information on energy efficiency.

ENERGY EFFICIENCY

American Council for an Energy-Efficient Economy (ACE³)
http://solstice.crest.org/efficiency/aceee/index.html
This is another good home page for information on energy efficiency.

EcoNet
http://www.econet.apc.org/econet/
This is the oldest environmental Internet provider. It is full of information on topics ranging from energy efficiency, recycling, and smart products to conflict resolution.

EcoWeb
http://ecosys.drdr.virginia.edu/EcoWeb.html
This is a full-service smart office and other environmental information source.

Electric Power Research Institute (EPRI)
http://www.epri.com/
EPRI offers information on electricity, including energy efficiency.

Energy Effiiciency and Renewable Energy Clearinghouse (EREC)
http://eren.doe.gov/erec/factsheets
DOE's EREC is a great source for information on energy efficiency and renewables. It contains a variety of topics, from landscaping for energy efficiency to energy-efficient water heaters.

Energy Efficiency and Renewable Energy Network (EREN)
http://www.eren.doe.gov/
Here is DOE's online source of energy efficiency and renewables information.

Energy Technologies
http://www.pnl.gov:2080
This Pacific Northwest National Laboratory program was created to offer a variety of energy information to users.

National Renewable Energy Laboratory (NREL)
http://www.nrel.gov/
This home page offers information on energy efficiency and on renewable energy technologies.

Rocky Mountain Institute (RMI)
http://www.rmi.org
RMI's home page is great for the latest information on energy-efficient technologies, from lightbulbs to hyper-cars, as well as the economics of smarter living and working.

Solstice
http://www.crest.org
Solstice informs on topics related to energy efficiency, renewable energy, and sustainable living.

FIBERS

Linen Flax
http://www.linen-flax.com
This Web page offers information in English and French regarding the versatility of linen and flax as fibers in paper, clothing, and for other uses.

GENERAL INFORMATION

Essential Information
http://www.essential.org/monitor/monitor.html
This site has maps made using satellite and computer data and offers information on white collar crime

EnviroLink
http://www.envirolink.org
This is one of my favorite home pages. Not just for the diverse and useful information but also because of its design.

Galaxy
http://galaxy.einet.net/galaxy
This is a great source for general information on nearly anything you could think of, from ergonomics and environmental illness to alternative fuels.

Global Environmental Options
http://www.geonetwork.org
This is a great clearinghouse for information on everything from renewable energy and energy efficiency to building design.

In Business
http://www.inbusiness.com/
This magazine is a great source of information about smarter technologies, investing, and companies.

GOVERNMENT PROGRAMS

Center of Excellence for Sustainable Development
http://www.sustainable.doe.gov
This home page offers information about how communities and sustainable development.

Department of Energy
http://www.eh.doe.gov/oepa
This Department of Energy home page offers regulatory information that you may need for your business.

Environmental Protection Agency
http://www.epa.gov/epahome/programs.html
Use this home page to search for information on Energy Star programs.

Enviroene
http://es.inel.gov/
Check out this home page for information on several smart federal programs.

HEALTH

EPA
http://earth1.epa.gov/chemfact/
This is a great source of fact sheets and chemical summaries on a variety of chemicals.

INVESTING

Better World Investing
http://www.betterworld.com

Calvert Group
http://www.calvertgroup.com

Co-op America Financial Planning Handbook
http://www.coopamerica.org/$links.htm

DBC
http://www.dbc.com/
DBC provides free stock and mutual fund quotes and current information on investing.

Discussion Groups
To take part in USENET discussion groups on investing, contact: misc.invest, misc.invest.stocks, or misc. invest. funds

GreenMoney Journal
http://www.greenmoney.com/
This is a great home page for information on smarter investing. It lists socially responsible mutual funds, offers information on financial planning, and even has a business guide. GreenMoney publishes its journal on socially responsible business and investment issues, and the home page also includes an events calendar, a guide to good Internet sites, and publications.

Franklin Research & Development Corp.
http://www.frdc.com
This is the Internet site for the publishers of *Insight: Investing for a Better World*.

Lombard
http://www.lombard.com
Like DBC, Lombard offers quotes and graphs for stocks, mutual funds, and other investments. In addition, there is a wealth of information on investing in general.

MIT's Experimental Stock Market Data Server
http://www.ai.mit.edu/stocks/prices/html

Ohio State University
Financial Data Finder:
http://www.cob.ohiostate.edu/dept/fin/osudata.htm
Investment FAQ (Frequently Asked Questions):
http://www.cis.ohiostate.edu/hypertext/faq/usenet/investment-faq/general/top.html

Social Investment Forum
http://wwww.socialinvest.org

OFFICES

SmartOffice
http://www.smartoffice.com
This is our home page. As with this book, SmartOffice provides information to help you improve your resource

efficiency and the overall health of your workplace while saving money.

PRODUCTS

AFM
http://www.greenmarket.com/COMPANIES/
Several companies offer healthier or or more efficient products and services.

EcoMall
http://www.ecomall.com
This is another fun site that offers a variety of information. Here, you can get names of some companies that make recycled or tree-free papers as well as data on renewable energy. (While the company listings don't represent everything that's available on the market with regard to smarter products, they do offer some insight into what's out there.)

EcoExpo Online
http://www.ecoexpo.com
This Web page offers information about upcoming EcoExpos (i.e., location, time, date, exhibitors).

Environmentally Sound Products
http://virtumall.com/ESP/ESPmain.html

Greenmarket
http://www.greenmarket.com/
This is a great home page for a vast listing of different home pages. Many of them are hyperlinked, so you can just click on the name of the home page you want to see, and it will take you right there.

Modern World Design
http://www.user.interport.net/~webcrawler/web.html

RECYCLING

EnviroSense
http://us.incl.gov
This is a great site for pollution prevention and waste exchanges.

Global Recycling Network
http://www.branch.com/grn/
This is another one-stop place for recycling information. Not only does this home page stock quotes and commodity prices, but it also gives recycling-company directories and associations. It has a career center and lists

business opportunities, news, events, and stock information on publicly traded recycling companies as well.

National Materials Exchange

http://www.earthcycle.com/g/p/earthcycle//
This is another good source of information about uses for your waste materials.

National Recycling Council (NREC)

http://www.nben.org
This is an information clearinghouse that discusses regional recycling issues and state programs.

Recycler's World

http://www.recycle.net/recycle/
Created to be a source of global information, Recycler's World covers everything from recycling investment opportunities to online market prices and a calendar of events. In addition, you can find information here on recycling associations, recycling and waste equipment, information and materials exchanges, and publications.

United States Environmental/Recycling Hotline

http://www.1800cleanup.org
This site offers free information, in English and Spanish, on recycling programs by zip code. Just type in your zip code and find out what type of recycling is available in your area.

TRANSPORTATION

Alternative Fuels Data Center

http://www.afdc.nrel.gov
The Department of Energy's Alternative Fuels Data Center is a centralized source of information for those using vehicles that run on alternative fuels. Not only are there refueling site maps for various types of alternative fuels available in the U.S., but there is also basic information on biofuels, alternative transportation vehicles and fuels, and a National Alternative Fuels Hotline.

Alternative Fuels Sites

http://www.alt.com/altlinks.htm
This home page provides links to alternative fuels information.

Biofuels Information Center

http://www.biofuels.nrel.gov/
Use this home page to access information regarding biofuels.

National Renewable Energy Laboratory (NREL)

http://info.nrel.gov/
NREL provides informtion on renewable energy.

This is only a partial list of home pages that may be useful in your evolving, smart office. New information and home pages appear continually, so check in routinely to find out what's new.

PART SIX

• • • • • • • • •

APPENDICES &
REFERENCES

DIRECTORY OF SUPPLIERS

A

A-1 Products Corp.
19-342 Bronte Street South
Milton, ON L9T 5B7
Canada
800-777-0979/ 416-875-2588
Fax: 416-875-0979

AEG, Andi-Co Appliances, Inc.
65 Campus Plaza
Edison, NJ 08837
800-344-0043

ASKO
800-367-2444

Abkit, Inc.
207 E. 94th St.
Suite 201
New York, NY 10128
212-860-8358

Absolute Environmental's Allergy
Products & Services
2615 South University Drive
Davis, FL 33328
800-329-3773/ 305-472-3773

A. E. Sampson & Son
P.O. Box 1010
Warren, ME 04804
207-273-4000

AERT
P.O. Box 1237
Springdale, AR 72765
501-750-1299

AFM Corporation
P.O. Box 246
Exelsior, MN 55331
800-255-0176

AFM Enterprises, Inc.
1140 Stacy Court
Riverside, CA 92507
714-781-6860

AFM Corporation
24000 W. Highway 7
Suite 201
Shorewood, MN 55331
612-474-0809

Abitibi-Price Corp.
P.O. Box 98
Highway 268
Roaring River, NC 28669
919-696-2751

Action Packaging Systems
374 Somers Road
Ellington, CT 06029
800-635-5364/ 203-872-6311
Fax: 203-875-4293

Advanced Photovoltaic Systems,
Inc.
195 Clarkesville Road
Lawrenceville, NJ 08648
609-275-5000

Advanced Wood Resources
34363 Lake Creek Drive
Brownsville, OR 97327
541-466-5177/ 800-533-3374
Fax: 503-466-5559

Aeolian Enterprises, Inc.
1 Lloyd Avenue
Latrobe, PA 15650
412-539-9460

Aged Woods Inc.
2331 East Market Street
York, PA 17402
800-233-9307/ 717-840-0330
Fax: 717-840-1468

AgriBoard Industries
P.O. Box 645
Fairfield, IA 52556
515-472-0363/ Fax: 515-472-0018

Agripulp
Arbokem
1773 H Street

Suite 330-133
Blaine, WA 98230
604-322-1317/ Fax: 604-322-5865

Agwa Systems
801 South Flower Street
Burbank, CA
800-473-9426/ 815-562-1449

Air Krete, Inc.
P.O. Box 380
Weedsport, NY 13166
315-834-6609

Aireox Research Corp.
P.O. Box 8523
Riverside, CA 92515
714-689-2781

Airxchange, Inc.
401 VFW Drive
Rockland, MA 02370
617-871-4816

Aldan Lane Company
P.O. Box 990
Kalona, IA 52247
319-656-3620

Allegro Rug Weaving
802 South Sherman St.
Longmont, CO 80501
800-783-1784/ 303-651-0555
Fax: 303-651-1444

Allen Special Products
P.O. Box 605
Montgomeryville, PA 18936
800-848-6805/ 215-997-9077

Allen's Naturally
P.O. Box 514
Farmington, MI 48332
800-352-8971/ 313-453-5410

Allermed Corp.
31 Steel Road
Wylie, TX 75098
214-422-4311/ 214-492-4897

ALLERX
P.O. Box 239
Fate, TX 75132
800-447-1100

Allied Thermal Systems
800-810-4307/512-443-4466
Fax: 512-443-3938

Allmilmo Corp.
70 Clinton Road
P.O. Box 629
Fairfield, NJ 07006
201-227-2502

Allure Rug Studio
1719 Wazae Street
Denver, CO 80202
800-658-8056/ 303-292-5661

Almquist Lumber
100 Taylor Way
Blue Lake, CA 95521
707-668-5454

Alte Schule USA
704 E. Palace Avenue
Santa Fe, NM 87501
505-983-2593

Alteschuler Wallpapers
346 N. Justin
Chicago, IL 60607
312-243-7227

Amati bambu
201 Don Park Road
Markham, Ontario
Canada L3R 1C2
905-477-8822/ Fax: 905-477-5208

American Aides Ventilation Corp.
4537 Northgate Court
Sarasota, FL 34234
813-351-3441/ Fax: 813-351-3442

American Air Filter
P.O. Box 35690
215 Central Avenue
Louisville, KY 40232
800-678-4356/ 502-637-0011

American Aldes Ventilation
7 Northgate Court
Sarasota, FL 34234

813-351-3441

American Council for An Energy-
Efficient Economy
2140 Shattuck Avenue
Suite 202
Berkeley, CA 94104

American Environmental Health
Foundation
8345 Walnut Hill Lane
Suite 225
Dallas, TX 75231-4262
800-428-2343

American Excelsior
850 Avenue H, East
Arlington, TX 76011
817-640-1555

American Forests
1516 P Street NW
Washington, DC 20005
202-667-3300/ Fax: 202-667-7751

American Iron and Steel Institute
Cold-Formed Steel Construction
1101 17th Street, NW
Suite 1300
Washington, D.C. 20036
202-452-7100

American Olean Tile
1000 Cannon Road
Lansdale, PA 19446-0271
215-855-1111

American Recreational Products
30-1 Raynor's Avenue
Ronkonkoma, NY 11779
800-663-4096/516-588-4545

American Soil Products
2222 3rd Street
Berkeley, CA 94710
510-540-8011

American Solar Network
12811 Bexhill Court
Herndon, VA 22071
703-620-2242/ Fax: 703-435-2636

American Solar Service & Sales
Carpenter Drive
Sterling, VA 22170

703-435-2669

American Standard
P.O. Box 6820
Piscataway, NJ 08855
800-752-6292/ 201-980-3000

American Stud Co.
2525 North 27th Ave.
Phoenix, AZ 85009
800-877-8823

Amoco Foam
375 Northridge Road
Atlanta, GA 30350
800-241-4402/ Fax: 404-594-5235

Andersen Windows
100 Fourth Avenue, N
Bay Port, MN 55003
612-439-5150

Andy Johanneson
P.O. Box 24
Whitehorn, CA 95589
707-986-7465

Angeles Metal Systems
4817 East Sheila Street
City of Commerce, CA 90040
213-268-1777/ Fax: 213-268-8996

Approved Equal
1538 Gladding Court
Milpitas, CA 95035
408-942-8191

Aptech Detectors
547 Courtenay Avenue
Ottawa, ON K2A3B4
Canada
613-837-4470

Aquapore Moisture Systems
610 South 80th Avenue
Phoenix, AZ 85043
800-635-8379/ 602-936-8083

Arbokem (maker of Agripulp)
Canada
604-322-1317/ Fax: 604-322-5865
Internet://www.agripulp.com

Architectural Forest Enterprises
1030 Quesada Avenue

San Francisco, CA 94124
800-483-6337/ 415-822-7300

Architectural Openings, Inc.
16 Garfield Avenue
Somerville, MA 02145
617-776-9223

Armor All
4055 Faber Place Drive
Charleston, SC 29405
800-398-3892/ 803-566-0766

Artesian Industries
201 East 5th Street
Mansfield, OH 44901
419-522-4211

Asahi Electronics
30 Alden Road
Unit 4
Markham, ON L3R 2S1
Canada
416-477-3320

Association of Foam Packaging
Recyclers
Washington, D.C.
800-944-8448

Atlantic Recycled Paper
P.O. Box 39179
Baltimore, MD 21212
800-323-2811/ 410-323-2676
Fax: 410-323-2681

Atlantic Solar Products
9351J Philadelphia Road
Baltimore, MD 21237
301-686-2500

Attic Technology Inc.
15548 95th Circle NE
Elk River, MN 55330
612-441-3440

Aubrey Organics, Inc.
4419 N. Manhattan Ave.
Tampa, FL 33614
800-282-7394

Auro, Sinan Co.
P.O. Box 857
Davis, CA 95617-0857
916-753-3104

Autumn Harp, Inc.
61 Pine Street
P.O. Box 267
Bristol, VT 05443
802-453-4807

The Aveda Corporation
4000 Pheasant Ridge Dr.
Blaine, MN 55449
800-328-0849

Avonite Inc.
5100 Goldleaf Circle
Suite 200
Los Angeles, CA 90056
800-428-6648/ 213-299-9900
Fax: 213-292-1441

Aztec International
2417 Aztec Road N.E.
Albuquerque, NM 87107
505-884-1818

B

BASF
800-477-8147

B & E Energy Systems
3530 Franklin Road
Bloomfield Hills, MI 48013
313-540-9617

B.R Enterprises
27 W 084 Walnut Drive
Winfield, IL 60190
800-949-6182/ 708-260-9097
Fax: 708-690-6220

BTW Industries, Inc.
2000 SW 31st Avenue
Pembroke Park, FL 33009
305-962-2100/ Fax: 305-963-4778

Baby Bunz and Company
P.O. Box 1717
Sebastopol, CA 95473
707-829-5347

Bainings Community-Based
Ecoforestry Project
Rabaul, Papua New Guinea.
Contact:
B & Q Plc.

Portswood House
One Hampshire Corporate Park
Chandlers Ford
Eastleigh
Hampshire SO5 3YX
England
011-44-0703-256-256

Baltimore Aircoil Co.
P.O. Box 7322
Baltimore, MD 21227
410-799-6200

Bangor Cork Co.
P.O. Box 1251
Penn Argyl, PA 18072
215-863-9041/ Fax: 215-863-6275

Barclay Recycling, Inc.
75 Ingram Drive
Toronto, ONT M5M 2M2
Canada
905-372-6183

Bard Manufacturing
1914 Randolph Drive
Bryan, OH 43506
419-636-1194

Barlowe Tyrie, Inc.
1263 Glen Avenue
Suite 230
Moorestown, NJ 08057
800-451-7467

Basic Coatings
2124 Valley Drive
Des Moines, IA 50321
800-247-5471

Be Earthlike
2012 W. Ash Street, #P15
Columbia, MO 65203
314-445-9301

Becker Zyko Kitchens
1030 Marina Village Parkway
Alameda, CA 94501
510-865-1616/ Fax: 510-865-1148

Bedford Industries, Inc.
1659 Rowe Avenue
P.O. Box 39
Worthington, MN 56187
507-376-4136

Internet:
http://www.bedfordind.com

Bedrock Industries
Seattle, WA 98103
206-781-7025

Bellbridge Inc.
1940-C Olivera Road Concord, CA
94520
800-227-3408/ 510-798-7242
Fax: 510-689-9674

Bellcomb Technologies
70 N. 22nd Avenue
Minneapolis, MN 55411
612-521-2425

Benjamin Moore Paints
51 Chestnut Ridge Rd.
Montvale, NY 07645
201-573-9600

Best Paint Co.
5205 Ballard Avenue, NW
Seattle WA 98124
206-783-9938

Biobottoms
Box 6009
Petaluma, CA 94953
707-778-7945

Biofac Incorporated
P.O. Box 87
Mathis, TX 78368
512-547-3259

Biofire, Inc.
3220 Melbourne
Salt Lake City, UT 84106
801-486-0266

Biological Urban Gardening
Services
P.O. Box 76
Citrus Height, CA 95611-0076

BioLogic Natural Pest Control
P.O. Box 177
Willow Hill, PA 17271
717-349-2789

Bio-Sun Systems, Inc.
RD #2, Box 134A

Millerton, PA 16936
717-537-2200/ Fax: 717-537-6200

Blackfeet Indian Writing Co.
251 1/2 Grove Avenue
Verona, NJ 07044
201-239-6480

The Blue Earth
2899 Agoura Road
Suite 625
Westlake Village, CA 91361
818-707-2187

Bomanite Corporation
209-673-2411

Bosch
2800 South 25th Ave.
Broadview, IL 60153
800-866-2022/ 708-865-5200

Bosch Custom Kitchens
11602 Knott Street, #4
Garden Grove, CA 92641
800-474-3353

Bostik
211 Boston Street
Middleton, MA 01949
800-221-8726/ 508-777-0100
Internet: http://www.bostik.com

Bellcomb Technologies
70 North 22nd Avenue
Minneapolis, MN 55411
612-521-2425/ Fax: 612-521-2376

Bentley Mills
14641 East Don Julian Road
City of Industry, CA 91746
818-333-4585

The Bio-Integral Resource Center
1307 Acton Street
Berkeley, CA 94706
510-524-2567

Boise Cascade
Timber and Wood Products
P.O. Box 62
Boise, ID 83707
800-762-2237/ 208-384-7158

Bonakemi USA, Inc.
14805 East Moncrieff Place
Aurora, CO 80011
800-872-5515/ 303-371-1411
Fax: 800-572-0211/ 303-371-6958

Boston Jojoba Company
4 Gregory Street
Middleton, MA 01949
508-777-9332

Brayton Int.
P.O. Box 7288
High Point, NC 27263
910-434-4151/ Fax: 910-434-4240

Bremworth Carpets
1940 Olivera Road
Suite C
Concord, CA 94520
510-798-7242

Briggs Plumbingware
4350 West Cypress St.
Suite 800
Tampa, FL 33607
800-627-4447/ 813-878-0178

The Brightwork Oat and Lumber
Company
5380 Farmco Drive
Madison, WI 53718
608-244-8780

Bronx 2000
1809 Carter Avenue
Bronx, NY 10457
718-731-3931
E-mail: bcf2000@aol.com

Brookside Soap Co.
P.O. Box 55638
Seattle, WA 98155
206-742-2265

Brownlee Lighting
3071-K N. Orange Blossom Trail
Orlando, FL 32804
407-297-3677/ Fax: 407-297-3705

Buckley Rumford Company
710 Foster Street
Port Townsend, WA 98368
800-447-7788/360-385-9974

Burns-Milwaukee Inc.
4010 West Douglas Ave.
Milwaukee, WI 53209
414-438-1234

C

C-Cure Chemical Co.
305 Garden Oaks
Houston, TX 77018
713-697-2024

CDC Carpets & Interiors
3425 Bee Cave Road
Austin, TX 78746
512-327-8326

CYA Products, Inc.
211 Robbins Lane
Syosset, MI 11791-6004
516-681-9394

CECOR, Inc.
102 S. Lincoln Street
Verona, WA 53593
608-845-6771

CEMCO
263 Covina Lane
City of Industry, CA 91744
818-369-3564

Caldwell Building Wreckers
195 Bayshore Blvd.
San Francisco, CA 94124
415-550-6777

California Building Systems
4817 East Sheila Street
Los Angeles, CA 90040
213-260-5380

Canac Cabinets
360 John St.
Thornhill, ONT L3T 3M9
Canada
800-CANAC-4U (226-2248)

Canvasmaker, Inc.
(House of Hemp)
P.O. Box 14603
2111 East Burnside St.
Portland, OR 97293
503-232-1128/ Fax: 503-232-0539

Card Recycling
100 St. Jude St.
Post Office Box 60100
Boulder City, NV 89006

Carpet Cushion Associates
1248 Palmetto Street
Los Angeles, CA 90013
800-344-6977

Carlisle Tire & Rubber
Box 99
Carlisle, PA 17013
717-249-1000

Carousel Carpets
1011 N. Main Street
Logan, UT 84341-2215
801-752-1210

or:
3315 Superior Lane
Bowie, MD 20715-2650
301-262-2650

Carrier Corp.
7310 W. Morris Street
P.O. Box 70
Indianapolis, IN 46241
317-243-0851

Carrysafe
920 Davis Road
Suite 101
Elgin, IL 60123
847-931-4771

Carsonite International
1301 Hot Springs Road
Carson City, NV 89706
800-648-7974

Carter Carpets
617 Excelsior Street
Rome, GA 30161
800-848-7941/ 706-235-8657
Fax: 706-235-6235

Cedar Works
P.O. Box 990-SS
Rockport, ME 04856
800-60-CEDAR (23327)

Cellulose Insulation Manufacturing
Association

136 South Keowee Street
Dayton, OH 45402
513-222-1024

Centercore Inc.
435 Devon Park Drive
Wayne, PA 19087
800-220-5640/ 215-975-9099
Fax: 215-975-9098

Chapman Studio Lighting
2133 Yarmouth Avenue
Boulder, CO 80301
303-449-2165

Chatham Brass Company, Inc.
5 Olsen Avenue
Edison, NJ 08820
800-526-7553/ 908-494-7107

Chem-Safe Products
P.O. Box 33023
San Antonio, TX 78265
210-657-5321

Chicago Adhesive Products Co.
4658 West 60th Street
Chicago, IL 60629
800-621-0220/ 773-581-1300
Fax: 312-581-2629

Chicagoland Processing
501 W. Algoquin Road
Mount Prospect, IL 60056
847-981-0310

The Children's Furniture Co.
P.O. Box 27157
1234 Leaden Hall Street
Baltimore, MD 21230
410-243-7488

Chinquapin Mountain Designs
13401 Highway 66
Ashland, OR 97520
541-482-6220

Chris Craft Industrial Products Inc.
P.O. Box 70
Waterford, NY 12188
518-237-5850/ Fax: 518-237-6629

Chronomite Labs, Inc.
21011 Figueroa Street
Carson, CA 90745-1998

310-320-9452

Clarus Technologies
172 Cameray Heights
Laguna Niguel, CA 92677
800-223-1998

Clean Way Co. (Lead Alert kits)
P.O. Box 173
Allentown, PA 18103
800-862-5323/ 215-432-8289

ClimateMaster
P.O. Box 25788
Oklahoma City, OK 73125
405-745-6000

Cloverdale Inc.
P.O. Box 268
5 Smith Place
West Cornwall, CT 06796
800-421-4818/ 203-672-0216

Coastline Products
43 New Brunswick Avenue
Perth Amboy, NJ 08861-2238
908-442-1955

Colin Campbell & Sons
1428 West 7th Avenue
Vancouver
British Columbia V6H 1C1
604-734-2758/ Fax: 604-734-1512

Collins and Aikman
Floor Coverings Division
P.O. Box 1447
311 Smith Industrial Blvd.
Dalton, GA 30722-1447
800-248-2878

Collins Pine Co.
P.O. Box 796
Chester, CA 96020
916-258-2111

Colonial Craft
2772 Fairview Avenue North
St. Paul, MN 55113
612-631-3110

Command Air, Inc.
100 E. Industrial Park Blvd.
Beeville, TX 78102-7201
512-358-0162

Command Aire
Geothermal Heating Systems
P.O. Box 2015
Lower Burrough, PA 15068
412-335-3544

CompuMentor
89 Stillman Street
San Francisco, CA 94107
415-512-7784

Computer Recycling Center
1245 Terra Bella Avenue
Mountain View, CA 94043-1833
415-428-3700

or:
3243 S. 13th Street, #B
Lincoln, NE 68502-4517
402-421-3956

Conservation Concepts
37 Myrtle Street
Milford, NH 03055-3928
603-672-3039

or:
RR1
New Broomfield, PA 17608-9801
717-582-2402

Conservation Energy Systems
2525 Wentz Avenue
Saskatoon, SK 57K 2K9
Canada
800-667-3717

Conservatree Paper Co.
10 Lombard Street
San Francisco, CA 94111
415-433-1000/ Fax: 415-391-7890

Contour Paper Products
W 229 N. 1687 Westwood Drive
Unit D
Waukeska, WI 53186
414-896-2040/ Fax: 414-896-2060

Coon Manufacturing
P.O. Box 190
Spickard, MO 64679
816-485-6148

Cooperative Business International
(Indonesia)

Jalan Karimun Jawa III/1
Klaten
Jawa Tengah
Indonesia
62-21-272-21077/ Fax:
62-21-272-21356

Copper Brite, Inc.
P.O. Box 50610
Santa Barbara, CA 93150
805-565-1566

Copper Cricket
520 Commercial Street
Eugene, OR 97402-5308
541-485-8714

Copper Development Association
260 Madison Avenue
16th Floor
New York, NY 10016
212-251-7200

The Cotton Place
P.O. Box 59721
Dallas, TX 75229
800-451-8866/ 214-243-4149

Cotton Unlimited, Inc.
P.O. Box 760
Post, TX 79356
806-495-3511/ Fax: 806-495-3502

Corniche Carpet Mills
201 Covington Street
Oakland, CA 94605
510-568-8610

Corticeira Amorim
P.O. Box 1
Mozelos 4539
Lourosa Codex, Portugal
2-764-7509

Coyuchi
P.O. Box 845
Point Reyes Station, CA 94956
415-663-8077/ Fax: 415-663-8104

Crabtree & Evelyn
2 Bowens Wharf
Newport, RI 02840
401-849-3655

Crane Plumbing
1235 Hartrey Avenue
Evanston, IL 60202
847-864-9777

Crestron
101 Broadway
Cresskill, NJ 07626
800-237-2041/ 201-894-0660

Crocodile Tiers
402 North 99th Street
Mesa, AZ 85207
602-380-3416

Crosscut Hardwoods
3065 NW Front Avenue
Portland, OR 97210
503-224-9663

Crossville Ceramics
P.O. Box 1168
Crossville, TN 38557
615-484-2110

Crown Bedding Sleep Shops
250 S. San Gabriel Blvd.
San Gabriel, CA 91776
213-681-6356

Crown Corporation, NA
1801 Wynkoop Street
Denver, CO 80202
303-292-1313/ Fax: 303-292-1933

Crystal Cabinet Works
1100 Crystal
Princeton, MN 55371
612-389-4187

Culligan International
1 Culligan Parkway
Northbrook, IL 60062
847-205-6000

John Curtis
P.O. Box 697
Healdsburg, CA 95448
707-433-9549

Custom Materials
16865 Park Circle Dr.
Chagrin Falls, OH 44023
216-543-8284

Cut & Dried Hardwoods
241 Cedros
Solana Beach, CA 92075
619-481-0442

D

Dasun Company
P.O. Box 668
Escondido, CA 92033
800-433-8929/ 619-480-8929
Fax: 619-746-8865

DePeri Manufacturing
P.O. Box 280815
North Ridge, CA 91328
818-885-0011

Deep Diversity seed catalog:
505-438-8080

Deepa Textiles
333 Bryant Street
Suite 160
San Francisco, CA 94107
800-8-DEEPTX/ 800-833-3789/
415-621-4171

Deerfield Woodworking
400 Dwight Street
Holyoke, MA 01040
413-532-2377

Dellinger, Inc.
P.O. Drawer 273
1943 North Broad St.
Rome, GA 30162
706-291-4447

Delta T Corporation
10520 Route 6N
Albion, PA 16401
814-756-5848

Denarco Inc.
301 Industrial Park Drive
Constantine, MI 49042-9702
616-435-8404

Denny Sales Corp.
3500 Gateway Drive Pompano
Beach, FL 33069
800-327-6616/ 305-971-3100
Fax: 305-972-0910

Desert Essence
9510 Basser Ave., #A
Chatsworth, CA 91311
818-709-5900

Design Materials, Inc.
241 South 55th Street
Kansas City, KS 66016
800-654-6451/ 913-342-9796
Fax: 913-342-9826

Designers Fiber Protection
2119 W. March Lane
Suite C
Stockton, CA 95207
209-957-3332

Desso Carpets
P.O. Box 1351
Wayne, PA 19087
800-368-1515

Development and Technical
Assistance Center
Nonprofit Computer Consultants
Program
70 Audubon Street
New Haven, CT 06510
203-772-1345/ Fax: 203-777-1614

Dietmeyer, Ward & Stroud, Inc.
P.O. Box 323
Vashon Island, WA 98070
206-463-3722

DK Heating Systems, Inc.
819 South Wabash
Suite 610
Chicago, IL 60631
800-959-WARM/312-360-0040
Fax:312-360-0440
dkheatsy@mail.idt.net

Dodge-Regupol, Inc.
P.O. Box 989
715 Fountain Avenue
Lancaster, PA 17608-0989
800-322-1923/ 717-295-3400
Fax: 717-295-3414

Dolphin Engineering
19 Chestnut Avenue
Chelmsford, MA 01824-1140
508-256-1777

Domtar Gypsum
133 Peach Tree NE
Atlanta, GA 30303
800-947-4497

Dona Designs
825 Northlake Dr.
Richardson, TX 75080
214-235-0485

Donghia Furniture
485 Broadway
New York, NY 10013
212-925-2777/ Fax: 212-925-4819

Dow Chemical USA
P.O. Box 515
Granville, OH 43023
614-587-4382

Dr. Bronner's All-One Products Co.
P.O. Box 28
Escondido, CA 92033-0028
619-745-7069

Du Pont Flooring Systems
Walnut Run
Room 1ST15
P.O. Box 80722
Wilmington, DE 19880
800-4DUPONT

DuPont Co. – Tyvek
1-800-44-TYVEK (89835)

Duluth Timber Co.
P.O. Box 16717
Duluth, MN 55816
218-727-2145

Dumond Chemicals
1501 Broadway
New York, NY 10036
212-869-6350/ Fax: 212-398-0815

Dura Undercushion
8525 Delmeade Road
Montreal, Quebec
Canada H4T 1M1
514-737-6561

Duratech Industries
1138 4th Avenue
Lake Odessa, MI 48849
616-374-0240

Dwyer Instruments
P.O. Box 373
Michigan City, IN 46360
219-872-9141

E

E.L. Foust
851 Industrial Drive
Elmhurst, IL 60126-1117
630-834-4952

EPA Green Lights Program
401 M Street, SW (6202J)
Washington, DC 20460
202-775-6650/ 202-775-6680

Eswa Radiant Heating Systems
106 Blue Mountain Street
Coquitlan
BC
Canada
604-522-1322

EX
400 East 56th Street
New York, NY 10022
212-758-2593

E-Z Air and Vent Vent II
DesChamps Labs
P.O. Box 440
17 Farinella Drive
East Hanover, NJ 07936
201-994-4660

E Source, Inc.
1050 Walnut Street
Boulder, CO 80302
303-440-8500

Eaglebrook Products
2600 W. Roosevelt Rd.
Chicago, IL 60608
773-638-0006

Earth Care
555 Leslie
Ukiah, CA 95482
800-347-0070

Earth Care Paper
800-347-0070

Earth Care Products
Nc 90 Hwy
Statesville, NC 28687
704-878-2582

Earth Rite
92 Argonaut
Suite 275
Aliso Viejo, CA 92656
800-328-4408

Earth Safe
P.O. Box 1401
Marstons Mills, MA 02648-0014
508-420-5681

Earth Systems International, Inc.
258 McBrine Drive
Kitchener
Ontario
Canada N2R 1H8
800-GO-EARTH

Earth Wise
1790 30th Street
Boulder, CO 80301
303-447-0119

Earthbond 7000
600 N. Baldwin Park Blvd.
City of Industry, CA 91749
818-369-7371

Earth's Best, Inc.
Box 887
Middlebury, VT 05753
802-388-7974/800-442-4221

East-West Education Development
Foundation
49 Temple Place
Boston, MA 02111
617-542-1234/ Fax: 617-542-3333

Easy Heat, Inc.
31977 U.S. 20 East
New Carlisle, IN 46552
219-654-3144

Eco-Container Corp.
1822 Blake Street
Denver, CO 80202
303-296-2657/ Fax: 303-296-2763

Eco-Corporation
550 Queen Street East
Suite M 115
Toronto, ON M5A 1V2
416-360-4119/ Fax: 416-360-8430

Eco Design
1365 Rufina Circle
Santa Fe, NM 87501
800-621-2591/ 505-438-3448
Fax: 505-438-0199

Eco Enterprises
2821 Northeast 55th St.
Seattle, WA 98105
800-426-6937

Ecoprint
9335 Fraser Avenue
Silver Spring, MD 20910
301-585-7077/ Fax: 301-585-4899

Eco Specialties
3422 Janvale Road
Baltimore, MD 21244
800-666-9386

Ecosport
34 Van Wettering Place
Hackensack, NJ 07601-6939
201-487-2440

Eco-Tech LP
4004 Dayton
McHenry, IL 60050
815-363-8570

EcoTech Recycled Products
14241 60th Street, N.
Clearwater, FL 34620
813-531-5353

Ecological Engineering Associates
13 Marconi Lane
Marion, MA 02738
508-748-3224/ Fax: 508-748-9740

Ecological Trading Co., Ltd.
1 Lesbury Road
Newcastle on Tyne
UK NE6 5LB
United Kingdom
4491-278-5547

ECOS
152 Commonwealth Avenue
Concord, MA 01742
508-369-3951/ Fax: 508-369-2484

Ecos Paint
P.O. Box 375
Saint Johnsbury, VT 05819
802-748-9144

or:
Cyr Road
Littleton, NH 03561
603-444-5588

EcoTimber International
1020 Heinz Avenue
Berkeley, CA 94710
510-549-3000

Ecover
Santa Ana, CA 92707
714-556-3644

EcoVision, Blackhawk Computers
38 Main Street
Chatham, NY 12037
518-392-7007

Ecowise International
1714-A S. Congress
Austin, TX 78704
908-220-1307
http://www.ecowise.com

Ecoworks
Barton Creek Mall
Austin, TX 78764-6422
512-328-6422

or:
Baltimore, MD 21207
410-448-3319/ Fax: 410-448-3317

Edensaw Woods
211 Seton Road
Port Townsend, WA 98368
800-950-3336/ 206-385-7870
Fax: 206-385-5215

Eldon Rubbermaid
1427 William Blount Dr.
Maryville, TN 37801
615-977-5477

Electron Connection
P.O. Box 442
Medford, OR 97501
916-475-3401

Eljer Industries
901 10th Street
Plano, TX 75074
800-4ELJER2/ 214-881-7l77

Emerald 2000
Guertin Brothers Industries, Inc.
9701 Turk Drive
Marysville, WA 98271-6411
360-653-5505

Encapsulation Technologies Corp.
310-312 N. Charles Street
Fourth Floor
Baltimore, MD 21201
410-962-5335

Ener-Grid
512-264-3462

Eneready Products
6860 Antrim Avenue
Burnaby, BC V5J 4M4
604-433-5697/ Fax: 604-438-8906

Energy Concepts Co.
627 Ridgely Avenue
Annapolis, MD 21401
410-266-6521

Energy Conservation Services of
North Florida
6120 SW 13th Street
Gainesville, FL 32608
352-373-3220

Energy Technology Labs, Inc.
2351 Tenaya Drive
Modesto, CA 95354
800-344-3242/ 209-529-3546

Englehard Corp.
Specialty Metals Division
235 Kilvert Street
Warwyck, RI 02886
800-225-2130

Enjo USA
Austin, TX
512-451-3635

Environ Technologies Corp.
17 Corporate Plaza
Newport Beach, CA 92660

Environmental Air Ltd.
50 Sheridan Road
P.O. Box 2000
Baouvctouche, New Brunswick
Canada E0A 1J0
506-576-6672

Environmental Applied Products
2029 North 23rd Street
Boise, ID 83702
800-531-0102/ 208-368-7900
Fax: 208-368-7900

Environmental Construction
Outfitters
44 Crosby Street
New York, NY 10012
212-334-9659

Environmental Flooring Products
P.O. Box 125
Lithonia, GA 30058
800-828-2675/ 404-448-1694
Fax: 404-484-0893

Environmental Light Concepts, Inc.
3923 Coconut Palm Dr.
Suite 101
Tampa, FL 33619
800-842-8848/ 813-621-0058
Fax: 813-626-8790

Environmental Plastics
4981 Keelson Drive
Columbus, OH 43232
614-861-2107

Environmental Purification
Systems
P.O. Box 191
Concord, CA 94522
800-829-2129/ 510-682-7231

Environmental Recovery Systems
1400 Brayton Point Road
Somerset, MA 02725
508-677-0252

Environmental Recycling, Inc.
8000 Hall Street
St. Louis, MO 63147

314-382-7766

Environmental Specialty Products
2807-C Guasti Road
P.O. Box 1114
Guasti, CA 91743
800-775-2784

Environmental Technology
South Bay Depot Rd.
P.O. Box 365
Fields Landing, CA 95537
800-368-9323/ 707-443-9323
Fax: 707-443-7962

Environmentally Responsible
Envelope System
P.O. Box 1267
Bangor, Maine 04402-1267
207-947-2250/ Fax: 207-947-6487

Environmentally Safe Products,
Inc.
313 West Golden Lane
New Oxford, PA 17350
800-BUY-LowE/ 717-624-3581

Enviroclean
30 Walnut Avenue
Floral Park, NY 11001-2404
800-466-1425

Envirowise
130 North Hardman Ave
South St. Paul, MN 55075
612-450-4757

Envirowood Corp.
501 W. Algonquin Road
Mt. Prospect, IL 60056
800-323-0830

Eternit, Inc.
Excelsior Industrial Park
P.O. Box 679
Blandon, PA 19510
800-233-3155/ 610-926-0100

Etex Ltd.
3200 Polaris Avenue
Suite 9
Las Vegas, NV 89102
800-543-5651/ 702-364-5911
Fax: 702-364-8894

Euro-Tap
12228 Venice Blvd., #146
Los Angeles, CA 90066
800-388-9255/ 213-398-7033
310-398-7033

Evanite Fiber Corporation
P.O. Box E
Corvallis, OR 97339
800-633-3838/ 503-655-3383

Evenson, Michael
P.O. Box 202
Redway, CA 95560
707-923-2979

Executive Office Concepts
1705 Anderson Avenue
Compton, CA 90220
213-537-1657

Exotic Gifts
P.O. Box 4665
Arcata, CA 95521
707-725-9798

F

Fabritex, Inc.
1122 Del Paso Blvd.
Sacramento, CA 95815

Fairfield Engineering
P.O. Box 139
Fairfield, IA 52556
515-472-5551

Falcon Products
9387 Dielman Industrial Dr.
St. Louis, MO 63132
314-991-9200

i play
200 Riverside Drive
Suite 9
Asheville, NC 28804
800-876-1574/704-254-9236

Faswall Building Systems
7322 Southwest Fwy
Houston, TX 77074-2010
713-270-1249

Feeny Manufacturing
P.O. Box 191
Muncie, IN 47308
317-288-8730/ Fax: 317-288-0851

Fiberiffic Energy System
2185 South Jason
Denver, CO 80223-4004
303-922-8277/ Fax: 303-934-2177

Fibrelam
P.O. Box 2002
Doswell, VA 23047
804-876-3135

Fieldcrest Cannon, Inc.
1 Lake Circle Drive
Kannapolis, NC 28081
704-939-2000

FILTRX Corporation
11 Hansen Avenue
New City, NY 10956
914-638-9708

Flecto Company
1000 45th Street
Oakland, CA 94608
800-635-3286/ 510-655-2470
Fax: 510-652-7135

Flexi Wall Systems
P.O. Box 89
208 Carolina Drive
Liberty, SC 29657
800-843-5394

Floorworks
231 Rowntree Dairy Road
Woodbridge, ON L4L 8B8
416-961-6891

Florida Playground & Steel Co.
4701 S. 50th Street
Tampa, FL 33619
800-444-2655

Florida Solar Energy Center
(FSEC)
300 State Road 401
Cape Canaveral, FL 32920-4099
407-783-0300

Forbo Industries, Inc.
Humboldt Industrial Park

Maplewood Drive
P.O. Box 667
Hazleton, PA 18201
800-233-0475/ 717-459-0771
Toronto: 416-661-2351

Ford Technologies, Inc./ACO
3250 South Susan Street
Suite A
Santa Ana, CA 92704
714-751-1152/ Fax: 714-754-4088

Foreign Accent
2825 Broadbent Pkwy, NE
Albuquerque, NM 87107
800-880-0413/ 505-344-4833

Forest Trust Wood Products
Brokerage
P.O. Box 519
Santa Fe, MN 87504
505-983-8992

Franklin International
2020 Bruck Street
Columbus, OH 43207
800-347-GLUE (4583)/ 614-443-0241

Free-Flow Packaging Corp.
1093 Charter St.
Redwood City, CA 94063
800-866-9946/ 415-364-1145
Fax: 415-361-1713

Frigidaire Company
800-451-7007

Furnature
319 Washington Street
Boston, MA 02135-3395
617-783-4343/617-782-3169
Fax: 617-787-0350

The Futon Shop
491 Broadway
New York, NY 10012
212-226-5825

G

G.E. Plastics Roofing Systems
One Plastics Avenue
Pittsfield, MA 02101

413-448-7383

G.E.S. Roofing
801 South Flower Street
Burbank, CA 91502
818-843-0544/ Fax: 818-843-7132

G.R. Plume Company
Bellingham, WA
360-676-5658/ Fax: 206-738-1909

Garden City Seeds
406-961-4837

Gardens Alive!
5100 Schenley Place
Lawrenceburg, IN 47025
812-537-8650

Gardener's Eden
P.O. Box 7307
San Francisco, CA 94102
800-822-9600/ Fax: 415-421-5153

Gardener's Supply
128 Intervale Road
Burlington, VT 05401
802-660-3500/ Fax: 802-660-3501

Garnet Hill
262 Main Street
Franconia, NH 03580
800-622-6216

Gemplers
P.O. Box 270
Mt. Horeb, WI 53572
800-272-7672/608-437-4883

General Ecology, Inc.
151 Sheree Boulevard
Lionville, PA 19353
610-363-7900

Georgia Pacific
10515 SW Allen Blvd.
Beaverton, OR 97005
503-643-8612

Gerber Plumbing Fixtures Corp.
4600 West Touhy Ave.
Chicago, IL 60646
847-675-6570

Gerbert Limited
P.O. Box 4944
Lancaster, PA 17604
717-299-5035

Gilmer Wood
2211 NW Saint Helens Road
Portland, OR 97210
503-274-1271

The Glidden Co.
General Offices
925 Euclid Avenue
Cleveland, OH 44115-1402
216-344-8000

Global Environmental Technologies
P.O. Box 8839
Allentown, PA 18105
215-821-4901

Global Technology Systems
Badger Cork Division
P.O. Box 25
Trevor, WI 53179
800-558-3206/ 414-862-2311
Fax: 414-862-2500

Global Zero, Inc.
Community Drive
Sanford, ME 07073
207-324-5200

Gloucester Company
P.O. Box 428
Franklin, MA 02038
800-343-4963/ 508-520-3851
Fax: 508-520-3851

Gold Mine Natural Food Co.
1947 30th Street
San Diego, CA 92102
800-475-3663/619-234-9711

Golden Rabbit
c/o Indo Trade
22455 Davis Drive
Suite 109
Sterling, VA 22170
703-406-3236

Goodkind Pen Co., Inc.
15 Holly Street, #112
Pine Point Park
Scarborough, ME 04074

207-883-1250

Goodwind Heartpine Co.
Route 2
Box 119-AA
Micanopy, FL 32667
800-336-3118

Granny's Old Fashioned
P.O. Box 256
Arcadia, CA 91006
818-577-1825

Great States Corporation
P.O. Box 369
Shelbyville, IN 46176
317-392-3615/ Fax: 317-392-4118

GreenCo Products
239 Old Ferry Rd.
Unit 2
Brattleboro, VT 05301
800-326-2897

GreenDisk
800-305-DISK(3475)/ 206-489-
2550/ 514-395-6060 (in Canada)

Green Earth Natural Foods
2545 Prairie Avenue
Evanston, IL 60201
847-475-0205

Green Earth Office Supply
P.O. Box 719
Redwood Estates, CA 95044
800-327-8449

The Green Office
810-737-0971
Fax: 810-737-2079/800-644-5044

Greenstone
3264 Villa Lane
Napa, CA 94510
800-862-7599

GreenStone Industries
390 W. Ray Road
Chandler, AZ 85225
800-237-7668/ Fax: 602-821-9820

Green Thumb
Lithius Springs, GA
800-666-3590/ 404-344-3590

Fax: 404-344-6113

Greenwood Cotton Insulation
Products, Inc.
P.O Box 1017
Greenwood, SC 29648
800-546-1332/ 404-998-8888

Gridcore Systems International
1400 Canal Avenue
Long Beach, CA 90813
562-901-1492/ Fax: 562-901-1499

Guardian Protection Products, Inc.
812 Ciernan Avenue
Modesto, CA 95356
800-527-8487

Guilford of Maine Textile
Resources
4710 44th Street, NE
Grand Rapids, MI 49512
800-544-0200

H

H. B. Fuller Company
315 South Hicks Road
Palatine, IL 60067
800-323-7407/ 312-358-9500

Hach Co.
P.O. Box 389
Loveland, CO 80539
800-227-4224

Hammermill Paper
Memphis, TN
800-242-2148

Hammer's Plastic Recycling
RR 3
Box 182
Iowa Falls, IA 50126
515-648-5073

John W. Hancock, Jr.
2535 Diuguids Lane
Salem, VA 24153
540-389-0211

Handloggers Hardwood Lumber
135 East Sir Frances Drake Blvd.
Larkspur, CA 94935

415-461-1180

Hanna Anderson
1010 NW Flanders
Portland, OR 97209
800-222-0544

Harbinger Company
1755 The Exchange
Atlanta, GA 30339
800-241-4216/ Fax: 706-625-4527

Hardware Designs
342 Main Street
Danbury, CT 06810
800-431-1904

Harmonious Technologies
P.O. Box 1865
Ojai, CA 93024
707-823-1999/ Fax: 805-646-7404

Harmony Farm Supply
P.O. Box 460
Graton, CA 95444
707-823-9125/ Fax: 707-823-1734

Haworth, Inc.
One Haworth Center
Holland, MI 49423
616-393-3000/ Fax: 616-393-1570

Health Magnetix, Inc.
20801 Biscayne Boulevard
Suite 302
Miami, FL 33180
800-989-SAFE (7233)
/305-932-3406

Healthy Kleaner
P.O. Box 4656
Boulder, CO 80306
800-327-8429/ Fax: 303-664-0825
E-mail: doug@the_greenspan.com
Internet: www.the_greenspan.com

Heart of Vermont
The Old Schoolhouse
Route 132
P.O. Box 183
Sharon, VT 05065
800-639-4123/ 802-763-2720

Heartsong Store
170 Professional Center Drive

Rohnert Park, CA 94928
800-533-4397

Heatway
3131 W. Chestnut Expressway
Springfield, MO 65802
417-864-6108

Helios Carpets
P.O. Box 1928
Calhoun, GA 30703
800-843-5138

Henry Flack International
P.O. Box 865110
Plano, TX 75086
800-527-4929/ 214-867-5677

Herman Miller
8500 Byron Road
Zeeland, MI 49464
616-772-3300

Hoechst-Celanese
2300 Archdale Drive
Charlotte, NC 28209
704-554-2000

Holaday Industries
14825 Martin Drive
Eden Prairie, MN 55344

Hold Everything
3250 Van Ness Avenue
San Francisco, CA 94109
415-421-7900

Homasote Company
Box 7240
W. Trenton, NJ 08628
800-257-9491/ 609-883-3300
Fax: 609-530-1584

Home Automation, Inc.
2313 Metairie Road
P.O. Box 9310
Metairie, LA 70055-9310
504-833-7256

Home Couture, Natural Fabrics
893 S. Lucerne Blvd.
Los Angeles, CA 90005
213-936-1302

Home Manager
Unity Systems, Inc.
2606 Spring Street
Redwood City, CA 94063
800-85-UNITY/ 415-369-3233

Homespun Fabrics & Draperies
P.O. Box 4315
Thousand Oaks, CA 91359
805-642-8111

Honeywell, Inc.
Honeywell Plaza
Minneapolis, MN 55408
800-345-6770

Hope's
84 Hopkins Avenue
P.O. Box 580
Jamestown, NY 14702-0580
716-665-5124

Horizon/Mowhawk Industries
5 S. Industrial Blvd.
Calhoun, GA 30701
706-629-7721

Hugg -A-Planet
247 Rockingstone Avenue
Larchmont, NY 10538
914-833-0200

Hurd Millwork Company, Inc.
575 South Whelen Avenue
Medford, WI 54451
715-748-2011

Hybrivet Systems, Inc.
P.O. Box 1210
Framingham, MA 01701
508-651-7881
Lead information hotline:
800-262-5323

I

I & J Construction
410 Broadway
Suite B
Santa Monica, CA 90401
310-392-4775

ICI
216-344-8000

Ida Grae
424 LaVerne Avenue
Mill Valley, CA 94941
415-388-6101

Image Industries
Box 5555
Armuchee, GA 30105
800-722-2504/404-235-8444
Fax: 706-234-3463

Inchcape Laboratories/ITS
101 West 31st Street
15th Floor
New York, NY 10001
212-868-7090

Indoor Air Quality Information
Clearinghouse
P.O. Box 37133
Washington, D.C. 20013-7133
800-438-4318/ Fax: 301-588-3408

Industries Maibec, Inc.
Contact:
Charles Tardif
Rue de l'Eglise Est
St.-Pamphile
Cte. l'Islet, Quebec
Canada G0R 3XO
418-356-3331

Insulcot Cotton Insulation Products
555 Sun Valley Drive
Suite J4
Roswell, GA 30076
770-998-6888

Insul-Tray
East 1881 Crestview Dr.
Shelton, WA 98584
360-427-5930/ Fax: 206-427-5930

Integrated Fertility Management
333 Ohme Gardens Rd.
Wenatchee, WA 98801
509-662-3179

Integrid Building Systems
1396 Campus Drive
Berkeley, CA 94708
510-845-1100/ Fax: 510-845-6886

Integrity Electronics and Research
558 Breckenridge Street

Buffalo, NY 14222

Interbath, Inc.
665 North Baldwin Park Blvd.
City of Industry, CA 91746
800-423-9485/ 800-828-7943
in California/ 818-369-1841

Interface Flooring Systems
Chicago, IL
312-822-9640

Interface Research
100 Chastain Center Blvd.
Suite 165
Kennesaw, GA 30144
770-421-9555/ Fax: 404-424-1888

Inter-Island Supply
345 N. Nimitz Highway
Honolulu, HI 96817
808-523-0711

International Plastics
2029 Budd Lane
Lexington, KY 40511
606-388-9116/606-254-7068

International Plastics Equipment
Ltd. (formerly Humphrey Plastic
Machinery)
29885 Second Street
Unit J
Lake Elsinore, CA 92532
909-471-1310/ Fax: 909-471-1313

Into the Woods
300 North Water Street
Petaluma, CA 94952
707-763-0159

Iowa Plastics, Inc.
3464 Goldfinch Ave.
Hull, IA 51239
712-722-0692

J

JH Baxter
1700 S. El Camino Real
San Mateo, CA 94402
415-349-0201

J.P. Stevens & Co.
1185 Avenue of the Americas
New York, NY 10036
212-930-3800

Jack Lenor Larsen
41 East 11th Street
New York, NY 10003
212-462-1300

James Hardie Building Products
10901 Elm Avenue
Fontana, CA 92335
800-426-4051/ 714-356-3600

James River Corporation
Oakland, CA
510-452-3100

Janice Corporation
Box 198, Route 46
Budd Lake, NJ 07828
800-JANICES/ 201-691-2979

Jefferson Recycled Woodworks
P.O. Box 696
McCloud, CA 96057
916-964-2740

Jervert Enterprises, Inc.
320 Chestnut
Roselle, NJ 07203
908-298-8555

Johnson Controls
507 E. Michigan Street
Milwaukee, WI 53201
414-274-4000

The Joinery Co.
P.O. Box 518
Tarboro, NC 27886
919-823-3306

Junckers Danish Beech
Flooring USA
4920 E. Landon Drive
Anaheim, CA 92807
800-878-9663/ 714-777-6430
Fax: 714-777-6436

K

K&B Associates
P.O. Box 35605
Monte Sereno, CA 95030
408-395-3394

KP Products, Inc./Vision Paper
P.O. Box 20399
Albuquerque, NM 87154
505-294-0293

Kachelofens Unlimited
P.O. Box 202
Williams, OR 97544
541-846-6196

Karen's Non-toxic Products
322 St. John Street
Havre-de-Grace, MD 21078
800-527-3674

Kaupert Chemical & Consulting
P.O. Box 430
Walterville, OR 97489
541-747-2509

Kelly-Moore Paint Co.
5101 Raley Blvd.
Sacramento, CA 95838
916-921-0165/ Fax: 916-921-0184

Kentrel Corporation
P.O. Box 173
Avoca, PA 18641
800-437-9200/ 717-451-0622

Kimball International
1600 Royal Street
Jasper, IN 47549
800-482-1616

Kingsley-Bates, Ltd.
5587 B Guinea Road
Fairfax, VA 22032
703-978-7200/ Fax: 703-978-7222

Klean Strip
Box 1879
Memphis, TN 38810
901-775-0100

The Knoll Group
105 Wooster Street

New York, NY 10012
212-343-4167

Knorr Steel Framing Systems
5073 Salem Dallas Highway
P.O. Box 5267
Salem, OR 97304
503-371-8033

Kohler Co.
444 Highland Drive
Kohler, WI 53044
800-456-4537/ 414-457-4441

Kurfees Paints/KCI Coatings
201 East Market St.
Louisville, KY 40202
502-584-0151

L

Latitude 16 Designs
c/o French Harbor Yacht Club
Isla Roatan, Honduras
504-45-0342/ Fax: 504-45-1459

Lennox Industries
P.O. Box 799900
Dallas, TX 75379
214-497-5000

The Libra Company
Pentacon Business Estate
Cambridge Road
Linton
Cambridge CB1 6NN
U.K.
44-0223-893839

Life Tree
P.O. Box 1203
Sebastopol, CA 95472
707-588-0755

Lister
1900 The Exchange
Suite 655
Atlanta, GA 30339
770-952-4272

Lite-Form, Inc.
P.O. Box 774
Sioux City, IA 51102-0774
800-551-3313/ 712-252-3704

Fax: 712-252-3259
Litetouch
3550 South 700 West
Salt Lake City, UT 84119
801-268-8668

Live Oak Structural
801 Camelia Street, #B
Berkeley, CA 94710
510-524-7101

The Living Source
P.O. Box 20155
Waco, TX 76702
817-776-4878

Living Technologies
431 Pine Street
Burlington, VT 05401
802-865-4460/ Fax: 802-865-4438

Living Tree Paper Products
1430 Willamette St.
Suite 367
Eugene, OR 97401
800-309-2974

Lotus Brands
P.O. Box 325
Twin Lakes, WI 53181
414-889-8561

Louisiana-Pacific
111 SW 5th Avenue
Portland, OR 97204
800-365-7672/503-221-0800
Call for referral to local branch
Fax: 503-796-0204

The Lowenstein Furniture Group
1801 North Andrews Avenue Ext.
Pompano Beach, FL 33069
954-960-1100/ Fax: 305-960-0409

Lowry Aeration Systems
P.O. Box 1239
Blue Hill, ME 04614
919-544-9080

M

Mack, Steve P. and Associates
Chasehill Farms
Ashaway, RI 02804

Trus Joist MacMillan
9777 West Chinden Blvd.
Boise, I D 83714
208-375-4450/ Fax: 208-378-4754

MacMillan-Bloedel
Trus-Joist MacMillan
Vancouver Plant
1272 Derwent Way
Annacis Island, BC V3M 5RI
Canada
604-526-4665/ Fax: 604-526-3157

Maharam
251 Park Avenue, S.
New York, NY 10010
212-995-0115

Mai'bec Corp.
P.O. Box 1249
Greenville, ME 04441
207-695-3255

Mansfield
150 East 1st Street
Perrysville, OH 44864
419-938-5211

Mansion Industries Inc.
P.O. Box 2220
14711 Clark Avenue
City of Industry, CA 91746
800-423-6589/ 818-968-9501
Fax: 818-330-3084

Marc's Furniture Restoration
18 Central Avenue
Norwich, CT
203-887-1035

Master Builder Technologies, Inc.
23700 Chagrin Blvd.
Cleveland, OH 44122
800-227-3350/ 216-831-5500
Fax: 216-831-6910

The Masters Corporation/SEAS
Corporation
289 Mill Road
P.O. Box 514
New Canaan, CT 06840
203-966-3541

Mat Factory, Inc.
760 West 16th Street

Suite E
Costa Mesa, CA 92627
714-645-3122

Maxi Tile
17141 South Kingview Ave.
Carson, CA 90746
800-338-8453

Maxon Corporation
920 Hamel Road
P.O. Box 253
Hamel, MN 55340
612-478-647/ Fax: 612-478-2431

Maya Romanoff Corp.
1730 West Greenleaf
Chicago, IL 60626
773-465-6909

Maze Nails
P.O. Box 449
Peru, IL 61354
800-435-5949/ 815-223-5290
Fax: 815-223-7585

Meadowood Industries, Inc.
33242 Red Bridge Road
Albany, OR 97321
541-259-1303/ Fax: 541-259-1355

Medite Corporation
P.O. Box 4040
Medford, OR 97501
800-676-3339/ 541-773-2522
Fax: 541-779-9921

Melard Mfg. Corporation
153 Linden Street
Passaic, NJ 07055
201-472-8888

Mellinger's, Inc.
2310 W. South Range Rd.
North Lima, OH 44452
330-549-9861

Menominee Tribal Enterprises
P.O. Box 10
Neopit, WI 54150
715-756-2311

Merida Meridian
643 Summer Street
Boston, MA 02210

800-345-2200/ 617-464-5400
Fax: 617-464-5417

Meridian
18558 171st Avenue
Spring Lake, MI 49456
616-846-0280/ Fax: 616-846-9236

Metal Sales Manufacturing
7800 State Road 60
Southersburg, IN 47172
812-246-1866

Metropolitan Ceramics
P.O. Box 68
Ozona, FL 34660
813-786-3828

Mia Rose
1374 Logan, Unit C
Costa Mesa, CA 92626
714-662-5465/800-292-6339

Michael Elkan Studio
22364 North Fork Road
Silverton, OR 97381
503-873-3241

MicroCentre
5300 N. Irwindale Avenue
Irwindale, CA 91706

MicroMenders
410 Townsend Street
Suite 408
San Francisco, CA 94107
415-543-0500/ Fax: 415-543-3845

Miele Appliances, Inc.
22D Worlds Fair Drive
Somerset, NJ 08873
800-289-MIELE (64353)/ 908-560-
0899

Millbrook Custom Kitchens
Route 20
Nassau, NY 12123
518-766-3033

Miller Paint Co.
317 S.E. Grand Ave
Portland, OR 97214
503-233-4491/ Fax: 503-233-7463

Miller SQA, Inc.
10201 Adams Street
Holland, MI 49424
800-253-2733/ Fax: 616-772-4129

Mitchell Instrument Co.
1570 Cherokee Street
Marcos, CA 92069
619-744-2690

Mobil Chemical Co.
Composite Products Division
800 Connecticut Avenue
P.O. Box 5445
Norwalk, CT 06856
203-831-4200

Mobil Oil Corporation
3225 Gallows Road
Fairfax, VA 22037
703-846-3000

Moen Incorporated
25300 Al Moen Drive
North Olmsted, OH 44070
216-962-2000

Monel
P.O. Box 291
Oakland Gardens, NY 11364
718-225-8535/ Fax: 718-423-4806

Monitor Detection Systems
4704 Harlan #245
Denver, CO 80212
303-480-0486

Motherwear
P.O. Box 114
Northhampton, MA 01061
413-586-3488

Mountain Ark Trading Co.
799 Old Leicester Hwy
Asheville, NC 28806
800-643-8909

Mountain Energy and Resources,
Inc.
15800 W. 6th Avenue
Golden, CO 80401
303-279-4971

Mountain Lumber
P.O. Box 289

Ruckersville, VA 22968
800-445-2671/ 804-985-3646

Multi-Pure Drinking Water Systems
P.O. Box 368
Barre, MA 01005

Murco Wall Products
300 NE 21st Street
Fort Worth, TX 76106
817-626-1987

N

N-Viro Products Ltd.
610 Walnut Avenue
Bohemia, NY 11716
516-567-2628

N.E.E.D.S.
527 Charles Avenue 12-A
Syracuse, NY 13209
800-634-1380/ 315-488-6312
Fax: 315-488-6336

NEW Plastics Corp.
P.O. Box 480
Luxemburg, WI 54217
414-845-2326

Nada-Chair
2448 Larpenteur Ave. West
St. Paul, MN 55113
800-722-2587

Narda Microwave Products
435 Moreland Road
Hauppauge, NY 11788

Nathenson Fine Furnishings
28 Industrial Street
Rochester, NY 14614
716-956-8342

National Cancer Institute
Building 31, Room 10A24
9000 Rockville Pike
Bethesda, MD 20892
800-4-CANCER (226237)

National Cristina Foundation
591 West Putname Avenue
Greenwich, CT 06830
800-274-7846/ Fax: 203-622-6270

National Institute for Occupational
Safety & Health
4676 Columbia Parkway
Cincinnati, Ohio 45226-1998
800-35-NIOSH (64674)

National Testing Labs
6555 Wilson Mills Road
Suite 102
Cleveland, OH 44143
800-458-3330

Native Seed/SEARCH
2509 N. Campbell Avenue, #325
Tucson, AZ 85719
520-327-9123

Natural Animal Inc.
P.O. Box 1177
St. Augustine, FL 32085
800-274-7387/ 904-824-5884

The Natural Bedroom
P.O. Box 3071
Santa Rosa, CA 95402
800-365-6563/ 707-823-8834

Natural Chemistry, Inc.
76 Progress Drive
Stamford, CT 06902
800-753-1233

Natural Cotton Colours
P.O. Box 66
Wickensburg, AZ 85390
602-684-7199

Natural Cotton Colours
P.O. Box 791
Wasco, CA 93280
805-758-3928

Natural Lifestyle Supplies
16 Lookout Drive
Asheville, NC 28804
800-752-2775

Natural Lighting Company
7021 W. Augusta
Suite 106
Glendale, AZ 85303
800-960-LITE (5483)/ 602-435-6542

Natural Resources
Network/Allergy
264 Brookridge
Palmer Lake, CO 80133
800-536-5308

Natural Way Natural Body Care
820 Massachusetts St.
Lawrence, KS 66044
913-841-0100

The Natural Baby
RD 1, Box 160S
Titusville, NJ 08560
609-737-2895

The Natural Gardening
217 San Anselmo Ave.
San Anselmo, CA 94960
707-766-9303

The Naturalist/J.C. Enterprises
P.O. Box 1431
Provo, UT 84603
801-377-5140

Nature's Control
P.O. Box 35
Medford, OR 97501
541-899-8318

Naturlich
P.O. Box 1677
Sebastopol, CA 95473-1677
707-824-0914 (for catalogue)
7120 Keating Avenue
Sebastopol, CA 95472-3741
707-829-3959 (showroom)

Necessary Organics/Trading Co.
422 Salem Avenue
P.O. 305
New Castle, VA 24127
800-447-5354/ 540-864-5103

Neff Kitchens
6 Malanie Drive
Brammton
Ontario
Canada L6T 4K9
800-268-4527/ 905-791-7770

New England Solar Electric
131 Bashan Hill Road
Worthington, MA 01098
413-238-5974

New York Recycled Paper, Inc.
170 Varick Street
New York, NY 10013
212-645-2300

Niagara Conservation Corp.
45 Horse Hill Road
Cedar Knolls, NJ 07927
800-831-8383/ 201-829-0800

Niagara Fiberboard
P.O. Box 520
Lockport, NY 14095
716-434-8881

Nigra Enterprises
5699 Kanan Road
Agoura, CA 91301
818-889-6877

Nonprofit Computing
40 Wall Street
Suite 2124
New York, NY 10005
212-759-2368

Non-toxic Environments, Inc.
P.O. Box 384
Newmarket, NH 03857
800-789-4348/603-659-5919
Fax: 603-659-5933

Norcold
600 South Kuther Road
Sidney, OH 45365
800-752-8654

Nordic Builders
162 North Sierra Court
Gilbert, AZ 85234
602-892-0603

North American Adhesives
530 Industrial Drive
West Chicago, IL 60185
800-637-7753/ 708-231-7175

North American Cellular Concrete
3 Regency Plaza
Suite 6
Providence, RI 02903
401-621-8108

North American Philips Information
and Literature Center

114 Mayfield Avenue
Edison, NJ 08837
800-631-1259

Northern Hardwood Lumber
520 Matthew Street
Santa Clara, CA 95050
408-727-2211/ Fax: 408-727-0215

Northern Lights
P.O. Box 35
Topsfield, ME 04490
207-796-0798

Nuclear Free America
325 East 25th Street
Baltimore, MD 21218
410-235-3575/ Fax: 410-235-5457

O

Old Fashioned Milk Paint Co.
436 Main Street
P.O. Box 222
Groton, MA 01450
508-448-6336/ Fax: 508-448-2754

Optical Coating Laboratory, Inc.
2789 Northpoint Parkway
Santa Rosa, CA 95407-7397

Organic Control, Inc.
5132 Venice Boulevard
Los Angeles, CA 90019
213-937-7444

Osram-Sylvania Inc.
100 Endicott Street
Danvers, MA 01923
800-255-5042/ 508-777-1900

Outwater Plastic Lumber
4 Passaic Street
Woodridge, NJ 07075
800-631-8375/ 201-340-1040
Fax: 800-888-3315

Owens Corning
1 Owens Corning Parkway
Toledo, CH 43659
419-248-8000/ Fax: 419-248-6227

P

Pace Chemical Industries, Inc.
P.O. Box 1946
Santa Ynez, CA 93460
800-350-2912/805-499-2911

or:
779 South La Grange Avenue
Newbury Park, CA 91320
Pace Environs, Inc.
207 Rutherglen Drive
Cary, NC 27511
919-467-7578

Pacific Environmental Marketing &
Development
421 South California Street #D
San Gabriel, CA 91776
800-243-8775/ 818-292-3855

Pacific Gas & Electric
San Francisco, CA 94106
415-973-8212

Palmer Industries
10611 Old Annapolis Road
Frederick, MD 21701
301-898-7848

Panasonic Industrial Co.
Two Panasonic Way
Secaucus, NJ 07094
201-348-5380

Papa Don's Toys
Walker Creek Road
Walton, OR 97490
541-935-7604

Paperdirect, Inc.
205 Chubb Avenue
Lyndhurst, NJ 07071
800-272-7377/ 201-507-5488
Fax: 201-507-0817

Pastorini Spielzeug of Zurich
Industriestrasse 4
Postfach
8600 Dubendorf
Switzerland
01-821-55-22

Pavestone Company
P.O. Box 1868
Grapevine, TX 76099
800-245-PAVE (7283)

Peaceful Valley Farm Supply
P.O. Box 2209
Grass Valley, CA 95949
916-272-4769

Peerless Pottery
P.O. Box 145
Rockport, IN 47635-0145
800-457-5785/ 812-649-6430

Pegelli Forest
Dyfed, Wales, England
Contact:
Dyfed Wildlife Trust
7 Market Street
Haverford West SA61 INP
England
011-44-0437-765-762

Perfect Aire
Research Products Corp.
P.O. Box 1467
Madison, WI 53701
608-257-8801

Perlite Institute
88 New Dorp Plaza
Staten Island, NY 10306
718-351-5723

Perma-Chink Systems
1605 Prosser Road
Knoxville, TN 37914
800-548-3554

Phenix Biocomposites
P.O. Box 609
Mankato, MN 56002-0609
507-931-9787

Phillips Lighting
200 Franklin Square Dr.
Somerset, NJ 08875
908-563-3000/ Fax: 908-563-3641

Photocomm, Inc.
7735 East Redfield Rd.
Scottsdale, AZ 85260
800-544-6466

Photron, Inc.
1220 Blosser Lane
P.O. Box 578
Willits, CA 95490
707-459-3211

Pittsford Lumber
50 State Street
Pittsford, NY 14534
716-586-1877/ 716-381-3489
Fax: 716-586-1934

Planet Natural
1612 Gold Avenue
P.O. Box 3146
Bozeman, MT 59772
800-289-6656

Planetary Solutions
P.O. Box 1049
Boulder, CO 80306
303-442-6228/ Fax: 303-442-6474
E-mail: paula@planetearth.com

Plastic Lumber Co.
540 South Main Street
P.O. Box 80075
Akron, OH 44311-1010
330-762-8989

Plastic Pilings, Inc.
1485 S. Willow
Realto, CA 92376
909-989-7685

The Plow and Hearth
P.O. Box 830
301 Madison Road
Orange, VA 22960
800-627-1712/ 703-672-361

Poly-wood
207 N. Huntington Street
Syracuse, IN 46567
219-457-3284/ Fax: 219-457-4723

Pompanoosuc Mills
Route 5
P.O. Box 38A
East Thetford, VT 05043
802-785-4851/ Fax: 802-785-4485

Porcher Inc.
3618 E. LaSalle
Phoenix, AZ 85040

800-359-3261/ 602-470-1005

Positive Growth Organic Lawn
Care
P.O. Box 7662
Little Rock, AR 72217-7662
501-223-2237

Prestige Mills
83 Harbor Road
Port Washington, NY 11050
516-767-1110

Presto Products
Geosystems Division
P.O. Box 2399
Appleton, WI 54913
800-548-3424/ Fax: 414-739-9471

Pure Air Systems, Inc.
P.O. Box 418
Plainfield, NJ 46168
317-839-9135

Pure Water Place
P.O. Box 6715
Longmont, CO 80501
303-776-0056

Q

Quaker Jobbing
1722 North Hancock
Philadelphia, PA 19122
215-739-9233

Quality Custom Cabinetry
125 Peters Road
P.O. Box 189
New Holland, PA 17557-0189
717-656-2721

Quantum Group
11211 Sorrento Valley Road
Suite D
San Diego, CA 92121
619-457-3048

Quantum Electronics Corp.
3100 Graystone Street
Warwick, RI 02886
800-966-5575

R

RB Rubber Products
904 East 10th Avenue
McMinnville, OR 97128
800-525-5530/ 503-472-4691
Fax: 503-434-4455

RMS Electric, Inc.
2560 28th Street
Boulder, CO 80301
303-444-5909

R Value West
10926-B Grand Avenue
Temple City, CA 91780
818-448-4833

Rachel Perry, Inc.
9111 Mason Avenue
Chatsworth, CA 91311
800-966-8888

Rainbow Organic Fiber Mill
P.O. Box 744
N. Bennington, VT 05257
802-442-0871/ Fax: 802-442-6478

Rastra Building Systems, Inc.
6421 Box Springs Blvd.
Riverside, CA 92507
909-653-3346

Real Goods Trading Corp.
966 Mazzoni Street
Ukiah, CA 95482-3471
800-762-7325/ Fax: 707-468-0301

Rector Mineral Trading
9 West Prospect Avenue
Mt. Vernon, NY 10550
914-699-5755/ Fax: 914-699-5759

Recycled Office Products, Inc.
27 Walnut Street
Peabody, MA 01960
800-814-1100/508-977-4851
Fax: 508-977-4856

Recycled Plastics Industries, Inc.
1820 Industrial Drive
Green Bay, WI 54302
414-433-0900

Recycled Polymer Associates
152 W. 26th Street
New York, NY 10001
212-463-8622

Reflectix
P.O. Box 108
Markleville, IN 46056
800-879-3645/ Fax: 317-533-2327

Regency USA Appliances, Ltd.
P.O. Box 3341
Tustin, CA 92680
714-544-3530

Reprocell
9189 DeGarmo Street
Sun Valley, CA 91352

Research Products Corp.
P.O. Box 1467
Madison, WI 53701
608-257-8801

Re-Source Building Products, Ltd.
920 Davis Road
Suite 101
Elgin, IL 60123
800-231-9721/ 708-931-4771
Fax: 708-931-1771

Resource Conservation
Technology, Inc.
2633 North Calvert Street
Baltimore, MD 21218
410-366-1146/ Fax: 410-366-1202

Resources Conservation
P.O. Box 71
Greenwich, CT 06836-0071
800-243-2862/ 203-964-0600

Rincon Vitova Insectaries
P.O. Box 1555
Ventura, CA 93002
805-643-5407

Ringer Corporation
9959 Valley View Road
Eden Prairie, MN 55344
800-423-7544/ 612-941-4180

Rio Rivuma
326 A Street, #2C
Boston, MA 02210

617-451-2549

Rising Sun Enterprises
P.O. Box 1728
Basalt, CO 81621
970-927-8051

Roberts Consolidated Industries
600 N. Baldwin Park Blvd.
City of Industry, CA 91749
800-423-9467/ 818-369-7311

Roche-Bobois
200 Madison Avenue
New York, NY 10016
212-725-5513

Rocky Grove Sun Company
HC 65, Box 280
Kingston, AR 72742
501-677-2871

Rocky Mountain Institute
1739 Snowmass Creek Road
Snowmass, CO 81654
970-927-3851
Internet: http://www.rmi.org

Rodman Industries
P.O. Box 76
Marinette, WI 54143
715-735-9509/ Fax: 715-735-6148

Roman Adhesives, Inc.
824 State Street
Calumet City, IL 60409
800-356-5595/ 708-891-0188

Ron Fisher
P.O. Box 1208
Marshalltown, IA 50158
515-753-3414/ Fax: 515-753-0977

The Roof Tile and Slate Co.
1209 Carrol
Carrollton, TX 75006
214-446-0005/ Fax: 214-242-1923

Royal-Pedic Mattress
119 North Fairfax Ave.
Los Angeles, CA 90036
800-487-6925/ 213-932-6155
Fax: 213-932-6158

Ruby & Coco
RD1, Box 185A
Leaman Road
Cochranville, PA 19330
610-593-8143/ Fax: 610-593-2581

Runtal North America
187 Neck Road
Ward Hill, MA 01835
800-526-2621

Russell Wold
2025 Westover Drive
Pleasant Hill, CA 94523

S

Safe Environments
2512 Ninth Street, #17
Berkeley, CA 94710
510-549-9693

Safe Technologies
1950 NE 208 Terrace
Miami, FL 33179
800-262-3260

Safeco Products Co.
9300 West Research Center Road
New Hope, MN 55428
612-536-6700/ Fax: 612-536-6777

Safer HomeTest Kit
325 North Oakhurst
Beverly Hills, CA 90210

Sancor Industries, Ltd.
140-30 Milner Avenue
Scarborough, Ontario
Canada M1S 3R3
Canada: 800-387-5245
U.S.: 800-387-5126

Sandoz Agro Inc.
1300 East Touhy Avenue
Des Plaines, IL 60018
800-527-0512/ 708-699-1616

Gordon T. Sands
40 Torbay Road
Markham, Ontario
Canada L3R 1G6
905-475-6380

Santana, Inc.
P.O. Box 2021
Scranton, PA 18501
800-368-5002/ 717-343-7921
Fax: 717-348-2959

Savogran
P.O. Box 130
Norwood, MA 02062
800-225-9872

Schuller International, Inc.
P.O. Box 5108
Denver, CO 80217
800-654-3103

Scientific Developments, Inc.
P.O. Box 2522
Eugene, OR 97402
800-824-6853/ 503-686-9844
Fax: 503-485-8990

Seed Savers Exchange
RR3, Box 239
Decorah, IA 52101
319-382-5990/ Fax: 319-382-5872

Seeds of Change
P.O. Box 15700
Santa Fe, NM 87506-5700
505-438-8080/ Fax: 505-438-7052

Septic Care
420 Commercial Avenue
P.O. Box 335
Palisades Park, NJ 07650
800-505-8800

Sessile Paper Company
125 Lincoln Avenue
Bronx, NY 10454-4432
718-401-0483

Seventh Generation
360 Interlocken Blvd.
Broomfield, CO 80021
800-456-1177/ Fax: 303-464-3700

Alison T. Seymour
5423 W. Marginal Way SW
Seattle, WA 98106
206-935-5471

Shaker Shop West
P.O. Box 487

Inverness, CA 94937
415-669-7256

Shaker Workshops
P.O. Box 8001
Ashburnham, MA 01430
617-646-8985

Siemens Fuller Solar Industries
P.O. Box 6032
Carmarillo, CA 93011
800-272-6765

Sigma Designs
46515 Landing Parkway
Freemont, CA 94538
510-770-0100

Signature Marketing
134 West Street
Simsbury, CT 06070
860-658-7172
Fax: 860-651-8376/ 800-841-7826
Internet:
http://www.logomall.com/sigcycle

Simplex Products
P.O. Box 10
Adrian, MI 49221
517-263-8881

Skanvahr Coatings
18646 142nd Avenue NE
Woodinville, WA 98072
206-487-1500/ Fax: 206-486-9663

Smith & Fong Company
2121 Bryant Street
Suite 203
San Francisco, CA 94110
415-285-4889/ Fax: 415-285-8230

Smith & Hawken
117 E. Strawberry Drive
Mill Valley, CA 94941
800-776-5558/ 415-383-2000
415-383-4415/ Fax: 415-383-8971

Solar Design Associates
P.O. Box 242
Harvard, MA 01451
508-456-6855

Solar Electric of Santa Barbara
232 Anacapa Street

Santa Barbara, CA 93101
805-963-9667

Solar Electric Systems
2700 Espanola NE
Albuquerque, NM 87110
505-888-1370

Solar Energy Industries
Association
122 C Street NW
4th Floor
Washington, DC 20001
202-383-2600

Solar Energy Systems
1244 Bell Avenue
Fort Pierce, FL 34982
407-464-2663

Solar Light Company, Inc.
721 Oak Lane
Philadelphia, PA 19126-3342
215-927-4206/ Fax: 215-927-6347
Internet: http://www.solar.com

Solar Works
64 Main Street
Montpelier, VT 05602
802-223-7804

Solec International, Inc.
12533 Chanron Avenue
Hawthorne, CA 90250
310-970-0065

Southwall Technologies
1029 Corporation Way
Palo Alto, CA 94303
800-365-8794/ 415-962-9111

Southern Humboldt Builders
Supply
690 Thomas Drive
Garberville, CA 95442
707-923-2781

Spectra, Inc.
1943 North Broad St.
P.O. Box 273
Rome, GA 30162-0273
706-291-7402

St. Charles Manufacturing Co.
1611 E. Main Street

St. Charles, IL 60174
630-584-3800

St. Jude Polymer Corp.
1 Industrial Park
Frackville, PA 17931
717-874-1220

Staber Industries, Inc.
4411 Marketing Place
Groveport, OH 43125
614-836-5995/800-848-6200
Fax: 614-836-9524

Steelcase, Inc.
901 44th Street SE
Grand Rapids, MI 49508
616-247-2710

Steeler
10023 Martin Luther King Way S.
Seattle, WA 98178
206-725-2500

Story Enterprises Co.
East 1881 Crestview Drive
Shelton, WA 98584
360-427-5930/ Fax: 360-427-5930

Structural Plastics Corp.
2750 Lippincott Blvd.
Flint, MI 48507
800-523-6899

Summit Furniture, Inc.
5 Harris Court
Ryan Ranch Building "W"
Monterey, CA 93940
408-375-7811/ Fax: 408-375-0940

Summit Solutions
381 Casa Linda Plaza, #194
Dallas, TX 75218
214-388-0006

Summitville Tile
P.O. Box 73
Summitville, OH 43962
330-223-1511

Sun Frog Products
17865 82nd Drive
Gladstone, OR 97027
503-650-8774

Sunelco
P.O. Box 787
Hamilton, MT 59840
406-363-6924

Sunfrost Refrigerator
Box 1101
Arcata, CA 95521

Sun-Mar Corp.
600 Main Street
Tonawanda, NY 14150-0888
905-332-1314/ Fax: 905-332-1315
Internet: http://www.sun-mar.com

5035 North Service Road, C9-C10
Burlington, Ontario
Canada L7L 5V2
compost@sun-mar.com

SunPipe
P.O. Box 2223
Northbrook, IL 60065
847-272-6977

Sunrise Lane
780 Greenwich Street
New York, NY 10014
212-242-7014

Sunrise Habitat
5001 Joerns Drive
Stevens Point, WI 54481
800-388-4083

Suntek, Inc.
6817 Academy Parkway East
Albuquerque, NM 87109
505-345-4115

Super Tech Wood
P.O. Box 242
Schoolcraft, MI 49087
616-323-3570

Superior Clay Corp.
P.O. Box 352
Uhrichsville, OH 44683
800-848-6166

Superior Fireplace Co.
4325 Artesia Avenue
Fullerton, CA 92633
714-521-7302

Superwood of Alabama
P.O. Box 2399
Selma, AL 36702
334-874-3781

Sureway Trading
826 Pine Avenue
Suites 5 & 6
Niagara Falls, NY 14301
416-596-1887

Sutherland Carpet Mills
342 Westway
Orange, CA 92665
714-447-0792

Swanstar
Box 2596
Vista, CA 92085
619-945-1050/ Fax: 619-945-2108

Swede-Tech
4031 NE 17th Terrace
Fort Lauderdale, FL 33334
954-565-7059/ Fax: 954-565-4929

Sylvania GTE
35 Vulcan Street
Rexdale, ON M9W 1L3 Canada

Syndesis
2908 Colorado Avenue
Santa Monica, CA 90404
310-829-9932/ Fax: 310-829-5641

T

21st Century Water Systems
1314 Main Street
Morro Bay, CA 93442
805-772-2951

THP/3, Phenix Heat Pump
Systems
8390 Gerber Road
Elk Grove, CA 95828
916-689-8111

TW Industries, Inc.
2000 SW 31st Avenue
Pembroke Park, FL 33009
305-962-2100

Tack Fast
15 Wertheim Court, #710
Richmond Hill ONT L4B 3H7
Canada
905-886-0785

Talisman Mills
6000 West Executive Drive
Mequon, WI 53092
800-482-5466

Tallon Termite and Pest Control
1949 East Market Street
Long Beach, CA 90805
800-779-2653/ 310-422-1131

Tarkett, Inc.
800 Lanidex Plaza
Parsippiny, NY 07054
201-428-9000

Technical Development
Nonprofit Computer Connection
30 Federal Street
Boston, MA 02110
617-728-9138/ Fax: 617-728-9138

Techrite
P.O. Box 19
Marblehead, MA 01945
800-875-0767

Temp-Cast
3332 Young Street
P.O. Box 94059
Toronto, ON M4N 3R1
800-561-8594/ Fax: 416-486-3624

Teron Lighting Corp.
33 Donald Drive
Fairfield, OH 45014
513-858-6004
Fax: 513-242-4228

Terra-Green Technologies
1650 Progress Drive
Richmond, IN 47374
317-935-4760/ Fax: 317-935-3971

Terra Verde
120 Wooster Street
New York, NY 10012
212-925-4533

Terressentials
2650 Old National Pike
Middletown, MD 21769-8817
301-371-7333
E-mail: antler@hotmail.com
Internet: http://www.tool-box.com/
rc/owa/freeweb.page?id=1049645

Testfabrics
200 Blackford Ave.
Middlesex, NJ 08846
908-469-6446/ Fax: 908-469-1147

Tetco (Thermal Energy Transfer
Corp.)
1290 U.S. 42 North
Delaware, OH 43015
800-468-3826/614-363-5002

Texas Kiln Products
Rt 2, Box 171D
Smithville, TX 78957
800-825-9158

Thai Silks
252 State Street
Los Altos, CA 94022
800-722-7455/ 415-948-3426

Tharco
2222 Grant Avenue
San Lorenzo, CA 94580
800-772-2332/ 510-276-8600
Fax: 510-276-4862

Thermacore
3200 Reach Road
Williamsport, PA 17701
800-935-3667/ 717-326-7325
Fax: 717-326-9017

Therma-Star Products Group, Inc.
P.O. Box 8050
Madison, W1 53708
800-533-7533

Thermax, Kooltronic
57 Hamilton Avenue
P.O. Box 300
Hopewell, NJ 08525-0300
800-929-0682/ 609-466-8800

Thermo Products
401 East Ray Road
Chandler, AZ 85225

800-882-7007/ Fax: 602-821-9047

Thermoguard Insulation Co.
451 Charles Street
Billings, MT 59101
800-821-5310/ Fax: 406-252-5019

Thomas Moser Cabinets
P.O. Box 1237
Auburn, ME 04211
207-784-3332/ Fax: 207-784-6973

Thoro System Products
7800 NW 38th Street
Miami, FL 33166 3
305-592-2081

Titon Industries
P.O. Box 566848
Atlanta, GA 31156
404-399-5252

Dr. John Todd
Ocean Arks International
233 Hatchville Road
E. Falmouth, MA 02536
508-563-2792/ Fax: 508-563-2880
bjosephs@cape.com

Tom's of Maine
P.O. Box 710
Kennebunk, ME 04043
207-985-4961
www.toms-of-maine.com

Tosten Brothers Saw Mill
P.O. Box 156
Miranda, CA 95552
707-943-3093/ Fax: 707-943-3665

Trade Winds HCR
Box 64
Grafton, VT 05146
802-843-2594

Traulsen & Co., Inc.
114-02 15th Avenue
College Point, NY 11356
718-463-9000

Tree Free Ecopaper
One World Trade Center
121 SW Salmon Street
Portland, OR 97204
503-295-6705/ Fax: 503-464-2299

Treecycle Recycled Paper
P.O. Box 5086
Bozeman, MT 59717
406-586-5287

Trendway
P.O. Box 9016
Holland, MI 49422
800-748-0234/ 616-399-3900

Trimax of Long Island
2076 5th Avenue
Ronkonkoma, NY 11779
516-471-7777/ Fax: 516-471-7862

TuliKivi Swedish Soapstone
Heaters
P.O. Box 300
Schuyler, VA 22969
800-843-3473/ 804-831-2228

Tulip
Natick, MA 01760

U

US Axminster Inc.
1856 Artistry Lane
Greenville, MS 38702
601-332-1581/ Fax: 601-332-1581
or 601-332-1594

U.S. Posco
900 Loverdge Road
Pittsburg, CA 94565
510-439-6000

Ultracel
Arco Chemical
P.O. Box 27902
Knoxville, TN 37927
800-234-5115

Under the Canopy
P.O. Box 393
Navaro, CA 95463
707-895-3203

Unicel Inc.
88 de Vaudreuil
Boucherville, QU J4B 5G4
Canada
514-655-1580/514-655-0162

(Don't be intimidated if Unicel answers the phone in French; the operators do speak English.)

Uni-group USA
4362 Northlake Blvd., Suite 207
Palm Beach Gardens, FL 33410
407-626-4666/ Fax: 407-627-6403

Union Carbide Corp.
Urethane Intermediates
39 Old Ridgebury Road
Danbury, CT 06817

Uniquely Australian
1202-865 View Street
Victoria, BC V8W 3E8
Canada
800-661-6607/ Fax: 604-388-5110

United Receptacle
P.O. Box 870
Pottsville, PA 17901
800-233-0314/ 717-622-7715
Fax: 717-622-3817

United Recycling, Inc.
3558 Second Street N.
Minneapolis, MN 55412
612-521-1111/ Fax: 612-521-1112

United Sanitation
6734 Highway 141 North
Jonesboro, AR 72401
501-932-3500/ Fax: 501-932-3537

United Solar
1100 W. Maple Road
Troy, MI 48084-5352
810-362-4170

United Technology Carrier
P.O. Box 70
Indianapolis, IN 46206
317-243-0851/ Fax: 317-240-5253

Universal Rundle Corporation
217 North Mill Street
New Castle, PA 16101
412-658-6631

Urban Ore
1333 Sixth Street
Berkeley, CA 94710
510-559-4454/ Fax: 510-528-1540

(For those of you visiting Urban Ore, it's located on the corner of Sixth and Gilman.)

U.S. Plastic Lumber Corp.
2300 Glades Road
Suite 440 W
Boca Raton, FL 33431
800-653-2784

U.S. Power Climate Control, Inc.
881 Marcon Boulevard
Allentown, PA 18103
610-266-9500

Utex Trading Enterprises
111 Peter Street
Toronto, Ontario
Canada M5V 2H1
716-282-4887

V

Vanbesuw
P.O. Box 692
Northport, AL 35476
800-562-8797

VanEE
Conservation Energy Systems
2525 Wentz Avenue
Saskatoon, SK Canada S7K 2K9
800-667-3717

Vari-Cool
P.O. Box 548
Hastings, NE 68902
402-463-9821

Venmar Ventilation
1715 Haggerty Street
Drummondvill, Quebec
Canada J2C 5P7
819-477-6226

Vent-Aire
Engineering Development, Inc.
4850 Northpark Drive
Colorado Springs, CO 80918
719-599-9080/ Fax: 719-599-9085

Vermont Country Store
Route 100
Weston, VT 05161

802-824-3184

Vermont Country Store
P.O. Box 3000
Manchester Center, VT 05255

Victorian Reproductions
P.O. Box 54
La Ceiba, Honduras
504-42-0342/ Fax: 504-43-1362

Vital Systems
1091 Gordon Drive
Kelowna, BC V1Y 3E3
Canada
800-661-2602/ 604-861-8381

Vulcraft
P.O. Box 169
Fort Payne, AL 35967
205-845-2460/ Fax: 205-845-1090

W

W.F. Taylor Co.
11545 Pacific Avenue
Fontana, CA 92337
800-397-4583/ 909-360-6677
Fax: 909-360-1177

W.H. Porter, Inc.
4240 N. 136 Ave.
Holland, MI 49424
616-399-1963/ Fax: 616-399-9123

WMX Technologies Recycling Services
18500 Von Karmen Ave
Irvine, CA 92612
714-474-2311/ Fax: 714-757-2508

Walnut Acres
Penns Creek, PA 17862
717-837-0601

Wambold Furniture
6800 Smith Road
Simi Valley, CA 93063
805-526-5200/ Fax: 805-526-0284

Wastenot
1720 E. Garry Avenue
Suite 109
Santa Ana, CA 92705

714-863-7133/ Fax: 714-863-7135

Waterforms, Inc.
P.O. Box 930
Blue Hill, ME 04614
207-374-2384/ Fax: 207-374-2383

Water Furnace International
Roanoke, VA 24012
540-366-2384

Water Tech Finishes
800-293-5249

Water Treatment Systems
4145 Via Marina
Suite 324
Marina del Ray, CA 90292
310-39-WATER (92837)

Watershed Sales Corp.
P.O. Box 31588
New Braunfels, TX 78131
512-629-4246

Weather-Bos Stains and Paint
316 California Ave., #1111
Reno, NV 89509
702-789-2691

Weleda
P.O. Box 769
Spring Valley, NY 10977
914-352-6145

Wellman, Inc.
P.O. Box 31331
Charlotte, NC 28231
704-357-2281/ Fax: 704-357-2272

Wesco Used Lumber
911 Ohio Avenue
Richmond, CA 94804
510-235-9995/ Fax: 510-236-2863

West Point Pepperell
P.O. Box 609
Westpoint, GA 31833
800-435-1199

Western Metal Lath
P.O. Box 39998
Riverside, CA 92519
909-360-3500/ Fax: 909-685-4685

Western Pottery
11911 Industrial Avenue
Southgate, CA 90280
213-636-8124

Westgate Enterprises
310-477-5891/ Fax: 310-478-1954

Westmont Building Products
200 E. Quincy
Westmont, IL 60559
630-968-3420/ Fax: 630-968-0285

Weyerhaeuser
4111 W. Four Mile Road
Grayling, MI 49738
517-348-2881/ Fax: 517-348-8226

Whedon Products, Inc.
21A Andover Drive
West Hartford, CT 06110
800-541-2184/ 860-953-7606
Fax:860-953-4510

Whirlpool Corp.
Consumer Assistance Center
Pipestone
2303 Pipestone Road
P.O. Box 0120
Benton Harbor, MI 49022-2400
800-253-1301

Whirlpool Fulfillment
Appliance Information Service
P.O. Box 85
St. Joseph, MI 49085

Whitfield Advantage WP-2
Pyro Industries, Inc.
695 Pease Road
Burlington, WA 98233
360-757-9728

Whole Earth Landscape Design, Inc.
P.O. Box 812-022
Wellesley, MA 02181
508-655-0722

Wild Iris Products
P.O. Box 1580
Redway, CA 95560
707-923-2344/ Fax: 707-923-4257
wit@isf-sw.org

Wildwoods Co.
1055 Samoa Blvd
Arcata, CA 95521
707-822-9541

Will-Seal
Pre-Formed Sealants
18780 Cranewood Parkway
Warrensville Heights, OH 44128
216-587-6067

William Lamb Corp.
10615 Chandler Blvd.
North Hollywood, CA 91601
818-980-6248

William Zinsser & Co.
173 Belmont Drive
Somerset, NJ 08875
908-469-8100

Willsboro Wood Products
P.O. Box 509
Keeseville, NY 12944
800-342-3373/518-834-5200
Fax: 518-834-5219

Wilson Woodworks
108 Hydeville Road
Stafford, CT 06075
203-684-9112

Winrich International
8601 200th Avenue
Bristol, WI 53104
414-857-7800

Winter Silks
2700 Laura Lane
P.O. Box 130
Middleton, WI 53562
608-836-4600/800-648-7455

Wirsbo Company
5925 148th Street West
Apple Valley, MN 55124
612-891-2000

Wise Woods
P.O. Box 1271
McHenry, IL 60050
815-344-4943

Wood Recycling, Inc.
3 Wheeling Avenue

Woburn, MA 01801
800-982-8732/ 617-937-0855
Fax: 617-932-0945

Woodburning Handbook
1991 California Air Resources
Board
P.O. Box 2815
Sacramento, CA 95812
800-952-5588

Woodcastle Forest Products
34030 Excor Road
Corvallis, OR 97330
541-926-5488

Wooden Workbench
202B Airpark Drive
Fort Collins, CO 80524
970-484-2423/ Fax: 970-482-1572

Woodmode
1 Second Street
Kreamer, PA 17833
717-374-2711

Woodworkers Source
5402 South 40th Street
Phoenix, AZ 85040
800-423-2450/ 602-437-4415
Fax: 602-437-3819

Y

Yemm & Hart
RR 1, Box 173
Marquand, MO 63655
573-783-5434

Z

Zia Cosmetics
410 Townsend Street
San Francisco, CA 94107
800-334-7546

Zemos Technology
43260 Christy Street
Fremont, CA 94538
510-657-0278

Zoo Doo Co.
281 E. Parkway North

Memphis, TN 38112
800-I LUV DOO/ 901-276-1200
Fax: 901-278-7031

HELPFUL GOVERNMENT PROGRAMS

"Our goal is to serve the American public, to prevent pollution at a profit, to create jobs, and to foster private initiative. Please join us."
John S. Hoffman, Director, Global Change Division, Office of Air and Radiation

There are several government programs that were set up to help businesses become more resource efficient. All of those described here are voluntary Environmental Protection Agency (EPA) programs. They cover a wide variety of industries, once again showing that environmental health is necessary for the long-term health of businesses.

The following are the EPA programs' guiding principles:

1. "Voluntary Participation: We seek partners who want to work with us to prevent pollution by increasing the productivity of energy systems.

2. Strong Technical Support: We will provide strong assistance to partners to help them decide how to accomplish their goals, but we will never try to dictate solutions.

3. Profitable Upgrades: We only ask partners to make investments that are profitable and that sustain or improve quality.

4. Minimal Bureaucracy: We only seek practical solutions and promise to minimize paperwork and red tape in all our efforts."

VOLUNTARY POLLUTION PREVENTION PROGRAMS

There are a number of voluntary programs by which the EPA helps businesses prevent pollution and save money in the process. I won't go into detail here, but I think that you should be aware of them. The programs include:

- 33/50 Program (for reduction of toxins pollution based on Toxic Release Inventory [TRI])
- Accounting Program (environmental cost accounting)
- AgStar Program (encourages dairy/swine industries to use methane for energy production in manure man-

agement)
- Building Technologies Program (window, glazing, lighting technologies for reduced energy use and improved visual and thermal comfort for building occupants)
- Coalbed Methane Outreach Program (removes obstacles to investment in coalbed methane recovery projects)
- Design for the Environment Program (building design)
- Environmental Leadership Program
- Energy Star Program (energy-efficient buildings and equipment)
- Indoor Environment Program
- Initiative on Joint Implementation (establishes approaches for joint implementation of greenhouse gas emissions)
- Landfill Methane Outreach Program
- Ruminant Livestock Methane Program
- Natural Gas Star (works with the natural gas industry to reduce methane emissions)
- Pesticide Environmental Stewardship Program
- State and Local Outreach Program (helps state/local governments with climate change)
- Transportation Partners (improves efficiency of transportation systems/reduces demand for vehicle travel)
- Waste Minimization National Plan (emphasizes source reduction and environmentally sound recycling over waste management)
- Water Alliances for Voluntary Efficiency (WAVE) (encourages efficient water use)

CONTACT INFORMATION

There are many government programs that have been designed to help businesses and individual citizens. Only a few are listed here. If you have access to the Internet, you can find a wealth of information on various government programs without having to wait for the agencies to send it to you through the mail. Some even have fax-back systems, which will allow you to use your telephone keypad to request information.

Don't forget to check the following Internet sites:

http://www.epa.gov/epahome/programs.html
http://es.inel.gov/partners

EPA PROGRAMS

Acid Rain Hotline
202-233-9620

AgStar
202-233-9041

Coalbed Methane Outreach
Manager, Coalbed Methane Outreach Program
US EPA Atmospheric Pollution Prevention Division
401 M Street SW (6202J)
Washington, DC 20460
Tel: 202-233-9468
Fax: 202-233-9569
Fax-back system: 202-233-9659
schultz.karl@epamail.epa.gov

Design for the Environment (DfE)
To order DfE documents contact:
Pollution Prevention Information Clearinghouse (PPIC)
400 M Street, SW
Mail Code 3404
Washington, DC 20460
202-260-1023

For more information contact:
Irina Vaysman
US EPA (7406)
401 M Street, SW
Washington, DC 20460
202-260-1312

Endangered Species Program
EPA's Public Information Center
202-260-1755.

Energy Star Programs (An EPA/DOE Program)
Energy Star Programs
U.S, EPA Atmospheric Pollution Prevention Division
401 M Street SW, (6202J)
Washington, DC 20460
Tel: 202-233-9190
Toll Free: 888-STAR-YES
Fax: 202-233-9569
Fax-back system: 202-233-9659

Residential "Golden Carrot" Programs
202-233-9230

Green Chemistry Challenge
U.S. EPA
Office of Pollution Prevention and Toxics
202-554-1404/ TDD: 202-554-0551
Internet: http://www.epa.gov
(Select "Offices," then "Prevention, Pesticides, and Toxic Substances," then "Toxics.")

Green Lights
Manager, Green Lights Program
U.S, EPA Atmospheric Pollution Prevention Division
401 M Street SW, (6202J)
Washington, DC 20460
Tel: 202-233-9190
Toll Free: 888-STAR-YES
Fax: 202-233-9569
Fax-back system: 202-233-9659
Federal Program
202-233-9485

Landfill Methane Outreach Program
Landfill Methane Outreach Program
US EPA Atmospheric Pollution Prevention Division
401 M Street SW (6202J)
Washington, DC 20460
Tel: 888-STAR-YES (782-7937)
Fax: 202-775-6680
Fax-back system: 202-233-9659

National Lead Information Center (NLIC)
1-800-424-LEAD

Natural Gas Star
Manager, Natural Gas STAR Program
US EPA Atmospheric Pollution Prevention Division
401 M Street SW (6202J)
Washington, DC 20460
Tel: 202-233-9793
Fax: 202-233-9569
Fax-back system: 202-233-9659

Ozone Protection Hotline
800-296-1996/ 301-614-3396

Office of Radiation and Indoor Air
Radiation Protection Division
Internet: http://www.epa.gov/radiation/

REFIT
U.S. Environmental Protection Agency
Reinvention For Innovative Technologies Program
MC 2173

401 M Street, SW
Washington, DC 20460
(202-260-2690

Ruminant Livestock Methane Program
Manager, Ruminant Livestock Methane Program
US EPA Atmospheric Pollution Prevention Division
401 M Street SW (6202J)
Washington, DC 20460
Tel: 202-233-9043
Fax: 202-233-9569
Fax-back system: 202-233-9659

or:
USDA-SCS, Ecological Sciences Division
P.O. Box 2890
Washington, DC 20013
Tel 202-720-0436
Fax 202-720-2646

U.S./GAZPROM
US/GAZPROM Working Group
US EPA Atmospheric Pollution Prevention Division
401 M Street SW (6202J)
Washington, DC 20460
Tel: 202-233-9044
Fax: 202-233-9569
Fax-back system: 202-233-9659

or:
US/GAZPROM Working Group
US Department of Energy
1000 Independence Avenue, S.W.
Washington, DC 20585
Tel. 202-586-5903
Fax 202-586-0823
This working group was developed as a public/private initiative to help Russia's natural gas industry be more efficient and environmentally sound.

DEPARTMENT OF ENERGY PROGRAMS

Advanced Lighting
202-586-1856

Affordable Housing
202-586-9167

Air Conditioning/Refrigeration Equipment
202-586-7425

Building America
202-586-9472

Central AC/Heat Pumps/Refrigeration
202-586-9611

Climate Challenge
202-586-6210

Commercial Codes/HERS
202-586-7892

Commercial Office Equipment/Dishwashers
202-586-8459

Cool Communities Program
202-260-6405

Cost-Shared Demonstration of Emerging Technologies
202-586-5253

Electric Motors
202-586-8654

Efficiency Standards for Electric Transformers
202-586-2828

Energy Audits
202-586-2193

Energy Analysis and Diagnostic Centers
202-586-7258

Energy Efficiency Programs and Housing Technology Centers
202-586-5253

Energy-Efficient Process Technologies
202-586-8296

Energy Efficiency and Renewable Energy Information and Training Programs
202-586-9389

Energy Market Mobilization Collaborative with Technology Demonstrations
202-586-1720/ 202-586-5389

Federal Commercial Standards
202-586-7935

Federal Residential Standards
202-586-9209

Fuel Economy Labels for Tires
202-586-1197

Furnaces and Combustion
202-586-9136

HERS/Financing
202-586-7819

High Efficiency Gas Technologies
301-903-2832

Home Energy Rating Systems and Energy-Efficient Mortgages
202-586-9204

Hydroelectric Generation at Existing Dams
202-586-5659

Indoor Air Quality
202-586-9455

Integrated Analysis of Energy-Related Actions
202-586-5316

Integrated Resource Planning
202-586-1491

Lighting Equipment
202-586-1689

MEMP
202-586-9120

Methane Recovery from Coal Mining
202-586-5278

Methane Recovery from Landfills
202-586-5278

Motor Challenge Program
202-586-7234

Natural Gas Share of Energy Use Through Federal Regulatory Reform
202-586-2040

Passive Solar
202-586-2996

Plumbing/Direct Heating
202-586-9145

Refrigeration
202-586-6149

Rebuild America
202-586-9424

Residential Appliance Standards
202-586-9142

Residential Building Codes
202-586-6262

State Grants
202-586-9495

State Revolving Fund for Public Buildings
202-586-8295

Transmission Pricing Reform
202-586-4871

Water Heaters
202-586-

Windows and Glazing
202-586-9214

ADDITIONAL FEDERAL PROGRAMS

Depletion of Nonindustrial Private Forests
USDA: 703-235-9018

Efficiency of Fertilizer Nitrogen Use
EPA: 202-260-6351
USDA: 703-235-9018

Federal Tax Subsidy for Employer-Provided Parking
EPA: 202-260-3761

Landfill Rules
EPA: 919-541-5393

Residential Building Standards
HUD: 202-708-3295
DOE: 202-586-9870

Seasonal Gas Use for the Control of Nitrogen Oxides (NO)
EPA: 919-541-3292

Transportation System Efficiency Strategy and Telecommuting
EPA: 202-260-3761
DOE: 202-586-1197
DOT: 202-366-4540

Tree Planting in Nonindustrial Private Forests
USDA: 703-235-9018

Upgrade Residential Building Standards
HUD: 202-708-3295
DOE: 202-586-9870

U.S. Forest Service
202-205-1052

GLOSSARY

4-Phenylcyclohexane (4-PC) – a compound inadvertently created through the breakdown of SB latex. It is chemically similar to 1-PC, which is formed when the hallucinogenic drug PCP ("angel dust") is heated.

ACC – autoclaved cellular concrete

ADA – Americans with Disabilities Act

AFUE – annual fuel utilization efficiency

ASHRAE – American Society of Heating, Refrigeration, and Air Conditioning Engineers.

Ballast – regulates electric current in lighting

BEPAC (Building Environmental Performance Assessment Criteria) – a Canadian, third-party, building audit system that studies the energy use, indoor quality, and other factors in a building

BREEAM (Building Research Establishment Environmental Assessment Method) – a British building audit program that, like BEPAC, offers feedback to building owners and occupants regarding their buildings' impacts on such things as global warming, ozone depletion, and rainforest destruction

BSA – Building for a Sustainable America

Building envelope – all external surfaces of a building that are subject to climatic influence. These would include exterior walls, roof, doors, and windows.

CD-ROM – compact disk

CERES (Coalition for Environmentally Responsible Economies) – a voluntary organization of people with diverse backgrounds who believe that global economic activity must be environmentally sustainable

CERES Principles – Designed by CERES, this set of voluntary principles has been embraced by companies large and small to show their commitment to environmental health and restoration.

CFC – chlorofluorocarbon

CFL – compact fluorescent light

CS – see Chemical Sensitivity

Chemical Sensitivity – a disease caused by the body's exposure to toxins, resulting in one or more damaged systems (e.g., immune, neurological)

CO – carbon monoxide

CO_2 – carbon dioxide

CRT – cathode ray tube

CTS – carpal tunnel syndrome

Dioxin (2,3,7,8-tetrachlorodibenzo-p-dioxin, or TCDD) – highly toxic in miniscule amounts – a byproduct of organochlorines.

DOE – Department of Energy

Dot matrix – like a typewriter, this technology uses an inked ribbon to imprint text on paper.

DDT – a highly toxic substance that, once banned in the U.S., sometimes is used as an ingredient in pesticides and other materials

DPI (dots per inch) – this is a measurement of the number of dots per inch that a computer printer prints. The higher the number, or dpi, the higher the resolution of the image.

EEG – electro-encephalogram

EER – energy efficiency rating

Efficiency – the complete use of resources in which their is little or no waste.

E-mail (electronic mail) – a means of communicating with others via a computer and modem

EMF – see Electro-magnetic Field

Energy Star Program – a voluntary EPA program through which businesses can save money by using efficient equipment and building electrical and mechanical systems.

EPA – Environmental Protection Agency

EPACT – Energy Policy Act

EPRI – Energy Policy Research Institute

EPS – expanded polystyrene, an ingredient used to make foam insulation board

Ergonomics- the study of humans' relations with their environments, particularly comfort, stress, and well-being

FDA – Food and Drug Administration

Fluorescent lighting – electrons inside a tube run into mercury while flowing between cathodes (electrodes) and emit light.

Golden Carrot Program – EPA's voluntary program encouraging the production of smart refrigerators

Green Lights Program – a voluntary program through which the EPA works with businesses to save money through energy-efficient lighting retrofits. Green Lights Partners sign a Memorandum of Understanding to show their commitment to efficient practices that will benefit them financially.

Green Seal – a non-profit certification organization that creates standards for smarter products. Look for the company's Green Seal of approval on products that have passed muster.

Hannover Principles – Created by architect William McDonough as a guide to the design of Hannover, Germany's World Fair in the year 2000.

HCFC – hydrochlorofluorocarbon

HID (high-intensity discharge) lighting – These are similar to fluorescent lights in how they work, but the electrical discharge occurs in a smaller area, and they produce a brighter light.

HVAC (heating, ventilation, and cooling) system – a building's mechanical system that incorporates heating, ventilation, and cooling rather than having separate systems for each

Hz (hertz) – the standard measurement of frequency per second

IAQ – indoor air quality

Incandescent lighting – an electric current heats a thin, metal filament until it glows and emits light.

Ink jet – the technology of spraying tiny ink droplets onto paper to create text or graphics

kWh – kilowatt-hour

LAN – local area network

Laser jet – the technology of fusing toner powder onto paper to create text or graphics

LCD – liquid crystal display

LED – laser/light emitting diode

Low-e (low-emissivity) – used in reference to a material's ability to conduct heat

Milk paint – a natural paint containing casein, a milk enzyme, and lime wash or distemper

Milligauss – the standard measurement of electro-magnetic radiation

MRI – multiple resonance imaging

MSDS (material safety data sheets) – lists the active ingredients found in products

NASA – National Aeronautic and Space Administration

Ni-cad battery – nickel-cadmium battery

NIOSH – National Institute of Occupational Safety and Health

NMH battery – nickel-metal-hydride battery

NRDC – Natural Resources Defense Council

NWF – National Wildlife Federation

OSB (oriented strand board) – board made of ground tree fibers that have been glued together.

OSHA – Occupational Safety and Health Administration

PC – personal computer

PCB – polychlorinated biphenyl

pCi/l (picocuries per liter) – the standard measurement of radon

PET – a type of plastic often recycled into carpets, fabric, and other products

Photovoltaics – active solar power uses mechanical systems to collect and distribute the sun's heat.

Polychlorinated biphenyls (PCBs) – a pernicious, highly toxic organochlorine found in many products.

PV – see Photovoltaics

PVC – polyvinyl chlorine, a type of plastic

PVP – vinyl plastic

Radon – a radioactive, invisible, underground gas. A cause of lung cancer, radon gas rises from the earth and lays concentrated in the lower levels of some buildings.

Reel mower – engine-less lawn mower

R value (resistance value) – a material's ability to resist the transfer of heat. The higher the R value (e.g., R-35), the higher a material's insulating capacity.

SAS (solar aquatic system) – a small ecosystem designed to break down wastes and treat water

SB (styrene-butadiene) latex – using in paints and carpets (to bind fibers). All carpets using SB latex emit some 4-PC.

SBS – see Sick Building Syndrome

Scientific Certification Systems – a certification organization that creates standards for certain products. Approved products carry the SCS Green Cross.

SCS – see Scientific Certification Systems

SEER – seasonal energy efficiency rating

Sick Building Syndrome – a temporary illness caused by exposure to toxins. Continued toxic exposure, however, can result in Chemical Sensitivity.

Smart Office – a highly efficient workplace characterized by little or not waste and toxicity.

SOC – synthetic organic compound

SRI – socially responsible investing

TCDD – dioxin

TCF – totally chlorine-free, a term often applied to paper that has been bleached without chlorine

THM (trihalomethane) – formed when natural, organic material comes in contact with chlorine

Telecommuting – working from a location other than a company's office (generally at home)

Transportation Partners Program – a voluntary EPA program that supports public and private initiatives to reduce the negative environmental impacts of transportation

ULF toilet – ultra-low flush toilet

UV – ultra-violet light

VDT – video display terminal (computer terminal)

VOC – volatile organic compound

WasteWi$e Program – EPA's voluntary program that helps companies prevent waste, purchase recycled products, and recycle

Wh – watt-hours

WWF – World Wildlife Fund

Xeriscape – smart landscaping that relies on native plants and little water or fertilizer

Zeolite – a mineral used in air fresheners to absorb bacteria and some contaminants

REFERENCES

American Academy of Arts and Sciences and the Aspen Institute.
1993 *Avoiding the Collision of Cities and Cars: Urban Transportation Policy for the Twenty-first Century.* Chicago: Kirkland and Ellis.

American Council for an Energy-Efficient Economy
1996 Guide to Energy-Efficient Office Equipment. Washington, D.C.: ACEEE.

Anderson, Bruce N., ed.
1991 *The Fuel Savers: A Kit of Solar Ideas for Your Home, Apartment, or Business.* Lafayette, CA: Morning Sun Press.
1990 *Ecologue: The Environmental Catalogue and Consumer's Guide for a Safe Earth.* NYC: Prentice Hall Press.

Andruss, Van, Christopher Plant, Judith Plant, and Eleanor Wright
1990 *Home! A Bioregional Reader.* Philadelphia: New Society Publishers.

Anzovin, Steven
1993 *The Green PC: Making Choices that Make a Difference.* NYC: Windcrest/McGraw-Hill.

ASHRAE
1995 "Florida's Energy Center is Lesson in Efficiency," in *ASHRAE Journal,* p. 6. October 1995.

Barnett, Dianna Lopez and William D. Browning
1995 *A Primer on Sustainable Building.* Snowmass, CO: Rocky Mountain Institute.

Bemish, Paul
1984 *Building Your Own Home for Less than $15,000.* Quill (NYC: William Morrow and Co.)

Berle, Gustav
1991 *The Green Entrepreneur: Business Opportunities that Can Save the Earth and Make You Money.* NYC: Liberty Hall Press.

Berthold-Bond, Annie
1990 *Clean & Green: The Complete Guide to Nontoxic and Environmentally Safe Housekeeping.* Woodstock, NY: Ceres Press.

Bloyd-Peshkin, Sharon
1990 "Taming the Waste Stream in Your Office" in *Vegetarian Times.* July 1990.

BioCycle
BioCycle: Journal of Composting & Recycling (monthly publication). Emmaus, PA: The JG Press, Inc.

Borman, F.Herbert, Diana Balmori, and Gordon T. Geballe
1993 *Redesigning the American Lawn: A Search for Environmental Harmony.* New Haven: Yale University Press.

Bower, John
1993 *The Healthy House.* NYC: Carol Publishing Group.

Bristol, Tim
1992 "Edge of the Woods" in *Turtle Quarterly.* Fall 1992.

Brown, Lester R., Christopher Flavin, and Sandra Postel
1991 *Saving the Planet: How to Shape an Environmentally Sustainable Global Economy.* NYC: W.W. Norton & Company, Inc.

Browning, William
1992 "NMB Bank Headquarters," in *Urban Land*, pp. 23-25. June 1992.

Buss, Dale D.
1997 "Pure Profit" in *Bloomberg Personal*, pp. 102-109, March/April 1997. Skillman, NJ: Bloomberg L.P.

CALMAC
1996 "Florida Regional Service Center" on CALMAC Manufacturing Corporation's Internet home page, http: www.calmac.inter.net/pages/opac1/awards/FRSC.htm. Englewood, NJ: CALMAC Manufacturing Corp.

Carless, Jennifer
1992 *Taking Out the Trash: A No-Nonsense Guide to Recycling.* Washington, D.C.: Island Press.

Celotex
1996 Composite Wall Design Fact Sheet.

Center for Renewable Energy and Sustainable Technology
1994 Fact/information sheets. Washington, D.C.: SEREF.

Chemical Injury Information Network
1993-1995   *Our Toxic Times* (a monthly publication). White Sulphur Springs, MT: Chemical Injury Information Network.

City of Austin
1994 *Sustainable Building Guidelines.* Austin: City of Austin.

City of Portland
1994 *Sustainable City Principles.* Portland: City of Portland.

Coffel, Steve and Karyn Feiden
1990 *Indoor Pollution.* NYC: Fawcett Columbine.

Consumers Digest
July/Aug. 1993   "Green Cleaning" and "From Glass to Fiberglass" under "The Environment" section, *Consumers Digest.* Chicago, IL: Consumers Digest.
Sept./Oct. 1993   "Before You Renovate, Interrogate," and "Unsafe Drinking Water" under "The Environment" section, *Consumers Digest.* Chicago, IL: Consumers Digest.

Co-op America
1994 *Co-op America Quarterly.* Winter 1994. Washington, D.C.: Co-op America.
1995 *You, Your Money & the World.* Washington, D.C.: Co-op America.
1996 *Who We Are and What We Do* fact sheet. Washington, D.C.: Co-op America.

Corbett, Judith
1994 "The Ahwahnee Principles: Toward More Liveable Communities" reprinted from *Western City Magazine.* September, 1994. Sacramento: Local Government Commission.

Crowley, Carolyn Hughes
1994 "Scents & Sensitivity" in *The Washington Post.* April 26, 1994: E5. Washington, D.C.

Dadd, Debra Lynn
1990 *Nontoxic, Natural, & Earthwise.* Los Angeles: Jeremy P. Tarcher, Inc.

Delicious!
1994 "Easy Alternatives to Chemical Cleaners" and "Look for the Eco-Label" in *Delicious!.* April 1994.

Dillon, Patricia S.
1994 "Salvageability by Design" in *IEEE Spectrum.* August 1994. New York, NY: The Institute of Electrical and Electronics Engineers, Inc.

Dreyfuss, Joel
1993 "Inside" in *PC Magazine.* May 25, 1993. New York, NY: Ziff-Davis Publishing Co.

Durning, Alan
1992 *How Much Is Enough?: The Consumer Society and the Future of the Earth.* NYC: W. W. Norton & Company, Inc.

The Durst Organization
1996 "A Responsible Addition to the Skyline" Fact Sheet. New York: The Durst Organization.

Earthword
1992 & 1994   *Earthword Journal* (published irregularly). Volumes 4 and 5. Laguna Beach, CA: Eos Institute.

Earth Works Group, The
1990 *The Recycler's Handbook.* Berkeley: EarthWorks Press.
1991 *Fifty More Things You Can Do to Save the Earth.* Berkeley: EarthWorks Press.

Ecological Engineering Associates
Fact Sheets on their Solar Aquaticsä System for Wastewater Treatment. Marion, MA: EEA.

Environmental Building News
"Checklist for Environmentally Sustainable Design and Construction." Brattleboro, VT: Environmental Building News.

Environmental Construction Outfitters
Pamphlet. New York: ECO.

Environmental Defense Fund Letter Staff
1992 "Leaving Grass Clippings on Lawn Helps the Environment" in *EDF Letter.* XXIII:3. June 1992.

Environmental Health Watch and the Housing Resource Center
1990 *Healthy House Catalog: National Directory of Indoor Pollution Resources.* Cleveland, OH: Environmental Health Watch and the Housing Resource Center.

Environmentally Sustainable Design and Construction
Environmental Building News (a bimonthly publication). Brattleboro, VT: West River Communications, Inc.

Faulkner, Grant
1997 "Building with Grain Instead of Lumber" in *In Business* (a bimonthly publication). January/February 1997. Emmaus, PA: The JG Press, Inc.

Fedrizzi, S. Richard
1995 "Going Green: The Advent of Better Buildings" in *ASHRAE Journal,* pp. 35-38. December 1995.

Flynn, Mary Kathleen
1993 "Ergonomics of Input" in *PC Magazine.* May 25, 1993. NYC: Ziff-Davis Publishing Company.

Franta, Gregory, Kristine Anstead, and Gregg D. Andor
1997 *Glazing Design: Handbook for Energy Efficiency.* Washington, D.C.: American Institute of Architects.

Franta, Gregory and Kristine Anstead
1994 "Daylighting Offers Great Opportunities," pp. 40-43, in *Window & Door Specifier.* Spring 1994.

Global Tomorrow Coalition
1990 *The Global Ecology Handbook.* Boston: Beacon Press.

Goodman, David
1993 "Working with What You've Got," in *Inc. 1994 Guide to Office Technology.*

Green Alternatives
Green Alternatives (a bimonthly publication). Rhinebeck, NY: Greenkeeping, Inc.

Green Seal, Inc.
1994 *Campus Green Buying Guide.* Also, Green Seal information sheets and pamphlets.
Washington, D.C.: Green Seal.

G.R. Plume Company
1994 "The G.R. Plume Company Reclaimed Douglas Fir Architectural Timbers Specification Sheet." February 1994.
     Bellingham, WA: The G.R. Plume Company.

Hamilton, Kim and Bill Browning
     "Village Homes: A Model Solar Community Proves its Worth," in *In Context,* No. 35, pp. 33-35.

Hawken, Paul
1993 *The Ecology of Commerce.* NYC: Harper Business.

Holmes, Hannah with Bill Breen
1993 "Getting the Lead Out" in *Garbage* (a bimonthly publication). November/December 1993. Gloucester, MA:
     Dovetale Publishers.

Holusha, John
1996 "For Office Towers, Being Green Can Be Beneficial," in *The New York Times,* Real Estate section, The New York
     Times Internet Web site. June 30, 1996.

In Business Magazine
1996 Internet Web site: www.ecoexpo.com/inbusiness/noframe/. January 1997.
1993 "Report from Eco-Timber," in IC newsletter, May/June 93, p.7. Emmaus, PA: The JG Press, Inc.

Ivanovich, Michael G., James A. Wise, Judy H. Heerwagen, and David B. Lantrip.
1996 *Development of a Protocol for Identifying and Assessing Potential Benefits of Green Buildings.* Seattle: Pacific
     Northwest National Laboratory.

Kourik, Robert
1993 "In Bob's Garden" in *Garbage* (a bimonthly publication). November/December 1993. Gloucester, MA: Dovetale
     Publishers.

Landis, Scott
1992 "Seventh-Generation Forestry" in *Harrowsmith Country Life.* November/December 1992. Charlotte, VT: TM
     Communications.

Lane, Hilary
1994 "Coffees with Conscience" in *E: The Environmental Magazine.* January/February 1994. Norwalk, CT: Earth

Action Network, Inc.

Lappe, Frances Moore and Paul Martin DuBois
1994 *The Quickening of America: Rebuilding Our National, Remaking Our Lives.* San Francisco: Jossey-Bass, Inc. Publishers.

LeClair, Kim and David Rousseau
1992 *Environmental by Design, Volume I: Interiors: A Sourcebook of Environmentally Aware Material Choices.* Point Roberts, WA: Hartley and Marks.

Ledbetter, Marc and Loretta A. Smith
1993 *Guide to Energy-Efficient Office Equipment.* Berkeley, CA: American Council for an Energy-Efficient Economy.

Lelen, Kenneth
1994 "Magnetic Fields Are No Dreams to Some Buyers" in *The Washington Post.* April 30, 1994: E1. Washington, D.C.

Lloyd, Nancy
1991 "Lethal Grass" in *The Washington Post.* Monday, September 16, 1991, p. D5. Washington, D.C.

Kruger, Anna
1991 *H Is for EcoHome: An A to Z Guide to a Safer, Toxin-Free Household.* NYC: Avon Books.

MacNeill, Jim, Pieter Winsemius, and Taizo Yakushiji
1991 *Beyond Interdependence: The Meshing of the World's Economy and the Earth's Ecology.* NYC: Oxford University Press.

Makower, Joel
The Green Consumer. NYC: Tilden Press (Penguin Books).

Manning, Richard
1993 *A Good House: Building a Life on the Land.* NYC: Grove Press.

Matthews, Bonnye L.
1992 *Chemical Sensitivity.* Jefferson, NC: McFarland & Co.

Menominee Tribal Enterprises
1995 Fact sheets, pamphlets. Neopit, WI: Menominee Tribal Enterprises.

Miller, Alan S.
1991 *Gaia Connections: An Introduction to Ecology, Ecoethics, and Economics.* Savage, MD: Rowman & Littlefield Publishers, Inc.

Mintz, John
1997 "Splendor in the Grass?" in *The Washington Post, Business* section, p. H1. Sunday, January 5, 1997. Washington, D.C.: The Washington Post.

Moore, Fuller
1993 *Environmental Control Systems: Heating Cooling Lighting.* NYC: McGraw-Hill, Inc.

Moquin, Michael
1994 "Ancient Solutions for Future Sustainability" in *Adobe Journal.* Albuquerque, NM: Adobe Journal.

Motavalli, Jim
1996 "The Virtual Environment," in *E Magazine,* pp. 29-35. May/June 1996. Norwalk, CT: E Magazine.

Nadel, Brian
1993 "The Green Machine" in *PC Magazine.* May 25, 1993. NYC: Ziff-Davis Publishing Company.

National Audubon Society and Croxton Collaborative, Architects
1994 *Audubon House: Building the Environmentally Responsible, Energy-Efficient Office.* NYC: John Wiley & Sons, Inc.

National Commission on the Environment
1993 *Choosing a Sustainable Future: A Report of the National Commission on the Environment.* Washington, D.C.: Island Press.

Nesper, Larry and Marshall Pecore
1993 "The Trees Will Last Forever" in *Cultural Survival Quarterly.* Cambridge, MA: Cultural Survival Quarterly.

New Settler, The
1993 "Tree-Free Paper" in *Whole Earth Review.* Fall 1993, No. 80. Sausalito, CA: POINT.

Northern Virginia Soil and Water Conservation District
"Cleaning House; Cleaning the Bay" in *Chesapeake Challenges.*

O'Neal, Edward J.
1996 "Thermal Storage System Achieves Operating and First-Cost Savings" in *ASHRAE Journal,* pp. 59-64. April 1996.

Pacific Gas & Electric Company
1995 "Heating and Cooling Measures at the VeriFone Office Site" Fact Sheet. December 1995. San Ramon, CA: Pacific Gas & Electric.

Panayotou, Theodore
1993 *Green Markets: The Economics of Sustainable Development.* San Francisco: ICS Press.

Pathways
1994 "Traffic-weary Europeans Looking at Car-free Cities" in *Pathways.* Fall 1994. Washington, D.C.: Pathways.

Pearson, David
1989 *The Natural House Book: Creating a Healthy, Harmonious, and Ecologically-Sound Home Environment.* NYC: Simon & Schuster, Inc.

Pecore, Marshall
1992 "Menominee Sustained Yield Management: A Successful Land Ethic in Practice" in *Journal of Forestry.* July 1992. Wisconsin.
"Menominee Woodland: 135 Years of Sustained Yield Management" in *Turtle Quarterly.* Wisconsin.

Perry, Tekla S.
1994 "Green Refrigerators" in *IEEE Spectrum.* August 1994. New York, NY: The Institute of Electrical and Electronics Engineers, Inc.

Planetary Solutions
Planetary Solutions (a quarterly newsletter). Boulder, CO: Planetary Solutions.

Plotkin, Mark and Lisa Famolare
1992 *Sustainable Harvest and Marketing of Rain Forest Products.* Washington, D.C.: Island Press.

Rensberger, Boyce
1993 "Environment: Fiber Problems in Sick Buildings" in *The Washington Post*. November 22, 1993: A2. Washington, D.C.

Rheingold, Howard, ed.
1994 *The Millenium Whole Earth Catalog*. New York: Harper Collins Publishers.

Rieland, Randy
1988 "Is Your Office Making You Sick?" in *The Washingtonian*, March 1988. Washington, D.C.: Washington Magazine, Inc.

Rifkin, Jeremy , ed.
1990 *The Green Lifestyle Handbook: 1001 Ways You Can Heal the Earth*. NYC: Henry Holt & Company.

Rittner, Don
1992 *EcoLinking: Everyone's Guide to Online Environmental Information*. Berkeley: Peachpit Press.

Rhode Island Lung Association and the Rhode Island Department of Health
1994 *Managing Indoor Air Quality: A Guide to Maintaining the Indoor Air Quality of Commercial Buidings*. January 1994.

Rocky Mountain Institute
Rocky Mountain Institute Newsletter (published three times yearly). Snowmass, CO: Rocky Mountain Institute.

Romm, Joseph J.
1994 *Lean and Clean Management: How to Boost Profits and Productivity by Reducing Pollution*. NYC: Kodansha International.

Romm, Joseph J. and William D. Browning
1994 "Greening the Building and the Bottom Line." Snowmass, CO: Rocky Mountain Institute.

Rothstein, Steven M.
1992 "Investing in the Earth" in *In Business* (a bimonthly publication). August 1992. Emmaus, PA: The JG Press, Inc.

Rousseau, David
1995 *EcoBuilding Times*. Summer 1995.

Sabulis, Jill
1996 "Home a Model of Energy-wise Efficiency," in *The Atlanta Journal-Constitution*.

Schaeffer, John and Real Goods Trading Company Staff, eds.
1994 *Solar Living Source Book: The Complete Guide to Renewable Energy Technologies & Sustainable Living*. White River Junction, VT: Chelsea Green Publishing Company.

Schmidheiny, Stephan
1992 *Changing Course: A Global Business Perspective on Development and the Environment*. Cambridge: The MIT Press.

Schultz, Warren
1994 "Greener Than Grass," in *Harrowsmith Country Life*. September/October 1994. Charlotte, VT: TM Communications.

Seims, Shelby
1994 "Boston Hotels Lead "Green" Push," in *The Christian Science Monitor*. May 20, 1994.

Shulman, Seth
1996 "Houses to Save the Earth," in *The Washington Post Parade Magazine*, pp. 4-5. March 3, 1996.

Smith, Carol
1994 "Protect the Environment at Little Cost," in *Seattle Post-Intelligencer*, p. B-1. Friday, March 25, 1994. Seattle: Seattle Post-Intelligencer.

Social Venture Network
1993 *Best Practices Source Book: Volume II.* San Francisco: Social Venture Network.

Solar Energy Research and Education Foundation
1994 "CD-ROM Captures Greening of the White House Initiative" in *ReSource.* Washington, D.C.: Solar Energy Research and Education Foundation.

Southface Energy Institute
1996 "ECOS Technology Fact Sheet: AFM Diamon Snap-Form System." May 1996. Atlanta: Southface Energy Institute.

Southface Energy Institute
1996 "ECOS Technology Fact Sheet: AFM R-Control Structural Building Panels." May 1996. Atlanta: Southface Energy Institute.

Southface Energy Institute
1996 "ECOS Technology Fact Sheet: Passive Solar Design." July 1996. Atlanta: Southface Energy Institute.

Stein, Sara
1993 *Noah's Garden: Restoring the Ecology of Our Own Back Yards.* NYC: Houghton Mifflin Company.

Steinman, David
1993 "The Architecture of Illness" in *Vegetarian Times.* January 1993.

Taplin, Philip and Richard Foraker
1989 "Radon – A Homeowner's Guide" videotape produced by NUS Training Corp.

Teal, John M. and Susan B. Peterson
1993 "A Solar Aquatic System Septage Treatment Plant" in *Environ. Sci. Technol.* Vol. 27: No. 1.

Thayer, Burke Miller
1996 "Way Station," pp. 23-26, in Buildings for a Sustainable America Case Studies. Boulder, CO: American Solar Energy Society.

Thompson, Claudia G.
1992 *Recycled Papers: The Essential Guide.* Cambridge, MA: The MIT Press.

Upton, Arthur C., MD and Eden Graber, MS, eds.
1993 *Staying Healthy in a Risky Environment: How to Identify, Prevent or Minimize Environmental Risks to Your Health.* NYC: Simon and Schuster.

U.S. Department of Energy
1995 "Clean Cities," "Energy Efficiency and Renewable Energy Clearinghouse," and "Energy Efficiency and Renewable Energy Network" fact/information sheets. Washington, D.C.: US DOE.

U.S. Department of Energy
1997 Programs for Your Community: Office of Energy Efficiency and Renewable Energy. Washington, D.C.: U.S. Department of Energy.

1997   Sustainable Building Technical Manual. Washington, D.C.: Department of Energy.

U.S. Environmental Protection Agency
1993 Xeriscape Landscaping: Preventing Pollution and Using Resources Efficiently booklet from the Office of Water series, #WH-556-F.   April 1993.
  "Secondhand Smoke" pamphlet/poster from the Air and Radiation series, #6203J. July 1993.
  "WasteWi$e: EPA's Voluntary Program for Reducing Business Solid Waste" booklet from the Solid Waste and Emergency Response series, #5306.   Oct. 1993.
1994   *WasteWi$e Update.* Dec. 1994.
1995   "EPA's Transportation Partners" pamphlet. Washington, D.C.: US EPA.

Watkins-Miller, Elaine
1996   "Right of Salvage," in *Buildings*, May 1996, pp. 32-36. (www.buildingsmag.com)

U.S. News & World Report
1994   "Diving for Abandoned Treasure" in *U.S. News & World Report.* May 30, 1994. New York: U.S. News & World Report.

Vajda, Deborah
1994   "Birth of the ecohotel," in *Utne Reader*, p. 35. September/October 1994.

Villatoro, Bobbi, ed.
1993   "Certifying Forest Sustainability" in *Menominee Tribal Enterprises Newsletter.* August 5, 1993. Neopit, WI: Menominee Tribal Enterprises.

Wall Street Journal
1992   "EC Proposes Packaging Recycling" in the *Wall Street Journal.* July 16, 1992.

Watson, Donald and Kenneth Labs
1983   *Climatic Building Design: Energy-Efficient Building Principles and Practice.* NYC: McGraw-Hill, Inc.

Wells, Malcolm
1981   *Gentle Architecture.* NYC: McGraw-Hill Book Company.

Westerman, Martin
1993   *The Business Environmental Handbook.* Grants Pass, OR: The Oasis Press.

William McDonough Architects
1992   *The Hannover Principles: Design for Sustainability*. New York: William McDonough Architects.

Wilson, Cynthia
1993   *Chemical Exposure and Human Health.* Jefferson, NC: McFarland & Co. (919-246-4460)

Woods, Charles G. and Malcolm Wells
1992   *Designing Your Natural House.* NYC: Van Nostrand Reinhold

World Watch
1994   "Public Investment: Some Choices" under "Matters of Scale" section in *World Watch.* May/June 1994.

Yakutchik, Maryalice
1993   "A New Jolt of Concern," in *USA Today, Weekend* section, p. 5, January 3, 1993.